DATE			
NOV 13 '79	JAN 28 '91	MAY 13, 2013	
FEB 21 '79	FEB 19 '91		
NOV 13 '79	JAN 13 '93	MAY 06 2014	
OCT 26 '81	JAN 15 '93		
NOV 03 1986			
JUL 26 1988			
JUL 26 1988	NOV 14 1994		
AUG 12 1988	FEB 29 1995		
APR 18 1990	AUG 26 1996		
OCT 11 1990			

Relationships in Marriage and Family

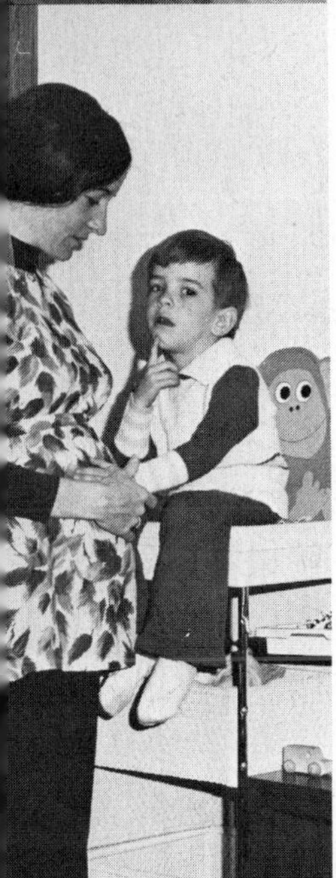

Relationships in Marriage & Family

NICK STINNETT *Oklahoma State University*

JAMES WALTERS *University of Georgia*

Macmillan Publishing Co., Inc.
NEW YORK
Collier Macmillan Publishers
LONDON

Printed in the United States of America

Macmillan Publishing Co., Inc.
866 Third Avenue, New York, New York 10022

Collier Macmillan Canada, Ltd.

Library of Congress Cataloging in Publication Data

Stinnett, Nick.
Relationships in marriage and family.

Includes index.
1. Marriage. 2. Family. 3. Interpersonal relations. I. Walters, James, joint author. II. Title.
HQ734.S873 1977 301.42'7 76-4966
ISBN 0-02-417530-7

Printing: 2 3 4 5 6 7 8 Year: 7 8 9 0 1 2 3

Dedicated with love to our families

Preface

The focus of this book is on relationships between people who come together for the purpose of loving each other. It includes consideration of the young before marriage, those who choose not to marry, relationships between couples who are married, parents and their children and other relatives, the middle-aged, and the elderly.

Few things in life are more important to people throughout the world than the loving relationships within their families. The late Richard Klemer, a leading family life educator, once observed that following an atomic explosion the first thing that most of us would do when the all-clear signal was given would be to search for the members of our families.

Most people marry, hoping that the love within their relationship will endure forever. Those who terminate their marriages usually marry again, hoping that the second marriage will afford them the love they seek. And most people who choose not to marry still wish for a close, intimate relationship with someone.

We grow up learning to value success in relationships with others, yet many fail in their relationships because they cannot accept themselves, or others, or the tasks which living requires. Success in relationships is especially dependent upon the person-to-person skills we learn in interacting with others. People who develop skills in interaction can better guide the course of their lives. They help others to appreciate themselves and, as a result, they are loved.

This book identifies those factors that make for successful relationships with others. Success in relationships results from a rational decision to make the best of whatever situations in which we may find ourselves. It is based on a recognition that we need not be victims of a life over which we have no control but that we can learn to improve our person-to-person skills and can develop realistic expectations and understandings of the tasks required of each of us at every stage of life.

It is our hope that this book will assist you in the development of the sensitivity, the understanding, and the insight which loving relationships require, and that the relationships you develop will enrich your life.

The authors gratefully acknowledge the cooperation of the Office of Public Relations at the University of Georgia, which permitted us to reproduce many of the photographs found in the text.

N. S.
J. W.

Contents

14

Parent-Child Relationships 291

15

The Later Years 317

16

Family Relationships in the Later Years 337

Relationships in Marriage and Family

1 Relationships

Photo by Walker Montgomery

If the relationship between two people can be made creative, fulfilling, and free of fear,

Then this can work for *two* relationships,

Or for relationships that affect entire social groups

Even nations.

Dan Drake

A Potential for Happiness

Of all the things that make living worthwhile, few equal the importance of the relationships we have with others: they determine and are a reflection of how we are loved. Our relationships reveal to others the state of our emotional health [1] and our mastery of the environment in meeting our physical and emotional needs,[2] and they are of paramount significance in terms of the happiness we attain.

Although research in human development and family studies has clearly emphasized the importance of the relationships we experience early in life, we need not become victims of our past lives. Most people, if they are sufficiently motivated, can play an active part in modifying their behavior so as to change the direction of their lives. Yet millions of couples find marriage unsatisfying, coexisting as strangers throughout a lifetime of unhappiness. However, there is hope for those who develop an awareness of the forces shaping their relationships; who, according to Eric Berne, founder of *transactional analysis*, learn to engage in spontaneous, warm, game-free interaction characterized by thoughtfulness, support, and concern.[3]

This book is designed to help you examine your own behavior, analyze the consequences of your behavior, and monitor your responses in such a way so that you can help yourself attain the goals you seek. It is based on the assumption that you can best achieve your goals by concentrating on *your* behavior in relation to others rather than concentrating on the behavior of *others* in relation to you. And it is based on the recognition that for you to gain control of your behavior, you must assume complete responsibility for it and work daily to improve your interaction with others.

Interaction in marriage and family life is influenced by a variety of factors, for example, attitudes about the use of the resources of money, time, and energy; roles assumed within and outside of the family; how one feels about having and rearing children; commitment to spouse and children. Each area considered in this book offers opportunities for trouble and potentials for happiness. Those wishing to be successful in each of the areas will learn the behavior skills necessary to control their interaction with their children and their spouses in such a way as to attain their goals while serving as a source of psychological support to others.

We cannot realistically expect to achieve satisfying relationships with others, within or outside a family, until we understand ourselves and our interpersonal interactions. Human relationships have tremendous potential for giving meaning to life. In the process of growing up, we learn a great many response patterns from our encounters with family members. Not all early experiences prepare us to achieve happiness in relationships; some of our learned behavior must be modified if we are to reach the potential of which we are capable.[4]

For example, if we have been reared so that we feel awkward, inhibited, or ashamed about our sexual feelings, we may need to modify our attitudes in order to please our spouse as well as to please ourselves. Sexual relationships can contribute much to the building and the maintenance of a successful marriage.[5]

A man reared in a home where his mother has assumed a traditional wife-mother role (preparing all of the meals, doing the laundry, and making the beds) may need to sharpen his homemaking skills if he marries an occupationally oriented woman who prefers that homemaking be a shared responsibility. Few men appreciate the time that is actually spent in the care of a home. Much of the routine of household maintenance is socially isolating, and many women of this generation will view the tasks involved very differently than their mothers did. They may find that they are as ill prepared psychologically for the day-to-day routines of homemaking as their husbands are.

A personal change is not easy, but it often is required if a marriage is to endure or if it is to be satisfying. Those who are successful in making the necessary attitudinal and behavioral changes are couples who are determined to make their marriages work. In spite of the fact that few couples reach marriage unmindful of its hazards, far too many approach marriage with unrealistic perceptions of what is required for their future together.

Couples nearing marriage might well consider that everyone can improve his or her interpersonal skills and then decide which skills need the most attention. There is real skill, for example, in responding patiently when one is angry, and in responding rationally when one's feelings are hurt.

Understanding Relationships

Ask yourself, "What do I want most from my relationships with others?" You may answer, "It depends. What I want from my employer is different from what I desire from my parents or my marriage partner." As you think about this question more deeply, however, you will probably discover that you desire one basic thing from all of your relationships—a *good feeling*. We hope our relationships with others will make us feel OK about ourselves.[6] This is exactly what others want from their relationships with us. They want us to make them feel OK.

An important key to building successful relationships is to design our interaction in such a way that we help others feel worthy and good about themselves. This is what Erich Fromm [7] calls a productive orientation toward relationships. The individual with a productive orientation is able to see the best in others and is aware of their needs. Such a person establishes loving relationships characterized by acceptance, appreciation of others, and helpfulness.

Unfortunately, we may attempt to elicit acceptance, recognition, and love in immature, self-defeating ways. One example of this is the girl who is sexually promiscuous in an effort to prove her desirability. Trying to obtain a good feeling about ourselves by relating to others in destructive ways is described by Fromm as a nonproductive orientation toward relationships. Persons with nonproductive orientations establish interactions characterized by exploitation, hostility, extreme competition, rejection, and defensiveness.

Improving Relationship Skills

It is not enough to develop insight into why people behave as they do; it is also important to decide that regardless of how well we interact now, we can always improve.[8] Essential to the development of successful relationships is an understanding of the principle that we are most likely to experience satisfying relationships by concentrating on our own responses rather than on the responses of others. In concentrating on our responses we direct attention *not* to what *others* do that is right or wrong, but to what *we* can do to strengthen relationships. In this way we assume responsibility for making relationships better. When we concentrate on the responses of another person, we are likely to place responsibility for the direction of the relationship in the hands of that person.

For example, in arguments many couples reach a level of anger where they care little about what is right; rather, they care about being hurt or humiliated.

Relationships

Frequently, we fail to consider the long-range consequences of our behavior in conflicts with others and concentrate on winning. At these times we focus on the responses of others to determine their vulnerability rather than focusing on how our responses can promote the welfare of the relationship. We may win the argument but destroy the relationship.

There is danger in regarding this approach to human interaction simplistically. Yet that is precisely what some people will do. Others will consider that it involves nothing more than controlling one's behavior in order to manipulate the behavior of others. In reality, however, this approach to human interaction includes profound regard for the worth of others and a willingness to concentrate on our own responses and to assume responsibility for our behavior.

Structuring Time

The manner in which we structure time with others influences the quality of our relationships. Three common ways of structuring time, according to transactional analysis, include rituals, pastimes, and games.[9]

RITUALS

In this society time is filled with rituals, highly patterned forms of interaction in which everyone knows what to say and says it regardless of whether he means it or not:

"Good morning, Mattie."
"Good morning, Richard."
"How are you?"
"I'm just fine. How are you?"

Obviously, rituals serve a purpose; however, when people consistently retreat to this level of formal interaction, they rarely become assured that they are worthy or are valued by others.[10]

A recent study by David Haun of bereaved persons indicated that following the death of a family member the visiting of friends in the home of the bereaved was deeply appreciated. It was significant that many of the respondents could not remember what had been said during the visits but valued them nonetheless. Clearly, it was not what was said that was important but the feelings of warmth, regard, and esteem that had been conveyed.[11]

Rituals can be useful, but only if used to communicate support. Frequently, rituals of everyday living become perfunctory, stripped of feelings that reflect understanding and concern. When we limit our responses to the polite, inexpressive patterns that are culturally prescribed, our behavior may be deemed appropriate but it will rarely touch the hearts of people.

PASTIMES

Similarly, if we limit our interaction to pastimes, which facilitate discourse but are noncommittal, there is little opportunity to reaffirm the esteem of others. Thomas Harris, in *I'm OK—You're OK*, describes our pastimes which include "General Motors," the comparison of automobiles; "Who Won," discussions of sports events; and "Grocery" and "Wardrobe," usually played by women when they are exchanging recipes and talking about clothes. The interaction of other pastimes described by Harris [12] is suggested by their titles:

"All Great Men Were"
"Ever Been?"
"How Much?"
"It's the Society We Live In"
"Me Too"
"What Became"

Pastimes involve little risk. By limiting discourse to this kind of interaction, we rarely communicate to people that we like them. Some people are afraid to tell others they like them for fear that their affection will not be reciprocated.[13] Whenever interaction reflects affection, risk is involved, for we cannot always predict the responses of others.

In order to protect themselves from disappointment, people learn to become inexpressive, keeping their feelings to themselves, and fearful of expressing affection. Much of our socialization has stressed caution in interaction so as not to become too vulnerable. As a result, we play it safe, avoiding contacts with people who might welcome a close, open friendship.[14]

GAMES

Games, so common in social discourse that Berne [15] devoted a whole book to them, are psychologically destructive forms of interaction. Psychological games contain a concealed motive and a well-defined psychological payoff. The behavior appears to be perfectly legitimate, but underneath there is a hidden motive that seeks to hurt or injure. Not only do games prevent people from attaining intimacy in their relationships, they also destroy whatever intimacy may exist. Berne describes dozens of games. Once identified, it is easy to recognize them and to see how common they really are. The underlying motives and the nature of the interaction are apparent in the titles of games:

"Why Does This Always Happen to Me?"
"Ain't It Awful?"
"Bum Rap"
"I Told You So"
"If It Weren't for You"
"I'm Only Trying to Help You"
"Look How Hard I've Tried"
"See What You Made Me Do"
"They Let Me Down"

Stroking

We all need recognition from others or we feel ignored and insignificant. The need to be recognized can be met through stroking. Psychological games replace positive strokes. A stroke refers to any interpersonal act that implies recognition of an individual's presence.[16] To a great extent we arrive at a particular life position as a result of the strokes we receive and give. Strokes may be either positive or negative.

Positive strokes are behaviors such as a smile, expression of affection, a word of praise, or simply listening with interest, which leave the other person feeling OK and worthy. Positive strokes enhance a person's sense of well-being and significance:[17]

"You are a lot of fun to be with."

"You look beautiful tonight."

"It is very thoughtful of you to help me with the report. I'll be able to make the deadline. You're a lifesaver."

"I love you."

A negative stroke is any type of behavior that leaves the other person feeling bad about himself. Criticism, sarcasm, and ridicule are examples of negative stroking.[18]

Negative strokes make people feel hurt and insignificant. All kinds of marital problems arise when couples consistently give negative strokes and make each other feel worthless. Not surprisingly, they enjoy being with one another less and less. Their relationship begins to focus upon the negative qualities in each other.

Just as strokes may be positive or negative, strokes may be conditional or unconditional. Positive strokes delivered only when a spouse conforms to the other's expectations are conditional. Positive strokes intended to communicate that you are liked just because you are you are unconditional. Satisfying marriages usually involve a great deal of unconditional stroking.[19]

It is possible to receive no strokes at all. An individual who receives neither positive nor negative strokes feels deserted. Understandably, such a state of nothingness can be devastating. Complaints of marriage difficulties often indicate a lack of stroking:

"He acts as though I'm not alive."

"She doesn't listen to me. She doesn't talk with me either. It's more like she talks *at* me."

Positive strokes are needed for both mental and physical health. As adults, we depend less upon physical contact—although we should not underestimate its importance—and more upon symbolic or word stroking than we did as children. By providing one another with genuine positive strokes, we do much to build satisfying interpersonal relationships.

Impact of Early Socialization

Berne [20] indicates in his book *Games People Play* that "parents, deliberately or unaware, teach their children from birth how to behave, think, feel, and perceive."

We are products of our socialization experiences and we *may* be ill equipped to attain satisfaction in relationships. However, the thesis of this book is that we can improve our interpersonal skills. We need not remain victims of early, negative experiences throughout life.

Life Scripts

A life script is much like a theatrical script for a character in a play—it is a life plan that dictates where we are going in life and how we are going to get there.[21] Each one of us has a life script.

From very early in life you have received information and formed impressions about yourself. The impressions become so pervasive as to be habitual. Impressions are similar to a tape in a computer memory bank. The tape of impressions continually transmits messages concerning the type of person you are, the kind of life you lead, what other people are like, and how you relate to others. In a sense, you are programmed by your tape.

A life script influences the quality and nature of interpersonal relationships. For example, if you have incorporated a life script of being unlovable, you may attract coplayers who will not love you, while shunning those who would love you. If your life script leads you to see yourself as a "victim," you may seek situations and relationships in which you are the victim of some discrimination or exploitative act. You may invite a hostile act or interpret an event so that you, in fact, become a victim just as your life script dictates.

People select marriage partners who are compatible with their life scripts. Muriel James and Dorothy Jongeward [22] in their book *Born to Win* note,

> An ambitious, young executive who is scripted to get to the top needs a marriage partner who is motivated to help him get there. He seeks out a properly educated, hostess-oriented, equally ambitious woman who will not foul up his dramatic plans. In turn, she selects him to fit a required role in her script. Even when planning a party, they are likely to include others who can play roles that advance their scripts.
>
> The same process of selection happens when a woman, who has taken the position "Men are bums," marries a sequence of "bums." Part of her script is based on "Men are not OK." She fulfills her own prophecy by nagging, pushing, complaining, and generally making life miserable for her husband (who has his part to play). Eventually, she manipulates him into leaving. Then she can say, "See, I told you. Men are bums who leave you when the going gets rough."

In order for us to improve the quality of our own interpersonal relationships, it may first be necessary to change our life script, particularly if the script calls for unsatisfying, negative relationships. It is difficult to change a life script; however, by altering the habitual thought pattern it *can* be done, and is being done every day. In fact, a major tenet of transactional analysis is that people *can* change their life scripts and move in a more positive direction. A person who has learned to think of himself and his relationships with people in a negative manner can redecide and rewrite his life script.

Paramount to an understanding of human relationships is the way we feel about ourselves because it influences the way we think of and interact with others. Each of us adopts what Thomas Harris [23] has called a life position, a way of looking at ourselves, others, and life in general. According to Harris's view, people adopt one of four major life positions: "I'm not OK—You're OK," "I'm not OK—You're not OK," "I'm OK—You're not OK," or "I'm OK—You're OK."

I'M NOT OK—YOU'RE OK

In the "I'm not OK—You're OK" position, an individual basically feels unworthy and experiences a sense of inferiority in relationships with others. Such a reaction to this self-perceived position may include living in a way that proves it:

A thirty-year-old woman felt lonely and friendless. She believed that no one liked her. She destroyed several friendships by telephoning two or three times a day and talking for long periods of time about the bad things people had done to her.

This life position also engenders the attitude, "I can be OK if . . ." with the sense of being OK depending upon pleasing others or attaining certain achievements. As Harris [24] states, a person in this position is committed to a lifetime of mountain climbing or achievement seeking. However, the sense of accomplishment is not lasting because the basic position has not changed. No matter how great his achievement, this person still feels *not OK*; he also often feels depressed.

Many children, because of their small size and comparative helplessness, learn to perceive themselves inferior to the adult parent and look to this adult (whom they consider OK) for their rewards.

I'M NOT OK—YOU'RE NOT OK

In the "I'm not OK—You're not OK" position people conclude they are not worthy and neither is anyone else. According to Harris, [25] this type of person has been deprived of positive strokes of affection or support. As a result of being abandoned in this way, the individual concludes, "I'm not OK—You're not OK." Such a person often gives up and feels there is no hope. He feels that life is no good and, as a result, may be destructive in relationships. In extreme cases this position may be manifested in suicide or schizophrenia. [26]

I'M OK—YOU'RE NOT OK

In the "I'm OK—You're not OK" position a person feels that he is OK and worthy but others are not. Often this person has experienced early in life very negative interactions with others but has learned to protect feelings of personal worth. As a result of past experience, he develops the general outlook that "Others have hurt me. I can't depend on others. The only person I can trust is myself." Other persons are viewed with suspicion. Individuals in this position may feel persecuted and victimized and blame others for their problems.[27]

I'M OK—YOU'RE OK

According to transactional analysis, the most healthy, desirable life position is "I'm OK—You're OK." In this position the individual feels that he is a person of worth and that others are worthy. Interaction with others is normally very positive. Of the four positions discussed, it is safe to say interaction that reflects an "I'm OK—You're OK" position will most often promote satisfying interpersonal relationships.

Ego States and Relationships

Relationships are influenced by the ego states of participants. An ego state is a consistent pattern of thinking, feeling, and behaving. Three major ego states influence the nature of your relationships: parent, child, and adult.[28]

PARENT

The *parent* in you is composed of the attitudes, values, and behaviors that have been internalized from outside sources, primarily from your parents. Your *parent* feels and acts very similar to your mother and father. The *parent* in you includes the set of rules that guides your behavior. It influences your views of how you should behave. Your *parent* can be helpful and nurturant. It can also be judgmental and unnecessarily critical.[29]

CHILD

The *child* ego state is composed of the same feelings and behavior patterns you had when you were very young. The *child* in you contains your natural impulses. It is the part of you that wants to have fun and experience pleasure. It is your *child* that wishes to avoid demanding responsibilities and painful experiences.

Your *child* state emerged early in life when your awareness centered around your own comforts and needs. Your *child* now includes recordings of your early experiences, how you responded to them, and the positions you took toward yourself and others.[30]

ADULT

The *adult* is the part of you that uses facts to make decisions. The *adult* is oriented toward reality and the objective gathering of information. It is, in a sense, your computer. The *adult* acts to keep your *parent* and *child* in balance.

Each of us may respond differently to a particular situation according to the particular ego state from which we are operating.

An Expensive Suit

Parent: I shouldn't want anything that expensive. It's selfish and silly of me to want that.

Child: I want this suit. I don't care how much it costs.

Adult: This suit is pretty but it costs $300. This is much more than I can afford.

A Broken Date

Parent: Jane doesn't know how to have fun. She studies too much. It's ridiculous for her to stay home and study instead of going to this party with me.

Child: Jane has ruined my evening. I really wanted to go to the party.

Adult: Jane needs to study for her chemistry test and feels she doesn't have time to go out. I will have to go by myself or take someone else.

Your *parent* can give nurturance, and it is your *parent's* job to treat your *child* with respect and love. It is your *child* that has fun, experiences pleasure, and appreciates beauty. It is your *adult's* job to make decisions objectively and to keep the *parent* and *child* in balance. Your *adult* has the task of meeting your *child's* needs without getting into trouble.[31]

IMPACT UPON RELATIONSHIPS

The manner in which *parent*, *child*, and *adult* are expressed influences the quality of interpersonal relationships. If your *parent* comes across as bossy, domineering, and "know it all," your *parent* will offend the *child* in other people. If, on the other hand, your *parent* is nurturing, warm, and concerned, the impact upon others will be positive.

Your *child* can have a positive influence upon others by being fun and loving. In contrast, if your *child* comes across as irresponsible and inconsiderate, it will elicit a negative response from others.

Types of Transactions

Parent, *child*, and *adult* interact in three ways: complementary, crossed, or ulterior.

COMPLEMENTARY TRANSACTIONS

A sense of security is experienced when a particular verbal or nonverbal message sent from one of our ego states brings the expected response from the other person. Most of the time we prefer predictable responses from others. Predictable interaction between any two ego states is complementary.[32] For example, a transaction may occur between husband and wife.

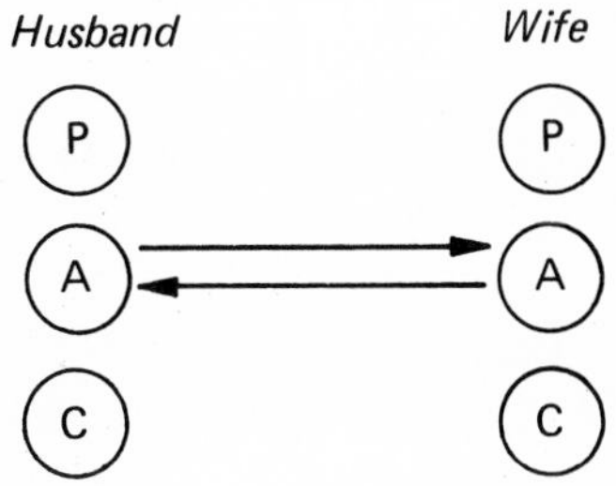

Adult and Adult

1. How much was the telephone bill this month?
2. It was $40.

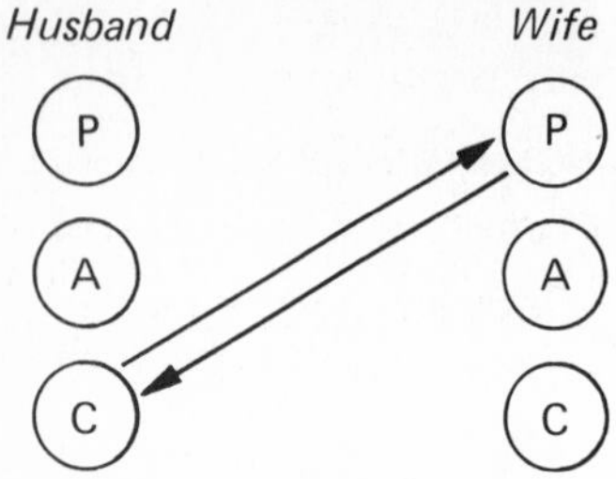

Parent and Child

1. I'm really tired and I don't feel like working on this paper anymore.
2. You've worked on it a long time today. Why don't you relax the rest of the evening. I'll take you out to dinner and then we'll go see a movie.

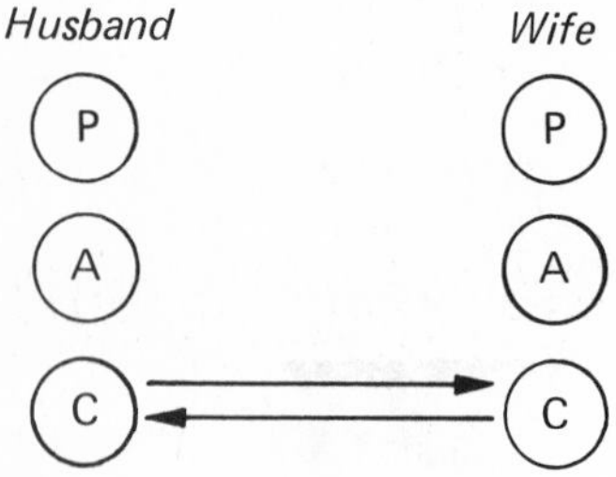

Child and Child

1. You're really a great guy.
2. I think you're great, too.

The communication in each of the described transactions is complementary because the responses were expected and appropriate to the original stimulus. This does not always occur in day-to-day interactions. When transactions are not complementary, confusion and misunderstanding often result.

CROSSED TRANSACTIONS

Sometimes people do not respond to us in an expected manner. Messages are misinterpreted and responses are negative. This offends or confuses us and may cause withdrawal. When two people interact and an inappropriate ego state is activated in one of them, their lines of transaction literally become crossed and communication breaks down.

Crossed transactions reflect and are a source of human relationship problems.[33] A husband may initiate an *adult-adult* transaction with his wife, expecting and wanting a positive response from her *adult*. Instead, the transaction becomes crossed and he receives a reprimanding response from her *parent*. This leaves him feeling confused and hurt. He may withdraw from his wife or retaliate. Withdrawal and retaliation perpetuate negative interaction patterns.

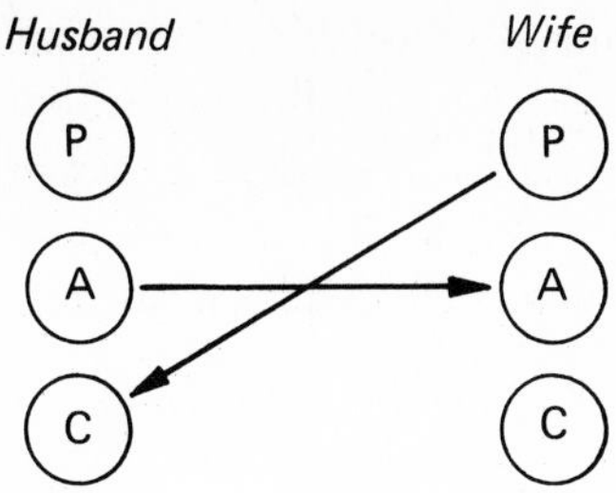

1. *Husband*: Why don't we plan a trip together this next weekend?
2. *Wife*: Don't be ridiculous! We can't afford it.

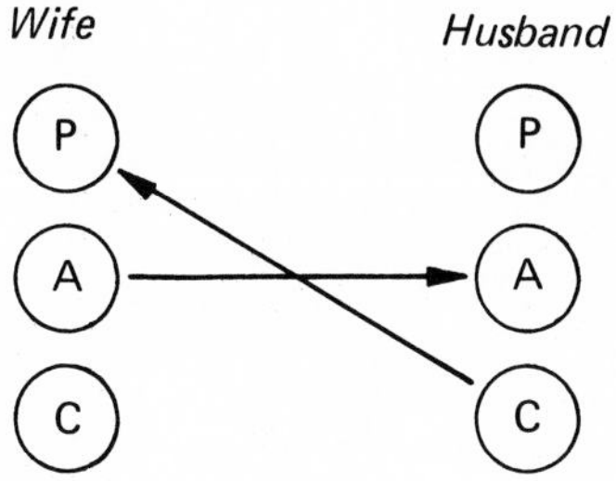

1. *Wife*: You look like you don't feel well (concerned)
2. *Husband*: Stop mothering me. I can take care of myself.

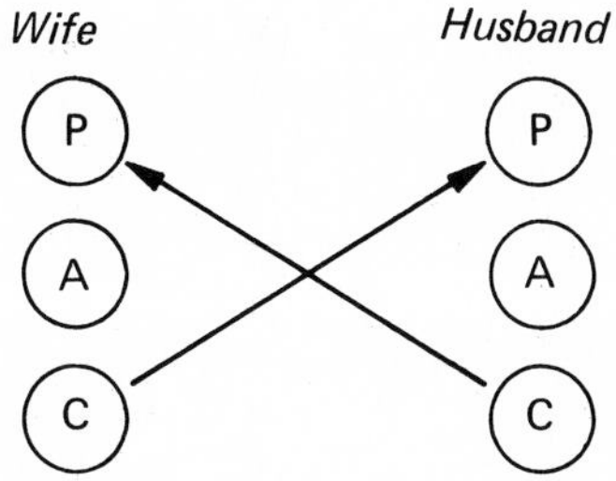

1. *Wife*: I've had a bad day. I could sure use some cheering up.
2. *Husband*: You think you're the only one who ever has a bad day? I don't feel good either.

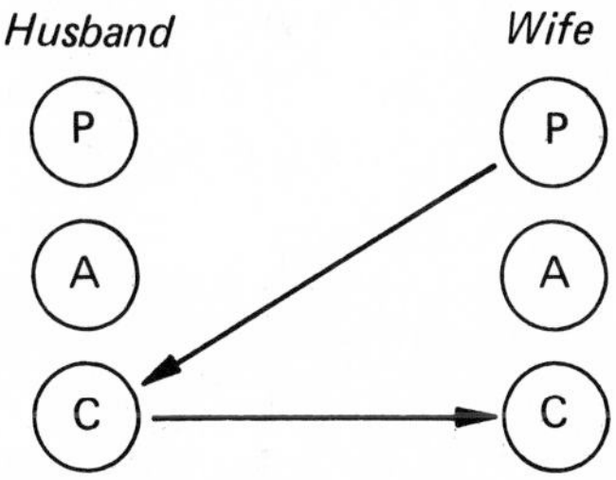

1. *Husband*: Hey, how's my little girl today? (in a jovial mood)
2. *Wife*: Don't call me little girl. You sound stupid. I'm a grown woman.

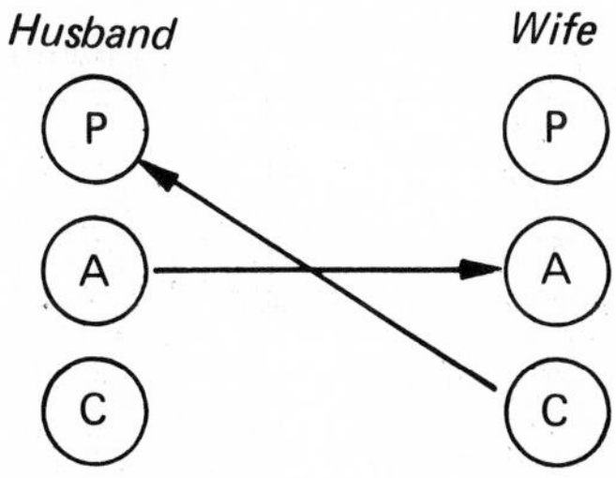

1. *Husband*: Why don't we go over to the Smith's party tonight?
2. *Wife*: I've cleaned house, cooked dinner, driven the kids to music practice, and you expect me to get dressed up and go to a party tonight?

In each of the described instances the transactions are crossed. The person initiating the interaction received an unexpected response instead of the parallel one that was desired. Crossed transactions frequently stimulate conflict. One task of couples in marriage is to get their transactions uncrossed. Interpersonal relationships can be improved by minimizing the frequency of crossed transactions and clearing up those that do occur.

ULTERIOR TRANSACTIONS

Many relationships are impaired because of the use of ulterior transactions that contain hidden messages involving more than two ego states.[34] The person initiating an ulterior transaction appears on the surface to be sending one message, but beneath the surface there is a different one. The motive is often to manipulate the other person to enable the instigator to achieve a goal with little concern for the welfare of others. Ulterior transactions are the kind used when people play psychological games. Because of their residual consequences, they are often more harmful to interpersonal relationships than many people suspect. They result in exploitation.

An example of an ulterior transaction would be the saleslady who says with a smile, "This is one of our finest dresses but it may be too expensive for you." This message may be heard by the customer's *adult* ego, in which case she may respond, "Yes, you are right. It is too expensive considering my present financial situation." However, the message may also be received by the customer's *child.* If the *child* ego state becomes activated, she may think, "I'll show this lady what I can afford," and then responds by saying, "It's beautiful. I'll take it." This appeared to be an *adult* to *adult* transaction, but there was a hidden message from the saleslady to the customer's *child.* In this way the saleslady manipulated the customer into buying the dress.

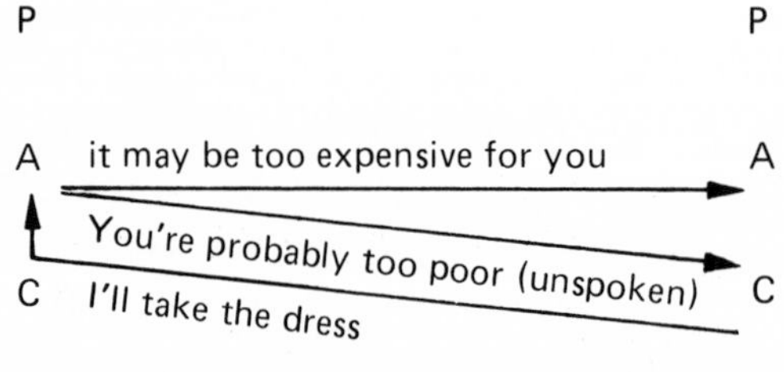

Unfortunately, some husbands and wives spend a great deal of time in ulterior transactions with each other, for example, "I guess we'll never be able to afford a house like that!" This can breed resentment, distrust, and can prevent an intimate, enjoyable relationship.

Analyzing Personal Interaction

One benefit of analyzing our behavior in relationships is that when errors are recognized, responses can be corrected; that is, we increase our chances of behaving differently next time.

For example, as a young couple was walking to the front door after a date, the girl handed her boyfriend the key to the door. After unlocking the door, he kept the key until she had kissed him good-night. Later he realized that he did not want to control his girlfriend's behavior; that is, he wanted to be kissed only if *she* wanted to kiss *him*. The next evening he handed his girlfriend the key *before* he kissed her good-night. In the first situation he assumed the *parent* role and his behavior revealed an attitude, "If you do what I want you to, then you may have your key." In the second situation he assumed the *adult* role and left the decision to his girlfriend.

Relationships are seldom destroyed by single big events. Rather, they are destroyed slowly by small things that, in themselves, seem too trivial to mention. Thus, our attention needs to be focused on daily interaction.

The man who says, "If she can't take me as I am, then she doesn't want *me!*" is incredibly naïve. No two people are so matched that they are perfect together. All relationships require accommodation. There may be, however, some aspects of your personality that are so basic to your being *you* that it will not be possible for you to change. Some differences, for all practical purposes, will have to be accepted. Still, many aspects of interaction can be improved to promote the development of a satisfying relationship, not with the idea that we are sacrificing, but with the intent to do our share to build the best relationship possible.

References

1. Johnson, David W. *Reaching Out: Interpersonal Effectiveness and Self-Actualization.* Englewood Cliffs, N.J.: Prentice-Hall, 1972.
2. Minuchin, Salvador. *Families and Family Therapy.* Cambridge, Mass.: Harvard University Press, 1974.
3. Berne, Eric. *Games People Play.* New York: Grove Press, 1964.
4. Ibid.
5. McCary, James L. *Freedom and Growth in Marriage.* Santa Barbara, Calif.: Wiley/Hamilton, 1975.
6. Harris, Thomas. *I'm OK—You're OK.* New York: Harper & Row, 1969.
7. Fromm, Erich. *Man for Himself: An Inquiry into the Psychology of Ethics.* New York: Holt, Rinehart and Winston, 1947.

8. LAIR, JESS. *I Ain't Much, Baby—But I'm All I've Got.* Greenwich, Conn.: Fawcett Publications, 1969.
9. BERNE, ERIC. *What Do You Say After You Say Hello?* New York: Grove Press, 1972.
10. HARRIS, op. cit.
11. HAUN, DAVID. "Perceptions of the Bereaved, Clergy, and Funeral Directors Concerning Bereavement." Ph.D. dissertation, Oklahoma State University, 1976.
12. HARRIS, op. cit.
13. Ibid.
14. BERNE, 1964, op. cit.
15. Ibid.
16. JAMES, MURIEL, and DOROTHY JONGEWARD. *Born to Win.* Reading, Mass.: Addison-Wesley, 1971.
17. MEININGER, JUT. *Success Through Transactional Analysis.* New York: Grosset & Dunlap, 1973.
18. Ibid.
19. Ibid.
20. BERNE, 1964, op. cit., p. 182.
21. MCCORMICK, PAUL, and LEONARD CAMPOS. *Introduce Yourself to Transactional Analysis: A TA Handbook.* Berkeley, Calif.: Transactional Publishers, 1969.
22. JAMES and JONGEWARD, op. cit.
23. HARRIS, op. cit.
24. Ibid.
25. Ibid.
26. JAMES and JONGEWARD, op. cit.
27. Ibid.
28. BERNE, 1964, op. cit.
29. STEINER, CLAUDE M. *Scripts People Live: Transactional Analysis of Life Scripts.* New York: Grove Press, 1974.
30. JAMES and JONGEWARD, op. cit.
31. MCCORMICK and CAMPOS, op. cit.
32. HARRIS, op. cit.
33. Ibid.
34. MCCORMICK and CAMPOS, op. cit.

2 Choosing a Mate

Photo by Walker Montgomery

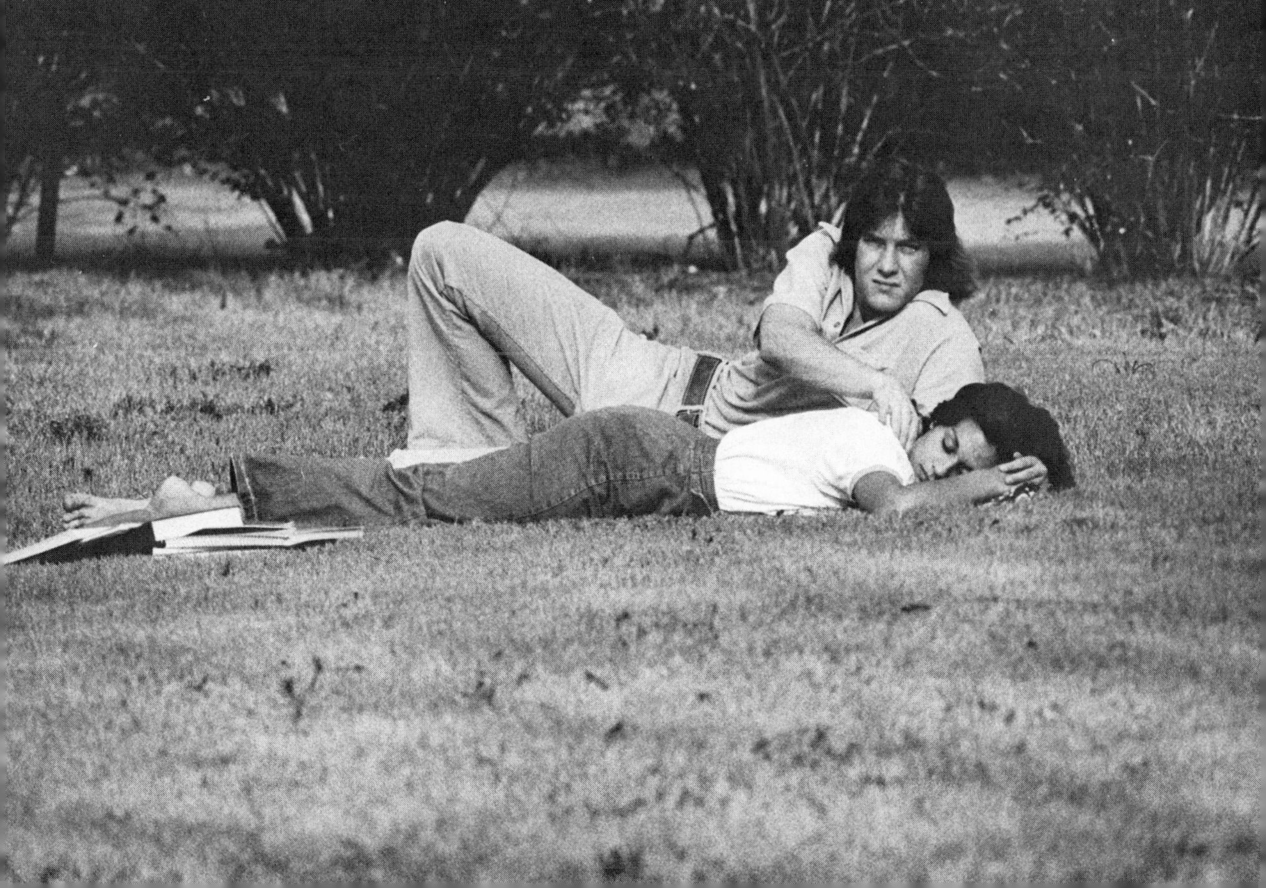

We are shaped by what we love.

Seignat

An Important Decision

One of the most significant decisions that most of us make is the selection of a marriage partner. We choose a mate hoping that person will give us positive psychological strokes and support our OK position. Our mate hopes to receive the same from us. However, these expectations are sometimes not fulfilled; instead, a couple may reinforce each other's "I'm not OK" position because they were not compatible from the beginning. Unfortunately, we may make this decision without sufficient understanding of ourselves or why we choose to marry a certain person.

Society is filled with couples who are poorly matched and with couples who are separated or divorced, trying to understand what went wrong with their lives. Many other couples are more fortunate. They engaged in the mate-selection process with greater insight into how to pair themselves successfully or were simply fortunate to have made a good choice without rational thought.

We receive few cues from society regarding the complexity of mate selection while we are in the process. The standard recommended questions of compatibility often seem irrelevant in the face of strong attraction, and the reasons for attraction are largely unknown. Some are related to life positions and basic types of interaction. Interaction emanating from a "not OK" life position will influence how we respond to others and how they will respond to us. Life scripts further determine the interaction process on which mate selection is based. It seems reasonable to assume that an understanding of ourselves and how we interact facilitates this choice that will affect the rest of our lives.

The mate-selection process that lasts a maximum of ten years for most of us affects the next thirty to fifty years of our lives. Anything we can learn that might aid us in this important decision would seem to be desirable. The mate-selection process, although not fully understood, involves (1) a general pattern followed by most couples and (2) influences affecting the selection of a mate.

The General Pattern

INITIAL ATTRACTION

People tend to be drawn to each other initially by such attributes as personality, physical appearance, and social characteristics.[1] One individual may be attracted to another because of beauty, a warm smile, or a pleasant voice; because the individual has a desirable personality; because their values are compatible; because of high social status; or for a variety of other reasons. Initial interest may be superficial or may from the beginning involve a deep attraction. The important point is that there is a mutual attraction that motivates two people to get to know each other better.

RAPPORT AND INCREASED UNDERSTANDING

Once attracted, a couple establishes rapport through continued interaction. Rapport enables the couple to communicate more freely about their values and life philosophies. The bases for mutual understanding are developed during this period of the mate-selection process.

COMPATIBILITY TESTING

As courtship continues, a couple learns to recognize how they respond to each other emotionally, socially, and physically. Through a variety of experiences they examine their values, life goals, and personality characteristics. Brief or deceptive courting relationships often serve as a deterrent to a successful marriage.

There is great variability in the length of time couples spend in this period of mate selection, and marriage may ensue whether a couple is compatible or not. Sometimes even the couple does not know why they married. However, couples with a high degree of compatibility are more likely to achieve marriage success than couples with a low degree. Some couples discover that they are not compatible and terminate the relationship.

Influences upon Mate Selection

What causes an individual to select a particular marriage partner? Many of our life experiences influence this decision. Some major influences on mate selection have been identified.

PSYCHOLOGICAL COMFORTABLENESS

Perhaps no factor is more important in the mate-selection process than the degree to which the couple feels psychologically comfortable with each other. We are attracted to people with whom we feel safe. We are comfortable with those who are supportive and nonthreatening to us.

Although psychological comfort results from many unknown forces, it is possible to identify some of the characteristics that tend to promote it. These include the inclination to:

1. See things from another's viewpoint (empathy).
2. Be natural; have freedom from extreme guardedness.
3. Have a helpful attitude toward others (supportiveness).
4. Refrain from being judgmental and critical.
5. Show respect and considerateness for others.
6. Be genuinely interested in the other person.
7. Refrain from putting on a front.
8. Be honest and sincere.
9. Avoid playing psychological games and trying to manipulate others.
10. Be trustworthy and dependable.[2]

Most people prefer marriage partners with whom they are comfortable; however, some individuals date and marry persons with whom they do not feel psychologically at ease. In some instances, people marry for reasons such as sexual attraction, status, or escape from an undesirable situation. They may or may not know that many of the qualities that promote comfortableness within relationships contribute to marriage success.

VALIDATION OF SELF-IMAGE

Our choice of a mate is strongly influenced by the image we have of ourselves. Whether we recognize it or not, we all have an opinion of what we are like. Frequently, an individual selects a marriage partner who supports his self-image.[3] For example, a man who sees himself as OK and a winner will probably select a wife who maintains this self-image by being supportive and relating to him in a way that makes him feel competent.

Selecting a spouse who validates our self-image is related to the life-script phenomenon (what we have decided about the kind of person we are, the way we interact with others, and what kind of life we will have), discussed in Chapter 1. We tend to be attracted to those who fit our life script. Similarly, we may be chosen as a marriage partner because we support the self-image part of our partner's life script.

FAVORABLE RESPONSE

It is often assumed that mate selection is determined to a large extent by the favorable response we receive from the prospective mate. Generally, we like people who make us feel good about ourselves, who see the best in us, and who are positive and supportive in their responses toward us.[4] We generally are attracted to those who reinforce our OK position. However, there is a great possibility that we will marry someone who supports our life position and fits our life script even though they may be negative.

IDEAL-MATE IMAGE

We all grow up with an image of what an ideal mate would be like. Perhaps the ideal wife is seen as having dark hair, a warm smile, a supportive manner, and a college education. The perfect husband may be seen as tall, handsome, blond, aggressive, and achievement-oriented. The "ideal type" we construct for ourselves (with the help of society) influences our choice of a marriage partner and may or may not reflect our values.[5]

One study [6] suggests that the ideal-mate image changes in response to new relationships. If so, the ideal-mate image may be the result rather than the determinant of mate selection.

A study by Anselm Strauss [7] found that most of the men and women in his research reported that their real mates and ideal mates were similar both in personality and in physical characteristics. It is interesting to note that more similarity between ideal and real mates seemed to occur in personality traits.

CULTURAL, SOCIAL, AND PHYSICAL HOMOGAMY

People tend to select marriage partners who have similar social characteristics, such as socioeconomic background, religion, race, education, and age.[8] Also, the divorced and widowed often marry others who have been divorced or widowed.[9] Some individuals even tend to select mates who are similar to themselves in physical characteristics, such as height.[10]

Usually, people with common social and cultural characteristics have grown up in similar environments and share the same symbolic environment—words have the same meaning to them and are associated with similar emotions and behavior.[11] Those who live in the same symbolic environment are more apt to like and understand each other than people who live in very different symbolic environments. This is one reason why the research evidence indicates that couples with similar social and cultural characteristics have a much higher rate of marriage success than couples who are very dissimilar.

PSYCHOLOGICAL HOMOGAMY

We enjoy being with people who are psychologically like us. Perhaps we are comfortable with a person who has a similar psychological makeup because we are more apt to share a frame of reference that makes mutual understanding and communication easier. It is not surprising that mate selection is strongly influenced by psychological homogamy. There is some evidence that divergence in specific personality patterns between partners can be emotionally destructive to one or both.[12]

Individuals tend to select marriage partners who have a similar degree of self-acceptance. Those who have a high degree are likely to select a spouse who also has a high degree of self-acceptance; whereas those with a low level often select a marriage partner who also has a low level of self-acceptance.[13]

Research examining mate-selection factors in computer-matched marriages indicates that people tend to select marriage partners with similar personality traits.[14] Computer dating programs, which have emerged in recent years, attempt to match couples on the basis of their preferences and similarities. A study by Ronald Sindberg, Allyn Roberts, and Duane McClain [15] compared two groups of couples who had been paired by a computer dating agency. One group of couples subsequently married, the other group did not. The couples who married were much more homogamous on the personality trait of pessimism-optimism than were those who did not marry. The married group also showed more homogamy on other personality traits, such as reserved-outgoing, trusting-suspicious, and submissiveness-dominance.

The impact of psychological homogamy becomes even more apparent when we recognize that people tend to select mates who are similar in mental health. A study by Bernard Murstein [16] found that couples alike in the degree of neuroticism progressed further in courtship than did couples who were dissimilar in this respect.

PROPINQUITY

Considerable research evidence shows that propinquity, or geographical closeness, is a major factor influencing the selection of a mate.[17] People usually meet because they live relatively close to each other and have some form of daily contact. They may live in the same community, attend the same church, go to the same school, or work in the same office.

PARENTAL INFLUENCE

Parents have a strong influence upon our choice of a mate. Parents provide us with values, a life philosophy, likes and dislikes, and examples of ways to relate to others.[18]

Wilma grew up in a lower middle-income family. Neither of her parents had gone to college. It was their dream that Wilma would complete a college education. Her father had an unfulfilled ambition to become a doctor. This ambition he projected on Wilma and encouraged her from an early age to go to medical school. She internalized this goal and took all of her education very seriously. She developed friendships with others who put a high priority on their education, which further reinforced her goal. She was accepted in medical school and became a pediatrician. During her last year of internship she married another intern. Wilma's selection of a mate was strongly influenced by the aspirations her parents had for her.

Frequently, people select marriage partners who are similar to their parents. The similarity may be physical, but more often it is the partner's values or personality traits that are similar to the individual's parents. A child who has had a positive relationship with a parent may wish to match the parent's personality traits in a marriage partner. If, on the other hand, the relationship with a parent has been negative or hostile, the individual may seek completely different characteristics in a mate.[19]

It should not be concluded that mate selection is predestined by parents. They exert an influence upon the choice of a marriage partner because they are a major agent of socialization for the child and the parents and child tend to hold similar values.[20]

COMPATIBILITY

All of the influences on mate selection mentioned in this chapter contribute to compatibility in a couple's relationship. Two specific forms of compatibility should be considered. The first is *need compatibility,* or compatibility of the couple's predominant psychological needs.

A couple's needs may be considered compatible if they are similar. For example, a man who aspires to consistent recognition in his job must spend a great deal of time at work. He may be compatible with either a wife who understands the desire to achieve or a wife who wishes to have a highly esteemed husband. A woman with a low need for achievement for herself or her husband might not encourage his attempts to get ahead. In fact, she might resent the time he devotes to his work.

A man with a strong need for affiliation (to be close to other people) and a low need for achievement probably would be most compatible with a woman who has similar needs. If he marries a woman with a strong drive for achievement who spends her time and energies outside of the marriage, he may feel neglected and frustrated. Also, the wife in this combination might be dissatisfied with her husband's lack of ambition. Couples generally must be oriented in the same direction to be compatible.[21]

However, a couple's needs may also be harmonious if they are *complementary*. Two people may choose each other on the basis of their ability to fulfill opposite types of needs in each other. Examples of complementary needs might be the following:

1. A man who has a strong need to express hostility selecting a wife who needs to have hostility directed toward her.
2. A man with a high need for dominance being attracted to a submissive woman.
3. A woman with a strong need for recognition being attracted to a man who stays in the background.
4. A woman who needs to be the center of attention choosing a man who admires her and does not compete with her for attention.

Some research supports the thesis that mate selection sometimes occurs on the basis of complementary needs.[22] However, the evidence indicates that mate selection on the basis of similar needs is more prevalent.[23]

The second form of compatibility is *value compatibility*. We tend to seek out and enjoy people who have values similar to ours. Research evidence indicates that we usually develop the closest friendships with people who share our values concerning such issues as sex, religion, and politics.[24] Value similarity is important because it helps us feel accepted by the other person. Many of the convictions we have are so important and personal to us that rejection of the value is interpreted as a rejection of self.[25] Value similarity promotes a feeling of comfort between people and provides a common frame of reference for easier and more effective communication.

Apparently, similarity of values promotes greater enjoyment of a dating relationship from the first date.[26] Studies have shown that couples with similar values find it easier to talk to each other, they are more satisfied with their relationship, and they consider marriage to each other more seriously than do couples without similar values.[27] Similar values are positively associated with marriage success.[28]

No two people, of course, hold identical views on everything, and it is certainly not necessary for a couple to agree always. In fact, some people regard value differences as interesting and stimulating. Value differences may enhance a relationship if great differences do not occur on issues of particular importance to one partner and if partners do not differ on too many issues.

Many marriages fail because individuals ignore major value incompatibilities during courtship. It is important for couples to detect them before marriage and to resolve them, or if they cannot be resolved, decide if it is possible to live with the discrepancies.

Importance of Dating

Dating is the predominant method of mate selection in the United States. Although most people begin dating with no conscious motive of mate selection, it prepares a person as follows:

1. *Providing opportunities to meet and develop relationships with a number of potential marriage partners.*
2. *Increasing self-understanding.* Dating offers an opportunity for an individual to become more aware of personal values, emotional needs, interests, goals, and likes and dislikes as they relate to interaction with others of the opposite sex.[29]
3. *Developing human relationship skills.* When persons first begin dating, they are motivated to develop fundamental social skills such as being good listeners, carrying on a conversation, and being considerate, which benefit human relationships in the future. They learn how to relate well so they can continue to date. Dating stimulates, in a sense, motivation toward self-improvement.
4. *Developing comfort in associating with the opposite sex.* Dating provides an opportunity to gain a greater knowledge and understanding of the opposite sex, thereby assisting a person in becoming more comfortable and confident with the opposite sex. A surprisingly large number of people are not comfortable in associating with the opposite sex. For example, in their study of 3,189 college students, Judson and Mary Landis [30] found that only 25 per cent of the students felt very confident in interaction with the opposite sex. More than 50 per cent reported some difficulty in associating with the other sex.
5. *Providing an opportunity to test compatibility.* The most important way that dating prepares for mate selection is by providing the individual with an opportunity to observe many different personality types. Dating helps people identify the types of individuals with whom they are most and least compatible.[31]

Dating behavior sometimes fails to provide optimum preparation for marriage. One reason for this failure is that much dating behavior involves interaction that does not assist couples in learning how to develop and maintain vital relationships.[32]

Another reason dating does not provide adequate preparation for marriage is that qualities considered desirable in a date and those desirable in a marriage partner are often different. Qualities desired in a date are frequently superficial and irrelevant to an enduring, intimate relationship like marriage. A person may choose a date on the basis of popularity, social poise, or sex appeal. Yet, the same person may desire understanding, support, love, and companionship in a marriage partner. When an individual begins to think seriously of marriage, qualities that are assumed to be more desirable in marriage should be sought in dates.

Couples considering marriage should allow time for resolving difficulties in their relationship during the dating stage rather than waiting until after the wedding. In order to accomplish this task, the dating relationship should be open and honest rather than what has been termed the "traditional dating game." [33]

Poor Mate-Selection Practices

Playing the "dating game" is only one problem in the mate-selection process. Consider some other problems encountered in mate selection.

OMITTING STAGES IN THE MATE-SELECTION PROCESS

Many couples do not go through the stages of mate selection discussed earlier, but stop at mutual attraction. Their attraction for each other is so strong, they do not feel the need to go through the other stages. This may lead to marriage early in the relationship without developing enough mutual understanding of the ways in which they are compatible. Brief courtships can result in a couple discovering after the wedding that they have different ideas and tastes. Length of acquaintance before marriage is positively associated with marriage success.

EARLY MARRIAGES

Unsuccessful marriages are often the result of picking a mate at too early an age. The number of teen-age marriages is increasing, and these marriages have a high divorce rate and the greatest frequency of reported problems of any age group. One explanation for difficulties in adolescent marriages is that the individuals may not have matured enough to be aware of their strongest needs or the types of persons with whom they are most compatible.

Randall and Kay married the summer after high school graduation. They had dated for a little over a year and neither was college-bound. Many of their friends who were not going to college were getting married, and it seemed a logical thing to do. They loved each other and Randall's father had made it possible for Randall to take over one of his farms. Kay had a secretarial position in a local real estate firm. Financially, they would be fine, they thought.

After a year they found themselves fighting constantly, although their basic values were similar. They fought over little things that, they both agreed, really were not important. Both wanted to win, to prove the other wrong, to show that he or she would not be bossed. They were both defensive, thoughtless, and responded in terms of how they felt at the moment rather than thinking through the consequences of their interaction.

As a result, they were unhappy, not quite certain why, but convinced it was the other's fault. They magnified differences out of proportion, were too proud to admit that they were sorry, and within a year had gone heavily in debt purchasing a new automobile, stereo, color television, and other furniture.

Their question was: "What happened to us? We loved each other and now we hate each other!"

LACK OF EMPHASIS UPON BEING THE RIGHT PARTNER

The desire to select a mate who is right for ourselves may mask the importance of choosing one for whom we will be the right partner. It is imperative that we be aware of and strive to meet our partner's needs.

These questions should be considered: Can you respond in a way that brings out the best in your prospective mate? Can you put yourself in your partner's place and see things from his or her point of view? Do you accept your partner or do you plan to change him or her? Do you make this person feel good about himself or herself? Are you understanding and accepting of your prospective mate?

As much emphasis should be placed on giving as on receiving. A satisfying relationship is mutual; a one-sided relationship provides little happiness for either participant.

PLAYING A FALSE ROLE AND CAMOUFLAGING NEEDS

One frequent difficulty in mate selection is the attempt to camouflage real needs while dating. People put on fronts and assume roles that do not reveal their real feelings. A man may have an "I'm not OK" position and believe that a prospective mate who knows what he is truly like (how he sees himself) would not find him attractive. As a result he pretends to be something he is not and may succeed in giving a false impression. Such behavior decreases the possibility of mutual understanding. Virginia Satir gives an example of this in *Conjoint Family Therapy:* [34]

> Joe acted self-confident and strong on the outside but felt uncertain, helpless, and frightened on the inside. When Mary looked at Joe she could say, "Here is a strong person who can take care of me."
>
> Mary acted self-confident, outgoing, talkative on the outside but felt uncertain, helpless, frightened on the inside. When Joe looked at Mary he could say, "Here is a strong person who can take care of me."
>
> After marriage, each found the other was not the strong person for which he hoped. Frustration, disappointment, and anger were bound to result.

A couple like Joe and Mary enter marriage with erroneous impressions and a low level of mutual understanding. Working out patterns of compatibility is much more difficult after marriage than it is before the wedding. Many people have learned the hard way that marriage at any cost is really not better than no marriage at all.

Criteria for Mate Selection

Mate selection is not an entirely conscious process. Many of our reasons for picking a particular individual are unknown even to ourselves. For this reason, time is an important asset. Over time we can, in a relaxed fashion, examine ourselves, our prospective mate, *and* the reasons why we want to marry. We can consider some important criteria that can increase our chances of wise mate selection.

KNOW YOURSELF

Knowing ourselves is not easy. We are continually in the process of understanding ourselves. This is perhaps the most important step in wise mate selection.

What are your most important needs? Do you have a strong need to achieve? Do you need lots of attention and want others to admire you?

What type of person do you seem most compatible with? Do you prefer an outgoing or deferent person? Why are you most compatible with this type of person?

When you are considering marriage, it is helpful to examine your motives.

Why do you wish to marry? Is it because you genuinely like the other person and want him or her to share your life? Is it because you share many interests and goals? Is it primarily because of sexual attraction? Is it because you want to escape something?

It is also wise to examine your expectations of marriage. What kind of marriage do you want? What do you expect of your marriage partner and of yourself?

These questions may be difficult to answer, but they can help you gain a greater understanding of yourself and a greater awareness of the type of person with whom you are most compatible.

KNOW THE PROSPECTIVE MARRIAGE PARTNER

It is also quite important to gain a thorough understanding of your prospective mate. This sounds obvious but many couples marry with very little knowledge or understanding of each other.

What kind of person is your prospective mate? Is he or she the type of person with whom you are compatible? Do you feel comfortable together? What are your prospective mate's most important needs? What are his or her major values? Are those values compatible with yours?

Such information can be gained by listening to your prospective mate and by observation. By talking about things that are important to you, much can be learned about the other person's views and values.

CONSIDER THE EFFECTS OF THE RELATIONSHIP

One important way to improve mate selection is to consider the probable effects the relationship will have upon you and the other person. Does the relationship bring out the best in both of you? Can you promote each other's welfare and happiness in the future? Try to project the relationship ten years from now. What will it be like?

EXAMINE THE COMPATIBILITY

It is important, too, to understand how you are compatible. Are your needs similar or complementary, or both? If incompatibilities exist, are they ones that you can accept and live with?

CONSIDER THE PSYCHOLOGICAL COMFORTABLENESS FACTOR

A study by David Haun and Nick Stinnett [35] indicated that the degree of psychological comfortableness among engaged couples was an important factor in predicting marriage success. The greater the psychological comfortableness of a couple, the more favorable was their prediction for marriage success.

Although comfort cannot always be assessed in concrete terms, it is possible to recognize some aspects of living that make couples more or less comfortable. Do you feel at ease with your prospective mate? Can you be yourself and act natural around this person or do you feel that you must maintain a certain image? Do you feel free to confide in each other? Do you trust each other? Do you feel confident that your prospective partner is committed to you? Two important reasons that couples do not feel comfortable in their relationship is that they do not trust each other and are uncertain of each other's commitment.

IS IT LOVE?

The most commonly stated reason for selecting a mate is "love." Love is the ideal relationship and we are taught from childhood that it characterizes marriage. Certainly, love is desirable, but careful attention should be given to the behavior of love so that we are not mislead by infatuation.

Infatuation is a relationship based on a strong attraction to one aspect of a person to the exclusion of mutual care and companionship. It is assumed by some that infatuation is essentially sexual in nature.[36] We can be physically attracted to many people with whom we would not necessarily have a loving relationship. By itself, strong physical attraction is a poor indication of love.

When we first met, it was like love at first sight. The sexual attraction was intense and we became involved. We had a whirlwind romance and were married five months after we started dating. About three months after the wedding, it began to dawn on me that we had very little in common and that I really didn't even like him. By that time I don't think he liked me either.

Regardless of the source of attraction, a relationship that begins with infatuation may broaden into love as the relationship expands to embrace the partner's total personality.

Few words have been discussed more than love. It has always been a popular topic of poets and novelists. Yet, it has been one of the most misused words in the dictionary. Popular music reflects some of the confusion and misconceptions commonly associated with love. Some songs portray love as a perplexing illusion while others suggest that love is a game with a winner and loser in which someone must get hurt.

The view that love is something a person "falls into" and there is nothing to learn about it is very common. Psychoanalyst Erich Fromm suggests in *The Art of Loving* [37] that such ideas are largely responsible for unwise mate selection and unsuccessful relationships. Regarding love as something one receives rather than gives results in self-centered attitudes that prevent genuine loving relationships. Fromm maintains that a great deal *can* be learned about love. He states that it is an art and, like any art, must be practiced and developed. To practice the art of loving, we must become aware of the components of love. According to Fromm, the four major components are care, responsibility, respect, and knowledge. To these might be added a fifth component: commitment.

Care. We are concerned about the persons we love, wishing to promote their well-being and happiness, wanting the best for them, and wanting them to grow and develop in a positive manner.

Responsibility. We behave responsibly toward those we love. We do not hurt them by acting irresponsibly. This responsibility does not come primarily from a sense of duty and obligation; rather, it is voluntary, involving becoming sensitive to the needs of others and being responsive to those needs.

Respect. A basic component of love is respect. Some couples show less respect for each other than for anyone else. The Greek root of the word *respect* means "to look at." Respect involves "looking at" someone closely enough to be aware of his or her needs and feelings; it communicates an interest in the other person and involves accepting him or her as a unique individual.

Knowledge. We gain an awareness of the needs, values, goals, and feelings of the person we love. With this knowledge comes an understanding of the loved one.

We can know people on a superficial level or we can know them more deeply. For example, on a superficial level we can listen attentively to a person's words. On a deeper level we can become sensitive to the person's feelings as well as words. You may know that a friend is irritable and moody today. On a deeper level you may know it is the result of studying for a big test, feeling a great deal of pressure, and having had too little sleep.

Unfortunately, many couples do not expend the time or effort required to develop a deep understanding of each other before marriage. They marry before knowledge and understanding have developed.

Commitment. Love is much more than a strong physical and emotional attraction. It involves a *conscious* decision to be committed to the other person.[38] To be committed means promoting the welfare, happiness, and growth of the other person and is vital to the growth of trust and security in the relationship.

Couples might gain insight into the question of whether they have a loving relationship by using Fromm's four components as criteria. Do we genuinely care for each other's welfare and growth? Are we aware of and responsive to one another's needs? Are we respectful and considerate of each other? Do we have a deep knowledge and understanding of each other?

According to Fromm, we can also develop a loving response not just toward one person but toward people in general by mastering the major components of love.

WILL THE MARRIAGE LAST?

Most couples at the time of marriage are convinced that they do, indeed, love each other and expect they will find a reasonable degree of happiness together throughout life. Most people still think of their own marriages in terms of permanence.

Although it is reasonable to assume that couples normally love each other at the beginning of their marriages, it is *not* reasonable to assume that all marriages have the same chance of enduring. Research indicates that the probability of a marriage lasting over a period of time is dependent upon numerous factors many people are aware of but do not always attend to when considering marriage.

Joining someone in marriage is often the result of strong emotional factors that, in terms of transactional analysis, trigger the *child* in a person, while rendering one's *adult* relatively ineffective. Such factors as sexual attraction, our needs to be *with* someone rather than be alone, and our desire for security often take precedence over a rational decision to give someone up. The question, as one student put it, is not whether you can face a life together with someone, but whether you can face life without that person.

There is folly in disregarding the odds against the establishment of an enduring marriage just because you are very much in love. Intensity of affectional feeling is a poor criterion on which to base marriage. Many people love each other with absolute fervor but should not marry.

Admittedly, prediction of whose marriage is going to endure is a tenuous business, for individuals vary in their motivations to succeed, in their ability to withstand stress, and in their capacity to find happiness amidst whatever conditions they find themselves. But to abandon all logic and all reason simply because of strong emotional attraction may invite disaster.

Clearly, marriage involves a complex relationship between two people who, normally, need to be headed in the same direction or who have considerable tolerance for their respective differences. Marriage without love may not be desirable, but entrance into marriage requires more than love. Love must be supported with careful evaluation of the relationship and planning for the process of living together.

Choosing to Be Single

For some persons, dating and other mate-selection processes will not lead to marriage. Many men and women do not find the "right person" or simply discover that they prefer the single life-style.

The fact that there are approximately 24 million single adults, eighteen years of age and over, in our society (about 17 per cent of the total population) [39] suggests that singles are not the "leftovers" but people who have opted for a viable alternative to marriage—at least for a while.

Some research indicates that there is little difference between the married and unmarried. One study, for example, found that the feeling of personal fulfillment was about the same among married and single women.[40] Of course, not all life conditions are perceived the same by married and unmarried people; but increased education, employment opportunities, and financial independence for women [41] have relieved the pressure to marry for both men and women. Also, remaining unmarried carries less stigma in our society than it did in the past.

Highly career-oriented people may prefer not to marry. Women who are financially at the top of their occupations are likely to be single.[42] The emotional requirements of a family may deter from marriage people who wish to devote more time and energy to a career.

Financial obligations are also a deterrent to marriage for some. Not only is the single person freer to come and go at will, greater affluence made possible by fewer family financial obligations also may make the freedom more fun. Possibilities for travel and entertainment are increased. Much of the single person's social life includes activities with a relatively consistent group of other singles. The group provides companionship, emotional support and, in general, many of the advantages of a family.

Many persons who do not marry set up a one-person household at an early age, whereas others develop a pattern of living alone after parents have died. Few live with relatives or siblings.[43] Some single people share apartments either with members of the same or opposite sex; fewer choose to live in some form of commune. There has been an increase in "singles only" apartments, although many people report they do not prefer this living arrangement because they see it as a form of exploitation.[44]

Obviously, some people choose to be single and are happy with their decision. However, not all singles are happy. Often their unhappiness stems from the fact that they did not choose to be single and still wish to marry. Regardless of the reasons why people are single, many experience a high degree of loneliness and do not find from other sources the companionship and emotional support they desire. Living singly at any age, but particularly in the later years of life, usually means having no one to provide care when sick or disabled.

References

1. ROGERS, CARL R. *Becoming Partners: Marriage and Its Alternatives.* New York: Delacorte Press, 1972.
ROSENBLATT, PAUL C., and PAUL C. COZBY. "Courtship Patterns Associated with Freedom of Choice of Spouse." *Journal of Marriage and the Family,* vol. 34, 1972, pp. 689–695.
2. HINDMAN, NORA. "Interpersonal Comfortableness Orientation." Masters thesis, Oklahoma State University, 1972.
3. CHAMBLISS, WILLIAM J. "The Selection of Friends." *Social Forces,* vol. 43, 1965, p. 370.
4. CURRY, TIMOTHY J., and RICHARD M. EMERSON. "A Balance Theory: A Theory of Interpersonal Attraction." *Sociometry,* vol. 33, 1970, pp. 216–237.
5. COOMBS, ROBERT H. "Value Consensus and Partner Satisfaction Among Dating Couples." *Journal of Marriage and the Family,* vol. 28, 1966, pp. 166–173.
6. UDRY, J. RICHARD. "The Influences of the Ideal Mate Image on Mate Selection and Mate Perception." *Journal of Marriage and the Family,* vol. 27, 1965, pp. 477–482.
7. STRAUSS, ANSELM. "The Influence of Parent-Image upon Marital Choice." *American Sociological Review,* vol. 11, 1946, pp. 554–559.
8. SCHULZ, DAVID A. and STANLEY F. RODGERS. *Marriage, the Family, and Personal Fulfillment.* Englewood Cliffs, N.J.: Prentice-Hall, 1975.
LANDIS, PAUL. *Making the Most of Marriage.* Englewood Cliffs, N.J.: Prentice-Hall, 1975.
9. MOSS, J. JOEL, FRANK APOLONIO, and MARGARET JENSEN. "The Premarital Dyad During the Sixties." *Journal of Marriage and the Family,* vol. 33, 1971, pp. 50–59.
10. MURSTEIN, BERNARD I. "Physical Attractiveness and Marital Choice." *Journal of Personality and Social Psychology,* vol. 22, 1972, pp. 8–12.
11. MOSS, APOLONIO, and JENSEN, op. cit.

12. Boxer, Louis. "Mate Selection and Emotional Disorders." *The Family Coordinator*, vol. 19, 1970, pp. 173–179.
13. Murstein, Bernard I. "Self–Ideal-Self Discrepancy and the Choice of Marital Partner." *Journal of Consulting and Clinical Psychology*, vol. 37, 1971, pp. 47–52.
14. Sindberg, Ronald M.; Allyn F. Roberts; and Duane McClain. "Mate Selection Factors in Computer Matched Marriages." *Journal of Marriage and the Family*, vol. 34, 1972, pp. 611–614.
15. Ibid.
16. Murstein, Bernard I. "The Relationship of Mental Health to Marital Choice and Courtship Progress." *Journal of Marriage and the Family*, vol. 29, 1967, pp. 447–451.
17. Moss, Apolonio, and Jensen, op. cit.
    Rosenblatt and Cozby, op. cit.
18. Coombs, op. cit.
19. Strauss, op. cit.
20. Coombs, Robert H. "Reinforcement of Parental Values in the Home as a Factor in Mate Selection." *Marriage and Family Living*, vol. 24, 1962, pp. 155–157.
21. Blood, Robert O. *Marriage.* New York: The Free Press, 1969.
22. Winch, Robert F. "Mate Selection: A Study of Complementary Needs." New York: Harper & Row, 1958.
    Huntington, Robert M. "The Personality-Interaction Approach to Study of the Marital Relationship." *Marriage and Family Living*, vol. 20, 1958, pp. 43–46.
    Kerckhoff, Alan C., and Keith E. Davis. "Value Consensus and Need Complementarity in Mate Selection." *American Sociological Review*, vol. 27, 1962, pp. 295–303.
    Winch, Robert F. "Another Look at the Theory of Complementary Needs in Mate Selection." *Journal of Marriage and the Family*, vol. 29, 1967, pp. 756–762.
23. Murstein, Bernard I. "Empirical Tests of Role Complementary Needs and Homogamy Theories of Mate Selection." *Journal of Marriage and the Family*, vol. 29, 1967, pp. 689–696.
    Moss, Apolonio, and Jensen, op. cit.
24. Moss, Apolonio, and Jensen, op. cit.
25. Murstein, Bernard I. "Stimulus-Value-Role: A Theory of Marital Choice." *Journal of Marriage and the Family*, vol. 32, 1970, pp. 465–481.
26. Blood, op. cit.
27. Kerckhoff and Davis, op. cit.
    Coombs, 1966, op. cit.
28. Murstein, 1970, op. cit.
    Kirkpatrick, Clifford. *The Family: As Process and Institution.* New York: Ronald Press, 1963.
29. Womble, Dale L. *Foundations for Marriage and Family Relations.* New York: Macmillan, 1966.
30. Landis, Judson T., and Mary G. Landis. *Building a Successful Marriage.* 6th ed. Englewood Cliffs, N.J.: Prentice-Hall, 1973.
31. McCary, James Leslie. *Freedom and Growth in Marriage.* Santa Barbara, Calif.: Wiley/Hamilton, 1975.
32. Olson, David H. "Marriage of the Future: Revolutionary or Evolutionary Change?" *The Family Coordinator*, vol. 21, 1972, pp. 383–393.
33. Ibid.

34. Satir, Virginia. *Conjoint Family Therapy.* Palo Alto, Calif.: Science and Behavior Books, 1967.
35. Haun, David L., and Nick Stinnett. "Does Psychological Comfortableness Between Engaged Couples Affect Their Probability of Successful Marriage Adjustment?" *Family Perspective,* vol. 9, 1974, pp. 11–18.
36. Blood, op. cit.
Havens, E. M. "Women, Work and Wedlock: A Note on Female Marital Patterns in the U.S." *American Journal of Sociology,* vol. 78, 1973, pp. 975–981.
37. Fromm, Erich. *The Art of Loving.* New York: Harper & Row, 1956.
38. Ibid.
39. U.S. Bureau of Census. *Statistical Abstract of the United States, 1975.* 96th ed. Washington, D.C., 1975.
40. Baker, Luther G. "The Personal and Social Adjustment of the Never-Married Woman." *Journal of Marriage and the Family,* vol. 30, 1968, pp. 473–479.
41. Kieren, Dianne; June Henton; and Ramona Marotz. *Hers & His: A Problem Solving Approach to Marriage.* Hinsdale, Ill.: Dryden Press, 1975.
42. Bowman, Henry A. *Marriage for Moderns.* New York: McGraw-Hill, 1974.
43. Bell, Robert R. *Marriage and Family Interaction.* Homewood, Ill.: Dorsey Press, 1971.
44. Rodin, M. "Tuesdays and Saturdays: A Preliminary Study of the Domestic Patterns of Young Urban Singles." *Urban Anthropology,* 1973, pp. 193–212.

3 Marriage

Photo by Walker Montgomery

At the end only two things really matter to a man, regardless of who he is; and they are the affection and understanding of his family.

Richard E. Byrd

Why People Marry

Marriage is among the oldest of all institutions in history. Century after century people have married. Your parents, grandparents, and great-grandparents chose to marry; and probably you will marry. Why? What is there about marriage that attracts the majority of people generation after generation?

COMMITMENT

We receive positive psychological strokes when we experience the commitment of another person to us. That person's commitment communicates the message that we are OK persons, that we are important. The deep need for a high level of commitment is illustrated by the responses anthropologist Margaret Mead received after her proposal of the two-step marriage. The first stage, which she called *individual* marriage, would have involved easy divorce, no children, and limited economic responsibilities. The second stage, which she labeled *parental* marriage, would be undertaken when a couple desired children and wanted to assume a lifetime responsibility for them. After receiving many responses to her proposal, Margaret Mead stated,

> It now seems clear to me that neither elders nor young people want to make a change to two forms of marriage. They want to reserve the word marriage for a commitment that they can feel is permanent and final, no matter how often the actual marriages fail . . .[1]

Most people have a strong need for the deep commitment of another person. They want to feel that someone is dedicated to them without reservation. Marriage is an expression of this type of dedication and the marriage contract is an important symbol of this desired commitment. Although the absence of a marriage contract certainly may not mean a lack of commitment, as Nena and George O'Neill point out in their book *Open Marriage,*[2] it often does mean just that. If there were a high degree of mutual commitment and responsibility between people, the marriage contract might not be needed. But the fact is most people have not reached this level of development. For most people, the marriage contract remains the ultimate stage of commitment between men and women.

ONE-TO-ONE RELATIONSHIP

Most people wish to have an intimate, meaningful one-to-one relationship with another person. We desire to be with someone who will provide emotional support by meeting our basic needs for self-esteem, affection, respect, trust, and intimacy. We need to feel that we are important to someone. Throughout history, marriage has provided a successful way in which people fulfill these deep emotional needs.

COMPANIONSHIP

One of the primary reasons for marriage is companionship. Much loneliness and isolation have been created as our society has increasingly become more industrialized, urban, and mobile. This sense of loneliness and isolation has resulted in a longing for close emotional ties and companionship. In this respect, marriage has taken on a renewed importance and significance. It offers excellent potential for fulfilling the need for companionship: someone to talk with, to share problems, burdens, and dreams with, to work with toward common goals, and to enjoy recreational activities with.

LOVE

Perhaps the most common motivation for marriage is love. Our lives are most satisfying when they mean a great deal to others. We want someone who will provide us with unqualified love and to whom we can return that love. Marriage, more than any other relationship except the parent-child relationship, has the potential for fulfilling the basic need for mature love, which Erich Fromm has described in the following way:

> To give has become more satisfactory, more joyous, than to receive; to love, more important even than being loved. By loving, one has left the prison cell of aloneness and isolation which was constituted by the state of narcissism and self-centeredness. He feels a sense of new union, of sharing, of oneness. More than that, he feels the potency of producing

love by loving—rather than the dependence of receiving by being loved—and for that reason having to be small, helpless, sick—or "good." Infantile love follows the principle: "I love because I am loved." Mature love follows the principle: "I am loved because I love." Mature love says: "I need you because I love you." [3]

Unhappiness and disappointment in marriage can be the result of immature love, of entering marriage with the expectation that "the other person will give me love," and with little thought given to "my loving the other person." The expectation concerning love is too often one way—receiving love.

One can certainly expect to achieve the goal of love in marriage. But as in all human relationships, it must not be only one way.

HAPPINESS

Happiness is a major goal that people seek in all aspects of their lives: jobs, education, recreation, and community relations. It is not surprising, then, that happiness is a major expectation of marriage.

When people marry, there is a tendency to expect that the husband or wife will "make me happier than I was before." There is great potential for finding happiness in marriage if the two people are compatible, emotionally mature, considerate, and seek to promote each other's happiness. However, as with love, happiness is not one way. It is not just a matter of receiving. Unfortunately, people too often enter marriage with the expectation that the other person "will bring me happiness," with little thought given to promoting the happiness of the partner.

Unhappy people may marry hoping that marriage will eliminate their unhappiness, and some previously unhappy people do become happier as a result. The research evidence indicates, however, that people who are happy before tend to be happy in marriage, and people who are unhappy before tend to be unhappy in marriage. Aron Krich and Sam Blum have stated,

For marriage will not make an unhappy person happy. Marriage is the relationship that most adults find conducive to attaining satisfaction from life, but marriage in itself does not create happiness . . . Marriage can add to one's feeling of self-worth if one enters it feeling worth loving in the first place.[4]

Happiness does not lie in the institution of marriage. It lies within *people* and depends upon the way they relate to each other. The major issue, then, becomes how husbands and wives relate to one another so as to promote each other's happiness.

SEXUAL SATISFACTION

Sexual interaction is a contributing factor to happiness in marriage.[5] For many people, marriage provides the conditions that promote sexual enjoyment and pleasure more effectively than any other relationship. Marriage provides social approval, personal peace of mind, and, ideally, commitment and security with respect to sexual behavior. All of these factors tend to promote the enjoyment and intensity of a sexual relationship.

Marriage ideally symbolizes sexual relationships with love, support, and commitment without exploitation and dishonesty. Although exploitation and dishonesty can occur in marriage, they are less likely than in sexual relationships outside of marriage. This is largely due to the verbalized commitment required to enter marriage.

NEGATIVE REASONS FOR MARRIAGE

People marry for a variety of reasons, and some of them are negative. It is important to recognize the disadvantages of marriage based upon negative motivations.

Spite. There are people who marry for spite, to hurt, or to get back at a person. They try to salve hurt feelings by hastily marrying someone else.

June had been graduated from high school for about two months. She and the boy she had been steadily dating for two years broke up at that time. June was hurt and bitter over the breakup. She wanted "revenge" and "got back" at him by plunging into marriage with someone else a month later. She hardly knew the young man she married. They had little in common, and their marriage lasted one year.

Pity. Some people marry primarily out of pity. When pity is the major basis and there are few other positive reasons, the marriage is started on a less than stable foundation.

Paul was a senior at a major state university when he met Judy who was paraplegic. They became friends, then began to date. Paul possessed altruistic ideals. He resented the fact that most people would not date persons with handicaps. Finally, Paul "shocked" some of his friends by marrying Judy. He later revealed in counseling that he had derived pleasure from shocking them. In a sense he saw his marriage to Judy as a type of social movement. However, his primary attitude toward her had been pity and a major reason for the marriage was pity. Because of a lack of other positive reasons for the marriage on his part, the relationship suffered many problems.

Loneliness. In some instances people enter marriage because of an overwhelming sense of loneliness. Marriage represents a way of escaping isolation, but it is a poor solution because once married such an individual may become demanding and monopolize the spouse. This may have the effect of driving the spouse farther away. As a result, the feelings of loneliness may be intensified and the chances of marriage failure are increased.

Escape from an Unhappy Home Situation. Many young people have unhappy home situations. Some feel they can no longer bear it and move out. Others escape by getting married, seeing this as a way of getting away from conflict and dictatorial parents. They feel they will have greater freedom and independence in marriage. Because they received little affection, understanding, or emotional support at home, they hope to find these qualities in marriage.

Escaping unhappy home situations may help explain why so many youth from low-income families and large families marry early. Constant conflict with siblings, crowded living conditions, and authoritarian parents induce many young people to choose marriage as an escape.[6]

Escaping an unhappy situation is not a sound reason for marriage when it is the major motivation and may contribute to the high divorce rate among youth.

Premarital Pregnancy. Many women find themselves premaritally pregnant. Some cannot accept abortion for themselves and, to avoid an unwed pregnancy, decide to marry. Many such marriages have been successful. However, when the premarital pregnancy is the major motivation, a couple may enter marriage with feelings of resentment toward each other, their parents may not approve of the situation, they may have little in common and may not be compatible. That these conditions often exist is reflected in the high divorce rates among these marriages. The divorce rate is higher among couples where premarital pregnancy has occurred than among couples where pregnancy has not occurred before marriage.[7]

Has Marriage Failed?

Marriage has been more ridiculed, criticized, and blamed for individual failures than perhaps any other institution. It has become increasingly fashionable to criticize marriage and to predict that it will soon disappear. Critics point out that one out of every three marriages now ends in divorce. They cite the estimate of some counselors that over 50 per cent of marriages at any one time are in need of professional help.[8] This, they maintain, is evidence that marriage does not adequately meet the needs of people. Such viewpoints have left many confused and fearful of marriage.

Actually, for the majority, marriage is today more successful in meeting deep emotional needs than any other form of man-woman relationship. It has been one of the strongest, most durable, and most valued institutions in history. The current predictions of doom are not soundly based. Why?

ONE IN THREE IS MISLEADING

The often quoted divorce statistic that one out of every three marriages ends in divorce is misleading. This statistic is most often interpreted that one out of every three marriages in the population ends in divorce. This interpretation is inaccurate.

One of America's leading authorities on divorce rates, Paul Glick, has pointed out that the one-out-of-three statistic is a ratio of divorces to newly entered marriages for each year. Divorcing couples who have been married twenty or thirty years are included in this ratio. Glick has noted that this ratio of one to three is like taking a community and counting the number of divorces that occurred during the year 1976, also counting the number of marriages that occurred during that year, and then determining the ratio of divorces to marriages. As an example, let us suppose that 100 divorces and 100 marriages occurred in a small community during the year 1976. The divorce ratio for that community in 1976 would then be one to one, or 100 per cent. It can easily be seen how misleading this is as an indication of marriage failure for that community. Nevertheless, this is exactly the way the commonly quoted one-out-of-three divorce ratio is determined.

The divorce frequency can be determined more accurately by the number of divorces per 1,000 population or by the number of divorces per 1,000 married women. The divorce rate is today approximately 4.7 per 1,000 population annually and approximately 18 per 1,000 married women.[9] This hardly indicates an overwhelming rate of failure for marriage. It certainly does not point out the death of marriage. It reflects, specifically, that the majority of people stay married.

MOST PEOPLE MARRY

A variety of factors such as economic conditions and wars influence the marriage rate (see Figure 1 in Chapter 17). The marriage rate has slightly declined from 10.9 per 1,000 population in 1972 to approximately 10.3 per 1,000 population in 1975. Even though the marriage rate is currently dropping gradually and we live in a time when it is fashionable to criticize marriage, most people eventually marry. Census statistics show that over 90 per cent of all women have been married by the end of childbearing age. In 1975 there were 2,182,000 marriages as compared to 993,000 divorces, indicating that for any given year more people are marrying than divorcing.[10]

MARRIAGE LASTING LONGER

Many people are surprised to learn that the average marriage of today lasts longer than ever before. In the past, premature death was the major factor in terminating marriages. Today, divorce has replaced premature death as the major factor.

Regardless of the reason for the end of marriage, fewer are terminated early than at any time in history. Taking only the death rate into consideration, the chances of a golden wedding anniversary are approximately twice as likely now as in 1900.[11]

What Is Right with Marriage?

Often we slip into the habit of considering only what is wrong with marriage. Because we live in a problem-oriented culture, it is especially easy to focus only on marriage problems.

MOST MARRIAGES ARE HAPPY

Many people experience great happiness in their marriages. Research studies have consistently shown over the past forty years that the majority of couples are happily married.

A classical study reported in 1939 by Ernest Burgess and Leonard Cottrell [12] found that 63 per cent of 526 couples reported their marriages as being happy or very happy; 14 per cent, as average; and 29 per cent, as unhappy or very unhappy.

Judson and Mary Landis [13] conducted a larger study in 1967 involving 3,189 students in eighteen colleges. The students were asked to evaluate their parents' marriages. Sixty-six per cent rated their parents' marriages as happy or very happy. Only 11 per cent indicated them to be unhappy or very unhappy.

A more recent survey based upon 62,000 marriages was published in the April 28, 1972, issue of *Life*. In this survey 80 per cent of the respondents rated their marriages as happy or very happy.

There is evidence that the majority of older husbands and wives are happy in their marriages. In many instances they experience greater happiness during the later years than at any other time of life. Nick Stinnett, Linda Carter, and James Montgomery questioned 408 older husbands and wives and found that approximately 95 per cent indicated that their marriages were happy or very happy. Approximately 53 per cent felt their marriages had improved over the years.[14]

The research studies, then, give very clear indication that the majority of husbands and wives find happiness in their marriages. At least two thirds are happily or very happily married, although some research studies show much higher percentages. In the average marriage, couples find the benefits and joys worth the effort. Most are successful in achieving a happy, gratifying marriage relationship.

LONGEVITY AND EMOTIONAL HEALTH

Marriage seems to have a positive influence upon longevity. Married persons have a lower death rate at every stage of life than do single persons. Married persons also have a lower death rate than those who are divorced or widowed.[15]

Emotional health also appears to be related to marriage. Married persons have better emotional health and a lower suicide rate than do single persons. The presence of someone who cares, who loves, who is a good companion, and who provides emotional support and understanding contributes immensely to good emotional health.

MATERIAL ENVIRONMENT FOR MARRIAGE HAS IMPROVED

The material environment for marriage today is better than ever before. This is an asset because the environmental circumstances of marriage and family life are very important to success. A separate house and yard are enjoyed by more people in America than in any other Western nation. Home ownership increased from 33 million in 1960 to approximately 40 million in 1970.[16] The separate dwelling insures adequate privacy as well as desirable quantity and quality of environmental space. It also contributes much to reducing in-law conflict. The separate dwelling encourages husband and wife to depend more upon each other for the fulfillment of emotional needs.[17]

The high standard of living today enables many families to enjoy material goods and recreational and leisure time activities at a level that would not have been imagined fifty years ago. Increased affluence has also enabled more youth to obtain college educations. The health of children, especially in lower socioeconomic classes, has been promoted by school medical examinations and school lunch programs.[18]

Living conditions have improved for the later years of marriage. Social Security, Medicare, and pensions have helped to raise the level of living and to promote health during the later years. Such developments have also made it possible for many older persons to maintain separate households and live independently of their children when they so desire.[19]

Faster airplanes as well as improved roads and automobiles have increased mobility and made it possible for family members separated by hundreds of miles to visit each other within a matter of hours. Technological advancement has also increased entertainment and educational opportunities for families. This has particularly been accomplished through the development of television. Aside from the entertainment aspect, there are thousands of children from low socioeconomic homes who are exposed to world developments and many educational experiences through television they otherwise would be denied.

As a result of greater income, more couples are taking advantage of marriage and individual counseling services. There is now far less stigma attached to seeking such services than in the past. The increased amount of information gathered from research and study of marriage and family relationships provides individuals with greater opportunities to prepare for marriage.

The Myths of Marriage

As with most things in life, certain myths exist concerning marriage. These myths, if accepted, can influence a person's perceptions of what marriage is like as well as his actual behavior. Many people have experienced difficulties in marital adjustment because of belief in various myths about marriage. An examination of some of these common myths can help to minimize unnecessary conflict and problems as well as contribute to a more sensible approach to the marriage relationship.

MYTH 1: PROBLEMS GALORE

The problems-galore myth is extremely prevalent and consists of perceiving marriage as a relationship with more problems and conflict than anything else.

According to this myth, marriage becomes synonymous with trouble and one is left with the impression that about the best that can be hoped for is to keep the problems to a minimum and to coexist as peacefully as possible.

This myth has been responsible for many people viewing marriage with a negative attitude: "Marriage is not a bed of roses" or "Marriage is a hard road"; consequently, it contributes to problems in that people who internalize this myth tend to enter marriage expecting many problems. Because they expect problems so strongly, they often behave in such a way as to bring about problems. This is referred to as self-fulfilling prophecy behavior, which means that we tend consciously or unconsciously to behave in a manner that brings about what we expected.

The problems-galore myth has been greatly perpetuated by popular magazines, newspaper columns, cartoons, books, and movies that deal exclusively with problems and conflicts in marriage. As a result, the individual is left with the feeling, "Is this all there is to marriage? It's more trouble than it is worth."

Such a negative emphasis is false because it virtually ignores the happiness, fulfillment, and rewards that marriage offers. It ignores the great potential for human growth in marriage. In short, the problems-galore view is a myth because it is distorted and tends to present only one side of the picture. To achieve a realistic, rational approach to marriage, the positive as well as the negative aspects must be acknowledged.

MYTH 2: MARRIAGE IS A DOWN-HILL EXPERIENCE

Another common myth is that marriage is *necessarily* a down-hill experience. It maintains that as time passes the marriage relationship just naturally and inevitably becomes progressively less satisfying and exciting, and progressively more dull, boring, and empty.

Again, this view influences the attitudes of people and contributes to a reluctance and fear among many concerning the marriage relationship. This reluctance and fear are reflected in such statements as, "Sure, marriage is just fine at the beginning, but what about after you've been married awhile and begin to lose interest in each other?" or "I would rather not get married because marriage seems to destroy love. I mean, why start something that won't last?"

The popular media have portrayed the young married years as the happiest time of marriage. The middle and later years have been much less discussed; but when attention has been given to these later stages, it is usually the problems that are emphasized. The individual is left with the impression that the middle and later years of marriage are much less satisfying than the younger years and that this is just the way life is.

The notion that marriage satisfaction naturally and inevitably declines with time is a myth. Although some research indicates that marriage satisfaction declines with the passage of time among some couples, several research studies indicate that marriage satisfaction increases with the passage of time. Specifically, there is research evidence indicating that the marriage relationship is more satisfying in the later years than at any other period of life.[20]

Actually, whether a marriage relationship deteriorates, improves, or remains about the same depends largely upon the quality of the marriage at the beginning. In one of the most well-known and carefully controlled research studies on this topic, it was found that older husbands and wives whose marital satisfaction had increased or remained the same over the years had very satisfying marriages from the beginning. On the other hand, those whose marital satisfaction had decreased over the years tended to have had unsatisfactory marriages from the beginning.[21]

Contrary to the down-hill myth, there are many husbands and wives who find the joy and fulfillment in their marriage increasing with time. There are many reasons why this should be true. With the passage of time, a husband and wife have greater opportunity to increase their communication skills and understanding of each other. Their relationship has more chances to grow in depth and meaning. Of course, many factors can determine whether they take advantage of these opportunities. These factors will be discussed later. However, it can be concluded that there is no basis for the myth that marriage satisfaction declines with the passage of time.

MYTH 3: MARRIAGE IS A 50–50 PROPOSITION

The 50–50 myth is quite common and contributes to needless frustration, alarm, and conflict among couples. This myth contends that marriage should always be a 50–50 proposition and that in any disagreement or difficult situation each partner should meet the other halfway. This contributes to the unrealistic expectation that each marital situation can be settled on a 50–50 basis. As a result, when one partner perceives that the other is not going halfway, it is easy to become frustrated and resentful because the other is not doing a proper share of the compromising.

What is desirable is not that marriage partners have a 50–50 type relationship, but that each partner be willing to go 80 or 90 per cent to cope effectively in a disagreement or difficult situation. It is highly desirable that each partner be willing to do more than a "fair" share in trying to understand and accept the other's feelings, demands, and, at times, hostile behavior.

Human relationships do not function on a 50–50 basis. There are such situations as illness, a new job, or moving to a new town, when one partner will have to give more than 50 per cent. In other situations it is the other partner who will have to go more than halfway. In any conflict situation one partner is usually more able, emotionally and/or intellectually, than the other to go more than halfway in acceptance and understanding.

Patricia has just started teaching second grade. She feels the pressure of wanting to do well, and she is making several adjustments. As a result, she is more tense and irritable than usual. Her husband, Walt, is aware of the increased pressure she is temporarily experiencing. Because of this awareness he does not take offense at her irritableness and goes the "extra mile" in the conflict situations that arise. Walt has been much more flexible than Patricia. Consequently, he has avoided several serious quarrels. In addition, he has assumed more household tasks to give her extra time to do lesson plans. In time, Patricia will adjust to her new job and the pressure and irritableness will diminish. In the process, Walt, by being willing to go more than halfway, has made the transition easier for both of them.

MYTH 4: THE GREAT SEX DIFFERENCE

The idea that great innate emotional, intellectual, and spiritual differences exist between men and women is extremely common.[22] This myth is a leading factor in communication difficulties between men and women, particularly between husbands and wives. William Lederer and Don Jackson in *The Mirages of Marriage* [23] have presented the following list of ten false assumptions (many of which we hear expressed almost daily) that have evolved from the great-sex-difference myth:

1. Women are more emotional than men.
2. Men are better at abstract thinking than are women.
3. Women are more intuitive than men.
4. Men are more skillful with their hands (and in using tools) than women.
5. Women are more hypochondriacal than men, but men are little boys at heart, especially when they are ill.
6. It is almost always the man who indulges in infidelity and breaks up the marriage.
7. The female usually snares the male.
8. Women are slier and more cunning than men.
9. Men are bolder, physically more vigorous, more courageous than women.
10. Women are more loving than men.

By believing these false assumptions, some men and women fall into the trap of stereotyping each other and then responding to the stereotype rather than to the person. They conclude that all men are inconsiderate or that all women are scheming. By their behavior and by what they say, they pass on these myths to their children who in turn pass them on to their children. In this way the great-sex-difference myth passes from generation to generation, forming a real barrier to understanding between men and women. A self-fulfilling prophecy is set into motion in which men and women who believe in the great-sex-difference myth behave toward each other in such a manner that they unconsciously and consciously arrange life so that what they believe becomes fact.

Although there are physical and some psychological differences between males and females, it is difficult to measure these differences, and much more difficult to measure them accurately.[24] The important point is that most of the differences between men and women are learned rather than innate. As Margaret Mead indicates in her books *Male and Female* [25] and *Sex and Temperament in Three Primitive Societies*,[26] qualities we have traditionally regarded as feminine, such as passivity, have been established in some primitive tribes as the masculine model, whereas in other primitive tribes such qualities are regarded as appropriate for women only. Also, in some primitive societies women are the dominant sex and men are subordinate.

That most of the sex differences are learned rather than innate is further supported by research with hermaphroditic children. (A hermaphrodite is a person with both male and female sexual organs. Usually, one set of sex organs is rudimentary.) Hermaphroditic children make better adjustments to the sex with which their parents have identified them than to the sex to which they are biologically closer. This indicates that the psychological conditioning and expectations established by the parents are far more influential than any innate physiological differences.[27] It is not vast innate differences between men and women that cause most of the problems in marriage.

MYTH 5: CHILDREN WILL CURE A BAD MARRIAGE

Many people sincerely believe that when a marriage begins to have difficulties and becomes progressively unstable, one of the best things the couple, particularly a childless couple, can do to stabilize the marriage is to give birth to a child.

When Jack and I were having some very serious marriage problems, two of my aunts advised me to have a baby. They said having the baby would hold us together. I did have the baby but that only intensified our problems. Our marriage began to improve only when in desperation we began seeing a marriage counselor.

It is true that the advent of a child will improve some unstable marriages. Also, for couples who are happily married the birth of a child often brings them even closer together. However, clinical and empirical evidence indicate that having children does not generally improve an unsatisfactory marriage relationship, rather, it usually compounds the existing problems.

For example, a couple who are constantly in a power struggle with each other may, when a child arrives, begin to use the child as a pawn in their battle. Their relationship may deteriorate further as their communication becomes more indirect because of sending messages through the child.

Another example is of a young wife who feels that her husband might decrease his extramarital affairs by becoming a father. The husband is very pleased when the wife gives birth to a baby girl. In fact, he gives most of his affection to the baby and in a rather obvious way rejects his wife. The young daughter comes to prefer her father over her mother, a situation the father has encouraged.[28] As a result, the wife feels more alienated than before and begins to dislike the child.

MYTH 6: MARRIAGE IS A SOLUTION FOR PROBLEMS AND UNHAPPINESS

A common myth contributing to many marital difficulties is that marriage will solve one's inner problems and loneliness. Some individuals who experience personality problems and unhappiness believe that after they marry things will be much better, their problems will disappear, and their marriage partners will eliminate their unhappiness. Marriage is seen as a means of escape. Unfortunately, such individuals are usually disappointed and find that marriage does not eliminate their problems and unhappiness. In fact, as noted earlier, research shows that persons happy before tend to be happy after marriage, whereas those unhappy before tend to be unhappy after marriage.

MYTH 7: THE SUCCESSFUL MARRIAGE HAS NO CONFLICT

There is the belief among some that happily married couples have no conflict, or at least they do not openly express this conflict in direct confrontation or quarreling. This myth has been a stumbling block to many marriage relationships. Although it is true that a great deal of conflict can be destructive to a relationship, the idea that conflict should rarely or never be present in a successful marriage is unrealistic.

In fact, several family counselors have concluded that one of the biggest problems of many marriages is that couples do not communicate their dissatisfactions to one another. Instead, they hold their frustrations within, thinking that it is somehow not proper to express dissatisfaction directly. Unfortunately, frustrations can build up within an individual over a period of time, and eventually the accumulated hostility is expressed toward the mate in various subtle ways. Resentment may be felt toward the other spouse simply because dissatisfactions cannot be openly expressed. This rigid pattern tends to lead to a greater gap in communication over the years. As William Lederer and Don Jackson in *The Mirages of Marriage* [29] have stated,

> How can spouses trust each other if they never have any disagreements? How does each know what the other really thinks and feels if he is accommodating and thoughtful all the time? For all anyone can tell one spouse may secretly hate the other's guts.

Individuals within marriage have different personalities, different family backgrounds, different metabolic rates, different needs, and different fatigue thresholds. Therefore, it is not surprising that they are occasionally in conflict with each other. Any two people who interact in a relationship as intimate as marriage are certain to have some conflict situations. The goal is not to eliminate conflict completely but rather to learn to deal with such situations in a positive, effective manner.

MYTH 8: MARRIAGE IS MORE IMPORTANT TO WOMEN THAN TO MEN

A common and often subtle myth is that marriage is more important to women than to men. We may hear this belief expressed in many ways:

> "Monogamous marriage is unnatural to a man" (implying that it is natural and more needed by a woman).
>
> "When a woman gets marriage on her mind, look out."
>
> "She chased me until she caught me, only at the time I thought I was chasing her."
>
> "Bob is a pretty sharp playboy bachelor; he has ingeniously avoided getting trapped into marriage."

Such statements may be made in a joking manner, but underneath there is often a sincere unconscious if not conscious belief in the statements. Underlying them is the belief that bachelorhood and multiple sex partners constitute the natural and desired state for men. Also underlying these statements is the notion that marriage is a trap set by women to catch men. The idea that marriage is a trap set by women has important implications for the man-woman relationship because associated with this belief are feelings of hostility toward women. The message that is communicated to a man who believes this myth goes something like this: "Since marriage is a trap, a man who marries is trapped. A trapped man loses his freedom. A man who loses his freedom loses his virility." Such reasoning may be done largely on an unconscious level; but nevertheless, the attitude exists among many men and influences their behavior toward women.

A man who has gone through such reasoning since childhood naturally concludes that women need marriage much more than men. As Myron Brenton in *The American Male* [30] suggests, when a man believes that marriage is of greater benefit to the woman, then regardless of how much he desires to marry a woman, he is apt to resent her (and perhaps all women) unconsciously for placing him in this unfair position. In other words, he is likely to be resentful because he feels that he has received the worst end of the deal. All of us are inclined to feel more satisfied when we believe that we have received a bargain. It is easy to understand how subtle feelings of dissatisfaction are experienced by the husband who believes that marriage is of much greater benefit to his wife than to him, that it is she who is receiving the bargain.

Our society emphasizes the benefits and satisfactions of marriage for women more than for men.[31] Probably for this reason research studies have found that women have more positive attitudes toward marriage than men.[32] However, the lack of emphasis on the benefits and satisfactions that marriage can provide men does not mean that it is not equally as important to them in terms of the fulfillment of basic emotional needs. We all have basically the same emotional needs regardless of our gender. Marriage is an intimate relationship offering the potential for fulfilling these needs for either sex. To assume that marriage is more important to women than to men is to imply erroneously that men have a completely different set of emotional needs than women. Actually, some evidence suggests that marriage in some ways is particularly important to men in that they tend to have fewer close interpersonal relationships outside of marriage and family than women, therefore, they depend more extensively on their marriage and family relationships for the gratification of basic emotional needs than women. Also, some research indicates that men are more family oriented than women.

These observations are not included to try to prove that marriage is more important to men than to women. We simply have no definite basis for concluding that marriage is more important for one sex than for another. The marriage relationship is important to any person, regardless of sex, because it is an intimate relationship in which one person shares a life with another and in which there is great potential for the satisfaction of basic emotional needs.

MYTH 9: ALL PSYCHOLOGICAL NEEDS SHOULD BE FULFILLED BY MARRIAGE

A myth that has created much disillusionment and unhappiness is that marriage should fulfill all of a person's psychological needs.[33] The marriage relationship does meet many psychological needs. Many couples who have a very fulfilling, happy relationship find that their marriage fulfills more of their deep psychological needs than any other relationship. The error comes in expecting that marriage will fulfill all of a person's emotional needs. This is unrealistic. No single relationship or institution, regardless of how satisfying, will meet all of an individual's needs.

This myth poses another danger in addition to being unrealistic. It contributes to a self-centered orientation toward the marriage relationship. An individual thinks primarily in terms of having needs met by a spouse. As a result, the individual thinks very little in terms of meeting the spouse's needs. Such a self-centered orientation tends to contribute to unhappiness, conflict, and marriage failure.

MYTH 10: GOOD COMMUNICATION ELIMINATES ALL CONFLICT

Good communication increases understanding between people and strengthens relationships. Effective and clear communication patterns are associated with marriage success. Conflicts between husbands and wives can be reduced by good communication; however, the idea that conflict can be completely eliminated by even the best communication is a myth.

A certain amount of conflict arises in any close relationship, and some marriage conflicts cannot be resolved no matter how good the communication patterns.[34] But even when compromise fails, successful marriages can and do exist with unsettled conflicts. One way that couples can cope with unresolved conflicts is to realize that one indication of maturity is the acceptance of what cannot be changed.[35]

MYTH 11: ALL TROUBLED MARRIAGES CAN BE IMPROVED BY IMPROVING THE SEXUAL RELATIONSHIP

Many marriages are made better by improving the sexual relationship. Learning more effective sexual techniques that are enjoyed by both partners has helped in many instances.[36] However, the myth that a troubled marriage can be improved by improving the sexual relationship implies that sex is the cure-all for marriage. It ignores the fact that when two people are in tune with each other with respect to values, personalities, and communication patterns, the sexual problems become less crucial. A good sexual relationship is more likely to be the *result* of a good total marriage relationship rather than the cause of it.[37]

Types of Marriage Relationships

Innumerable kinds of marriage relationships develop. However, certain basic types of relationships have been identified as a result of research and clinical observation by psychiatrists and marriage and family counselors. Some of the best research available is reported by John Cuber and Peggy Harroff in *The Significant Americans.*[38] The five types of marriage relationships they identified are conflict-habituated, devitalized, passive-congenial, vital, and total. The cyclical relationship is another type that has often been observed.

THE CYCLICAL RELATIONSHIP

In the cyclical marriage relationship the husband and wife experience periods of sharp conflict, dissatisfaction, and maladjustment followed by periods of great happiness and serenity. Although all relationships are cyclical to a degree, an extreme up-and-down pattern is characteristic here, as stated by one husband:

> Our marriage, as well as our relationship before marriage, has been a series of ups and downs. Sometimes we have a long period of real satisfaction together . . . our marriage is just great and we feel about as close as two people could possibly feel. Then we will have a short time in which we are at each other's throats and are fed up with each other. After a while we get it worked out, and we kiss and make up. Then the whole thing starts all over again.

THE CONFLICT-HABITUATED RELATIONSHIP

Tension and conflict dominate the conflict-habituated relationship. The husband and wife engage in nagging and quarreling. There is a tendency for each to "throw up" the mistakes and offenses of the past to the other. The conflict may be confined to constant, private quarreling, or it may erupt at parties and social gatherings. Perhaps in its most unfortunate form husband and wife engage in a habitual pattern of "cutting" and ridiculing each other, and in general tearing each other down both privately and publicly.

The following case * from Cuber's and Harroff's research involves a middle-aged physician who presents an example of the conflict-habituated type of marriage relationship.

> You know it's funny; we fought from the time we were in high school together. As I look back at it, I can't remember specific quarrels; it's more like a running guerrilla fight with intermediate periods, sometimes quite long, of pretty good fun and some damn good sex. In fact, if it hadn't been for the sex, we wouldn't have been married so quickly. Well, anyway, this has been going on ever since . . . It's hard to know what it is we fight about most of the time. You name it and we'll fight about it. It's sometimes something I've said that she remembers differently, sometimes a decision—like what kind of car to buy or what to give the kids for Christmas. With regard to politics, and religion, and morals—oh boy! You know, outside of the welfare of the kids—and that's just abstract—we don't really agree about anything . . . At different times we take opposite sides—not deliberately; it just comes out that way.
>
> Of course we don't settle any of the issues. It's sort of a matter of principle not to. Because somebody would have to give in then and lose face for the next encounter . . .
>
> No—we never have considered divorce or separation or anything so clear-cut. I realize that other people do, and that I can't say that it has never occurred to either of us, but we've never considered it seriously.[39]

THE DEVITALIZED RELATIONSHIP

The devitalized marriage relationship appears to be rather common. In this relationship satisfaction and vitality have declined over the years. Such a husband and wife describe themselves at an earlier time (the beginning of their marriage) as having done many things together, having had a very satisfactory sexual relationship, and having experienced a close identification and feelings of emotional closeness with each other. In other words, their relationship during the early years was very close, meaningful and satisfying.

However, this couple views their marriage as having deteriorated over the years. Their relationship in the present is one in which they spend very little time together and do not particularly seem to enjoy being with each other. Their sexual relationship is less satisfying both quantitatively and qualitatively. Their relationship has become more superficial and less meaningful. The time the couple does spend together has, over the years, become duty time such as entertaining, participating in the children's activities at school, and taking part in civic activities. There is little overt conflict. The relationship has simply become apathetic, lifeless, and void.

Following are the comments of two middle-aged housewives reported in the

* Excerpts reprinted by permission of Hawthorn Books, Inc. from *The Significant Americans* by John F. Cuber and Peggy B. Harroff. Copyright © 1965. All rights reserved.

research by Cuber and Harroff.* These comments illustrate some common characteristics of the devitalized relationship.

Judging by the way it was when we were first married—say the first five years or so—things are pretty matter-of-fact now—even dull. They're dull between us, I mean. The children are a lot of fun, keep us pretty busy, and there are lots of outside things—you know, like Little League and the PTA, and the Swim Club, and even the company parties aren't so bad. But I mean where Bob and I are concerned—if you followed us around, you'd wonder why we ever got married. We take each other for granted. We laugh at the same things sometimes, but we don't really laugh together—the way we used to. But as he said to me the other night—with one or two under the belt, I think—"You know, you're still a little fun now and then" . . .

Now, I don't say this to complain, not in the least. There's a cycle to life. There are things you do in high school. And different things you do in college. Then you're a young adult. And then you're middle-aged. That's where we are now . . . I'll admit that I do yearn for the old days when sex was a big thing and going out was fun and I hung on to everything he said about his work and his ideas as if they were coming from a genius or something. But then you get the children and other responsibilities. I have the home and Bob has a tremendous burden of responsibility at the office . . . He's completely responsible for setting up the new branch now . . . You have to adjust to these things and we both try to gracefully . . . Anniversaries though do sometimes remind you kind of hard . . .[40]

THE PASSIVE-CONGENIAL RELATIONSHIP

The passive-congenial relationship is very similar to the devitalized one in that it seems apathetic and void. Husband and wife do few things together and do not seem to care deeply for each other. The major difference is that the passive-congenial relationship has been this way *from the beginning*, whereas the couple in a devitalized relationship have intense, exciting memories. In the passive-congenial relationship the husband and wife from the beginning have had minimal personal involvement with each other and usually indicate little feeling of disillusionment.

Cuber and Harroff, on the basis of their research, suggest that husbands and wives establish a passive-congenial relationship in two major ways. One way is by default in which the couple gradually drifts into this life-style by neglecting their relationship and taking each other for granted. Cuber and Harroff point out, however, that from the beginning there was so little the husband and wife cared about deeply in each other that a passive-congenial relationship becomes a sufficient life-style for them.

The second way is by deliberate intention. These passive-congenial relationships are deliberate arrangements by husbands and wives whose interests and emotions are centered not in the marriage relationship, but in other areas such as careers, homemaking, or community activities. Their emotional involvement is primarily directed away from the marriage relationship and both desire this. Such husbands and wives married each other for convenience or utilitarian purposes. An example would be a lawyer who married his wife primarily because she is a good hostess and entertainer and thus helps him advance in his career. The wife is content with her role of hostess. She married the lawyer mainly because he gives her financial security.

THE VITAL RELATIONSHIP

In the vital relationship husband and wife are intensely bound together psychologically and experience genuine sharing and togetherness. In fact, they find major satisfaction in their companionship with each other. They experience a feeling of vitality in their relationship. The presence of the partner seems necessary for one to experience real satisfaction with a particular activity whether this be hobby or career.

This is not a compulsive, false type of togetherness. It is genuine and the husband and wife enjoy being together so much that any activity is enjoyed more if it is shared. Husbands and wives who have established a vital relationship often sacrifice other valued goals in order to enhance their relationship. The following comment was reported by a husband interviewed in Cuber's and Harroff's research.*

> I cheerfully, and that's putting it mildly, passed up two good promotions because one of them would have required some traveling and the other would have taken evening and weekend time—and that's when Pat and I live. The hours with her (after twenty-two years of marriage) are what I live for. You should meet her . . .[41]

Another interesting description is as follows:

> We like this kind of life—where we can have almost all of our time together . . . We've been married over twenty years and the most enjoyable thing either of us does—well, outside of the intimate things—is to sit and talk by the hour. That's why we built that imposing fireplace—and the hi-fi here in the corner . . . Now that Ed is getting older, that twenty-seven mile drive every morning and night from the office is a real burden, but he does it cheerfully so we can have our long uninterrupted hours together . . . The children respect this, too.[42]

In summary, the husband and wife find each other's companionship vital in this type of relationship. However, as Cuber and Harroff have noted, this does not mean that there is no quarreling, nor does it mean that they lose their separate identities. There may very well be conflict; but when it occurs, it is usually over matters that are important to them and they tend to settle disagreements quickly. This is in contrast to the conflict-habituated relationship in which discord is often over trivial matters. Also, the conflict-habituated pair look forward to disagreement and operate by a policy that no conflict is ever to be completely settled.

THE TOTAL RELATIONSHIP

The total relationship is very similar to the vital relationship. The main difference seems to be that the total relationship involves even more mutual sharing and companionship; it is more multifaceted. As Cuber and Harroff state,

> We occasionally found relationships so total that all aspects of life were mutually shared and enthusiastically participated in. It is as if neither spouse has, or has had, a truly private existence.[43]

The various areas of the total relationship reinforce one another rather than being in competition. An example * of this reinforcement quality was given by an engineer:

> She keeps my files and scrapbooks up to date . . . I invariably take her with me to conferences around the world. Her femininity, easy charm, and wit are invaluable assets to me. I know it's conventional to say that a man's wife is responsible for his success and I also know that it's often not true. But in my case I gladly acknowledge that it's not only true, but she's indispensable to me. But she'd go along with me even if there was nothing for her to do because we enjoy each other's company—deeply. You know, the best part of a vacation is not what we do, but that we do it together. We plan it and reminisce about it and weave it into our work and play all the time.[44]

In the total relationships that emerged from Cuber's and Harroff's research, serious differences of opinion had often existed in the past, but these were settled as they *arose,* sometimes by compromise and sometimes by one partner yielding to the other. However, Cuber and Harroff made the important observation that in the total relationship the major consideration was not who was right or wrong, but how the problem could be solved without hurting the relationship.

Cuber and Harroff emphasize that these types of relationships represent different conceptions of marriage, and husbands and wives in each of these types may be happy, adjusted, and content. These relationships do not necessarily represent degrees of marriage happiness. A major purpose of classification such as this is to help us realize that there are different types of marriage relationships just as there are different types of people. Also, such classification makes us more aware that one important factor that differentiates marriage relationships is the variety of forces that integrates the husband and wife within a relationship.

Within a particular marriage, a husband and wife may move from one type of relationship to another. However, such changes are rather infrequent and there is a tendency for relationship types to persist over long periods of time. In fact, Cuber and Harroff found that the particular type of relationship characterizing the marriage of a husband and wife in the middle years was essentially the same they had established during courtship.

What Is a Successful Marriage?

What is a successful marriage? What criteria do you use to judge? Perhaps the best indication is how the husband and wife feel about it. If both spouses are happy and feel it is successful, then as far as they are concerned, their marriage is successful.

Several research studies show there is a high association between the way couples rate their own marriage happiness and happiness ratings assigned to their marriage by others, such as interviewing researchers or friends. Studies have also shown that when husbands and wives rate their marriage happiness independently of each other, there is a high percentage of agreement.[45]

But what are the components of a successful marriage? It is one in which:

1. Both partners are happy with the relationship.
2. There is mutual fulfillment of basic emotional needs.
3. Each partner enriches the life of the other.
4. The marriage environment enhances the personality of each partner and is conducive to each moving toward his or her full potential as a person.
5. There is mutual emotional support; neither spouse threatens the ego of the other; they are comfortable with one another.
6. There is mutual understanding and acceptance of each other as persons.
7. The relationship reflects a mutual (a) care and concern for the welfare and happiness of each other, (b) respect, and (c) a voluntary sense of responsibility for meeting many of the partner's needs.

There are many successful marriages that do not possess all of these components at any one time. A particular marriage may possess some from the beginning, whereas other components may be developed over a period of years. These components contribute to the success of a marriage by creating a positive, healthy, and supportive interpersonal and emotional climate.

References

1. Mead, Margaret. "A Continuing Dialogue on Marriage—Why Just Living Together Won't Work." *Redbook*, vol. 130, April 1968, p. 50.
2. O'Neill, Nena, and George O'Neill. *Open Marriage.* New York: Evans, 1972.
3. Fromm, Erich. *The Art of Loving.* New York: Harper & Row, 1956, pp. 40–41.
4. Krich, Aron, and Sam Blum. "Marriage and the Mystique of Romance." *Redbook*, vol. 136, November, 1970, pp. 65, 118–123.
5. Bell, Robert. *Marriage and Family Interaction.* Homewood, Ill.: Dorsey Press, 1971.
6. Landis, Paul. *Making the Most of Marriage.* Englewood Cliffs, N.J.: Prentice-Hall, 1975.
7. Christensen, Harold T., and Hanna H. Meissner. "Studies in Child Spacing: III—Premarital Pregnancy as a Factor in Divorce." *American Sociological Review*, vol. 18, 1953, pp. 641–644.
   Landis, Judson T., and Mary G. Landis. *Building a Successful Marriage.* 6th ed. Englewood Cliffs, N.J.: Prentice-Hall, 1973.
8. O'Neill and O'Neill, op. cit.
9. U.S. Department of Commerce. "Population Characteristics: Population Profile of the United States: 1974." *Current Population Reports.* Series P-20, no. 279, March 1975. Washington D.C.: U.S. Government Printing Office.
   Division of Vital Statistics, National Center of Health Statistics. "Births, Marriages, Divorces, and Deaths for March 1975." *Monthly Vital Statistics Report*, vol. 24, no. 3, May 27, 1975. Rockville, Md.: Public Health Service.
10. Cox, Frank D., ed. *American Marriage: A Changing Scene.* Dubuque, Iowa: Brown, 1972.
    U.S. Bureau of Census. *Statistical Abstract of the United States, 1975.* 96th ed. Washington, D.C., 1975.
11. Landis, Paul, op. cit.
12. Burgess, Ernest, and Leonard Cottrell. *Predicting Success or Failure in Marriage.* Englewood Cliffs, N.J.: Prentice-Hall, 1939.
13. Landis and Landis, op. cit.
14. Stinnett, Nick; Linda M. Carter; and James E. Montgomery. "Older Persons' Perceptions of Their Marriages." *Journal of Marriage and the Family*, vol. 34, 1972, pp. 665–670.
15. Landis and Landis, op. cit.
16. U.S. Bureau of Census. *Housing Characteristics by Household Composition*, February 1973, Washington, D.C.: U.S. Government Printing Office.
17. Landis, Paul, op. cit.
18. Ibid.
19. Ibid.
20. Stinnett, Carter, and Montgomery, op. cit.
    Stinnett, Nick; Janet Collins; and James E. Montgomery. "Marital Need Satisfaction of Older Husbands and Wives." *Journal of Marriage and the Family*, vol. 32, 1970, pp. 428–434.
    Bossard, James H. S. and Eleanor S. Boll. "Marital Unhappiness in The Life Cycle." *Marriage and Family Living*, vol. 17, 1955, pp. 10–14.

LIPMAN, AARON. "Role Conceptions and Morale of Couples in Retirement." *Journal of Gerontology*, vol. 16, 1961, pp. 267–271.

21. FRIED, EDRITA G., and KARL STERN. "The Situation of the Aged Within the Family." *American Journal of Orthopsychiatry*, vol. 18. 1948, pp. 31–54.
22. LEDERER, WILLIAM J., and DON D. JACKSON. *The Mirages of Marriage.* New York: Norton, 1968.
23. Ibid.
24. Ibid.
25. MEAD, MARGARET. *Male and Female.* New York: Morrow, 1949.
26. MEAD, MARGARET. *Sex and Temperament in Three Primitive Societies.* New York: Morrow, 1935.
27. LEDERER and JACKSON, op. cit.
28. Ibid.
29. Ibid.
30. BRENTON, MYRON. *The American Male.* Greenwich, Conn.: Fawcett Publications, 1967.
31. WHITE, LYNN. "The Changing Context of Women's Education." *Marriage and Family Living*, vol. 17, 1955, pp. 291–295.
    WILLIAMSON, ROBERT. "Dating, Courtship and the Ideal Mate: Some Relevant Subcultural Variables." *The Family Life Coordinator*, vol. 14, 1965, pp. 137–143.
32. WALTERS, JAMES; KAROL K. PARKER; and NICK STINNETT. "College Students' Perceptions Concerning Marriage." *Family Perspective*, vol. 7, 1972, pp. 43–49.
33. CROSBY, JOHN F. *Illusion and Disillusion: the Self in Love and Marriage.* Belmont, Calif.: Wadsworth, 1973.
34. CUTLER, BEVERLY R., and WILLIAM G. DYER. "Initial Adjustment Processes in Young Married Couples." *Social Forces*, vol. 44, 1965, pp. 195–201.
35. CROSBY, op. cit.
36. Ibid.
37. Ibid.
38. CUBER, JOHN F., and PEGGY B. HARROFF. *The Significant Americans.* New York: Appleton-Century-Crofts, 1965.
39. Ibid., pp. 45–46.
40. Ibid., pp. 47–48.
41. Ibid., p. 56.
42. Ibid., pp. 56–57.
43. Ibid., p. 60.
44. Ibid., p. 59.
45. LANDIS and LANDIS, op. cit.

4 Marriage Success Research

Photo by Walker Montgomery

The sign of a good marital relationship is that it can always get better.

Inge and Sten Hegeler

Marriage Success

Many people consider one of the most important goals in life to be the achievement of a successful marriage. Some attain this goal whereas others fail. Why? It is the purpose of this chapter to share some of the answers research has revealed.

Exactly what is a successful marriage? It involves more than permanence because there are permanent marriages in which the partners are miserable and maintain a destructive relationship with each other. Neither is a successful marriage necessarily one in which there is little conflict between the partners because there are many couples who "fight" a great deal but have a meaningful relationship. On the other hand, there are couples who have little conflict but are unhappy and dissatisfied.

Perhaps the best definition is that a successful marriage is one in which both partners receive a high level of personal satisfaction. In terms of transactional analysis it might be defined as one in which positive psychological strokes are maximized and negative psychological strokes minimized, and the interaction of husband and wife is such that they reinforce each other's "I'm OK" position. Marriage success occurs when both partners obtain at least the satisfaction they expected from marriage. In addition, as satisfaction is obtained above this minimum level of expectation, the greater is the success of the marriage relationship from the perspective of the partners themselves.[1]

Most of the research conducted in the area of marriage success has been based upon the use of marital happiness and marital adjustment scales. The scales contain questions designed to determine how happy and satisfied a person is with marriage and how well a couple has adjusted to each other and their marriage situation. These instruments are not perfect; indeed, no instrument would be perfect to measure a phenomenon as complex as marriage success. However, the use of these instruments has provided us with some helpful information. Findings from a large number of studies that have been compiled by Clifford Kirkpatrick,[2] as well as those completed more recently, indicate that there are certain common factors closely associated with marital success.

Premarital Factors Related to Marriage Success

HAPPINESS OF PARENTS' MARRIAGE

One factor that seems to be strongly related to marriage success is the happiness of the parents' marriages. If a couple's parents were happily married, they are more likely to be happily married and less likely to become divorced. If, on the other hand, the couple's parents were unhappily married or were divorced, the likelihood of being unhappily married or becoming divorced is greater. This finding from many different research studies emphasizes the importance of the parents' marriage as a model for their children because children tend to imitate parents both consciously and unconsciously. The way parents relate to each other influences the child's attitude toward marriage and also influences how that child relates and responds to others, particularly to a future marriage partner.[3] If a child grows up seeing parents give each other positive psychological strokes, he or she learns to view marriage as a pleasant relationship. The child also learns how to give positive strokes in relationships.

PERSONAL HAPPINESS IN CHILDHOOD

Another factor found to be strongly related to marriage success is an individual's personal happiness in childhood. An individual who was happy is more likely to have a happy, successful marriage. This finding reflects the importance of a positive parent-child relationship and the importance of parents relating to the child in a warm, accepting, and supportive manner to prepare him for successful and fulfilling relationships with others, particularly with a future marriage partner. Also, it is important for the individual to experience satisfying relationships with persons other than his parents during childhood.[4]

LENGTH OF ACQUAINTANCE

Research indicates that length of acquaintance before marriage is an important factor related to marital success. Generally, the longer the acquaintance, the more likely the marriage will be happy and adjusted. Specifically, those who have known each other over one year are more likely to experience a happy, adjusted marriage than those who have known each other less than a year. A longer acquaintanceship gives the couple a better opportunity to get to know each other and learn what each expects of life and marriage, and to establish effective communication patterns.[5]

AGE AT MARRIAGE

Age at marriage is related to marriage success. Young marriages (those entered at age nineteen or younger) have among the highest divorce rates and the most problems of any group of marriages. For example, one study found that when both spouses were nineteen years of age or younger at the time of matrimony, the marriages lasted only half as long as when the spouses were twenty years of age or older.[6] Young marriages have a higher rate of failure than those entered at a later age because of factors such as limited education, little income, low socioeconomic background, continued need for parental support, emotional immaturity, and lack of awareness of one's own personality needs and personality types with whom one is most compatible.

PARENTAL APPROVAL

Persons whose parents approve of their mates tend to have happier, better adjusted marriages than those whose parents do not approve of their mates. Couples need the approval and support of persons close to them, such as parents. It is particularly important to have this approval and support if the couple lives near the parents and must interact with them a great deal.[7]

REASON FOR MARRIAGE

The primary reason for marriage is an important factor in marriage success and adjustment. If the major reason is to alleviate loneliness or to escape an unhappy family situation, the chances for marital dissatisfaction and failure are greater. On the other hand, if one enters marriage primarily because of genuine love for the other partner and/or because of many common interests, marital success and happiness are more likely to be achieved.[8]

Postmarital Factors Related to Marriage Success

MARITAL ATTITUDES

Various studies indicate that the following attitudes by one or both marriage partners are strongly associated with dissatisfaction and low adjustment in marriage:

1. Husband is more dominant than wife.
2. Wife is more dominant than husband.
3. One partner is extremely jealous of the other.
4. One partner feels superior to the other.
5. One partner feels more intelligent than the other.

An equalitarian, democratic attitude is closely associated with marriage success and high marital adjustment.[9]

RELATIONSHIP WITH IN-LAWS

"I am marrying Joe, not his family," stated one coed in a discussion about in-laws. This statement reflects a common misconception because in reality one also develops a network of relationships with the partner's family. If relationships with in-laws are good, the marriage is more likely to be successful and characterized by a higher degree of satisfaction than if in-law relationships are not good. It is interesting that *not* living with in-laws is positively associated with marriage success.[10]

COMMON INTERESTS

Enjoyable companionship is desired by most people whether married or single. Virtually all who enter marriage hope to enjoy a close companionship with their spouse. Some do not achieve this, whereas others do. What makes the difference?

Many factors can determine whether two people enjoy close companionship. One important factor is common interests. Couples with shared interests are more likely to enjoy participating in activities together and because of their interests in the same types of things, they often have a greater understanding of, and empathy for, each other.[11]

CULTURAL BACKGROUNDS

"Differentness makes for more spice and enjoyment in marriage" is not a very sound philosophy, at least not after a certain point. Many studies agree that having similar cultural backgrounds, such as education, socioeconomic status, race, and nationality, is positively related to marriage success. Great differences in such areas are associated with marriage failure.[12]

DESIRE FOR CHILDREN

Couples with a desire for children reflect a higher degree of marriage satisfaction than those who do not want children. Perhaps the desire for children is an indication of satisfaction within the marriage and a desire to extend the relationship.[13]

It is interesting that *actually* having children is not positively associated with marriage success, even though a *desire* for children is. In fact, there is some evidence that childless couples tend to have a higher degree of marriage satisfaction than couples with children.[14] One study by John Hurley and Donna Palonen [15] among college-student parents found that marriage satisfaction decreased as the number of children born to a couple increased. Couples with children may experience decreased marital satisfaction because they become so involved in rearing the children that they allow themselves to become progressively less involved with one another. Some couples spend so little time with each other as the children are growing up that they become strangers and find it difficult to communicate when the children have left home.

It should be noted that children are one of the few sources of satisfaction in many unhappy marriages, according to research.[16] There are other indications that children may be associated with marriage stability; for example, the divorce rate decreases as the number of children increases.[17] One explanation is that some couples choose to continue to live together after the marriage has failed because of the children. In other cases, the divorce may have occurred early in the marriage before children were born. Another explanation is that children serve as a common bond to bring many couples closer. In summary, the research findings concerning the relationship of children to marriage success indicate that for some couples rearing children is associated with decreased marriage satisfaction, but they serve to insulate couples from divorce. Among the unhappily married, children serve as one of the few sources of satisfaction within the family.

RELATIONSHIP FACTORS

There is evidence that marriage happiness is a result of a satisfying interpersonal relationship between husband and wife in which positive psychological strokes are maximized and negative strokes minimized.[18] Mutual respect, understanding, and expressions of appreciation and affection are important factors in contributing to a positive marital relationship and to happiness.

Degree of involvement in the marriage relationship is another important factor. Partners who are very much involved in the marriage and with each other are more likely to be happily married than those who have little involvement in the relationship.[19] A study by Robert Blood [20] indicated that a prime factor related to marriage success is the wife's happiness with the amount of attention given to her by her husband.

A better understanding of the *types* of behavior that can adversely affect the marriage relationship may be obtained by examining the results of a study by Vincent Mathews and Clement Milhanovich.[21] They reported that unhappily married individuals felt

1. They were neglected by their mates.
2. They received little appreciation, affection, companionship, or understanding from their mates.
3. They were belittled and their self-respect attacked by their mates.
4. They were often falsely accused by their mates.

COMMUNICATION

Clear, effective communication is positively associated with marriage success.[22] The communication patterns of happily married couples have been found to differ from unhappily married couples in the following ways:

1. They talk to each other more often.
2. They more often convey the feeling that they understand what is being said to them.
3. They demonstrate more sensitivity to each other's feelings.
4. They preserve communication channels more effectively and keep such channels open.
5. They make greater use of nonverbal techniques of communication.[23]

COMPATIBILITY OF ROLE EXPECTATIONS

We are more apt to enjoy being with people whose expectations of us agree with our own. Friendships are more likely to develop with such persons than with individuals whose expectations of us are in sharp contrast to our own. The same principle applies to marriage relationships. Marriage success is negatively affected by incompatibility in marital role expectations.[24] The more important the roles are to the individuals involved, the more important it is that the role expectations are compatible. Much marital conflict and dissatisfaction is caused by one partner having different expectations of the mate than he has of himself.

I guess my marriage really busted up over the fact that my wife wanted me to be something I didn't want to be. I have always been very independent. I was before we were married and I intended to continue to lead an independent, individualistic life after we were married. I thought she knew that. I was wrong! After we were married, she expected me to stay home all the time and be a "family man." She wanted us to do everything together. That wasn't the real me. For example, I frequently wanted to spend the weekend with some friends of mine. She couldn't accept that. But she wouldn't go with me because she didn't like the friends. Anyway, we couldn't agree. She couldn't live with what I expected and I couldn't live with what she expected.

Research suggests that marriage satisfaction is *more* dependent upon the extent to which the wife's expectations of her husband agree with his expectations of himself than upon the degree to which the husband's expectations of his wife agree with hers of herself.[25] This may be explained by the findings of Wesley Burr [26] that women have greater tolerance than men for discrepancy between *role expectations* and actual *role behavior.* Wives have consistently been found by studies to possess a greater degree of adaptability than husbands.[27] This is largely due to the cultural expectation that wives should be more adaptable than husbands. With women's roles undergoing significant changes in our society, this relationship may not hold true in the future.

PERSONALITY CHARACTERISTICS

Several personality characteristics have consistently been shown to be associated with marriage success.[28] These include the following:

1. Emotional maturity and stability.
2. Self-control.
3. Ability to demonstrate affection.
4. Willingness to take on responsibility.
5. Ability to overcome feelings of anger.
6. Considerateness.
7. Tendency to be conventional.
8. Favorable self-perceptions.
9. Optimism.

The personality characteristic of adaptability has also been found to be strongly associated with marriage success.[29] There are many situations in marriage in which the flexibility (willingness to modify one's behavior) of one or both partners determines whether a particular conflict situation will be resolved or prolonged.

Some research [30] indicates that it is not the awareness of the effects of specific behaviors on the spouse that differentiate stable from unstable couples, but rather the willingness to change behavior. The stable and unstable couples were found to be equally aware of the effects of certain behaviors; however, the stable couples were much more willing to modify their behaviors.

Studies concerning personality traits of happily and unhappily married persons indicate that those who are happy possess personality traits that contribute to positive interpersonal relationships in general. Persons who are kind, considerate, cooperative, emotionally stable, and optimistic are more likely to have satisfying friendships as well as marriages than those who are inconsiderate, selfish, uncooperative, aggressive, and moody.[31]

How do individuals who are satisfied in their marriages view their spouses? What personality characteristics do they perceive their spouses to possess?

Satisfied individuals see their spouses as being considerate, cooperative, generous, conventional, and responsible. They see them as having moderate, not extreme, personality qualities. The dissatisfied individuals see their spouses as being impatient with the mistakes of others, extremely dictatorial or passive, unkind, blunt, aggressive, gloomy, complaining, slow to forgive, extremely skeptical, and distrustful.[32]

Many personality traits, when possessed by either marriage partner to an extreme degree, may contribute to marital dissatisfaction. For example, one study reported that extreme aggressiveness, dominance, independence, and self-centeredness in wives threatened the self-concepts of husbands and had negative effects upon the marriage relationships.[33]

Failures in human relationships are often explained by the comment, "They had a personality clash." Many marriage partners may possess personality traits that are not compatible. Research evidence indicates that a high degree of marital dissatisfaction and instability is associated with large differences between spouses in the personality traits of enthusiasm, sensitivity, outgoingness, and drive.[34]

You know it seems like a little thing. But it has really caused a lot of trouble between us. I'm kind of a low-key guy. I don't act real excited. My wife is very different. She constantly bubbles with enthusiasm and excitement. She wants to get involved in everything and seems to have an endless supply of energy. She doesn't seem to need much sleep. Five or six hours are plenty for her and she likes to go to bed late. I need about nine or ten hours of sleep and I like to go to bed early. This has caused some conflict. Enthusiasm is good, but there are many times when her enthusiasm just about makes me sick. I get very tired of it and become irritable, and then we find ourselves in a fight.

Marriage satisfaction and stability are associated with similarity in emotional stability, enthusiasm, social boldness, and conscience.[35]

INCOME

It has been said that the elimination of poverty is one development that would reduce the divorce rate.[36] There is much to consider in this statement because it is true that a leading cause of marital failure and unhappiness involves economic problems. When a couple has inadequate income to meet their needs, a situation is created that is conducive to conflict and hostility. Marriage stability is positively related to higher levels of income and to income stability.[37] One study indicates that income has a far greater effect upon marriage stability than either education or occupation.[38]

Financial management is a major source of conflict even in those marriages that have a stable or adequate income. Much disagreement can arise over how money is to be spent. This problem can be particularly frustrating for couples who cannot or do not coordinate their purposes, goals, and interests in life.

OCCUPATION

Occupation seems to be a very important influence upon marriage success. In one study based upon census statistics, the highest proportion of stable marriages was found to exist among professional and technical workers, managers, officials, and proprietors; the highest proportion of unstable marriages, among laborers and service workers.[39]

There are, of course, minor variations from study to study concerning which occupations have the highest proportion of happy and stable marriages and which the lowest. The studies generally agree, however, that marriage stability and happiness are higher among the more stable and higher-paid occupations. Marriage satisfaction is positively associated with job satisfaction, particularly for men.[40] This connection is stronger for men because they have been socialized more than women to view their work success as important to their sense of self-worth. But as the socialization of women changes, this difference may no longer be apparent.

The degree to which one or both spouses are involved in their occupations may affect the marriage relationship. One thirty-eight-year-old wife of a business executive stated:

> I feel like he is more married to his job than to me. He spends about fourteen hours a day with his work. When we're together and supposed to be relaxing that's usually what he talks about. Even on vacation he's preoccupied with his job. I often feel very lonely even when we are together.

Research has shown that the degree of involvement in the work role (time directed to occupational role performance in addition to the normal workday) is associated with marriage happiness. A study by Carl Ridley [41] found that marriage happiness and satisfaction are highest when there is a *low* degree of involvement by both husband and wife with their respective jobs or when the husband has a *medium* and the wife has a *low* degree of job involvement. Ridley's research indicates that when either the husband or the wife becomes highly involved in his or her job, it tends to adversely affect the marriage. These results are consistent with other research [42] indicating that if the husband is more family oriented than career oriented, there is more mutual enjoyment of everyday activities by both spouses than if the husband is more career oriented.

EMPLOYMENT OF THE WIFE

A frequent question students ask is, "Does employment of the wife outside the home make a difference with respect to marriage success?" There is no simple answer.

Several studies, particularly early ones, indicate that less satisfactory marital adjustment exists when the wife is employed outside the home.[43] Employment of the wife may have an adverse effect upon the marriage relationship for several reasons. For some women, being employed and also attempting to be a full-time homemaker is too great a physical strain. They become fatigued, feel pressured to get too many things done, and, as a result, become increasingly irritable. Some wives must work but dislike their jobs, which may adversely affect the marital relationship. In some cases a husband may feel threatened by his wife working outside the home and thus feel resentful toward her.

Employment of the wife is not likely to have a negative effect upon marital adjustment if (a) she is working by choice, rather than because of financial necessity, (b) she enjoys her work, and (c) the husband approves of her employment. Many of the earlier studies did not control these contingent conditions.

More recent research indicates no difference in the marital adjustment of wives who are employed by choice and wives who are full-time homemakers.[44] However, the more recent evidence does reveal more favorable marriage adjustment among wives employed part-time than among wives employed full-time.[45]

Employment benefits the personal adjustment and marriage relationship of some women. For other women, employment has a negative effect on personal adjustment and marriage. Perhaps the best conclusion that can be reached is that the effect employment of the wife has on marriage satisfaction depends upon the particular woman, her husband, her reason for working, whether she enjoys her work or not, and her fatigue level. It should be noted that the research that has been done reflects the effects of an era in which men were considered to be the primary earners. In the future, hopefully, we will have studies conducted on how gainful employment of men affects their performance as househusbands.

RELIGIOUS PARTICIPATION

Many people ask, "Is religious participation really related to marriage success?" The answer is "Yes." There is a positive association between religious participation and marriage success. Couples with a strong religious orientation and participation have fewer divorces than nonreligious couples. Those with a high degree of religious orientation and participation have the highest rate of marriage success and happiness. Those with no religious orientation or participation, show, as a group, a higher rate of marriage failure. The relationship between religiosity and marriage success has been consistently found in numerous studies during the last forty years.[46]

One study, for example, found that where both spouses have no religious orientation, the probability of divorce, desertion, and child delinquency is four times as high as when there is religious orientation.[47] Religion seems to contribute to family cohesiveness. In a study of 3,810 high-school students and 1,469 college students, it was found that those *active* in church activities, in contrast to those who were inactive,

1. Experienced a more harmonious home life.
2. Had a larger circle of friends.
3. Were less worried and more optimistic toward life.
4. Were more interested in helping others.[48]

Religious training during childhood is positively associated with marriage success. Men and women who have had much religious training express greater marriage happiness than those with little or no religious training.[49]

Having a wedding in a place of worship has also been found to be positively associated with marriage success. Those who marry in a place of worship generally enjoy a more successful marriage than those who do not.[50] It is not, of course, the wedding itself that contributes to success, but those who have a church or synagogue wedding may have more serious religious convictions than those who choose to marry elsewhere. The church or synagogue wedding, particularly for those with religious convictions, adds a feeling of sacredness to the marriage relationship.

Why is religious belief positively associated with marriage success? Perhaps the most important reason is that the principal teachings of the major religions emphasize values that contribute to a successful marriage and family life. "Love your neighbor as yourself" is one such teaching. Abiding love and commitment are stressed. Respect is another value that is greatly emphasized. Mutual support and responsibility for the needs and welfare of others are taught as a requirement for the most desirable types of human relationships. "Bear one another's burdens" is a basic teaching of religion. Patience, service, and forgiveness are valued: "First be reconciled to your brother"; "Forgive seventy times seven"; "If a man asks you to go one mile with him, go two with him." The importance of fidelity is stressed: "What God has joined, let no man put asunder." These basic values, which religion generally idealizes and stresses, inspire and encourage people who take them seriously to make a greater effort to establish a high level of interpersonal relationships.

Another aspect of religious involvement that may contribute to marriage and family success is that church or synagogue attendance is for many families an activity they can share together. There is evidence that joint activity strengthens the family if it is rewarding and pleasant. Attendance by the whole family can provide a sense of group identity as they go out into the community together. Participating in activities provides a source of joy and companionship for many couples.[51]

Religious participation also provides friendship support for stable marriage and family living because it puts a couple in contact with other couples who tend to take seriously such values as commitment, respect, love, responsibility, fidelity, and forgiveness. These couples reinforce each other's beliefs and encourage each other to strive for a higher level of interpersonal interaction. They reinforce each other's desire for a stable, successful family life. Their friendship tends to discourage irresponsible behavior and provides a type of social control.[52]

A fourth aspect of religious participation that promotes marriage success for many couples is that awareness of God in the marriage relationship provides a sense of support and strength. This awareness acts to de-emphasize conflict and has a healing, forgiving, and reconciling influence. The awareness of God in the marriage contributes to the ability to forgive and to promote the welfare and happiness of the spouse and other family members.[53]

Problem Areas

There are certain areas about which husbands and wives have most frequently found themselves in conflict. The major problems couples experience in order of difficulty were revealed in a 1967 study by Judson and Mary Landis.[54] They were (a) sexual relations, (b) finances, (c) communication, (d) in-laws, and (e) child rearing. Many couples manage to adjust satisfactorily in the common problem areas as indicated in Table 4–1.

Table 4–1 Percentage of Couples Achieving Satisfactory Adjustments in Seven Areas of Marriage

Area	Satisfactory Adjustment (N = 409)
Sexual relations	63%
Children	71%
Social activities	72%
Religion	76%
Spending family income	77%
In-law relationships	77%
Mutual friends	82%

SOURCE: Judson Landis and Mary Landis, *Building a Successful Marriage*, 6th ed. (Englewood Cliffs, N.J.: Prentice-Hall, 1973), p. 248.

A tabulation of "help-request" letters received by the American Association of Marriage and Family Counselors has revealed eight major problem areas among the couples seeking help (see Table 4–2). Affection, sexual relationships, and personality relations were the three most frequently mentioned.[55]

Major problem areas in marriage were revealed in a study by Robert Blood and Donald Wolfe. The areas included money, sex, children, recreation, personality, in-laws, roles, and politics.[56]

An interesting study of marital problems that physicians reported indicated several important problem areas. These were sex, fear of pregnancy, money, expression of affection, inability to discuss problems, in-laws, failure to express appreciation, and inability to conceive.[57]

All of these studies on difficulties in marriage indicate that the most frequently mentioned problem areas are money, sex, in-laws, communication, and expression of affection. Some of these areas will be more fully discussed later. The possible problem areas in marriage are innumerable as in any relationship. Any area can become a problem. The most important factor in the final analysis is how a couple deals with a problem situation.

Table 4–2 Major Problems Revealed by Husbands and Wives in 1,412 Help-Request Letters

	Husband (Per cent)	Wife (Per cent)	Total (Per cent)
Affectional Relations	11.5	31.0	27.6
Spouse cold, unaffectionate			
Spouse is in love with another			
Have no love feelings for spouse			
Spouse is not in love with me			
Spouse attracted to others, flirts			
Excessive, "insane" jealousy			
Sexual Relations	42.1	20.6	24.4
Sexual relations "unsatisfactory"			
Orgasm inability; frigidity, impotence			
Sex deprivation; insufficient coitus			
Spouse wants "unnatural" sex relations			
Role Tasks—Responsibilities	0.0	6.0	4.9
Disagreement over who should do what			
Spouse's failure to meet material needs			
Parental-Role Relations	0.0	1.7	1.4
Conflict on child discipline			
Parent-child conflict			
Intercultural Relations	11.5	11.4	11.4
In-law relations troublesome			
Religion and religious behavior			
Situational Conflicts	4.0	3.4	3.5
Financial difficulties, income lack			
Physical illness, spouse or self			
Deviant Behavior	7.5	8.7	8.5
Heavy drinking, alcoholism of mate			
Own heavy drinking or alcoholism			
Spouse's "loose" sex behavior			
Own illicit sex behavior			
Compulsive gambling			
Personality Relations	23.4	17.2	18.3
Spouse domineering, selfish			
Own "poor" personality, instability			
Clash of personalities; incompatible			
Spouse's violent temper tantrums			
Spouse withdrawn, moody, "neurotic"			
Spouse quarrelsome, bickering, nagging			
Spouse irresponsible, undependable			

SOURCE: James E. DeBurger, "Marital Problems, Help-Seeking, and Emotional Orientation as Revealed in Help-Request Letters," *Journal of Marriage and the Family,* November 1967, p. 715. Copyright 1967 by National Council on Family Relations. Reprinted by permission.

References

1. Bowman, Henry A. *Marriage for Moderns*. New York: McGraw-Hill, 1974.
2. Kirkpatrick, Clifford. *The Family*. New York: Ronald Press, 1963.
3. Ibid.
4. Ibid.
5. Ibid.
6. Ibid.
   Burchinal, Lee G. "Trends and Prospects for Young Marriages in the United States." *Journal of Marriage and the Family*, vol. 27, 1965, pp. 243–254.
7. Kirkpatrick, op. cit.
8. Ibid.
9. Ibid.
10. Ibid.
11. Ibid.
12. Scanzoni, John. "Family Organization and the Probability of Disorganization." *Journal of Marriage and the Family*, vol. 28, 1966, pp. 407–411.
    Hicks, Mary W., and Marilyn Platt. "Marital Happiness and Stability: A Review of the Research in the Sixties." *Journal of Marriage and the Family*, vol. 33, 1970, pp. 553–574.
13. Kirkpatrick, op. cit.
14. Bernard, Jessie. *The Future of Marriage*. New York: World, 1972.
15. Hurley, John R., and Donna P. Palonen. "Marital Satisfaction and Child Density Among University Student Parents." *Journal of Marriage and the Family*, vol. 29, 1967, pp. 483–484.
16. Luckey, Eleanore B., and Joyce K. Bain. "Children: A Factor in Marital Satisfaction." *Journal of Marriage and the Family*, vol. 32, 1970, pp. 43–44.
17. U.S. Department of Commerce. "Population Characteristics: Population Profile of the United States: 1974." *Current Population Reports*. Series P-20, no. 279, March 1975. Washington, D.C.: U.S. Government Printing Office.
18. Hicks and Platt, op. cit.
19. Gurin, Gerald; Joseph Veroff; and Sheila Feld. *Americans View Their Mental Health*. New York: Basic Books, 1960.
20. Blood, Robert O. "Kinship Interaction and Marital Solidarity," *Merrill-Palmer Quarterly*, vol. 15, 1969*a*, pp. 171–184.
21. Mathews, Vincent C., and Clement S. Milhanovich. "New Orientations on Marital Maladjustment." *Marriage and Family Living*, vol. 25, 1963, pp. 300–304.
22. Karlsson, Georg. *Adaptability and Communication in Marriage: A Swedish Predictive Study of Marital Satisfaction*. Uppsala, Sweden: Almqvist and Wiksells, 1951.
    Locke, Harvey; Georges Sabagh; and Mary M. Thomes. "Correlates of Primary Communication and Empathy." *Research Studies of the State College of Washington*, vol. 24, 1956, pp. 115–124.
    Navran, Leslie. "Communication and Adjustment in Marriage." *Family Process*, vol. 6, 1967, pp. 173–184.
    Leninger, George, and David J. Senn. "Disclosure of Feeling in Marriage." *Merrill-Palmer Quarterly*, vol. 13, 1967, pp. 237–249.

23. NAVRAN, op. cit.
24. BURR, WESLEY R. "An Expansion and Test of a Role Theory of Marital Satisfaction." *Journal of Marriage and the Family*, vol. 33, 1971, pp. 368–372.
MURSTEIN, BERNARD I., and GARY D. BECK. "Person Perception, Marital Adjustment and Social Desirability." *Journal of Consulting and Clinical Psychology*, vol. 39, 1972, pp. 396–403.
25. HICKS and PLATT, op. cit.
26. BURR, op. cit.
27. KIEREN, DIANNE, and IRVING TALLMAN. "Spousal Adaptability: An Assessment of Marital Competence." *Journal of Marriage and the Family*, vol. 34, 1972, pp. 247–256.
28. LANTZ, HERMAN, and ELOISE SNYDER. *Marriage*. New York: Wiley, 1969.
HICKS and PLATT, op. cit.
MURSTEIN and BECK, op. cit.
29. HICKS and PLATT, op. cit.
KIEREN and TALLMAN, op. cit.
30. CLEMENTS, WILLIAM H. "Marital Interaction and Marital Stability: A Point of View and a Descriptive Comparison of Stable and Unstable Marriages." *Journal of Marriage and the Family*, vol. 29, 1967, pp. 697–702.
31. LANDIS, JUDSON T., and MARY G. LANDIS. *Building a Successful Marriage*. 6th ed. Englewood Cliffs, N.J.: Prentice-Hall, 1973.
32. LUCKEY, ELEANORE B. "Marital Satisfaction and Personality Correlates of Spouse." *Journal of Marriage and the Family*, vol. 26, 1964, pp. 217–220.
33. ALLEN, FLORENCE A. "Role of the Self-Concept in Student Marital Adjustment." *The Family Life Coordinator*, vol. 11, 1962, pp. 43–45.
34. CATTELL, RAYMOND B., and JOHN R. NESSELROADE. "Likeness and Completeness Theories Examined by Sixteen Personality Factor Measures on Stably and Unstably Married Couples." *Journal of Personality and Social Psychology*, vol. 7, 1967, pp. 351–361.
35. Ibid.
36. PARKE, ROBERT, and PAUL C. GLICK. "Prospective Changes in Marriage and the Family." *Journal of Marriage and the Family*, vol. 29, 1967, pp. 249–256.
37. HICKS and PLATT, op. cit.
38. CUTRIGHT, PHILLIPS. "Income and Family Events: Marital Stability." *Journal of Marriage and the Family*, vol. 33, 1971, pp. 291–306.
39. BERNARD, JESSIE. "Marital Stability and Patterns of Status Variables." *Journal of Marriage and the Family*, vol. 28, 1966, pp. 421–439.
40. RIDLEY, CARL A. "Exploring the Impact of Work Satisfaction and Involvement on Marital Interaction When Both Partners are Employed." *Journal of Marriage and the Family*, vol. 35, 1973, pp. 229–237.
41. Ibid.
42. RAPOPORT, RHONA; ROBERT RAPOPORT; and VICTOR THIESSEN. "Couples Symmetry and Enjoyment." *Journal of Marriage and the Family*, vol. 36, 1974, pp. 588–591.
43. AXELSON, LELAND. "Marital Adjustment and Marital Role Definitions of Husbands of Working and Non-Working Wives." *Marriage and Family Living*, vol. 25, 1963, pp. 189–195.
GOVER, DAVID A. "Socio-Economic Differential in the Relationship Between Marital Adjustment and Wife's Employment Status." *Marriage and Family Living*, vol. 25, 1963, pp. 452–456.

NYE, F. IVAN. "Maternal Employment and Marital Interaction: Some Contingent Conditions." *Social Forces*, vol. 40, 1961, pp. 113–119.
44. ORDEN, SUSAN R., and NORMAN M. BARDBURN. "Working Wives and Marriage Happiness." *American Journal of Sociology*, vol. 74, 1969, pp. 392–407.
HICKS and PLATT, op. cit.
45. HICKS and PLATT, op. cit.
46. BURCHINAL, LEE G. "Marital Satisfaction and Religious Behavior." *American Sociological Review*, vol. 22, 1957, pp. 306–310.
LANDIS, JUDSON T. "Religiousness, Family Relationships and Family Values in Protestant, Catholic and Jewish Families." *Marriage and Family Living*, vol. 22, 1960, pp. 241–247.
DYER, DOROTHY, and ELEANORE BRAUN LUCKEY. "Religious Affiliation and Selected Personality Scores as They Relate to Marital Happiness of a Minnesota College Sample." *Marriage and Family Living*, vol. 23, 1961, pp. 46–47.
LANDIS, PAUL. *Making the Most of Marriage.* Englewood Cliffs, N.J.: Prentice-Hall, 1975.
BLOOD, ROBERT O. *Marriage.* New York: Free Press, 1969*b*.
47. ZIMMERMAN, CARLE C., and LUCIUS F. CERVANTES. *Successful American Families.* New York: Pageant Press, 1960.
48. STONE, CAROL L. "Church Participation and Social Adjustment of High School and College Youth." *Washington Agricultural Stations Bulletin*, no. 550, Pullman, May 1954.
49. LANDIS, PAUL, op. cit.
50. LUCKEY, op. cit.
ALLEN, op. cit.
51. BLOOD, 1969*b*, op. cit.
52. ZIMMERMAN and CERVANTES, op. cit.
BLOOD, 1969*a*, op. cit.
53. BLOOD, 1969*b*, op. cit.
54. LANDIS and LANDIS, op. cit.
55. DEBURGER, JAMES E. "Marital Problems, Help-Seeking, and Emotional Orientation as Revealed in Help-Request Letters." *Journal of Marriage and the Family*, vol. 29, 1967, pp. 712–721.
56. BLOOD, ROBERT, and DONALD WOLFE. *Husbands and Wives.* New York: Free Press, 1960.
57. HERNDON, C. N., and ETHEL M. NASH. "Premarriage and Marriage Counseling." *Journal of the American Medical Association*, vol. 180, 1962, pp. 395–401.

5 Developing a Successful Marriage Relationship

Photo by Walker Montgomery

Love that does not renew itself every day becomes a habit and in turn a slavery.

Kahlil Gibran

Building a Fulfilling Marriage Relationship

A marriage relationship offers tremendous potential for two persons to enhance each other's "I'm OK" position—to contribute to each other's personal growth, self-respect, morale, and feeling of being loved. Perhaps no other relationship offers as great an opportunity for two individuals to achieve union with each other and to develop mutual commitment and understanding.

The very essence of our society is influenced by what happens in the marriage relationship. Psychotherapist Herbert Otto has said the challenge of the marriage relationship "is the adventure of uncovering the depth of our love, the height of our humanity." [1]

The ultimate desire of two persons interacting within marriage is to achieve emotional closeness. How can this best be accomplished? How can we build enduring, positive marriage relationships? How can we create growth and facilitate marriage relationships so that partners help rather than hinder each other and enhance rather than lower each other's morale? Some important ways for improving marriage have been identified by clinical and empirical research as well as by hundreds of years of observing human behavior.

Appreciation

William James, a famous psychologist, once wrote a book on human needs. Some years after the book was published, he commented that he had forgotten to include the greatest need of all—the need for appreciation. The need for appreciation is also recognized by the proponents of transactional analysis as one of the deepest psychological needs we have. The overt expression of appreciation is one of the most important positive psychological strokes people can give one another.

The records of marriage and family counseling clinics suggest that many marital complaints and problems stem from a lack of feeling appreciated. As one wife stated:

If my husband would just see my good points . . . if he would recognize the worthy things I do and compliment me or let me know he is aware of what I do, it would make me feel so much better about myself. As it is, he just complains and criticizes.

Many of the most intense conflicts and quarrels in marriage stem from one or both partners feeling unappreciated. Consider this example:

Husband: I came home from work and told my wife the good news about the congratulations I had just received from my boss about the big project I had finished. She said she was real happy but the way she said it sounded very disinterested. She started chatting about something else that had happened around the house. This hurt me and made me a little mad. I suggested that we go to a movie that night to sort of celebrate. Just as we were leaving, she started telling me about all the things I needed to fix and do around the house. I became angry and told her to forget about the movie. I was so mad I had to leave the house for a while.

Counselor: Why do you suppose that made you so angry? Of course, you were already a little angry before that happened.

Husband: I think . . . well, I know that I expected her to show some appreciation for my accomplishment. When she didn't even appear interested, this hurt me. Then when she started talking about all the things I hadn't done and needed to do, I just exploded.

A severe lack of appreciation for a partner can place the marriage relationship in danger of being terminated. For example, when a wife feels that her husband does not appreciate her, her ego is threatened. Her sense of worth is attacked. Lack of appreciation or ridicule can easily result in a wife feeling resentment, bitterness, and even hatred toward her husband.

Expressing sincere appreciation communicates the message, "You are a person of worth and dignity. You have much to contribute to others." Expressing appreciation also communicates, "I am interested enough in you to see and acknowledge your positive qualities." Expressions of sincere appreciation serve to strengthen relationships, and their importance cannot be overemphasized. Each of us can develop the art of expressing *genuine* appreciation because nearly every person has qualities that can be sincerely appreciated. The expression of appreciation involves important psychological strokes that help people feel, "I'm an OK person." Failure to receive simple psychological strokes has motivated many people to change jobs as well as marriage partners.

Seeing Each Other as Persons

Several family counselors and psychotherapists have observed that in the final analysis each person asks himself the question, "Who am I?" and seeks positive responses from others.[2] We all want others to reinforce our OK position. A vital challenge for each person within the marriage relationship is to see beyond a partner's outward appearance, to see beyond the partner's anger, hostility, or specific problems.

It is particularly necessary to see beyond the specific roles the partner plays. Husbands and wives sometimes become so accustomed to seeing each other as players of roles, such as father, lawyer, mother, wife, or a cub scout leader, that they stop seeing each other as persons and, unfortunately, stop interacting with each other as persons. Instead, they relate to each other superficially as players of roles, as labels, leaving each other yearning to have the core of his being touched by the other. Each is left desiring to be seen and interacted with as a person.

A marriage relationship can be stronger and more functional when the husband and wife respect each other as unique persons. When the marriage partners' understanding of each other goes beyond the daily roles each assumes, spouses feel closer to one another.

Minimizing Threat in the Relationship

A marriage relationship is enhanced when husband and wife relate to one another in such a way as to minimize making each other feel threatened. Sometimes a husband and wife threaten each other's self-esteem so badly that both become concerned with defending themselves and retaliating against the other. This type of interaction forms a vicious cycle in which each partner feels threatened by the other. Such couples can become so concerned with defending themselves that they may see very little good in each other or in their relationship. They become caught in a cycle of negative interaction that reinforces each other's "I'm not OK" position.

Perhaps the most common way husbands and wives threaten each other is through evaluating each other negatively. Consider the husband who made the following statement to a marriage counselor:

My wife really knows how to make me feel two feet tall. I guess this is the main reason I became involved with Irene. She made me feel I was ten feet tall. She didn't tear me down. She seemed to bring out my best qualities. For years my wife has been criticizing me for not advancing more and being more successful in my occupation. She has even done it in front of our friends a few times. I usually strike back in some way and we get into a big yelling fight. I feel like I have had all I can take.

Everyone has some characteristic he does not like and does not want presented to others. It is that part of ourselves we consider to be not OK, to be inadequate and unattractive. Many marriage problems are caused by husbands and wives exploiting and focusing attention upon each other's limitations. For example, a wife relates to her husband in such a way as to communicate to him the following message:

The part of you that you do not like and fear . . . this is the real you! You fear that because you are not as aggressive and successful in your work as your friends, that this somehow means you are inadequate. This is true. You are inadequate. This is the real you!

To relate to a person in a way that causes feelings like this is threatening to his self-esteem. Over a period of time, such messages could destroy the relationship.

The goal of the marriage counselor often becomes that of determining those areas in which husband and wife threaten each other's feared self-concept.[3] These areas, for example, may include physical appearance, sexual response, occupational performance, or social relationships. After these problem areas have been identified, the counselor's goal is to assist the couple to develop patterns of relating to one another that end the threats to each other's feared self-concepts and instead confirm positive or ideal self-concepts. In other words, to improve the relationship, the couple must find ways to enhance each other's OK position and stop reinforcing each other's "I'm not OK" position.

Recent experiments have indicated a person is most attracted to a particular individual when that individual's communicated evaluation of him or her is consistently positive. A person is least attracted to an individual whose communicated evaluation of him or her is consistently negative.[4] People, including husbands and wives, can alienate themselves from each other by developing a pattern of negative interaction with, and negative evaluation of, each other.

Providing Joy Experiences

Living should be a joyful experience. We should feel OK about ourselves and the part we play in that portion of the world we are able to influence. Each one of us has alternatives for bringing more joy into our daily lives. Our challenge is making use of these opportunities. Although there is great potential for the marriage relationship to be a most happy experience, many couples allow their marriages to get in a rut. Psychotherapist Herbert Otto indicates that because we believe joyful experiences are the result of luck or circumstances, we fail to realize that we can make joy happen and consequently needlessly miss out on much joy in marriage.[5]

We can create the climate and circumstances in which joy experiences become a part of our daily lives. A husband and wife can bring more joy into their daily lives in many ways. Following are just a few ways of providing joy experiences in marriage.

BEING RECEPTIVE TO NEW EXPERIENCES

One method of creating a joyful climate is to seek and welcome new experiences. A couple open to them has a greater probability of experiencing more joy in their daily lives. Many couples report that trying new experiences has helped get their relationship out of a rut and has been a positive influence on their marriage.[6] One husband stated:

> Since we decided to create our own experiences, we've tried more new, different things than we had the last four years of marriage. We've been to several great lectures, gone horseback riding, tried cooking together and enjoyed it, traded cars, read more, tried new ways of sex—I could go on and on. Trying things has made a difference to us.[7]

When daily life patterns become old to couples, it is easy for them to feel that they are old and that their marriage relationship is old. To maintain a degree of excitement, adventure, anticipation, and youthfulness, new experiences can be a big help.

MORE SPONTANEITY

One way of achieving greater satisfaction in marriage is through more spontaneous interaction between husbands and wives. The word *spontaneous* is derived from a Latin word that means "coming from within." Spontaneous interaction involves a sharing of inner feelings, thoughts, and ideas in which the inner self of one person reaches out to the inner self of another. The interaction is free of calculation, routine, and formality. A small increase in spontaneity in marriage can do much to create a more positive atmosphere in the relationship.

Many marriages and many lives are badly in need of more spontaneity. One factor that prevents couples from being more spontaneous is that they become victims of habit in interpersonal interaction and daily routines. When our responses become patterned, our behavior resists modification because it feels comfortable to stay as we are even though life may become boring.[8]

A factor that minimizes spontaneity in our interaction is the middle-class tendency to postpone pleasure and happiness in the present for possible gains in the future. Many people believe that pleasure and joy of the moment should be postponed in view of long-range goals that could be better achieved through this postponement. However, in far too many instances we postpone joy experiences without any real reason except that we have fallen into a habit of "putting off" enjoyment.[9]

Many husbands and wives are addicted to the "putting off" habit. They work hard for many years, postpone joy experiences for themselves, retire, and then find they cannot enjoy their retirement. They have become so addicted to postponing pleasure, they find it difficult to have fun even during retirement when they consider it is socially appropriate to do so.

If we allow ourselves to be more spontaneous, we will be less likely to "put off" joy experiences. As Herbert Otto suggests, the danger is not that we will become too spontaneous but that spontaneity will play too small a role in our lives. The more that spontaneity characterizes the marriage interaction, the greater is the possibility of mutual growth and joy.[10]

PARTICIPATING IN ENJOYABLE ACTIVITIES

One obvious way of bringing more enjoyment into a marriage relationship is for husband and wife to participate in activities that they like. If a couple enjoys playing tennis, then they can have more fun by structuring their schedules so that they play tennis together regularly. If a couple enjoys fishing, they should fish. If there is nothing a couple enjoys doing more than camping in the mountains, then they should certainly camp in the mountains periodically.

Many couples do not do the things they find fun, however, because they have fallen into the habit of "putting off" many things they view as frivolous and not of great importance. Both fresh vitality and interest can be added to a marriage relationship by a couple listing the activities they most enjoy in life, and then following through with those plans. As a husband who participated in a couple's discussion group said:

> Marjorie and I listed the five things we most enjoyed doing; I was really surprised to find that we rarely did any of them. None of them were a significant part of our active life-style. So we tried an experiment. For two months we actively participated in the five enjoyable activities. The vitality this brought into our relationship was amazing. We both feel younger and more energetic. We are less tense and have rediscovered the art of having fun.

PROVIDING SPECIFIC JOY EXPERIENCES FOR EACH OTHER

Husbands and wives can express love and appreciation for one another by providing pleasurable experiences for each other. The impact of this simple approach has been underestimated and, as a result, tends to be practiced little by couples. There are many ways in which couples can increase daily pleasure and happiness for each other. Herbert Otto in *More Joy in Your Marriage* [11] suggests some interesting ways couples might provide joy experiences for each other.

Biweekly Paradise. The biweekly paradise is a very simple and enjoyable practice in which on one day out of the month the husband does everything in his power to make his wife feel that she is in paradise. Then, on another day in the month the wife does everything in her power to create a day of paradise for him. Whatever pleases that partner is the appropriate behavior for the day. This might include cooking a favorite food, breakfast in bed, going to a concert, or even throwing a surprise party. The partner who is making this day of paradise for the other might appropriately think of himself or herself as a genie who fulfills the other's every wish and tries to think of surprises and activities to add to the fun and beauty of this day. As Otto states, the harder one partner tries to make this day truly one of paradise for the other, the more likely the other will want to give that partner the same kind of experience.

Love Gifts. The use of love gifts is a technique that many couples have found to be particularly fulfilling. A love gift is defined as anything one partner does for another that gives happiness or assistance. A husband's love gift to his wife might include washing dishes for her on a particular day. A wife's gift to her husband might include washing the car or mowing the lawn. Some couples find that trading love gifts on a daily basis is very enjoyable.

Many years ago when I was a graduate student at the University of Iowa, I was married. Although we had very little money, we never thought of ourselves as poor. It was impossible, however, for us to exchange the kind of gifts that we would have liked to have given, so we began exchanging "love gifts."

I remember one Christmas my wife gave me a box of pancake flour with a note that promised she would make pancakes for me each Sunday—a task she really disliked—for a year. It was another way of saying, "I love you." My gifts included pledges to do the household things she disliked. With the passing of years, we continued the "love gifts" at Christmas. In turn, when our children were very small, they would give a love gift that involved bringing in the milk each morning or the newspaper at night, and when my son grew to the age that he loved monster movies, my love gift one year was to take him to all the monster movies for a year.

Our love gifts were not limited to members of our family. When my son was in preschool, his love gift to his godmother was to collect pine straw and tie them in little bundles she would use to start fires in her fireplace.

As the years have passed, the love gifts have meant a great deal to the members of my family. Because they frequently involve pledges for an entire year, they are gifts that remind us throughout the year of our love for each other.

Joyful Happenings. Providing a joyful happening is one way of bringing happiness into a marriage. Herbert Otto suggests that there are too few joyful happenings in our daily lives and that we can remedy this by planning more of them.

An example of a joyful happening might be a wife planning a surprise party for her husband and inviting only his favorite people. In fact, any party can be a joyful happening if the husband and wife enjoy the people who are invited and if the party's activities are pleasant. Interestingly, parties designed to bring pleasure to the host and hostess are not as common as might be expected. Some studies show that more than 75 per cent of the parties given, especially by businessmen and professionals, are given either to repay obligations or for business and social status purposes.[12] Other examples of joyful happenings are a trip to the mountains or simply a much needed and desired evening of relaxation at home.

Reshaping the Marriage Environment

The quality of the marriage relationship is, as noted by Herbert Otto, greatly influenced by the marriage environment. The term *marriage environment* is here used to refer to the immediate physical surroundings; the network of relationships one has with friends, relatives, and acquaintances; and habitual marriage behavior patterns.

The quality of the relationship can be either positively or negatively affected by the marriage environment. Yet, couples having marital difficulties often ignore this. A particular couple may, after analyzing their situation, decide that certain aspects of their marriage environment have a negative influence upon their relationship. This couple can then do much to reshape their marriage environment in order to minimize the negative elements and promote the positive aspects.

RESHAPING THE HOUSING ENVIRONMENT

Many couples find that redecorating their home provides a refreshing lift and seems to have a beneficial effect upon their relationship. It is interesting that some couples report that redecorating their bedroom to make it more attractive has for a time had a positive influence upon their sexual relationship.[13]

Actually, how much of an effect redecorating a home has upon a marriage relationship is not known. However, it is a well-established fact that color influences emotions. Room arrangement and room size influence people. Yet many husbands and wives let their housing environment remain unchanged over long periods of time. A couple may purchase a picture they like, display it in a prominent place, and let it stay there for years, becoming so accustomed to seeing the picture in the same place that it loses its impact. Household accessories reflect and express the personality, which is constantly in a process of change. Esthetic needs change over the years as well.[14]

Couples need to re-examine periodically the impact upon them of their housing environment. Do they still get feelings of happiness from their surroundings? They might wish to consider the Japanese custom in which art pieces or accessories are periodically brought out of storage for appreciation.

When reshaping the housing environment occasionally, it is not necessary to do a complete job of redecorating. The couple should ask themselves, "How can we change our physical environment to create a more joyful, comfortable atmosphere?"[15] Much positive change can be accomplished simply and inexpensively by relocating the furniture, acquiring a few houseplants, or repainting a room.

RESHAPING RELATIONSHIPS WITH OTHERS

The network of relationships a couple establishes with friends, relatives, and acquaintances has strong influences upon the marriage relationship. Outside relationships can naturally have either a beneficial or negative influence upon a couple's marriage. Some relationships that a couple establish tend to have a long-range, deadening effect upon their marriage, as a husband indicated in this example:

We were a little surprised when we realized that some of our friendships we had maintained for some time were really not enjoyable at all. There were three couples whom we saw on a regular basis for no reason other than because we had been doing it for so long. I mean, we would go out with these couples and we would not look forward to it; we would not enjoy it. In fact, it was dull; there was no life in it. Because we spent too much time with these couples, they influenced our marriage in a bad way, and made us feel weary, disinterested, and oppressed. In fact, one of the couples was very pessimistic and cynical. They spent a lot of time putting people down, including each other. After spending an evening with them, we always went away feeling depressed and as if things were not at all well with us. My wife and I finally decided that we did not want to continue the relationships with these three couples in this manner any longer. We decided there was no reason why we could not change our circumstances to bring more positive experiences into our marriage. Gradually, we eased out of our relationships with these three couples and began to establish new friendships, starting with a new couple who were members of our church. They had many of the same interests we did, and we had more fun together than we had experienced with another couple in a long time. The change that we made in our friendships was a breath of fresh air in our marriage. We began to feel more alive and more interesting.

Husbands and wives need relationships with people who:

1. Promote their growth as individuals instead of retarding their growth.
2. Help them feel good rather than bad about themselves.
3. Are enjoyable to be with rather than unenjoyable or simply neutral.
4. Strengthen rather than weaken the marriage.

Herbert Otto recommends that couples analyze their relationships with others and ask themselves such questions as, "Which individuals or couples with whom we have established relationships have the most positive influence upon our marriage?" "Which individuals or couples bring out the best in us?" "Which persons have a negative influence upon our marriage or bring out the worst in us?" After this type of analysis, the couple might well decide to reshape their relationship patterns with others.

RESHAPING HABITS

We are all creatures of habit. Most of us do not realize the extent to which our lives are dictated by habits. Many of our habits are good; however, some may serve to minimize the joy and contentment in a marriage relationship. By analyzing their habits, both their daily routines and their interpersonal and emotional response patterns, a husband and wife can determine if reshaping their habit environment would increase the pleasure of their marriage. Herbert Otto suggests that husbands and wives discuss such questions as, "Would a change in certain habits make us feel more alive, more happy, more spontaneous, or better about ourselves?" "Would a change in certain habits help us to enjoy life more?" "Would a change in certain habits help us to be a more positive influence upon each other?"

Changing habits is not easy, but the benefit that can result from changing negative habits is worth the effort. Many couples who have analyzed their habits and made the effort to make desirable changes report very positive influences upon their marriage relationship, as this wife indicated:

We made a list of our habits and discovered that some of them were making our lives miserable. For example, we had been getting up in the mornings just early enough to dash off to work and barely be there on time. This gave us a feeling of being very rushed and disorganized. The worst thing about it was that it irritated us and we would quite often get in a spat with each other. We changed this habit by getting up two hours before we had to be at work. For a while it was hard to make the change because we wanted to sleep as long as we possibly could. However, gradually we started going to bed earlier. The change has improved things for us quite a bit. We have plenty of time to have breakfast and get dressed. We no longer start the day off rushed and irritated.

A husband discussed a habitual behavioral pattern that created problems in his marriage.

My wife and I identified two response habits that were preventing us from experiencing the maximum amount of satisfaction in our marriage. Whenever my wife would criticize me about anything, no matter how constructive her criticism was, I would always get mad and become sarcastic. This would result in a feud that lasted a couple of days. We decided this was stupid. I decided to change my habit of reacting to criticism by getting mad and sarcastic. This was very hard because I had always reacted to criticism in this way. But through very disciplined effort I was able to gradually change. Also, we had discussed the way my wife expressed her criticism and decided she needed to make some changes. She became more diplomatic and positive in her expression of criticism. This particular change by her was an immense help to me in changing my responses because her criticism was much less antagonistic. Our marriage relationship is improved due to better understanding between us and less bickering.

Commitment

Many students in high school or college whose academic records are less than outstanding later distinguish themselves in their vocational fields. Such persons develop a drive to succeed that sustains them during periods of crisis and enables them to persist regardless of the defeat they encounter. This commitment is as important in marriage as it is in one's vocation. Couples who are committed to one another and determined to endure in spite of temporary unhappiness during certain stages of their marriages may, in the long run, achieve greater happiness in life than those couples who decide to terminate their marriages because they find themselves in an unhappy period.

Divorce is seen as the solution to unhappiness in marriage by an increasing number of couples. Others, however, view their commitment in different terms and find that working toward solving their problems is a more satisfactory approach. Of course, to the woman who is being abused by an alcoholic husband, quite understandably, divorce may indeed be the best answer.

Commitment in marriage differs greatly. Some couples decide after a few weeks it is not worth the struggle. Others experience a commitment that is typified by the following:

My commitment to my wife is total. I am not a fair-weather husband. I accept her and love her when she is difficult as well as when she is loving. I don't expect to be happy all the time. I believe that in my role as a husband I should be a "builder," that is, I believe I should be *for* my wife and that my behavior should reflect that I support her. I assume responsibility for my behavior. I consider it irrational to become angry with her. Although I acknowledge that my behavior affects my wife, I do not hold myself responsible for *all* her behavior, so when she becomes angry, I do not blame myself unnecessarily, hence there is little need to become angry and defensive myself.

You may believe that such a philosophy is difficult to live by, but it isn't. For me it is practical since I do not like a great deal of conflict, and I recognize that I can influence the amount of conflict in my marriage by the way I respond.

I believe that the "total commitment" concept is an intelligent one in that it serves as a guideline on which to base my behavior. When I am in doubt, I usually choose the response that best supports my wife. I say "usually" rather than "always" because if I am forgetful and concerned about my personal world, I say and do things that damage us.

Few things are more important in building gratifying human relationships than the sincere commitment of one person to another. Commitment involves devoting oneself to promote the welfare and happiness of the other; a willful attempt to tolerate the other's shortcomings and focus instead upon strengths; and sincerely trying to understand and meet the needs of the other. When someone is truly committed to another, a powerful bond is formed, as this husband reports:

The greatest thing about our marriage is Ruthie's commitment to me. It is really a feeling of security and strength to me. I know that she is 100 per cent for me. I can always count on her. If I'm in trouble or need help, man, she is going to be there at my side to help me through it. If I am wrong or right, she is committed to me. Believe me that's not exactly common among the couples we know.

When someone is committed to us, we feel that person is for us. As a consequence, we trust the person to "do right" by us; we value that individual and, in turn, tend to be committed to him or her. In this way commitment contributes to strong relationships.

Commitment is sometimes lacking in a dating relationship, and in its place there is sometimes the attitude, "What can I get out of this person? What can this person do for me?" The lack of commitment in a dating relationship is often sensed and is a source of insecurity and distrustfulness. Students in two southern universities reported that lack of commitment by dating partners was the chief barrier to enjoying a good relationship.[16]

Sometimes this lack of commitment by one partner may not be obvious and only vaguely sensed by the other. Such a relationship may result in marriage where the commitment may or may not develop, as indicated in the following example:

> When Jeff and I were dating, I knew that his commitment to me was not great but I ignored it. I thought it would grow after marriage. It didn't. Jeff dated other girls even when we were engaged. He has continued this pattern in the form of extramarital relationships since we married. But even the extramarital relationships are casual. Jeff never shares his inner thoughts and feelings with me. I don't think he has with anyone. I believe he is afraid of becoming really involved with another person.

Commitment entails a decision to be involved with someone and to participate fully in making the relationship with that person as positive and fulfilling as possible. It entails a decision to be 100 per cent for that person and to be devoted to that person's welfare regardless of whether his or her behavior is good or bad. In a very real way, commitment indicates a willingness to love.[17]

Development of Trust

The development of trust is essential for a satisfying, enduring marriage relationship. The trust level between a husband and wife is a key determinant of the success of their emotional and sexual relationships.

When you trust someone, you feel comfortable and safe with that person. Consequently, you are more likely to share feelings and dreams with him or her. You don't feel inhibited or self-conscious around that individual.

When you don't trust someone, you feel uncomfortable, a little insecure, and defensive with that person. You feel as though you have to be on guard because of uncertainty that this person is for you or will "do right" by you. Unfortunately, some husbands and wives don't trust each other and are not comfortable together.

It is easy to say that we should be more trusting, but there must be a reason for trusting. How can husbands and wives increase the level of trust in their relationship? Perhaps we can best answer this question by observing that we have a higher degree of trust in someone when:

1. Our trust in that person has not been violated.
2. Confidentiality has not been violated.

3. That person's actions and attitudes toward us indicate that he or she is for us and will "do right" by us.
4. That person is emotionally supportive of us.
5. That person is interested in promoting our well-being.
6. There is an absence of exploitation or manipulative behavior on the part of that person toward us.
7. That person's behavior is honest, sincere, genuine, and consistently real.
8. That person expresses acceptance of us rather than rejection.[18]

Concentrating on Our Own Responses

"It's your fault. If you hadn't nagged so much, I wouldn't have got drunk at the party."

"You drive me crazy when you start arguing like that."

"How can you expect me to act civil when you talk to me like that?"

"If you wouldn't be so bitchy, I would stay home more and be a better husband."

We have all heard statements similar to these. Each may be true in a specific marriage situation. However, the important point here is that in each situation one marriage partner is concentrating upon the responses of his mate rather than upon his own response. Each statement indicates that one partner believes that his responses *depend* upon the behavior of the other.

Regardless of how desirable it would be for one spouse to change his behavior, it is undesirable for either to blame the other for *all* their problems. First, this is a destructive approach to human relationships in that it concentrates on criticizing the other partner. It focuses on the other person's inadequacies. Such an approach says in effect, "You are bad for these reasons." Second, this is a poor approach because it is a "cop-out." The "I-would-be-good-if-you-didn't-act-so-badly" attitude relieves one partner of any responsibility for the condition of the relationship by stating that everything depends upon the behavior of the other partner. Third, blaming the other partner is futile in that the person who is labeled as inadequate feels threatened and, therefore, usually responds by defending his actions. The blamed person may also launch a counterattack.

The practice of complaining and blaming is ineffective because it does not deal with the unwanted behavior at the time it occurs. An individual who concentrates almost entirely upon the responses of the other partner ignores the fact that his responses have a significant influence upon the relationship in general and the unwanted behavior in particular.[19]

The marriage relationship involves the interaction of two people, and the quality of that relationship depends upon the responses of *both* partners. We cannot make someone respond in a certain way, but *we can control our own re-*

sponses. It is, therefore, logical that we should be primarily concerned with our own responses in a relationship rather than upon the responses of the other person.

Accepting and Respecting Differences

There is a tendency for people to view qualities in others that are markedly different from their own as inferior and to reject them. This tendency helps to cause frustration, resentment, and deterioration in marriage relationships.

For example, a man whose mother always enjoyed cooking and took great pride in it may marry a woman who came from a home where the mother cooked very little and the family ate in restaurants most of the time. The husband and wife have come from different backgrounds in this respect; however, the husband may view this difference in his wife as an inferior quality. He may interpret the fact that his wife does not want to cook as laziness and disinterest in the home. If he views his wife's differentness in this way and criticizes her for not cooking, he communicates the message, "You are inferior. You are inadequate."

She may begin to think, "He criticizes my background, my family, my breeding. He does not think I am worthy." If the message is taken seriously by the wife, she may feel threatened and find some shortcoming in her husband. In this way the practice of criticizing each other's differences grows to the point where among some couples almost all of their interaction is spent in ridiculing and rejecting each other's differentness. The relationship can deteriorate into a pattern of each spouse depreciating the other and, at the same time, trying to prove self-worth.

Such negative and destructive interaction can evolve from the spouses' failure to accept and respect each other's differentness. Differences are, after all, simply *differences* rather than indicators of inferiority. In fact, many of the human-relationship problems between nations, races, and the generations are due to the failure to accept this simple principle.

Effort and Determination

We all know that it takes effort, a conscious attempt to perform at a high level, as well as determination to succeed in business, in school, or in athletics. However, we often fail to realize the importance of effort and determination in successful human relationships.

Effort is certainly necessary for success in marriage. Many marriages disintegrate and end partly because the partners fail to make the effort to keep their relationship pleasant and meaningful.

Effort may not appear to be greatly needed at the beginning of a marriage, particularly when the husband and wife are very compatible.[20] However, when the fascination of a new relationship begins to wear off, the partners may take each other too much for granted and no longer bother with little acts of affection and consideration toward one another. This can result in the partners slipping into a psychological stupor and indifference regarding their relationship. It does not have to be this way. If a person's professional career can show greater productivity and personal satisfaction as the years pass, then so can a marriage relationship grow in fulfillment and meaningfulness.[21] Effort can be a big factor in contributing to a marriage relationship that grows in happiness and harmony.

Unconditional Positive Regard

The everyday contentment and joy in marriage relationships are greatly enhanced when both spouses express positive regard for each other that is unconditional. This is what psychologists call noncontingent reinforcement. It means that the husband and wife express appreciation for each other regardless of their particular behavior at the present moment. The beauty and strength of this quality of interaction is that it communicates that each partner is OK in the eyes of the other. It involves giving positive psychological strokes unconditionally. Positive regard does not depend upon certain rigid demands and expectations being met. In short, positive regard does not depend upon the other person's performance. The person is simply loved and valued as he or she is. Often, the times when we are at our worst are the times when we need the greatest support from those who love us.

A relationship in which unconditional positive regard is present is greatly strengthened in that the person receiving the regard experiences feelings of security in knowing that he is valued for the person he is and that being loved is not dependent upon always pleasing the spouse. Such a person also tends to feel warmly toward the individual from whom the unconditional regard comes. Consider the following remarks of a middle-aged husband:

> I honestly feel our marriage is one of the happiest and most stable that I am aware of. I have been looking back over our marriage trying to determine what separates us from many other couples we know. I think one of the most important differences is that I have always known that my wife loves me regardless of my behavior. I have acted pretty rotten at times. She might not agree with my behavior, but her attitude toward me has not changed at all. Her love for me is truly unconditional. This has meant a lot to me.

References

1. OTTO, HERBERT. *More Joy in Your Marriage.* New York: Hawthorn Books, 1969, p. 62.
2. SATIR, VIRGINIA. *Conjoint Family Therapy.* Palo Alto, Calif.: Science and Behavior Books, 1967.
3. JOHNSON, KATHRYN P. "Self-Concept Validation as the Focus of Marriage Counseling." *The Family Coordinator,* vol. 17, 1968, pp. 174–180.
4. TOGNOLI, JEROME, and ROBERT KEISNER. "Gain and Loss of Esteem as Determinants of Interpersonal Attraction: A Replication and Extension." *Journal of Personality and Social Psychology,* vol. 33, 1972, pp. 201–204.
5. OTTO, op. cit.
6. Ibid.
7. Ibid., p. 15.
8. Ibid.
9. Ibid.
10. Ibid.
11. Ibid.
12. Ibid.
13. Ibid.
14. Ibid.
15. Ibid.
16. CONNOR, RUTH, and EDITH F. HALL. "The Dating Behavior of College Freshmen and Sophomores." *Journal of Home Economics,* vol. 44, 1952, pp. 278–281.
17. BLOOD, ROBERT O. *Marriage.* New York: Free Press, 1969.
18. JOHNSON, DAVID W., and M. PATRICIA NOONAN. "Effects of Acceptance and Reciprocation of Self-Disclosures on the Development of Trust." *Journal of Counseling Psychology,* vol. 19, 1972, pp. 411–416.
19. LEDERER, WILLIAM J., and DON D. JACKSON. *The Mirages of Marriage.* New York: Norton, 1968.
20. BLOOD, op. cit.
21. Ibid.

6 Communication in the Marriage Relationship

Photo by Walker Montgomery

It takes two of us to discover truth; one to utter it and one to understand.

Kahlil Gibran

Importance of Communication

A BASIC NEED

Nearly every person needs to achieve satisfying and meaningful communication with others. Erich Fromm [1] has noted we have a basic need to relate to others and to overcome our separateness, and that overcoming this sense of separation comes through communication with others. We have a need to share thoughts and feelings with other persons. We want to be understood. We enjoy being with individuals with whom we feel free and comfortable in disclosing thoughts and feelings. We enjoy the companionship of those who understand and empathize with us. We appreciate the person who gives us the benefit of a doubt and can overlook the silly or negative things we sometimes say. The nineteenth-century English novelist Dinah Maria Mulock Craik stated,

> Oh, the comfort, the inexpressible comfort of feeling safe with a person, having neither to weigh thoughts nor measure words, but pouring them all right out, just as they are, chaff and grain together; certain that a faithful hand will take and sift them, keep what is worth keeping, and then with the breath of kindness, blow the rest away.

The people who are close to us, such as spouse, parents, siblings, and friends, usually have a wholehearted concern for our welfare as well as true feelings of respect, appreciation, and love. However, it is not enough that they simply have these feelings; we need to have them expressed to us.[2] Family relationships—indeed, all interpersonal relationships—are more meaningful and enjoyable when empathy, understanding, respect, concern, and appreciation are mutually expressed.

In order that significant others, that is, persons who are important to us, may more effectively understand our feelings, it is necessary that we make our expectations, goals, likes, and dislikes clear to them. For example, if a husband wants his wife to accompany him on business trips, how can she be expected to know this unless he somehow communicates it to her? Similarly, if a wife expects her husband to assist her with some of the housework, how can he know this unless the expectation has been clearly communicated? Yet, much conflict and dissatisfaction in family relationships are the result of our failure to communicate expectations. Often, two individuals marry without ever having communicated their expectations of marriage or of each other. They have definite expectations but do not express them and may feel irritated and disappointed because the expectations are not fulfilled. For this reason, many couples find it helpful to write out informal marriage contracts prior to marriage in order to clarify their expectations concerning gainful employment of the partners, financial management, children, household care, and related subjects. Couples doing this for the first time often are surprised to find differences in their expectations for marriage.

COMMUNICATION AND EMOTIONAL HEALTH

Researchers and psychiatrists have long recognized the central role communication plays in the mental and emotional health of individuals.[3] For example, the research of Spitz [4] indicates that infants deprived of physical handling and other forms of communication tended to become emotionally unresponsive. Many also began a physical decline and succumbed eventually to disease. Experiments by Levine [5] found that in rats physical, mental, and emotional development as well as the biochemistry of the brain and resistance to leukemia were positively affected by physical handling, one of the most basic forms of communication. Similarly, adults who experience extreme communication deprivation may develop psychoses or a temporary mental distuıbance. Similar effects have been observed in persons confined for long periods of solitary imprisonment.[6]

There seems to be a direct relationship between emotional disturbance and communication difficulties. The emotional disturbance may interfere with the sending and receiving of clear messages by the individual and also makes it difficult for others to respond satisfactorily to his or her messages. Carl Rogers has stated,

> The whole task of psychotherapy is the task of dealing with a failure in communication. The emotionally maladjusted person, the neurotic, is in difficulty first because communication within himself has broken down, and second because as a result of this his communication with others has been damaged. If this sounds somewhat strange, let me put it in other terms. In the neurotic individual, parts of himself which have been termed unconscious, or repressed, or denied to awareness, become blocked off so that they no longer communicate themselves to the conscious or managing part of himself. As long as this is true, there are distortions in the way he communicates himself to others, and so he suffers both within himself and in his interpersonal relations.[7]

COMMUNICATION AND THE MARRIAGE RELATIONSHIP

Satisfying patterns of communication are a basic requirement for happy family relationships.[8] Yet, communication is one of the most neglected areas of marriage and family study. There is a real need for more research and instruction. For example, some evidence indicates that college students desire more information in the area of communication than in other aspects of marriage.[9]

The clinical experiences of family counselors lead many to suggest that marriage and family problems are primarily due to a lack of communication. Consequently, one major objective of the counselor is assisting marriage partners in learning to communicate more effectively.

The importance of communication as a factor involved in marital success is noted in several research investigations. In a study by Georg Karlsson,[10] communication of role expectations was found to be associated with marital satisfaction, suggesting that an important prerequisite for marital adjustment is that the partners' expectations are communicated to each other. Karlsson also found that communication of intentions is positively related to marital satisfaction. Logically, a couple with a reasonable knowledge of each other's intentions and motivations has a greater feeling of security. Perhaps most important was the finding by Karlsson that communication of love and respect is associated with marital satisfaction. Although this is not surprising, it needs to be emphasized: an important expectation in marriage is that one's mate will be loving and respectful and will *express* these feelings.

Other research evidence indicates that marital adjustment is positively related to the following aspects of communication: expressions of affection, talking things over, and joint participation in most outside activities and interests.[11]

In a study by Leslie Navran,[12] happily married husbands and wives significantly differed from unhappily married couples in that they:

1. Much more frequently talked over pleasant things that happened during the day.
2. Felt more frequently understood by their spouses; that is, their messages were getting across.
3. Discussed shared interests.
4. Were less likely to break communication off or inhibit it by pouting.
5. More often talked with each other about personal problems.
6. Made more frequent use of words that had a private meaning for them.
7. Generally talked most things over together.
8. Were more sensitive to each other's feelings and made adjustments to take these into account when they spoke.
9. Were freer to discuss intimate issues without restraint or embarrassment.
10. Were better able to tell what type of day their spouse had without asking.
11. Communicated nonverbally to a greater degree.

Researcher Harold Feldman found that the more time a couple spends talking with each other, the more likely they are to experience high marriage satisfaction. They were also found to feel closer to each other after the discussions.[13]

Most interpersonal and social relationships result from appeals for response from others. The marriage relationship might be viewed as a strong appeal for intimate response and positive, successful communication from another person. It is little wonder that disappointment and frustration occur when this appeal continually goes unheeded. Marriage offers one of the greatest opportunities for meeting an individual's need for intimate communication with another person.

What Is Communication?

COMMUNICATION: DEFINITION AND PROCESS

Communication is a process by which one understands others and in turn seeks to be understood by them. It is, according to David Schulz,[14] two people contacting each other. Communication is, in its highest sense, communion, a union of thoughts and feelings. This is perhaps the ultimate goal of communication within the marriage relationship, for true communion with another person necessarily includes mutual respect, trust, understanding, and empathy. Communication in marriage involves a sharing and companionship with each other, every day and in many ways. Such communication contributes immensely to the enjoyment of the relationship.[15]

Communication includes all nonverbal behavior used by individuals in giving and receiving messages.[16] We communicate not only by the spoken words we use in relating to another, but also by the spirit, attitude, and intention underlying the literal content of the message being sent. Feelings are often more clearly communicated by the tone of voice with which something is said than by the literal content of the verbal message. We also communicate nonverbally through facial expressions, [17] gestures, and posture of the body. For example, a wife may respond to her husband's request to go to a party by clearly communicating through her facial expression alone that she does not want to go.

A great deal of interplay of feelings, thoughts, and actions occurs through the nonverbal communication between individuals. Much of our communicated message is related through sight and touch. We communicate everyday with others through dress, physical touch, facial expression, and many other ways. Nonverbal communication is an extremely important aspect of the marriage relationship because so much of our interaction is affected by nonverbal messages.

Approximately 70 per cent of our communication is nonverbal.[18] Many feelings and thoughts are not easily expressed in words and can more easily and adequately be expressed in a nonverbal manner, such as a look. A husband and wife may often communicate a feeling of "I love you" more effectively through a smile, physical touch, thoughtful act, or gift than by verbalizing it. Frequently, husbands and wives find apologies difficult to verbalize so that "I'm sorry" is more easily communicated through a look or physical touch. A husband may simply say to his wife, "I enjoy our playing tennis together," yet the tone of voice with which this is said may communicate much more than simply the enjoyment of playing tennis. It may communicate the message, "I love you and I enjoy being with you."

The communication process involves the person sending the message, the message itself, the person receiving the message, and the social context within which the message is given. For example, the reactions of a wife receiving a message from her husband are influenced by the content of the message, the intention behind it, and the manner in which he sends the message. The husband, in turn, is influenced by the attitude with which the wife listens and by the way she responds to the message. The meaning and intent of the husband's message as well as the wife's reaction to it depend upon the social context within which the message is given. The husband's simple statement, "The bill for the stereo came today," may actually reflect strong emotions of hostility and resentment because he had objected to his wife purchasing the stereo. To an outside observer, the statement would appear to be a simple *adult-adult* transaction. However, considering the negative feelings of the husband and the social context, the statement actually represents a reprimanding *parent-child* transaction.

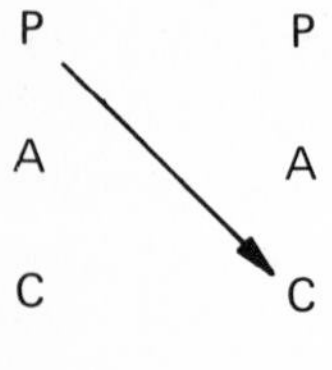

"The bill for the stereo came today."

PURPOSES OF COMMUNICATION

The general purpose of communication is to send and receive messages. Much communication between marriage partners is designed to send or request messages of information and to assist or contribute to the well-being of the other. Unfortunately, sometimes the purpose of communication is to hurt the other partner.[19] Marital communication often involves one partner asking something of the other or attempting to influence the behavior of the other spouse.[20] Some of the specific purposes of communication in marriage might be categorized as follows: (a) I value you, (b) value me, (c) I want to share these thoughts and feelings with you, (d) I want to hurt you, and (e) I want to control this situation.

I value you (You're OK). This general message is a basic factor in contributing to the meaningfulness of any close interpersonal relationship. This feeling is not communicated enough in many marriage relationships. This is indicated in marriage counseling by complaints of not receiving appreciation from one's mate or of being taken for granted. This purpose of communication involves expressing affection or respect and generally contributing to the well-being of the other person.

Value me (Tell me I'm OK). This desire is one of the strongest motivators of human behavior. A great deal of communication at its deeper level involves "validate me" messages.[21] This frequently takes such forms as "Agree with me," "Show me you are interested in me and my well-being," "Show me you appreciate me and my contributions," "Show me that you feel I am a worthy person." This purpose of communication becomes distorted when expressed in an immature, neurotic, or self-defeating manner.

I want to share these thoughts and feelings with you. This purpose of communication involves a desire to share thoughts, feelings, and experiences with another person. In its broadest sense this motivation involves a desire for companionship with someone who is understanding, appreciative, and interested.

I want to hurt you. When expressed over a long period of time, this purpose of communication can destroy a relationship. The expression of this message sometimes reflects temporary frustration, or it may reflect deep psychological and relationship problems. This message is commonly communicated in terms of sarcasm, ridicule, criticism, and actions that knowingly hurt another person. Such behavior makes the other person feel threatened and insecure and, as a result, can severely handicap the communication process.

I want to control this situation. Much of our communication reflects attempts to control situations or discussions.[22] The simple fact that we all have desires and needs motivates us to try to control situations and interactions with others, at least to some extent. However, the manner in which this desire to control is expressed influences the relationship. Many marriage problems result from husbands and wives trying to control their relationship in negative or destructive ways.

These purposes of communication are not exclusive categories in the marriage relationship but are frequently interrelated. For example, an individual may send an "I want to hurt you" message to a mate because he or she has not received an "I value you" message from that spouse.

Barriers to Communication

The husband-wife relationship is one in which the need for intimate communication should be satisfied. Yet, there is often a lack of communication between husbands and wives. Consider the following passage from John Steinbeck's *The Winter of our Discontent* concerning Ethan's relationship with his wife, Mary:

> When I am troubled, I play a game of silly so that my dear will not catch trouble from me. She hasn't found me out yet, or if she has, I'll never know it. So many things I don't know about my Mary, and among them, how much she knows about me . . .
>
> Does anyone ever know even the outer fringe of another? What are you like in there? Mary—do you hear? Who are you in there? . . .
>
> She doesn't listen to me either, and a good thing sometimes . . .[23]

How can a glaring lack of communication exist between husbands and wives? Quite a few factors interfere with clear, satisfying communication in the marriage relationship.

CULTURAL DIFFERENCES

One major factor that blocks communication in marriage is the existence of extreme cultural differences between husband and wife. Marriage partners who come from diverse national, racial, socioeconomic, or religious cultures face some obvious barriers to communication. Each brings from his or her own culture distinct and often quite different values, attitudes, aspirations, customs, and styles of living. Such cultural variations result in the marriage partners having different frames of reference that can make mutual understanding rather difficult. This seems to be indicated by the fact that mixed religious, racial, national, and socioeconomic marriages as a whole have a higher divorce rate than the more homogamous marriages.

Marriage partners who share the same national, racial, socioeconomic, religious, and cultural backgrounds may still be extremely different from each other in terms of their previous family orientation. Each partner comes from a family of orientation that has its own distinct values and culture, [24] customs, shared common experiences, rituals, views of life, and manner of communication. Each family has its own special words of praise and condemnation, gestures, favorite phrases, humorous stories, and particular topics of conversation. Different previous family cultures can sometimes interfere with communication between husband and wife.[25]

Of course, many couples overcome cultural differences and enjoy a satisfying marriage. However, extreme cultural differences between marriage partners require a high level of maturity and an initial ability of the partners to communicate clearly and effectively with each other so that they may be able to understand and accept their differences as well as to develop solutions to them.

DIFFERENCES IN SEX-ROLE LEARNING

Another obstacle to communication between husband and wife results from the different sex-role learning that takes place in childhood and adolescence.[26] While changes are taking place in our society resulting in sex roles becoming more similar,[27] the traditional sex-role learning is still dominant and will continue to be for the near future. These differences in sex-role learning are due to varying cultural expectations for males and females. Males have traditionally been expected to be adventurous, aggressive, active, and achievement oriented. In contrast, females have traditionally been expected to be more passive, dependent, affectionate, and nurturant. There is evidence that during the preschool years girls begin to express feminine roles overtly, and boys begin to express definite conceptions of masculine roles.[28] Many male children learn what it means to be male by learning to be antifeminine or just the opposite of what is supposedly characteristic of female behavior.[29] If the male child learns that the behavior of boys is supposed to be the opposite of girls, he may have perceptions such as these:

Little girls are affectionate and openly express affection; therefore, little boys are not affectionate and do not openly express affection.

Little girls are considerate and thoughtful; therefore, little boys are inconsiderate and thoughtless.

Little girls are good and well-behaved; therefore, little boys are bad and mischievous.

Little girls are polite; therefore, little boys are rude.

Little girls openly express emotions and feelings; therefore, little boys do not openly express emotions and feelings.

A male who internalizes such sex-role learnings during childhood and adolescence may carry these attitudes and patterns of behavior into the marriage relationship.

The tendency to associate femininity with expressiveness such as being empathetic, considerate and understanding, sensitive and affectionate results in many men failing to develop these expressive, supportive qualities that are so important to a marriage relationship.[30] If a male has learned that men do not express emotion, that it is unmanly to express affection or consideration, then it is not surprising that he tends to have difficulty in communicating these qualities to his wife. Neither is it surprising that he is uneasy about expressing or receiving warmth and tenderness. In many respects, antifeminine sex-role learning for the male discourages the development of qualities that can contribute to more fulfilling communication patterns and more satisfying marriage relationships.

Many of the differences in sex-role learning for males and females tend to lead to some distrust, avoidance, hostility, and general misunderstanding between the sexes during childhood and adolescence that sometimes carry over into marriage. Robert Harper has discussed this as follows:

> Since members of the other sex represent behavior patterns opposed to those each sex is encouraged to develop, boys and girls during the pre-adolescent years grow up under conditions that lead them to avoid and distrust one another. The girls come to resent boys because boys are permitted freedom not granted girls and because boys develop personality traits girls have been taught to think of as not nice. Boys, feeling tensions from frustrations met in their broader and more demanding experiences, come likewise to resent girls because girls manifest interests and attitudes that the boys have been taught are undesirable, and because girls have a socially enforced impunity from male attack. Both sexes then move into the period where romantic interest develops with a conditioning that has not equipped them either to understand or to admire the personality traits of the other sex.[31]

Probably one of the greatest difficulties such differences in sex-role learning pose for later husband-wife communication is that it can lead males and females to view each other stereotypically, as sex objects, or persons with sex roles such as "housewife" or "breadwinner," rather than as individual persons. When an individual is stereotyped, understanding of and communication with that person is severely impaired.

INDIRECT COMMUNICATION

Frequently, much confusion and frustration are produced in the marriage relationship because of indirect communication, which is the failure of one mate to let the other know clearly what he or she wants or expects. Instead of expressing directly the intended message, indirect communication hints at or evades the intended message, often leaving the receiver confused concerning the real meaning of the message.

For example, a wife who wishes to go to the movies may communicate this wish indirectly to her husband by saying, "A good movie is playing tonight," never stating directly that she would like to go to the movies. The husband may think she is simply making conversation, not realizing that she wants to go. When he does not respond by saying, "Let's go to the movies," she may feel her request has been rejected, when in reality the husband never realized it was a request. Similarly, the request to go to the movies might be indirectly communicated by presenting it as someone else's desire: "Our daughter would like to go to a movie," or "You'd like to see a movie tonight, wouldn't you?"

Often *adult-adult* communication is avoided because of a fear that the direct message or request will be rejected.

P P "I would like to go to a movie tonight."

A ——→ A

C C

Indirect communication can attempt to test another's feelings about something without risking rejection of the direct message in its entirety. It can be a means of saving face or avoiding embarrassment. In many instances, indirect communication serves the purpose of genuine protection and is not necessarily a dysfunctional method of communication. Indirect communication becomes dysfunctional when it is extreme and/or so frequent that others cannot understand the real meaning and intent of an individual's messages.

When a marriage partner uses a great deal of indirect communication with a mate, it may be primarily because he or she established this pattern in childhood and has simply not learned a more effective method of communication. However, it may be that indirect communication is employed primarily due to the manner in which the other mate responds.[32] The method of communication is often determined by the kind of response one marriage partner has learned to expect from the other. Sufficient freedom, trust, and acceptance in the marriage relationship will enable the partners generally to communicate in a direct, clear manner, and thus will promote greater understanding concerning the desires, expectations, and feelings of each other.

DIFFERENT USES OF WORDS

Some communication difficulties and misunderstanding in marriage are due to partners using the same word in a different way. Heated arguments sometimes take place simply because one person is using a word in a particular way and the other person is receiving and using the same word in an entirely different manner.

One difficulty is that the same word can have various connotations according to each person's frame of reference. To one person the word *school* may carry connotations of happiness, acceptance, and success. To another person, because of an entirely different past experience, *school* may carry connotations of unhappiness, rejection, and failure. Also, the same word can have different literal meanings. The following example from a marriage counseling session indicates a misunderstanding of expectations and desires that is largely due to differences in the definition of a word.

Husband: She never comes up to me and kisses me. I am always the one to make the overtures.
Therapist: Is this the way you see yourself behaving with your husband?
Wife: Yes, I would say he is the demonstrative one. I didn't know he wanted me to make the overtures.
Therapist: Have you told your wife that you would like this from her—more open demonstration of affection?
Husband: Well, no, you'd think she'd know.
Wife: Now, how would I know? You always said you didn't like aggressive women.
Husband: I don't like *dominating* women.
Wife: Well, I thought you meant women who make the overtures. How am I to know what you want?
Therapist: You'd have a better idea if he had been able to tell you.[33]

Because words are often unclear and can have different literal meanings as well as different connotations for each individual, the communication process is facilitated when each marriage partner frequently clarifies word usage and asks the other mate to clarify how he or she is using a particular word.

OVERGENERALIZATIONS AND INACCURATE ASSUMPTIONS

Communication is handicapped when people overgeneralize or make inaccurate assumptions.[34] An individual may assume that one instance or experience is typical of all instances and experiences. A woman, for example, may overgeneralize in the following ways: "All men are mechanically minded," or "All little boys want to play football." Such generalizations can lead to responding to another person not as an individual but in terms of a generalized stereotype. A mother may encourage her son to play football even though he does not want to play, thereby ignoring his individuality because of her generalization that all boys want to play football. Her faulty perception becomes the basis for her attitude: all boys *should* play football. A wife may expect her husband to make any repairs for the house and cars, even though he has neither the inclination nor the skill to do so, because of her generalization that all men are mechanically minded.

As adapted from Virginia Satir, the following are four inaccurate assumptions that often interfere with clear communication:

1. *Assuming the other person necessarily shares feelings and attitudes.* A husband may expect his wife to enjoy playing golf simply because he enjoys it and may feel angry when she does not share his enthusiasm. He is inaccurately assuming that she shares and should share his love of golf.
2. *Assuming that what has happened in the past or what is happening in the present can't change.* This leads to a fatalistic attitude toward behavior and is frequently a barrier to solving differences in marriage. A husband may say, "I have always been that way . . . I have always gotten drunk when I am angry. I guess I always will."
3. *Assuming that one knows the thoughts and feelings of another without ever checking the accuracy of these assumptions.* This leads to misinterpretations of the feelings, desires, and motivations of another person. Too often one marriage partner projects personal emotions and desires to the other mate without attempting to discover the actual feelings of that mate. For example, a husband who likes very practical and useful items may give his wife a vacuum cleaner as a gift. She—favoring something a bit more personal—may respond in anger, "You think I'm a drudge, your servant!" Both are guilty of "mind rape" (a term used by George Bach and Ronald Deutsch in *Pairing,* which refers to the practice of assuming you know another's thoughts and feelings without ever checking the accuracy of these assumptions).
4. *Assuming that another necessarily knows one's inner feelings and expectations.* Again this promotes misunderstandings, particularly when a marriage partner has never communicated feelings and expectations about a certain topic to the other mate. Yet, individuals frequently do not communicate their feelings and expectations but behave toward others as though they had.[35]

Consider the following example from a counseling session:

Mother: They never help around the house.
Therapist: Now you mean the kids?
Mother: Yes.
Therapist: Have you told them what you want them to do?
Mother: Well, I think so. They're supposed to know.
Therapist: But have you *told* them?
Mother: Well, no.[36]

Much misunderstanding could be avoided if expectations and feelings were clearly communicated so that husband and wife are aware of many of the major feelings and expectations of the other.

SELECTIVE PERCEPTION

A factor that contributes to communication breakdown is the practice of *selective perception*, which often results in selective distortion. Selective perception takes place when we have learned a rigid manner of viewing certain aspects of human behavior and seem incapable of perceiving them in any other way. Previously learned subjective images persist and resist change. Rather than change in the face of evidence that clearly contradicts the preconceived perceptions, we tend to be highly selective and screen out behaviors that do not coincide with those we believe. This sometimes results in distortion of factual data in order that the established image may remain undisturbed.[37]

A wife may have formed early an image that all men are interested in women only for physical sex and are not in the least interested in them as whole persons. Thus, she may disregard her husband's behavior which does not coincide with this image. When he makes sexual advances toward her, she may feel or actually say to him, "See, you aren't really interested in *me,* you're only interested in sexual gratification."

Frequently, selective perception and distortion are accompanied by behavior designed to prove the image, bringing about a self-fulfilling prophecy effect. For example, a husband with a selective perception that all women nag, and that his wife nags constantly, may act in a manner that he knows will cause his wife to nag. In this way he tends to confirm his selective perception about women.

Selective perception—in the sense of emphasizing the positive qualities of others and of life—is often a desirable practice as it can nurture and develop those positive qualities that contribute to satisfaction in interpersonal relationships. However, selective perception emphasizing negative qualities or vastly distorted images constitutes a barrier to clear communication and contributes to great dissatisfaction within interpersonal relationships.

CONTRADICTORY COMMUNICATION

Confusion is added to the communication process in the marriage relationship when partners communicate in a contradictory manner. This happens when two or more messages sent by the same person contradict each other.[38] Contradictory messages may occur on the same or on different communication levels. A wife may send contradicting messages on the same communication level, the verbal level, by saying to her husband that she would like to go shopping; then five minutes later, for no apparent reason, saying she does not want to go. Which message does she mean? How does she really want her husband to interpret and respond to her contradictory messages? On the other hand, a wife may send contradictory messages on different levels by verbally saying to her husband that she is looking forward to a camping trip with him. Yet, as she makes this verbal statement, she also sends a nonverbal message of boredom and disgust through her facial expression. Which message is her husband to take seriously, her words or her facial expression?

Sometimes contradictory communication has a double-bind effect for the individual receiving the message. A husband may indicate to his wife that he absolutely *does not* want her to go against his wishes in financial matters. Then, when she complies, he complains that she lacks the spirit to stand up to him. This places the wife in a double-bind situation. She is criticized regardless of which course of action she takes. Contradictory communication that produces a double-bind effect not only contributes to confusion in the communication process, but, if repeated over a long period of time, can also threaten the emotional health and stability of the individual receiving such messages.[39]

Contradictory communication requires an extra effort on the part of the receiver to try to understand and interpret what messages are being sent. Usually, such contradictory messages can be clarified if the receiver feels free to question their meaning. Such comments as "What did you mean by that?" or "You said you wanted to go camping but you look as though you don't want to go" can often encourage the other person to be more explicit and clarify the contradictory message.

MONOLOGUE

The practice of monologue inhibits effective communication and interaction between individuals.[40] In the monologue the assumption is made that communication is accomplished by simply *telling* another person something. This telling, or monologue, however, is an uncertain method of communication because it does not allow for exploration of the other person's feelings and ideas.

Although the monologue may later give way to dialogue between individuals, the monological communicator is often so preoccupied with his or her own self and with talking about personal experiences, problems, and desires that he or she loses touch with the other person.[41] Such monologue is often frustrating and meaningless as evidenced by such statements as these:

I have told my wife a thousand times, but it goes in one ear and out the other.

Many times when I come home from work I am tired and concerned about something that happened at work. My wife immediately begins to bombard me with all the details of her day, hardly giving me a chance to reply. You would think she would be able to detect my moods and feelings. It's as though sometimes she's not really talking to me, but at me.

Perhaps the best way of expressing the disadvantage of monologue is that it is talking *at* rather than *with* someone.

DEFENSIVE COMMUNICATION

Another factor that interferes with intimate, satisfying communication is defensiveness. Defensive behavior occurs when a person feels threatened or anticipates threat from others. A marriage partner who behaves defensively expends a great deal of communicative effort in defending himself rather than attempting to understand the other mate. The defensive person to a large extent

> . . . thinks about how he appears to others, how he may be seen more favorably, how he may win, dominate, impress, or escape punishment, and/or how he may avoid or mitigate a perceived or an anticipated attack.[42]

Defensive feelings tend to result in defensive listening in which the individual does not hear accurately what another is saying because of concern with defending his or her position.

A marital partner's defensive listening and behavior are expressed in verbal and nonverbal cues, which in turn may increase feelings of defensiveness in the other mate. The more defensive a person feels, the less he or she is able to perceive accurately the feelings, desires, and intentions of another. A study by Jack Gibb [43] found that as defensive feelings and behavior increase, efficiency in communication decreases. Specifically, the prevalence of defensiveness contributed to distortions in the communication process within the groups studied. On the other hand, in a supportive interpersonal climate where defensive feelings and behavior decrease, the communication process was found to become more efficient. As feelings of defensiveness are eliminated, the individual becomes better able to concentrate upon and perceive accurately the meaning of another's message. Also, the more secure a person feels in a relationship, the more likely he is to feel free to share his feelings. Security is a most important aspect of communication.[44]

Research provides evidence that families with severe relationship problems express a much higher degree of defensiveness-arousing communication toward one another than do families without severe relationship problems. The problem families have been found to engage much more frequently in behaviors that arouse defensiveness, such as being evaluative, controlling, and indifferent, acting superior, trying to manipulate through the use of strategies, attempting to dominate, and trying to impress others.[45] These types of behavior arouse defensiveness and create relationship problems largely because they communicate a "You're not OK" message to persons who are targets of such behavior.

It is evident from research that communication is impaired by defensiveness as well as by the types of behavior that arouse it.

Behavior That Promotes Defensive and Supportive Environments in Interpersonal Relationships. In Table 6–1 six pairs of defensive and supportive behavior categories are presented. These were developed by Jack Gibb[46] as a result of working over an eight-year period with observed and recorded interpersonal communications.

Evaluation-Description Behavior. When a marriage partner by verbal content, tone of voice, or mannerisms appears to be judging his or her mate, that mate can easily feel defensive and guarded. Behavior that places blame on someone, is extremely judgmental, and questions the values and motivations of another tends to cause the other person to feel defensive and uneasy. Such behavior represents a *parent-child* transaction, placing the person who is the object of the negative evaluation in the position of a child being reprimanded by the parent.

Speech sometimes sounds evaluative and judgmental when it is not meant to be. For example, "Why did you do that?" may be perceived as an accusation, when it was really only meant to be a request for information.

In contrast to evaluative behavior, descriptive behavior is seen by the listener as a genuine request for information or as a presentation of information or thoughts. There is no attempt, directly or indirectly, to evaluate the listener.

Table 6–1 Behavior Characteristics which Promote Supportive and Defensive Feelings Within Interpersonal Relationships

Behavior Promoting Defensiveness		Supportive Behavior Which Minimizes Defensiveness
Evaluation	versus	Description
Control	versus	Problem orientation
Strategy	versus	Spontaneity
Neutrality	versus	Empathy
Superiority	versus	Equality
Certainty	versus	Provisionalism

SOURCE: Jack R. Gibb, "Defensive Communication," *Journal of Communication,* Vol. 11, No. 3, 1961, pp. 141–148. Reprinted by permission of the International Communication Association.

Therefore, such descriptive behavior minimizes feelings of defensiveness and uneasiness.

Control–Problem-Orientation Behavior. Behavior of one marriage partner that has the purpose of trying to control the other is apt to evoke resistance in the other mate. The attempt to control the behavior of another implies an assumption by the one seeking to control that the person to be controlled is somehow inadequate, immature, uninformed, or holds wrong attitudes. This perceived assumption, in itself, tends to make the person who is the object of the controlling behavior feel threatened and defensive.

Problem-orientation behavior, in contrast to controlling behavior, communicates a desire to cooperate in defining what the problem is and seeking the best solution. The individual who expresses this type of behavior is implying to the other that he has no predetermined answer to force upon him. Problem-orientation behavior expressed by one person usually evokes the same type of approach in the other, thereby minimizing feelings of defensiveness.

Strategy-Spontaneity Behavior. When a marriage partner perceives the behavior of the other as characterized by manipulative and deceptive strategies, he or she tends to become defensive or uneasy and is careful to be on guard. Few people enjoy being the victim of hidden motivations.[47] A marriage partner who is perceived as playing a role, feigning, or trying to manipulate may well cause feelings of resentment in the other. The defensiveness and resentment aroused by the perception that another person is using strategies is largely due to the underlying feeling that such a person is deceitful and insincere. Also, when we perceive that someone is using a strategy with us, we tend to feel that the person is responding to us not as a human being, but as a role or an object to be manipulated. Such behavior reinforces our "not OK" position and we resent it.

In contrast to the use of strategies, behavior that is perceived as spontaneous and free of deceit or manipulation minimizes defensiveness and uneasiness. When we perceive another to be spontaneous, we tend to feel that we can trust that individual; therefore, we feel comfortable with that person.

Neutrality-Empathy Behavior. A marriage partner who believes the behavior or speech of the other is neutral, that is, communicating neither positive nor negative feelings, may easily feel defensive. Most partners desire to be loved, respected, and valued by their mate. Neutral speech or behavior conveys little warmth, concern, love, or feeling in general and communicates to the other person that he or she is being rejected. Such behavior often arouses defensive feelings.

When, instead of communicating neutrality, a marriage partner conveys empathy for the other, he or she communicates an attitude that the other person is OK as well as an interest in the feelings of the other. The communication of empathy is very reassuring. It provides a feeling of being supported, thereby reducing defensiveness.

Superiority-Equality Behavior. When a marriage partner behaves as though he or she is superior in some respect, feelings of inadequacy and defensiveness may be aroused in the other spouse. If an individual is perceived as feeling superior, it is often assumed that such a person does not need assistance, is not willing to enter into a shared problem-solving relationship, and does not value the feelings or ideas of the other. This behavior communicates an "I'm OK—You're not OK" message.

A person who acts superior seems to be saying, in effect, "I am better than you." A person receiving this message feels his or her own self-worth has been minimized. Quite naturally, the person who acts superior is resented. The other person may react by feeling threatened, resentful, jealous, or hostile. In summary, the consequences of such reactions are often that the person who perceives the other as feeling superior does not really listen to that person because he or she is too concerned with defending himself or herself.

In contrast to behavior that denotes superiority, defensiveness and feelings of inadequacy are minimized when marriage partners perceive each other as being equal and willing to enter into joint planning with mutual respect and trust.

Certainty-Provisionalism Behavior. The behavior of a marriage partner characterized by an extreme degree of certainty tends to contribute to defensiveness in the other partner. Such behavior implies an attitude of knowing all the answers and not needing additional information or ideas from others. The individual whose behavior is perceived in this manner is seen by others as a dogmatic person who must always be right, is more interested in winning an argument than solving a problem, and has a low tolerance for those persons who disagree. Such behavior tends to put others on guard.

In contrast, a marriage partner perceived as expressing provisional behavior, that is, as being open-minded, willing to change behavior and ideas, and willing to accept the attitudes and ideas of the other partner, reduces feelings of defensiveness. This behavior communicates an interest in the ideas of others and a desire to cooperate in examining issues and solving problems rather than arguing or debating.

Factors Contributing to Successful Communication

PRESENCE OF A POSITIVE INTERPERSONAL ETHIC FOR COMMUNICATION

Communication in marriage is, in its highest sense, a complete sharing between husband and wife. In the marriage relationship, mutual appreciation, trust, respect, and understanding are necessary to provide the atmosphere in which partners feel the freedom and willingness to share their innermost feelings and thoughts with each other most fully. But upon what is mutual appreciation, trust, respect, and understanding based? To a large extent such mutuality is based upon a positive interpersonal ethic—a commitment—shared by both partners that the conditions will be created and maintained in which the potential of the other mate is best realized.[48]

Fulfillment of personal potential requires a great deal of freedom to choose one's course of action. Therefore, communication based upon the interpersonal ethic that conditions be created and maintained in which the potential of the other mate is best accomplished will be characterized by acceptance of the mate's freedom of response. We sometimes have difficulty in accepting another person's freedom of response and want him or her to respond in a certain way. We become angry if that person does not, and in the process of subjugating him or her to our will, we produce conflict and misunderstanding.

Behavior in marriage that restricts the other mate's freedom of response is probably not guided by the ethic of creating and maintaining conditions for achievement of that mate's potential. Behavior that is guided by such an interpersonal ethic contributes not only to more mature communication, but also to a more satisfying marriage relationship.

MUTUAL REGARD

A quality that immeasurably facilitates effective, satisfying communication is the presence of high regard in the interpersonal relationship. This has the effect of reinforcing each other's OK position. When we feel that we are valued by another and are convinced that the other is genuinely interested in our welfare, we feel free to openly share our innermost feelings and thoughts. The honest expression of mutual high regard in marriage minimizes feelings of being threatened, thereby decreasing guarded and defensive communication. Mutual regard with its associated qualities of respect, trust, and acceptance establishes a favorable environment for positive communication within the marriage relationship.

However, if a marriage partner is not convinced that the other sincerely values him or her as a person, trust of that partner tends to decrease, contributing to guardedness. A person who does not trust another tends to conceal his or her own attitudes by such communication patterns as evasiveness or aggressiveness.[49]

SHARING A COMMON FRAME OF REFERENCE

Sharing a common frame of reference is an important factor contributing to clear communication. This is supported by evidence that, as a group, there is a higher degree of happiness and a much lower rate of divorce among marriages in which the partners share similar cultural backgrounds than among marriages with different cultural backgrounds.[50] The greater marital satisfaction and stability among couples with similar cultural backgrounds is due in part to better communication because of a more common frame of reference between the partners.

A frame of reference basically refers to a background of experiences, ideas, and attitudes. If two people are to understand and communicate with each other effectively on an intimate level, they need to share a somewhat common background of experiences, ideas, and attitudes.

One of the most common causes of a breakdown in communication is that people attach widely different meanings to the same experience or idea, primarily because of differences in past life experiences. Couples sometimes argue endlessly over a word for which each has a different frame of reference. When they become aware of each other's frame of reference, they often discover they are not really in disagreement. Such awareness is often obtained by asking each other why he or she feels a certain way, what a particular experience means to him or her, and how the other person is using a certain word.

LISTENING

Adequately expressing thoughts and feelings to another person is only one part of the communication process. Equally as important is the receiving of the message, or listening.[51]

Perhaps the best way to improve communication in interpersonal relationships is to develop a greater facility for listening. Sometimes people hear very little at parties or social gatherings. There is the story of the hostess who wanted to see if anyone was really listening at her tea party.

> She passed some cakes around to her guests and asked if they would like to try her homemade petit fours covered with arsenic! Everyone ate heartily and agreed that the icing was delicious.[52]

Husbands and wives may not listen to each other and, as a result, are sometimes unaware of each other's emotional needs, problems, and desires. Sometimes adolescents make the statement "My mom and dad are so involved in their own problems and interests that they never listen to each other or to me." One frequently hears such statements as "Talking to my husband is like talking to a brick wall," or "My wife can't stop talking long enough to listen to anything I have to say."

Listening constitutes a vital aspect of communication and of the marriage relationship. Listening, in and of itself, communicates a message of interest in and concern for the other person. When someone listens to another, he or she communicates, "I am sincerely interested in you and what you are saying. I want to share your thoughts and feelings." Also implied is the important idea that the listener values and respects the speaker as a person. This provides the type of environment in which the speaker is assisted to express his feelings more fully.

The need to be listened to and have our feelings acknowledged is basic to our emotional welfare. Often one of the strongest needs manifested by clients of psychiatrists and counselors is to have someone who will truly listen.

It is equally important to "listen" to the nonverbal communication and the tone of voice as it is to the verbal content of the message. Nonverbal signals and voice tone serve as a guideline to the listener's perception of the other person's state of feeling. For example, when a wife arrives home from work, a "listening" husband will be able to perceive from her facial expression and body movement whether she had a good day at the office or a tiring, irritating one.

Research studies show a positive association between accuracy of nonverbal communication and marriage satisfaction. Couples who accurately understand each other's nonverbal communication tend to have a greater degree of marriage happiness than do those who have little understanding of each other's nonverbal communication.[53] Listening to feelings as well as words increases understanding and strengthens a marriage.

CHECKING THE MEANING OF COMMUNICATION

An important aid to good communication in marriage is the ability of mates to check with each other the meaning of messages that are not clear. An unclear message can often be clarified by such comments as "I'm not sure I know what you mean by that," or "This is my understanding of what you mean by that . . . Is that correct?"

Inaccurate interpretation of messages often causes needless misunderstanding and conflict. A wife may misinterpret her husband's irritation with himself as irritation with and criticism of her. Therefore, she may feel hurt and resentful toward him. Establishing a pattern of checking the meaning of unclear messages improves the clearness of the communication process in the present and contributes to better communication in the future.

EMPATHY

Another important factor aiding successful communication between husband and wife is the quality of empathy. Robert Blood has stated,

> Communication is a two-way process. It begins with self-expression, but it is completed only if the partner receives the message. Empathy is the ability to perceive the partner's attitudes and feelings.[54]

In other words, empathy is the ability to sense the emotional state of the other. Individuals who are deeply involved in their own interests, problems, and needs may not sense or understand the feelings of others.

Newborn babies are egocentric and require several years of maturing to learn to be aware of the feelings of others.[55] Maturation of the whole person involves an increasing recognition and appreciation of the feelings and the identity of others. The marriage relationship is enhanced by empathy as each understands the feelings, moods, and desires of the other in small matters as well as large ones. A high degree of empathy enables marriage partners to sense each other's needs often without verbal communication, and it can help a marriage partner to see beyond the words of the other to his or her inner feelings.

ACKNOWLEDGING THE AWARENESS OF ANOTHER'S FEELINGS

Acknowledging the feelings of another person can greatly aid the communication process. We tend to feel better when we think others are aware of our thoughts and attitudes concerning things that are important to us.

Wife: I'm depressed. We never do anything together anymore.
Husband: Oh, but honey, that's really not true.
Wife: Yes, it is true, we don't do anything anymore.
Husband: Paula, don't you remember that last Friday night we went to a party and last Saturday we went to the football game together. And two weekends ago we went to the beach house.
Wife: (Silence)
Husband: You still feel depressed, don't you?
Wife: Yes, and lonely.
Husband: I guess it really doesn't matter how much we have done together

lately. The important thing is that you feel depressed and lonely. That's not a very pleasant way to feel.

Wife: Well, you're right, it really doesn't make much difference what we've done together lately. I guess that's not the real reason I'm feeling bad. I just feel depressed.

Husband: I wish there was something I could do to help.

Feelings are not always logical. Sometimes what we think to be the cause of our negative feelings is not the cause at all. But our negative feelings may be there just the same. It can be therapeutic if someone close to us acknowledges an awareness of how we feel. This is a very important part of empathy.

References

1. FROMM, ERICH. *The Art of Loving.* New York: Harper & Row, 1956.
2. WAHLROOS, SVEN. *Family Communication.* New York: Macmillan, 1974.
3. SATIR, VIRGINIA. *Peoplemaking.* Palo Alto, Calif.: Science and Behavior Books, 1972.
4. SPITZ, RENE. "Hospitalism: Genesis of Psychiatric Conditions in Early Childhood." *Psychoanalytic Study of the Child,* vol. I, 1945, pp. 53–74.
5. LEVINE, S. "Stimulation in Infancy." *Scientific American,* vol. 202, 1960, pp. 80–86.
6. BERNE, ERIC. *Games People Play.* New York: Grove Press, 1964.
7. ROGERS, CARL. "Communication: Its Blocking and Facilitation." In *Language, Meanings, and Maturity,* edited by S. I. Hayakawa. New York: Harper & Row, 1954, p. 53.
8. CHAPMAN, A. H. *Marital Brinkmanship.* New York: Putnam, 1974.
9. STINNETT, NICK. "Attitudes of College Students Toward Marriage." *Journal of Home Economics,* vol. 63, 1971, pp. 33–37.
10. KARLSSON, GEORG. *Adaptability and Communication in Marriage: A Swedish Predictive Study of Marital Satisfaction.* Uppsala, Sweden: Almqvist and Wiksells, 1951.
11. LOCKE, HARVEY. *Predicting Adjustment in Marriage.* New York: Holt, Rinehart and Winston, 1951.
12. NAVRAN, LESLIE. "Communication and Adjustment in Marriage." *Family Process,* vol. 6, 1967, pp. 173–184.
13. FELDMAN, HAROLD. *Development of the Husband-Wife Relationship.* Cornell University, Research Report to National Institute of Mental Health, Grant M-2931, 1965.
14. SCHULZ, DAVID A., and STANLEY F. RODGERS. *Marriage, the Family, and Personal Fulfillment.* Englewood Cliffs, N.J.: Prentice-Hall, 1975.
15. RUDD, O. J., and ROGER RUDD. "Husbands and Wives: Talking May Be Sharing." *New Catholic World Magazine,* May/June, 1973, pp. 125–129.
16. WAHLROOS, op. cit.
    CREEK, LEON VANDE, and JOHN T. WATKINS. "Responses to Incongruent Verbal and Nonverbal Emotional Cues." *The Journal of Communication,* Vol. 22, 1972, pp. 311–316.
17. BOUCHER, JERRY D., and PAUL EKMAN. "Facial Areas and Emotional Information." *The Journal of Communication,* vol. 25, 1975, pp. 21–29.

18. O'Neill, Nena, and George O'Neill. *Open Marriage.* New York: Evans, 1972.
19. Miller, G. R. "On Defining Communication: Another Stab." *The Journal of Communication*, vol. 16, 1966, pp. 88–98.
20. Satir, Virginia. *Conjoint Family Therapy.* Palo Alto, Calif.: Science and Behavior Books, 1967.
21. Ibid.
22. Ericson, Philip M., and L. Edna Rogers. "New Procedures for Analyzing Relational Communication." *Family Process*, vol. 12, 1973, pp. 245–267.
23. Steinbeck, John. *The Winter of Our Discontent.* New York: Viking Press, 1961.
24. Papajohn, John and John Spiegel. *Transactions in Families.* San Francisco: Jossey-Bass Publishers, 1975.
25. Bossard, James H. S. *The Sociology of Child Development.* New York: Harper & Row, 1954.
26. Bowman, Henry A. *Marriage for Moderns.* New York: McGraw-Hill, 1974.
27. Udry, J. Richard. *The Social Context of Marriage.* Philadelphia: J. B. Lippincott, 1974.
28. Smart, Mollie S., and Russell C. Smart. *Children: Development and Relationships.* New York: Macmillan, 1972.
29. Coombs, Robert. Paper given at National Council on Family Relations Conference, October, 1968.
30. Brenton, Myron. *The American Male.* Greenwich, Conn.: Fawcett, 1966.
    Farrell, Warren. *The Liberated Man.* New York: Random House, 1974.
31. Harper, Robert. *Marriage.* New York: Appleton-Century-Crofts, 1949, p. 67.
32. Satir, 1967, op. cit.
33. Ibid., pp. 72–73.
34. Ibid.
35. Ibid.
36. Ibid., p. 72.
37. Sebald, H. "Limitations of Communication: Mechanisms of Image Maintenance in Form of Selective Perception, Selective Memory and Selective Distortion." *The Journal of Communication*, vol. 12, 1962, pp. 142–149.
38. Satir, 1972, op. cit.
39. Satir, 1967, op. cit.
40. Tubbs, Stewart L., and Gail A. Tubbs. "Speaking and Listening." *Today's Education*, vol. 61, 1972, p. 23.
41. Howe, R. L. *The Miracle of Dialogue.* New York: Seabury Press, 1963.
42. Gibb, Jack R. "Defensive Communication." *The Journal of Communication*, vol. 11, 1961, pp. 141–148.
43. Gibb, Jack R. "Defense Level and Influence Potential in Small Groups." In *Leadership and Interpersonal Behavior*, edited by L. Petrullo and B. M. Bass. New York: Holt, Rinehart and Winston, 1961, pp. 66–81.
44. Smith, Rebecca M. *Klemer's Marriage and Family Relationships.* New York: Harper & Row, 1975.
45. Alexander, James F. "Defensive and Supportive Communications in Normal and Deviant Families." *Journal of Consulting and Clinical Psychology*, vol. 40, 1973, pp. 223–231.
46. Gibb, 1965, op. cit.
47. Ibid.

48. KELLER, PAUL W., and CHARLES T. BROWN. "Interpersonal Ethic for Communication." *The Journal of Communication*, vol. 16, 1968, pp. 73–81.
49. MELLINGER, G. E. "Interpersonal Trust as a Factor in Communication." *Journal of Abnormal Social Psychology*, vol. 52, 1956, pp. 304–309.
50. HICKS, MARY W., and MARILYN PLATT. "Marital Happiness and Stability: A Review of the Research in the Sixties." *Journal of Marriage and the Family*, vol. 33, 1970, pp. 553–574.
51. WIEMANN, JOHN M., and MARK L. KNAPP. "Turn-Taking in Conversations." *The Journal of Communication*, vol. 25, 1975, pp. 75–92.
52. NEWMAN, J. E. "Communication: A Dyadic Postulation." *The Journal of Communication*, vol. 9, 1959, pp. 51–58.
53. KAHN, MALCOLM. "Non-Verbal Communication and Marital Satisfaction." *Family Process*, vol. 9, 1970, pp. 449–456.
RISKIN, JULES, and ELAINE E. FAUNCE. "An Evaluative Review of Family Interaction Research." *Family Process*, vol. 11, 1972 pp. 365–455.
54. BLOOD, ROBERT. *Marriage.* New York: Free Press, 1969.
55. Ibid.

7 Psychological Games in Marriage

Photo by Walker Montgomery

Trickery succeeds sometimes, but it always commits suicide.

Kahlil Gibran

Psychological Games

Unfortunately, husbands and wives, instead of establishing mutually satisfying and helping relationships within marriage, sometimes play psychological games with each other. Many play psychological games as a way of dealing with "I'm not OK" feelings.[1] These games are destructive and retard growth-facilitating relationships.

Eric Berne, author of *Games People Play*,[2] suggests that husbands and wives often allow psychological games to become substitutes for genuine living and real intimacy. Psychological games have the effect of creating and maintaining a gap between husbands and wives rather than bringing them closer together.

In our search for ways to bring family members closer and bridge the gap that often exists in relationships, it is beneficial to examine what a psychological game is and to consider some of the common games husbands and wives employ with each other. The following definition and examples are taken from Eric Berne's *Games People Play*[3] and A. H. Chapman's *Put-Offs and Come-Ons*,[4] two of the more widely read books dealing with psychological games.

What Is a Psychological Game?

A psychological game is defined as a pattern of interaction between two or more persons that superficially appears legitimate or honest but actually has a concealed or ulterior motive. If a person is playing a psychological game with someone, his or her interaction with the other involves a "gimmick." A psychological game is basically dishonest. For example, if someone asks another person directly or indirectly for a compliment, and after the compliment is given, then takes it and uses it in a way that makes the giver look bad, or insincere, that is a game.

Another characteristic of a psychological game is a lack of spontaneity. The person who plays the game plans the interaction with another person to produce a desired effect. The game player's interaction is designed to manipulate and maneuver the other person into doing what he or she wants that person to do.[5]

Psychological games *should not* be considered fun or frivolous. Some are amusing and harmless, but others are vicious and destructive. Although all of us play psychological games to some extent, an intense and constant playing of these games may reflect an emotional disturbance in that person. Of course, the continual use of psychological games may also *cause* emotional disturbance.

Some Common Marital Games

Any number of psychological games are played within the marriage relationship; however, some appear more often than others. Following is a brief discussion of some common marital games.

CORNER

The corner game is frustrating to the partner who is "cornered." It can also be very destructive. Clinical research with mentally ill patients suggests that much emotional disturbance is caused by an individual having been continually cornered by a marriage partner or earlier in life by a parent.

The corner game involves a process by which one marriage partner interacts with the other in such a manner as to place him or her in a situation where anything he or she does is wrong or undesirable. The game player maneuvers the other into a corner so that the partner finds himself or herself in a situation described as "damned if you do and damned if you don't."

One example of this game is a husband who encourages or even badgers his wife to give parties for his friends at work; but when she hosts such parties, he severely criticizes her for the way the party was handled. In other words, the wife is forced into a corner; if she does not give parties, she receives this type of criticism from her husband:

> Why don't you give parties like my friends' wives do. You are the only one who doesn't. You are hurting my chances of climbing in the company by not being friendly. Doesn't it matter to you?

However, if she does give parties, she receives this type of criticism from her husband:

The roast beef was awful. Why didn't you talk more with Mrs. Anderson tonight? I don't see why you couldn't have done a better job of circulating among the guests.

TELL ME YOUR PROBLEMS

"Tell Me Your Problems" is a game in which one partner appears to be extremely interested in learning about the problems of the other. The apparent motive for this concern is to understand and to help; however, the real motive is to learn and expose the partner. By exposing the partner's weaknesses, the game player compensates for personal feelings of inadequacy. The game player increases his or her feelings of self-worth by "putting the partner down."

For example, a wife may appear to be very concerned with her husband's problems. In fact, she may appear overly interested. After listening to an enthusiastic report by the husband of a wonderful day at work, she may respond with, "Yes, but tell me how you *really* feel." With this response from her, he may begin to feel that she does not believe he is being honest and open unless he discusses some problems with her. She encourages him in many ways to reveal his troubles. She is a very attentive listener and tells him that she wants to help. However, after learning his vulnerable areas, she betrays his confidence by indiscriminately revealing his problems and weaknesses to neighbors and friends. She may also reveal his difficulties at social gatherings with or without his presence by dropping remarks such as these:

I am very worried about Edward. He has been working too hard lately. I hate to see him getting so tired and tense. He had some pretty bad emotional problems a few years ago, you know. He thought about suicide. He had psychiatric care for almost two years. I have given Edward a great deal of emotional support. It has been difficult for me. I don't think he would make it without me. It's a lot of responsibility when you have to "carry" someone emotionally like this.

In this case the wife puts her husband down by making him appear inadequate and emotionally unstable. At the same time she builds herself up in the eyes of others by presenting herself as the strong force that supports Edward and holds him together emotionally. She also presents herself as a martyr, a stance designed to gain sympathy and admiration from others.

WE SHOULD DO THIS FOR YOU

In the game "We Should Do This for You," one partner desires to do or have something, but attempts to achieve this particular goal by making it seem that the *other* partner needs to have or do this particular thing. For example, a wife may not feel like going to a particular party. Instead of straightforwardly telling her husband that she does not feel like going, she makes it appear that they should not go to the party for his sake. Her approach may be something like the following:

Honey, I think we had better stay home tonight for your sake. You have been having difficulty with the philosophy course you're taking at the college. I think you need to stay home and study tonight.

Perhaps it would be best for her husband to stay home and study, but the point is that she is not revealing her true reason for not wanting to go to the party. She makes the request to stay home in terms of her husband's need to study. This suggests that the wife may fear her request will be rejected if she discloses her real reason for wanting to stay home. Also, by making it appear that they are staying home for her husband's sake, she avoids feeling like or being seen by her husband as a "wet blanket." In a sense she maneuvers him into being the "wet blanket."

SWEETHEART

The sweetheart game is a process by which one partner indirectly ridicules or depreciates the other in public. This psychological jab is done in such an indirect manner that probably no one except the other partner is aware of what is happening. The motive for this game often is to make the other person feel badly about himself or herself. Also, the player of this game is trying to achieve feelings of superiority or worth at the expense of his or her mate.

For example, a husband who feels hostile about his wife earning more money than he does may express this hostility indirectly by accusing her of neglecting the children because of her career involvement. He may express this hostility by playing the sweetheart game at a party. During the party, he may, in the presence of his wife, tell a story about another working woman who greatly neglected her children. He concludes the story by commenting on how unfortunate it is when parents neglect their children, after which he casually turns to his wife and says, "Don't you agree, sweetheart?"

Because he appears to be talking about someone else and because it is an extreme case, the wife can hardly afford to object or retaliate in the presence of others. It would not seem reasonable. If the wife confronts the husband about this in private, he may dishonestly plead innocence and say, "But sweetheart, I wasn't talking about you," or "I was talking about someone else, but if you feel the story applies to you, perhaps you should do some thinking about this."

IT IS YOUR DECISION

In the psychological game of "It Is Your Decision," one marriage partner escapes the responsibility of making a decision about something by placing the burden of the decision completely upon the shoulders of the other partner. Although actually very much concerned about the outcome of the particular decision, the partner playing this game insists that he or she is not by making comments such as these:

> "It makes no difference to me."
> "Whatever you would like to do is fine with me."
> "But honey, you know so much more about this than I do, you make the decision."

By responding in this way the game player escapes the responsibility of facing the consequences of the decision. If it turns out to be wrong, it was, after all, the partner who made the decision.

An example of this game is a husband confronted with a decision of whether to go to a movie or stay home. For the most part, he would rather stay home and rest, but in a way, he would like to see an entertaining movie. If he goes to a bad movie, he will be disgusted; yet if he stays home, he will wonder if he is missing a good movie. Therefore, when his wife asks him if he wishes to go to the movie or stay home, he replies, "It makes no difference to me. Whatever you would like to do is fine." In this way he forces his wife to make the decision. If she makes the decision to stay home he can say, "We may have missed a good movie tonight but *you* really didn't want to go, did you?" However, if the wife decides to go to a movie that turns out to be boring, he does not need to be angry at himself since he did not make the decision. In a more destructive aspect of this game he may direct anger toward his wife and say, "Brother! You sure goofed that one. What a lousy movie. It would have been better if we had stayed home."

Husbands and wives frequently play this game with each other about their children. A husband, for example, may refuse to help his wife make decisions concerned with rearing their children. Then, when something seems to go wrong or one of the children gets into some kind of trouble, the husband, if he is playing a destructive version of this game, self-righteously blasts his wife with a charge of "You're not rearing our children right."

COURTROOM

Courtroom is often played in marriage relationships. Many times marriage counselors see husbands and wives play this game with one another. This game significantly interferes with satisfying communication and understanding because both marriage partners channel their effort in such a way as to justify their actions and prove the faults and shortcomings of the other partner.

The courtroom game typically involves three persons, including the two marriage partners. One partner assumes the role of the plaintiff and accuses the other of wrongdoing. The partner who plays the role of defendant insists on his or her innocence, justifies his or her behavior, and counters with accusations against the partner playing the plaintiff. The third member represents the judge to whom the plaintiff and defendant present their cases. Each partner wants the judge to approve *his* or *her* actions and to disapprove of the other partner.

The accuser often does not even hear the explanation of the defendant but simply continues the attack. Much of the communication of a husband and wife playing the courtroom game is directed toward the third person playing the role of judge rather than toward each other. This tends to prevent them from achieving better understanding and a satisfactory solution to the problem. Husbands and wives playing this game often seem to be more interested in proving themselves right and the other partner wrong before a judge than they are in solving the problem or achieving better understanding.

CAMOUFLAGE

The game of camouflage is common in marriage and serves as a stumbling block to clear communication. Camouflage is a process by which one partner sends a message that seems on the surface to communicate one idea but actually is intended to communicate something else. It is a pattern of interaction in which one partner gives the other an indirect hint about something rather than giving the message in a direct, clear manner. It is a devious game and is probably most often played in order to avoid confrontation or negative responses from the other person, thereby serving as a means of self-defense.

The unfortunate aspect of this game is that the hint may be so indirect that the person for whom it is intended never receives it. When this happens, the person playing the camouflage game may become frustrated and resent the other partner for being so "indifferent and stubborn."

An example of this game is a wife whose husband is slightly overweight and she wishes that he would watch his weight more closely. She feels that she cannot voice her concern directly for fear that it will injure his pride or that he might retaliate in some way. Instead, she camouflages her concern by saying, "Isn't it just unbelievable how many health problems that medical doctors say are due to overweight?" The husband may catch the hint, but the chances are high he may never realize that her remarks are directed at him and that she wants him to reduce.

Most husbands and wives who play psychological games in marriage have a deep need to achieve an intimate, satisfying relationship with each other that is characterized by clear communication and mutual understanding. Yet, playing psychological games tends to prevent mutual understanding and leads to confused, inaccurate communication. Playing psychological games within marriage has the opposite result of what most husbands and wives deeply desire. Rather than bringing them closer together and contributing to a deeply satisfying relationship, the use of psychological games is more likely to drive husbands and wives farther apart.

In view of the negative effects psychological games may have on the marriage relationship, it appears illogical that marriage partners would play such games. The question naturally arises, "Why do husbands and wives play psychological games with each other?"

DISTRUST

A common reason for manipulating others through game playing is a general lack of trust in others and in oneself. For example, a wife may strongly desire to go to the beach for a weekend but may not trust her husband to respond favorably to her direct request for the trip. Neither does she trust her ability to express this desire and achieve it in a direct manner, so she attempts to achieve this goal indirectly by playing the game of "We Should Do This for You." She may say to her husband something like this:

> Darling, I'm concerned about the way you've been working lately. You look very tired. I think you need a break. You know, I'll bet a weekend at the beach would do wonders for you.

She places more trust in manipulating her husband into thinking he needs to go to the beach for his health and that she wants to go for his sake than she does in requesting this as something she wants.

Everett Shostrom, author of *Man, the Manipulator,*[6] notes that we often do not trust ourselves to achieve desired goals; therefore, we rely upon others to achieve those goals for us. Yet, because we do not completely trust the other person, we often manipulate that person by game playing in an attempt to achieve our goals.

FEAR OF CLOSE RELATIONSHIPS

Fear of close relationships is another reason for playing psychological games and is related to the previously mentioned reason. Some individuals fear close relationships because they have been hurt, exploited, or disappointed in the past by someone close to them. For example, a woman who has been greatly disappointed in a past love affair may be reluctant to establish a close relationship with a man in the future because she fears being hurt again. Also, a person who experienced very unsatisfactory relationships during childhood may avoid close relationships in adulthood in order to protect himself or herself. Again, the reasoning would be, "If I don't get too involved with others, I won't get hurt."

We may also fear close relationships because of the responsibilities involved. When we avoid becoming closely involved with others, we avoid the responsibility of being concerned about their feelings and welfare as well as the responsibility of spending time with them.

Whatever the reason for being reluctant to establish close relationships, psychological games are often used either consciously or unconsciously by individuals as a way of keeping a distance between themselves and others.

LACK OF DIRECTNESS IN RELATING TO OTHERS

Individuals may rely on games because they feel they cannot have direct relationships with others. This can be due to a fear of revealing self-perceived inadequacies or due to a fear of being hurt or rejected by others. These feelings may lead a person consciously or unconsciously to resort to indirect patterns of relating to others. Such a person may associate danger with directness, and safety with indirectness, in interpersonal relationships. Psychological games may be utilized as a way of relating to others in an indirect, seemingly safe manner.

UNFAMILIARITY WITH ALTERNATIVE WAYS OF RELATING TO OTHERS

We may continue to play psychological games in marriage even though it is obvious that the games are contributing to a less than satisfactory relationship because we are not familiar with alternative ways of behaving. We tend to cling to that with which we are familiar. We all are prone to resist change. If an individual has grown into adulthood seeing parents manipulate each other by the use of psychological games, he or she will quite naturally be very familiar with this approach to interpersonal relationships and may have little knowledge of alternative ways of relating to others.

VIEWING OTHERS AS PERSONS TO BE USED

One of the most basic reasons that we attempt to manipulate others through psychological games is the tendency to view others as persons to be used. The emphasis our society places on economic production and industrial progress has led to an inclination to judge a person's worth in terms of what he or she achieves or produces.

Business organizations have traditionally been interested in their employees in terms of what the employees can do for the business and how much they can produce. The employee may be seen as a person to be controlled for the profit and good of the business organization. Some salesmen and manufacturers see the potential buyer only as a customer. The primary concern is how to manipulate the customer most effectively to buy a product. It is not surprising, then, that many individuals, even in intimate relationships such as marriage, view each other as persons to be manipulated and that each sees the other in terms of "What can this person do for me?" or "How can this person profit me?"

The Roots of Psychological Games

The psychological games used in marriage are often learned in childhood.[7] The child learns these games by imitating parents. Some clinical evidence suggests that game playing runs in families and that certain games appear to be passed from one generation to the next. If parents often use certain psychological games with each other as well as with the children, there is a good probability that the children will begin to play these games themselves. To a lesser extent one also learns to play games by imitating older brothers and sisters or peers.

A person may learn to play psychological games during childhood through trial and error. Children notice that when they use a particular psychological game, they usually get what they want. In this way children learn to utilize games to manipulate people and get them to do what they want. They then use the game over and over, and it becomes a habit that carries into adulthood.

Not all psychological games are learned in childhood. As a result of the manner in which a wife interacts with her husband, for example, the husband may learn to play a psychological game because it seems to be the best defense against a game the wife may be employing.

Psychological Games Reflect a Life-style of Manipulation

An unfortunate consequence of husbands and wives playing psychological games with each other is that they most likely will pass these games onto their children who will tend to play the same games as they become adults. In this way games are transmitted from generation to generation. This is particularly unfortunate when extremely destructive, vicious games are involved.

When children grow up seeing their parents playing psychological games, they learn to accept them as a way of life and are prone to participate in games themselves in an automatic, unthinking way.

We have been discussing individual games that husbands and wives sometimes use in their interaction with each other. It is important to realize that the use of individual psychological games is part of a broader style of life that we might label as manipulation. Manipulation can become a lifetime system of dealing with people characterized by trying to exploit, control, and use others for one's own profit and benefit.[8] Manipulation involves a maneuver to get others to give us the positive strokes we want.

Couples whose marriages are troubled by this problem are fortunate if they become aware of the adverse consequences these games can have upon their relationships. For example, during an intensive counseling session, a husband remarked with some insight to the marriage counselor, "It seems that the difficulty in our marriage is that we both try to outmaneuver each other. We always try to control each other. I guess we don't really understand why."

Manipulation is not only a basic problem in marriage, but also in human relations in general. It contributes to the strife among nations, races, employees, and employers.

We are all, to various degrees, guilty of manipulation. The child who throws a temper tantrum to make parents do what he or she wants, the boy who pretends he loves a girl for the sole purpose of having sexual relations with her, the person who pretends interest in what another is saying when not even listening, the person who always carefully says what others want to hear—they are all manipulators.[9]

Types of Manipulators

There are many methods of manipulation, and each one of us can manipulate others psychologically in a variety of ways. When we are aware of some of the various types of manipulations, we can better understand ourselves. Everett Shostrom in *Man, the Manipulator* [10] suggests some basic types of manipulators. These types, according to Shostrom, present a picture of a typical therapy group as well as a picture of each of us with our particular manipulative approaches to interpersonal relationships.

THE DICTATOR TYPE

An example of the dictator-type of manipulator is the husband who dominates and controls his wife by ordering her around. He may dictate to her how every penny of the family income is to be spent on the assumption that he knows best or is an authority in financial matters. The dictator-type, in relating to others, often projects a parent or boss image.

THE WEAKLING TYPE

An example of the weakling-type manipulator is the wife of a dictator-type husband. She allows, and in many ways seems to enjoy, her husband's domination. According to Shostrom, the wife, characterized as the weakling-type of manipulator, may appear to be relating to her husband in a manner that makes him responsible for her problems and failures in life. She seduces her husband to dictate, control, and abuse her; then she complains about how abusive and unjust he is in an attempt to make him feel guilty. She may also elicit sympathy and solace from her friends by complaining about the injustice she experiences from her husband.

THE CALCULATOR TYPE

The calculator-type manipulator characteristically controls others by deceiving, lying, and outwitting them. An example of this type is the compulsive "Don Juan" who is obsessed with seducing women. Other examples are the high-pressure salesman and the con artist.

THE CLINGING-VINE TYPE

The clinging-vine-type manipulator exploits and emphasizes his or her dependency upon others. An example of this is a husband who wants to be cared for and who wants his wife and friends to do his work for him. This type includes the husband or wife who persists in playing the "perpetual child" role. Other variations of this type given by Shostrom are the "hypochondriac," the "attention demander," and the "helpless one."

THE BULLY TYPE

The bully-type manipulator attempts to control others through hostility and cruelty. Examples are the wife who "cuts down" and humiliates her husband both publicly and privately, and the husband who tries to get his own way by consistently presenting his wife with an implied threat of divorce.

THE NICE-GUY TYPE

According to Shostrom, the nice-guy-type manipulator is a person who exaggerates caring and love for others and uses a kind approach as a very effective way of controlling and manipulating. In a sense his or her "niceness," rather than reflecting true caring and love, is on a superficial level and is designed primarily as a way of coping with people. An example is the person who feels it is important to please everyone at all times and always says what he or she thinks others want to hear.

THE JUDGE TYPE

The judge-type manipulator is demonstrated by the husband who attempts to control and dominate his wife by being extremely critical of and very adept at blaming her as well as comparing her unfavorably with others. Shostrom notes other variations of the manipulator who specializes in making others feel ashamed and guilty, such as the "resentment collector" and the "convictor."

THE PROTECTOR TYPE

According to Shostrom, the protector-type manipulator is the opposite of the judge type. The protector tends to be overprotective and oversupportive of others in that he or she does not allow them to mature and become independent. An example is a wife who plays the "mother hen" role with her husband to the extent that she makes him look like a child. Other variations of this type are the person who always suffers for others, the person who is always embarrassed for others, and the martyr.

These types all overlap each other and most of us have, to some degree, employed all of these types of manipulation at various times in our lives. However, when we primarily use one type of manipulation, we tend to project its opposite onto others and they become our targets. An example is the wife who is the weakling-type manipulator often choosing a dictator-type husband.[11]

The Problems of Manipulation

Manipulation is so common that we can be unaware that it is taking place. Why do we manipulate each other so much? Because we have learned from an early age that manipulation is an accepted, even respected way of life. Salesmen and television commercials manipulate us in various ways to buy the desired products. Other people attempt to control our behavior by making us feel guilty. Through the movies and television we learn to admire those who are masters at manipulating people.[12]

The practice of manipulation creates many problems in interpersonal relationships. Two problems are of particular concern to today's world.

One basic difficulty is that manipulation contributes to dishonesty and artificiality in human relationships. A person who manipulates another must maintain a false front in order to create a desired impression. He or she uses tricks and deceit in attempts to influence the behavior of others.[13]

The manipulator is not genuinely being himself or herself and is not honest with self or others. This dishonesty and phoniness leads to a general distrust between people. Perhaps the greatest problem of all is that manipulation contributes to people seeing one another as *things* instead of persons. When we manipulate another person, we view that person as an object to be controlled for our benefit.

The Actualizor Versus the Manipulator

There are other more satisfying approaches to interpersonal relationships than manipulation. Instead of being manipulative, phony, and attempting to control others as though they were things, each person has the potential to relate to another in ways that (a) reflect genuine interest in and appreciation for that person, (b) acknowledge the worth and potential of that person and bring out his or her positive qualities, (c) promote the welfare and growth of the other person.

This latter type of relationship could perhaps be called the actualizing relationship. The term *actualizing* has been made famous by Abraham Maslow's [14] concept of, and research on, the self-actualizing person. It is the thesis of Maslow that we can better understand psychological health and healthy relationships by studying the characteristics of people who possess an unusually high degree of mental health and personal fulfillment and who relate to others in a very satisfying, healthy manner. Such persons have been called self-actualizing.

It is helpful to compare some basic characteristics of the manipulator and the actualizor. Everett Shostrom has compiled the characteristics of both, and as Table 7–1 indicates, the manipulator's philosophy of life is characterized by the four basic qualities of deception, unawareness, control, and cynicism. In contrast the actualizor's philosophy of life is characterized by the four basic qualities of honesty, awareness, freedom, and trust.

Logically and ideally, family relationships should be the place where actualizing relationships begin. It is within the family that the child should learn to re-

Table 7–1 Fundamental Characteristics of Manipulators and Actualizors Contrasted

Manipulators	Actualizors
1. Deception (phoniness, knavery). The manipulators use tricks, techniques, and maneuvers. They put on an act, play roles to create an impression. Their expressed feelings are deliberately chosen to fit the occasion.	1. Honesty (transparency, genuineness, authenticity). Actualizors are able to express feelings, whatever they may be. They are characterized by candidness, expression, and genuinely being themselves.
2. Unawareness (deadness, boredom). Manipulators are unaware of the really important concerns of living. They have "Tunnel Vision." They see only what they wish to see and hear only what they wish to hear.	2. Awareness (responsiveness, aliveness, interest). Actualizors fully look and listen to themselves and others. They are fully aware of nature, art, music, and the other real dimensions of living.
3. Control (closed, deliberate). Manipulators play life like a game of chess. They appear to be relaxed, yet are very controlled and controlling, concealing their motives from "opponents."	3. Freedom (spontaneity, openness). Actualizors are spontaneous. They have the freedom to be and express their potentials. They are masters of their lives and not puppets or objects.
4. Cynicism (distrust). Manipulators are basically distrusting of self and others. Down deep, they don't trust human nature. They see relationships with humans as having two alternatives: to control or be controlled.	4. Trust (faith, belief). Actualizors have a deep trust in self and others to relate to and cope with life in the here and now.

SOURCE: Adapted from *Man, the Manipulator* by Everett Shostrom. Copyright © 1967 by Abingdon Press. Used by permission.

ceive and give positive strokes, to have his or her OK position affirmed, and to help others feel OK about themselves. The relationship between husband and wife is the cornerstone upon which the other relationships within the family are built. The husband-wife relationship sets the prime example and mood for the parent-child and sibling relationships to follow. There is great truth in the statement, "one of the most important things a mother and father can do for their children is to establish a loving relationship with each other."

References

1. CHAPMAN, A. H. *Marital Brinkmanship.* New York: Putnam, 1974.
2. BERNE, ERIC. *Games People Play.* New York: Grove, 1964.
3. IBID.
4. CHAPMAN, A. H. *Put-Offs and Come-Ons.* New York: Putnam, 1968.
5. TEDESCHI, JAMES T.; BARRY R. SCHLENKER; and THOMAS V. BONOMA. *Conflict, Power, and Games.* Chicago: Aldine, 1973.
6. SHOSTROM, EVERETT. *Man, the Manipulator.* Nashville, Tenn.: Abingdon, 1967.
7. BERNE, ERIC. *What Do You Say After You Say Hello?* New York: Grove, 1972.
8. SHOSTROM, op. cit.
9. Ibid.
10. Ibid.
11. Ibid.
12. Ibid.
13. Ibid.
14. MASLOW, ABRAHAM H. *Toward a Psychology of Being.* New York: Van Nostrand, 1962.

8 Dealing with Marital Conflict

Photo by Walker Montgomery

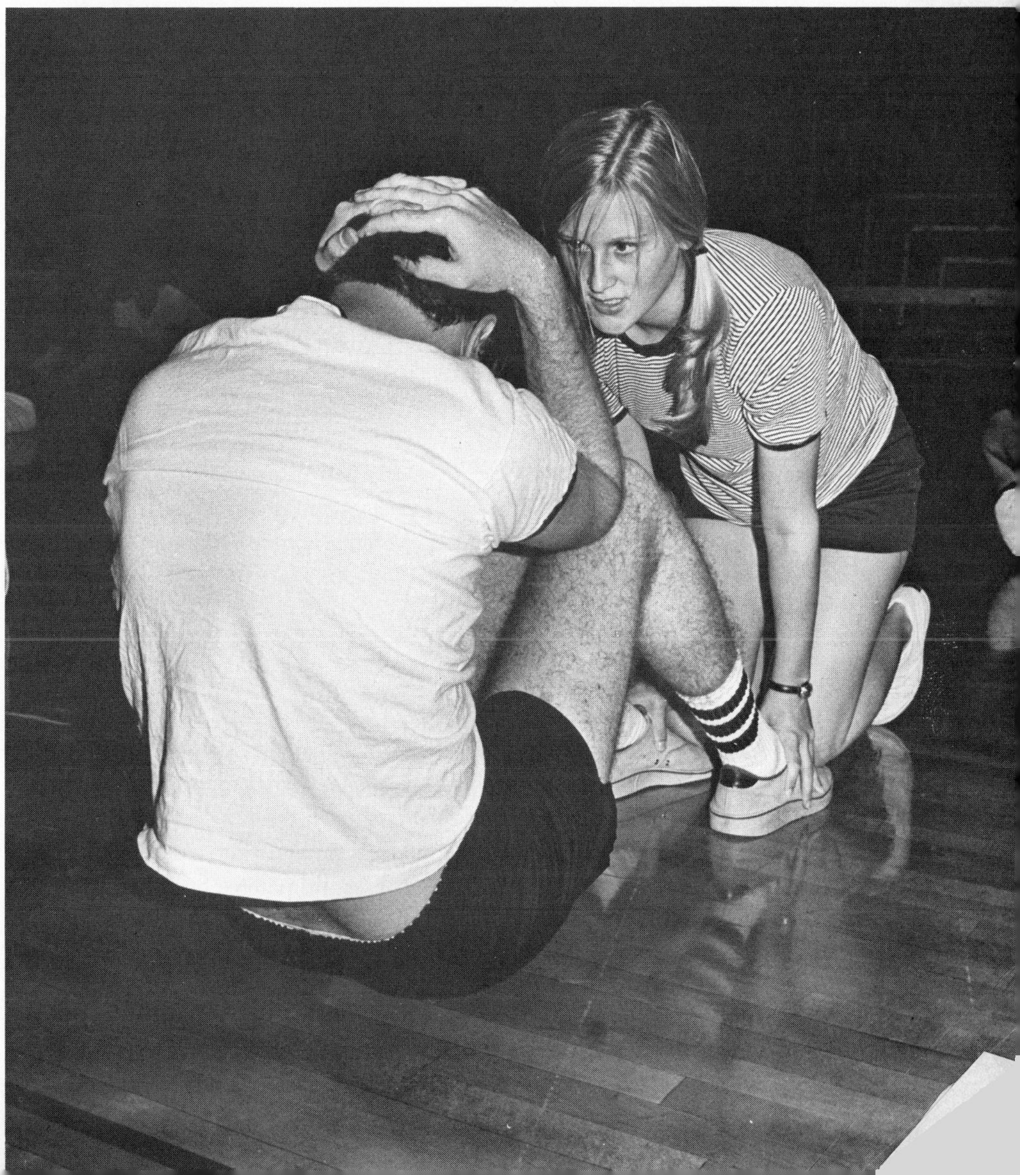

Hatred often consumes the container in which it is held long before it does violence to the victim for whom it is intended.

Unknown

Marital Conflict

Many people talk about conflict in marriages as if it is inevitable, as if couples were victims of marital interaction over which they have no control. In reality we can direct the course of our interaction with others. We need not be victims because we can consciously guide and change the course of our interaction to minimize conflict.

However, some couples do not minimize conflict; they cultivate it, thereby destroying their marriages in order to give expression to the hostility they feel. They recognize *what* they are doing and are often unhappy because they have not learned to cope with the hurt they feel. In time they regret that they did not identify the danger signals soon enough and find themselves on a course they despise. Unable to alter patterns they find personally threatening and self-defeating, they persist, year after year, in a life-style that makes them miserable. These couples are trapped not because they do not want to cope with and eliminate conflict, but simply because they do not know how.

Learning how to live with the hurt which each of us experiences in life and which leads to interpersonal conflict is one of the most important skills we can learn. Conflict often becomes a process by which a couple reinforces each other's "not OK" position. Extreme conflict destroys relationships and is a poor substitute for affection and appreciation in human interaction.

Although some conflict normally occurs in families, *it is not inevitable,* and it can be minimized. Because of differences in values, couples will not agree on everything, and mature couples will not expect to agree always. Couples who disagree have a choice as to whether their disagreements will produce conflict. They can choose, if they wish, *not* to fight. In a particular situation, couples may believe that fighting will improve their relationship in the long run, and they may choose to fight. It is important for a couple to evaluate responses in marital interaction in terms of whether or not the responses ultimately contribute to a satisfying marriage.

Each of us is aware that some conflict in an intimate relationship like marriage is normal and can be expected. To make our relationships as good as possible, it is important to learn how to deal with conflict effectively.

That we can learn how to deal successfully with conflict is illustrated by research with couples experiencing a moderately high degree of marital conflict. In one such study,[1] couples were taught the following skills in a series of training sessions:

1. To stop responding to each other in a destructive, hostile manner.
2. To increase the number of pleasant, supportive responses to each other.
3. To develop negotiating skills (for example, learning to specify exactly what they would like to change in the relationship, each person agreeing to alter some aspect of his or her behavior in exchange for changes in the behavior of the other).

Positive changes in the interaction of the couples were observed. A follow-up study of these couples one to two years after the training sessions had terminated found that most of the couples resolved conflicts more successfully, experienced fewer conflicts, and reported a higher degree of marriage happiness.

Benefits of Conflict

We usually talk about conflict as if it were very bad and to be avoided if at all possible. Conflict does have negative effects. However, psychiatrists and marriage counselors recognize some benefits of conflict.

RELIEF OF TENSION

The expression of conflict can have healthy and therapeutic effects by releasing pent-up tension and hostility. When these negative feelings are expressed openly it often lifts a great burden from the individual. Keeping tensions and negative feelings locked inside and never allowing expression of them can lead to hypertension, ulcers, high blood pressure, and extreme nervousness. In addition, bottled-up negative feelings have a tendency eventually to be expressed in the marriage relationship in subtle, less direct ways.

Tony and Martha have been married for two years. Martha came from a home in which her mother was the dominant family member. Her mother bossed her father. The father did not mind, so this was not a source of conflict. The mother and the father both made frequent use of sarcasm in their marriage relationship, even though they were happily married. They viewed sarcasm as a form of witty dialogue. Martha had identified with her mother's dominant role and had developed the habit of sarcasm. She minimized the sarcasm and dominance during her courtship with Tony, but these behaviors increased after marriage. Tony, in contrast, came from a home in which the relationship between his mother and father was equalitarian. Sarcasm was not used and was viewed as a very degrading, unattractive form of interaction.

Tony had been irritated by Martha's periodic use of sarcasm and bossiness before marriage but never said anything about it. As the dominance and sarcasm increased after marriage, Tony's dissatisfaction and anger grew. He saw her dominance and sarcasm as belittling him. His feelings were hurt. But he would not say anything about it. He kept his feelings to himself. By the second year of marriage, he developed high blood pressure and a pattern of periodic depression. His desire to have sexual relations with Martha had dwindled to almost zero. This created more problems between them. Finally, his physician recommended that they both see a marriage counselor.

After several weeks of counseling, the marriage counselor had helped them to see the pattern of interaction that was causing their problems. The turning point came when Tony, for the first time, openly expressed to Martha in a counseling session his negative feelings about her dominant behavior and use of sarcasm. Martha was quite surprised because she was really not aware of how strong his feelings were. Although it was not easy to break the habit, she did begin to reduce her dominating behavior and almost completely eliminated her use of sarcasm. Getting the conflict and negative feelings out in the open for the first time, and in this case getting the conflict resolved, had dramatic effects upon Tony. His high blood pressure and pattern of depression were completely eliminated. Their sex life gradually returned to normal and their total relationship is improved.

REDUCING RESENTMENT

Just as conflict in marriage can reduce tension, it can also reduce resentment. A person with negative feelings toward some behavior of a spouse who never openly expresses these feelings can easily develop feelings of resentment. For example, in the previously mentioned case of Tony and Martha, Tony had developed such strong resentment toward Martha that it had severely impaired their sexual relationship. Open expression of negative feelings and conflict is sometimes noisy and very intense for a period. However, it can benefit the marriage relationship by reducing resentment.

IDENTIFICATION OF PROBLEM

Conflict often serves the useful purpose of aiding precise identification of what the marital problem actually is.[2] Conflict can contribute to the real issues being brought out into the open. Extraneous issues can then be discarded and misunderstandings about the real issues can be clarified. When the actual problem is identified, both partners think more clearly about the situation and the chances of resolving difficulties are increased.[3]

Lance is a high school coach. His job is often hectic and tense. He started taking art lessons for relaxation. Sarah, his wife, had consistently maintained that they did not have enough money to afford art lessons as his salary was modest and they had incurred large debts. Lance continued with the art. Finally, one night, when Lance returned from art, Sarah gave full vent to her anger and resentment toward Lance for continuing to take the art lessons. A series of heated quarrels followed which continued into the next evening.

It gradually became apparent in the process of this conflict that Sarah was not really concerned about the money involved in the art lessons. Lance was quite busy as a coach and was extensively involved in community activities. Most of his evenings were taken up. He and Sarah had very little time together. The one night that had belonged to them alone was now taken by art lessons. This is what really bothered Sarah. When they both had identified the real problem, they began to appraise their life-style and decided they wanted to make some changes. Lance reduced his involvement in community activities and they regularly reserved three evenings a week to spend together. Lance continued in his art lessons with full support from Sarah.

INCREASING MUTUAL UNDERSTANDING

Conflict offers a very positive benefit if it results in a couple developing a greater understanding of each other. A greater appreciation for each other's past experiences and values often results from conflict situations.[4]

Veronica and Ross have been married for a year. Their marriage relationship is good. However, a major area of incompatibility concerns the attendance of concerts. Veronica has enjoyed going to them all her life. From childhood, concerts have been for her a source of pleasure, entertainment, and relaxation. Ross, in contrast, does not enjoy concerts. He refused to go despite Veronica's persistent requests. He told her to go with some of her friends or alone. Veronica became increasingly hurt and brooded about this.

Finally, she could no longer contain her negative feelings. She openly expressed her frustration and disappointment. Ross struck back. An intense quarrel erupted. However, in the quarrel, Ross pointed out that in childhood he had been forced to learn to play the violin. Much pressure was associated with his musical training. His parents insisted that he play well. They were extremely critical and were constantly nagging him as they felt he had not lived up to their expectations. Not surprisingly, Ross learned to hate music and concerts. They came to represent pressure, unpleasantness, and failure. When Veronica became aware of his past experiences she had a much greater understanding of why he did not want to go. As a result, she no longer felt angry or resentful about his refusal to attend concerts.

RENEWING APPRECIATION OF THE RELATIONSHIP

Conflict produces a beneficial by-product if it renews a couple's appreciation of their marriage relationship. Some couples go through a period of conflict and experience a feeling of being alienated from each other. They pass through this negative stage and find themselves with a renewed awareness of their positive emotional involvement with each other.[5]

Mr. and Mrs. Scott had been married for twenty years. They experienced severe conflict over an affair Mr. Scott was having with a younger woman. Mrs. Scott hurled insults at him and made guilt-inducing remarks. Mr. Scott threw insults back at her and brought up many grievances from the past. They talked about divorce. They visited a marriage counselor. At one of the sessions he had them list all the things they did not like about each other and their marriage as well as all the things they did like. They found that there really were many positive things about their relationship.

They began to think less about the hurts, problems, and negative aspects of their relationship and more about their positive emotional involvement with each other. They focused more on the enjoyment and positive memories of their twenty years together. They remembered vacation trips, funny times, hard times when money was tight, and projects they had worked on together. They decided they did not want a divorce. Mr. Scott decided to terminate his affair. They experienced renewed awareness of the deep loving feelings they had for each other.

Negative Aspects of Conflict

Conflict can, of course, be detrimental to a relationship. Intense, unresolved conflict creates a great deal of tension that can contribute to physical maladjustments. Conflict that involves a continued attack on the self-worth of the partner can result in the formation of a negative self-concept and can quickly cause alienation between two people. Whether conflict has primarily a positive or negative effect upon a marriage depends upon the way it is approached by the two people.

The Process of Conflict

Marital conflict generally follows a well-ordered pattern. There are certain stages within this pattern.[6] *The conflict may be stopped or reversed at any stage.* However, if the couple cannot resolve the conflict and the nature of it is serious, it may escalate through all the stages.

THE LATENT STAGE

There is usually a latent stage at the beginning of the conflict. In the latent stage, negative feelings lie hidden and unexpressed within the individual. Conflict and dissatisfaction are not brought out in the open and discussed.

There is, of course, little chance for the problem to be resolved at this stage. Irritation and resentment slowly build and lead to increased dissatisfaction and disenchantment until conflict finally erupts. Some people keep their irritations in a latent stage, but usually conflict progresses to a more advanced stage.[7] "You're not OK" messages are communicated subtly.

THE TRIGGER STAGE

The second stage comes about in the process of conflict when something happens to trigger the latent irritation out into the open. The incident may be so minor that it seems inconceivable it could result in such anger and conflict. But to the spouse who has been silently harboring irritation and resentment, the incident, however small, becomes the "straw that broke the camel's back." This event triggers or prompts the spouse to do something to reduce negative feelings and cope with the problem.[8]

THE CLASH STAGE

Prodded by the trigger event, the discontented spouse brings irritations and dissatisfactions out of hiding into the open. An open blowup or clash between the couple results.

This confrontation may come as a shock to the other partner, particularly if he or she had no clues about the spouse's latent discontent. The couple may react in several ways: They may quickly abandon the confrontation and return to an avoidance and denial of the problem; they may continue in the clash stage for a time and eventually resolve the problem; they may fluctuate between open conflict and reconciliation; or they may continue indefinitely in the clash stage, attacking and counterattacking and never resolving the problem.[9]

THE INCREASE-OF-CONFLICT STAGE

If the couple remains indefinitely in the clash stage and continues to attack and counterattack each other, the intensity of the conflict usually increases. There is also a tendency for the conflict to spread into other areas.

As hostile criticisms and disparaging, belittling remarks increase, feelings of anger and bitterness also grow and become deeply ingrained. Each partner feels rejected and threatened. As a result, each is prone to share the blame less. Each is less inclined to acknowledge his or her contribution to the problems. Increasingly, each partner projects blame onto the other. Each spouse tries to make himself or herself feel more adequate by tearing the other down.

Flexibility of the partners generally decreases and negative behavior is reinforced. A couple may realize that they are "spinning their wheels" and reduce the conflict by focusing on the problem rather than on each other. They may go on to resolve the problem. Other couples may have a temporary reconciliation. Still other couples may continue the intense and constant conflict that may spread to additional areas of the relationship.[10]

THE SEARCH-FOR-ALLIES STAGE

Conflict sometimes increases because a couple cannot resolve the difficulty alone. When this happens, each partner generally tries to find allies who will support him or her. Each seeks allies who will in effect say, "I am on your side. Your spouse is wrong. You are right. You have been mistreated. Your mate has been very inconsiderate."

Couples sometimes try to recruit their children as allies. Children may be brought into the conflict as mediators, judges, or confidants. A spouse may use a child as an accomplice to hurt the other spouse. The child may be used to send messages back and forth between the spouses. Allies may also be recruited from among friends and relatives. Some couples even go to a marriage counselor with the intention of using him or her as an ally.

The two spouses become more strongly opposed and hostile to each other and less willing to compromise as the circle of allies is expanded. The situation can develop into two armies opposed to one another.[11]

THE SEARCH-FOR-ALTERNATE-SOURCES-OF-GRATIFICATION STAGE

If the conflict continues through the stage of recruiting allies, the hostility may become so great and the satisfaction from the relationship so little that one or both partners may look for emotional fulfillment somewhere else. They may seek vicarious emotional satisfaction through their children. They may become absorbed in work or in social and community activities. It is at this stage that both partners are most susceptible to extramarital sexual relationships.

Seeking alternate sources of emotional fulfillment may give necessary emotional relief and serve to reduce the conflict level. It can, in a sense, serve as a diversion. However, it is also true that as each partner develops an independent life, the emotional investment in the marriage relationship is reduced.[12]

THE DISSOLUTION STAGE

The final stage in a severe conflict situation is a formal breakup of the marriage. One or both partners get to the point where they do not wish to tolerate the dissatisfaction any longer. They decide to separate or divorce. Lawyers are then employed in divorce proceedings, often serving as additional allies in the conflict.[13]

Barriers to Dealing with Conflict Successfully

Some behaviors prevent us from dealing effectively with conflict. We can recognize these behaviors and become aware of their negative influence in handling conflict. We can learn to minimize such behavior in our interaction with others.

ATTACKING THE PERSON

Nothing can fan the fires of conflict more rapidly than when a couple begins to attack each other. They throw insults, call each other names, make each other feel inadequate, and, in general, depreciate each other. This results in husband and wife feeling hurt, rejected, and defensive with each other. Attacking the person makes resolution of conflict more difficult because it shifts the concentration and communication away from the issue. The attention becomes focused on tearing each other down.

REFUSAL TO ACKNOWLEDGE THE EXISTENCE OF A PROBLEM

Some couples have difficulty resolving marital conflict because they refuse to acknowledge that a problem exists.[14] They may maintain a façade of well-being in their relationship even when there are obvious signs of trouble.

A couple who denies problems and negative feelings even though both know deep within themselves that problems do exist, in a sense tries to run away from the problems. The greatest disadvantage of constant refusal to acknowledge the existence of a problem is that it makes it almost impossible to clear up that problem.

AVOIDING RESPONSIBILITY

Another major barrier to dealing successfully with conflict is the tendency for either marriage partner to refuse responsibility for contributing to the conflict situation.[15] One partner may be inclined to blame the other for the problem.

Most of us intellectually agree that it is desirable to see the other person's point of view and to admit when we are wrong. Emotionally, however, some individuals have difficulty admitting they are wrong or acknowledging they have contributed to a conflict situation. These individuals may feel they are admitting something bad about themselves. For someone already sensitive about an unfavorable image or who is already in a "not OK" position, admitting even the slightest error is very disturbing. Such a person has difficulty in acknowledging any fault in a marriage problem.

Margaret and Gene had been married for three years. Their relationship had deteriorated to the point that they were seriously considering divorce. Gene began seeing a marriage counselor. Finally, at his urging, Margaret came with him to see the counselor. Part of their problem was caused by Margaret's destructive interaction. She belittled Gene in many ways. In subtle and not so subtle ways she made him feel inadequate. The counselor observed this after a few counseling sessions. When he pointed this out to Margaret, she became threatened and defensive. She denied it and angrily told the marriage counselor that Gene was the one who had the problems, and if he couldn't see that, he wasn't a very competent counselor. Margaret refused to return for counseling.

FOCUSING UPON SYMPTOMS RATHER THAN CAUSES

One common difficulty in coping effectively with conflict is a tendency to concentrate upon symptoms rather than the cause.[16] Very often couples are not aware of what the problem really is. In fact, one major function of marriage counseling is to assist the couple in identifying the actual problem.

Quite often a husband and wife spend much energy arguing about a symptom and never touch upon the cause of their problems. Couples sometimes spend a great deal of time in marriage counseling discussing symptoms rather than real problems. The tendency to substitute a superficial problem for the basic one results from the fact that couples find it difficult to face their real problems. It may be easier to project the conflict on a superficial issue.

One middle-aged couple began visiting a marriage counselor. They presented their problem as fighting over money. They talked at length to the counselor about their quarrels over money. As it turned out, conflict over money was not their real problem. The real problem was that the wife did not participate in sexual relations as much as the husband desired. His wife was an emotionally aloof person and did not appear very concerned about his wishes. The husband who already had feelings of insecurity felt personally rejected by his wife. Because of these feelings of being rejected, he became vindictive and attempted to get back at his wife by controlling her spending habits and complaining about how much money she was spending.[17]

OVERINTELLECTUALIZATION

Many couples approach problems and conflict from a strictly intellectual point of view: "We will deal with our problems rationally and objectively. We will not become emotional." To approch problems rationally and objectively is good. However, some couples overemphasize the rational and objective approach.[18] They reduce conflict to a simple matter of intellect.

When it is overintellectualized, a serious weakness is imposed that may prevent a couple from dealing most successfully with conflict. The weakness is that their feelings and emotions have been ignored. Each person continues to have feelings about the problem, but they may not be discussed because that would be considered too emotional.

Mere verbal or intellectual responses are not likely to bring about lasting changes. The most effective way to deal with marriage conflict is to acknowledge and come to terms with the underlying values, attitudes, and emotions that serve to guide behavior as well as to consider the rational and objective aspects of a problem.[19] Becoming too emotional or irrational is not effective. However, feelings and emotions must be considered in dealing with a conflict situation.

LACK OF COMMUNICATION

Lack of communication is one of the greatest barriers to dealing successfully with marriage problems. Many problems are prevented and many resolved when husband and wife maintain good communication patterns.[20] Some couples share surprisingly little of their goals, expectations, joys, preferences, dissatisfactions, and limitations with each other. A marriage problem may exist that frustrates both partners. Yet, they may not communicate their feelings about this problem. Why?

A couple may not communicate with each other about a problem because they are afraid of confrontation. They may willingly refrain from communicating marital grievances to each other to avoid conflict. A couple may also fail to mention grievances to each other because of insecurity about their relationship. They may feel that they risk rejection by their spouse if they communicate any dissatisfaction with the marriage.

Sometimes spouses have a sense of hopelessness and fatalism about a particular problem. They believe that nothing can change the situation, so there is no point in discussing it.[21]

It is nearly impossible to clear up a conflict or problem when there is no communication about it. Communication helps to identify the problem, clarify the feelings of each spouse, and enables them to consider the best alternative to solving the problem.

INABILITY TO ACCEPT DISAGREEMENT

Inability to accept disagreement from another is a major factor contributing to and intensifying conflict.[22] We may expect those close to us to agree with us on practically everything. Agreement is seen as support that makes us feel more secure. Disagreement may be viewed as rejection and may, therefore, promote feelings of insecurity. Our interpretation of the agreement or disagreement often runs far deeper than the importance the particular issue merits. An individual's feelings of self-worth may be associated with agreement or disagreement with the spouse. It is no surprise that such a person usually reacts to disagreement very strongly and perhaps with an extreme degree of hostility.

FATIGUE

Many couples try to resolve conflict situations and quarrels when they are very tired.[23] For some couples this seems to be the *only* time they try to resolve conflict. It is probably the worst possible time. When most of us are very fatigued, we don't feel good; our nerves are often on edge; our mental attitude may be gloomy or at least not at our usual level of optimism; and we tend to be quick-tempered.

A couple can approach a problem more objectively and positively when they are not tired. When both partners feel good and physically alert, they are much more likely to deal successfully with a troublesome situation.

When we were first married, we had most of our fights in the evening. I got into the habit of hitting him with a gripe in the evening, usually before dinner. Generally, the lid would really blow off and we would get into a grand-slam fight. It finally dawned on us that this was the worst time we could talk about problems or bring up gripes. This was the time of day when he was most tired and hungry. I am also tired at this time. In addition, my energy level is lowest at this particular time, which puts me in a less positive frame of mind. We agreed not to discuss problems in the evenings. We now usually bring them up in the mornings on the weekend. Not every weekend, of course, just when we have a gripe or problem to discuss. We operate much better at this time and get far less irritable with each other.

EXTREME ANGER

It may be therapeutic and desirable for couples to express their anger in a conflict situation. It may release tension, clear the air, and help to clarify feelings about the issue. However, as with most things, there is a limit to expression of anger. In the long run, more harm may be done to the relationship than the immediate benefit derived from the expression of anger.

Anger, beyond a certain point, can become a negative influence and serve as a barrier to resolving conflict effectively. Sometimes we get too angry to do anything except be destructive in our interaction. At such a time, perhaps the best action we can take is to remove ourselves from the conflict situation until we "cool off."

Reasons for Conflict

There are innumerable reasons for conflict. However, certain major reasons contribute to most of the marital conflicts that couples experience.

INTIMACY

One of the most basic reasons for marital conflict is the intimacy involved in the marriage relationship.[24] Any relationship as intimate and close as marriage will involve some conflict.

Couples become involved in marital conflict partly because they feel free to do so. Most of us feel more free to disagree with those persons who are closest to us. Also, in any close relationship, such as marriage, there are more opportunities for conflict regardless of how satisfying the relationship may be. There are more occasions for conflict because a couple spends so much time together and because they share so many different aspects of their lives.

BASIC DIFFERENCES

Perhaps the most obvious reason for conflict between husbands and wives is that they have basic differences. A husband and wife may come from very different family cultures. Each family has its own culture with its distinctive customs, attitudes, and habits.

A frequent source of conflict for Robert and Elaine has been behavior at dinner. Elaine was reared in a family where dinner was an occasion for visiting and talking about whatever was of concern to the family members. A major purpose of dinner was fellowship. Robert, in contrast, came from a family that primarily ate in silence. The only purpose of dinner was to eat, after which the family members got up and left. It was not an occasion for visiting. The family cultures of Robert and Elaine clashed on this issue. Elaine was disappointed and hurt over Robert's silence at dinner. Robert was irritated at Elaine's insistence on talking while he was trying to eat. Mutual understanding and tolerance were increased when they both became aware of their different family upbringing in this respect.

Broad cultural differences can contribute to marital conflict. Research evidence indicates that conflict and instability are more likely in marriage where there are great differences in education, socioeconomic backgrounds, racial and ethnic backgrounds, and religious beliefs. Conflict also results when couples have goals that are incompatible.[25]

TRYING TO MAKE A PARTNER OVER

Conflict may be caused by one partner trying to make the other over. Some individuals marry with the intention of remodeling their partner. They may try to change a partner's values, attitudes, likes and dislikes, interests, or certain personality characteristics. The result is usually conflict and resentment. Each of us is apt to resist being changed by another, especially when it is against our wishes. When one partner tries to change the other, it implies displeasure with that partner as a person. Feelings of resentment and rejection are common in the spouse who is the object of the attempted change.

Constructive criticism within moderation can be helpful and beneficial. However, extensive and persistent attempts to remodel a partner almost certainly are destined to end in trouble. Gentle requests for a partner to change can develop into nagging, which may develop into pointed attacks. Finally, open conflict can break out with each partner attacking and retaliating.

POWER STRUGGLES AND COMPETITION

Some of the most intense forms of marriage conflict result from power struggles. Each partner may have strong power needs, and interaction can become a contest to determine who exercises the most power. Conflict erupts and, in a sense, may be desired by one or both partners as a necessary part of the game. Either partner may enhance his or her feeling of self-worth and competency by dominating the other.

In American society, people compete constantly both in school and in the work world. It is not surprising that this competitive spirit sometimes carries over into marriage.[26] A husband and wife may have a large element of competition in their marriage, continually comparing themselves and competing with each other in terms of amount of income earned, promotions, prestige, community activities, and even the number of friends.

Achievements of one partner in work or in social life may be resented by the other who feels outdone. Instead of sharing the joy of that partner's accomplishment, the other mate may feel inferior, humiliated, or beaten. Instead of being supportive of the partner who has accomplished something desirable, the other mate may try to diminish that partner's achievements. He or she may belittle, ridicule, or ignore the partner's accomplishments.[27]

A competitive marriage relationship becomes much like the business world with a ruthless drive for success and quest for recognition. When competitiveness characterizes a marriage, the husband's and wife's sense of emotional security in each other usually is lost.[28]

TREMENDOUS TRIFLES

There is an adage, "It's not the great storms that destroy the oak tree, it's the little bugs." The little bugs might be compared to the tremendous trifles in marriage. The tremendous trifles can add up and damage the marriage relationship if they are not dealt with effectively.

Slurping coffee, leaving the cap off of the toothpaste tube, dirty clothes left on the floor, muttering, nervous mannerisms, jingling coins and car keys in the pocket, and irritating verbal expressions—these are examples of tremendous trifles. They are petty irritants.[29]

These petty irritants, however, result in conflict. Couples may feel that these trifles are too petty to mention; but eventually they become so irritated by them that they finally express their irritation openly. Individuals often feel petty for having expressed frustration over such trifles. This makes them more irritated and they proceed to complain in an even more angry and forceful manner.

Tremendous trifles are most damaging to a relationship when they are kept inside and resentment is allowed to build up over a period of time. They are most likely to be kept in perspective when they are realized for what they are—trifles. A couple can prevent trifles from gaining undue importance by discussing them as soon as they begin to be irritants.

DIFFERENT ROLE EXPECTATIONS

Husbands and wives bring different role expectations with them to marriage. Each has definite expectations of self, the other marriage partner, and the marriage. Sometimes these different expectations contrast sharply.

Herb grew up in a home where his mother was a full-time homemaker. His entire family had the attitude that it was very desirable for a wife and mother not to work. Herb internalized the attitude. His wife, Joan, grew up in a family where her mother was a career woman and actually had a higher income than her father. Joan identified with her mother and wanted to have a career herself. Yet, Herb expected her to be a full-time homemaker. These clashing expectations resulted in much conflict.

It sometimes helps to realize that a particular conflict is due mostly to role expectations that do not match rather than to the "bad" qualities of the marriage partners.

Importance of Adaptability

How can Herb and Joan, in the previously cited case, resolve their conflict of expectations? Joan could change her expectations and be a full-time homemaker; Herb could change his expectations and accept her pursuing a career; they could compromise so that Joan could work part-time; or they could both maintain their expectations and continue their interaction in conflict. In this case as in most conflict situations, one important quality necessary for dealing with conflict is adaptability.

Adaptability might be defined as a willingness of an individual to modify his or her own behavior. In fact, adaptability is one characteristic that distinguishes adjusted from maladjusted couples. Research evidence indicates that adjusted couples are more willing to modify their behavior than are maladjusted couples.[30] There is also evidence that divorced couples resort to mutual "give and take" much less as a way of dealing with disagreement than do happily married couples.[31] An experimental study of 180 couples undergoing family therapy found that those couples who resolved conflict situations most effectively and constructively viewed each other as being more cooperative than did those couples responding to conflict situations in a mutually destructive manner.[32]

Mr. and Mrs. Benson are on their first camping trip in the mountains. Mr. Benson is enjoying the experience, but Mrs. Benson is not. She does not like "roughing it." Aso, the mountain air is cooler than she expected and she is uncomfortable. Finally, Mr. Benson says, "Let's go. You're uncomfortable and not having a good time. We can do something else that we will both enjoy." Mrs. Benson replies, "But you are enjoying this very much. We will stay. It'll probably get better. We can buy a jacket for me tomorrow and I'll be more comfortable."

Both partners in this case are willing to concede to each other. The important result of this expression of adaptability is that it transforms conflict from a clash of wills to a courtesy contest.[33] Another important result is that each partner perceives that the other wants to please him or her. The willingness and desire to accommodate each other is appreciated regardless of which solution is selected.[34] The willingness to modify behavior communicates respect and consideration.

Adaptability seems to be more characteristic of wives than of husbands. The adaptability of wives appears to be more positively associated with the marital happiness of husbands than the adaptability of husbands is to the happiness of wives. The finding that wives adjust more in marriage than do husbands suggests that they possess the quality of adaptability to a greater degree.[35] If wives are more adaptable, it is most likely because they are expected to be. The skills associated with adaptability, such as empathy and flexibility, have traditionally been associated with feminine behavior. This is unfortunate because adaptability is an important quality in promoting good interpersonal relationships. Men need to internalize this quality as much as women.

Ways of Dealing with Conflict

THE AVOIDANCE PATTERN

Some people believe that a good marriage is one in which there is no open conflict. Open conflict implies disharmony and that they have somehow failed in their marriage. They may, therefore, become fearful of engaging in conflict as it symbolizes failure. Consequently, they repress feelings of conflict, dissatisfaction, and aggression.

Such repression of conflict frequently has adverse effects. The research evidence indicates suppressed hostility and conflict often are a greater threat to the relationship when they finally do break out into the open. Other studies show that there is less residual hostility among individuals who communicate their negative feelings to the person causing their frustration. Happily married couples more often discuss conflict situations, whereas unhappily married couples tend to avoid the issue.[36]

The avoidance pattern attempts to deal with marital conflict by refusing to acknowledge or be involved in it.[37] Even though a husband and wife may feel very much like disagreeing with each other, by using the avoidance of conflict pattern, they keep conflict and tension underground. They do not allow it to come out in the open.

Certain common attitudes are associated with this manner of dealing with conflict. One such attitude is a fear of alienating or hurting others, or of being hurt by others. Peace and harmony are seen by some individuals as a condition in which no conflict or divergence is expressed or allowed. Conflict is viewed as being cruel, vulgar, and as indicating a lack of love, largely because the individual learned to view conflict in this manner from parents. Therefore, such learned attitudes often motivate the individual to avoid conflict at any price.[38] Such an individual keeps the conflict within, refusing to express it.

Many family counselors view the avoidance pattern of dealing with marital conflict as unhealthy, creating a major barrier to effective communication between the marriage partners over a period of time.[39] Various family counselors also note that even though marriage partners attempt to avoid any open expression of hostility, the conflict eventually manifests itself in subtle, indirect ways that are often more destructive than direct expressions of conflict would have been. Such indirect, subtle expressions sometimes involve manipulation of the children to express the conflict they have not been willing to express openly to each other. Spouses may use their children to hurt each other.

THE CONFLICT-CENTERED PATTERN

The conflict-centered pattern focuses upon the conflict itself rather than upon the issue involved. When this pattern is engaged in, conflict becomes a game of wits where victory means the enhancing of one partner's ego by belittling the other person. This pattern usually becomes person-centered. The objective is not solving the problem or gaining insight about the issue, rather, the objective is attacking the person who takes a different viewpoint.

When communication becomes person-centered and one partner attacks the other, feelings of defensiveness and resentment are aroused in the other mate who, in turn, is likely to counterattack. Such a communication pattern is apt to result in each mate becoming hypnotized by his or her own rightness and virtue and by the other mate's shortcomings. This type of communication becomes a destructive game in which each mate looks for and exploits vulnerable areas in the other. Real issues get lost in the fray and any true understanding is prevented.

THE ISSUE-CENTERED PATTERN

The issue-centered pattern of dealing with conflict focuses on the issue involved. This pattern of communication deals with identifying and solving the problem and with clarifying the feelings of each mate about the issue. Conflict is neither unduly avoided nor utilized as a means of enhancing one's own ego and belittling another.

This pattern is not person-centered or concerned with attacking the other person. The prime concern is to arrive at a better understanding of the problem at hand. The issue-centered pattern of communication is a constructive and positive manner of dealing with conflict. It includes certain elements that contribute to clearer communication and greater effectiveness in handling conflict.

Respect for the Right to Disagree. The first element involved in the issue-centered pattern is an attitude of allowing the other mate the freedom and right to disagree. Such an attitude is an extremely important step in dealing with conflict effectively as it implies an awareness of and respect for the individuality of the other person.

Identifying the Problem and Clarifying Feelings. The second step involves identifying the problem and clarifying each mate's feelings about it. The focus, of course, should not be upon the other person *but upon the problem* because the more the emphasis centers on the issue, the easier and quicker it is to deal with it effectively.[40]

Identifying the problem involves bringing it out in the open, calling it to the attention of the other partner, clarifying exactly what the problem seems to be. After the problem is identified, it is important for each spouse to express his or her feelings about it and listen to and try to understand the other spouse's feelings. Many couples find it helpful for each partner, after listening to the other express his or her feelings, to verbalize what he or she thinks that the other partner has said. This facilitates the interchange between the two partners, enabling each to "get inside" the other's perception of the problem. Consider the following example:

> Over a five-hour period, a young couple quarreled in my presence . . . They were trying to work through a point of tension that had continued to plague them in their personal relationship . . .
>
> Each was quite open about feelings of hostility toward the actions of the other. There was no mock politeness nor sentimentality, but neither was there any attempt to undercut or diminish the other. Their aim seemed to be to understand their mutual problem while maintaining their relationship and undertaking honest communication.
>
> It required two and a half hours of patient interchange to discover what the fight was really about. Each stated what he felt to be the problem and the other "replayed" the statement until both agreed that each understood the other's viewpoint. They then tried to dig back to see why each felt as he did. Each was sharply critical of how the other had made him or her feel, yet both expressed such criticism in terms of a search for what caused the disagreement rather than a personal attack on the motives or actions of the other. Now and then one would attempt a summary of what had been achieved in the discussion, and the other would correct any misunderstanding or faulty interpretation.
>
> When one began to use methods that seemed unfair, the other was quick to say, "Now wait. You are trying to put me on the defensive. You are dragging in things that don't really help." When one began to be angry, he said so, or the other expressed it openly. "You're mad now, aren't you? What made you mad?" There was no attempt to hide strong feelings or to deny them. Such feelings were acknowledged rather than criticized, ignored, or repressed. Then the statement, replaying of the statement, restatement, replaying process began again.
>
> In a spirit of seeking to find the truth about a very troubling matter, they worked toward revelation and communication which bound them more closely to each other at the end of the evening despite the depth of their disagreement.[41]

Considering the Alternatives. After identification of the problem and clarification of each mate's feelings have been achieved, the third stage in the issue-centered pattern of coping with conflict is to consider the various solutions to the problem. The advantages and disadvantages of each alternative can be considered. The solution should ideally be chosen on the basis of the best alternative in the long run for everyone concerned.

Basic Principles for Dealing with Conflict

George Bach and Ronald M. Deutsch in *Pairing* recommend some basic principles for dealing with conflict that are adapted herein. These principles provide some simple and specific guidelines for handling conflict situations.[42]

1. Be specific when you introduce a complaint.
2. Don't just complain; ask for a reasonable change that will make the situation better.

3. Give and receive feedback of the major points to make sure you are understood; to assure your partner that you understand the issue.
4. Try tolerance. Be open to your own feelings, and equally open to your partner's.
5. Consider compromise. Many conflict issues involve no clear-cut right or wrong. Your partner may even have some good ideas.
6. Do not allow counterdemands to enter the picture until the original demands are clearly understood, and there has been clear-cut response to them. Deal with one issue at a time.
7. Don't mind-rape. Do not tell a partner what he or she knows or feels. Never assume you know what your partner thinks. Ask.
8. Attack the issue, not each other. Refrain from name-calling and sarcasm.
9. Forget the past and stay with the issue at hand. Hurts, grievances, and irritations should be brought up at the earliest moment, or the partner may suspect that they have been saved as weapons.
10. Do not burden your partner with grievances. To do so can make him feel hopeless and suggests that you have either been hoarding complaints or do not know what really troubles you.
11. Think about your real thoughts and feelings before speaking.
12. Remember that there is never a winner in an honest, intimate fight. Both either win more intimacy, or lose it.

Types of Solution to Conflict

CONSENSUS

One way couples may solve conflict is by consensus. After considering the advantages and disadvantages of the various alternatives, the husband and wife agree upon an alternative that would be best for both of them.[43] For example, a couple in conflict over where to vacation may come to a mutual agreement that Colorado is a wiser choice than Europe. They may base this decision on factors such as comparative costs of the two trips and time involved.

COMPROMISE

Couples may solve conflict through compromise. Part of each partner's view is adopted in the final decision. They meet each other halfway in a sense. For example, a couple may decide to spend one week of their vacation in Colorado and the other week in parts of Europe. Or they might travel in Europe this year and visit Colorado next year.

A compromise may leave both partners quite happy, or it may leave both of them somewhat dissatisfied with the final outcome.[44]

CONCESSION

A conflict situation may be ended by one partner conceding to the other.[45] The wife may finally agree with her husband to vacation in Colorado rather than in Europe (her vacation choice), but she does not agree because she thinks it would be most enjoyable to vacation in Colorado. She agrees primarily to end the conflict.

Concession can be a satisfactory solution to conflict particularly in situations where the issue involved is far less important to the spouse making the concession than it is to the other mate. One helpful question husbands and wives can consider in a conflict situation is, "How important is it to me to have my way in this situation? Is it more or less important to me than to my spouse?"

ACCOMMODATION

Sometimes a couple cannot agree and neither partner wants to give in. In such a situation, accommodation is a type of solution. Each partner holds to his or her own view about the situation and both agree to disagree. If a couple disagrees strongly on where to spend a vacation, the wife may go to Europe and the husband to Colorado. In a sense, this is what accommodation is—each partner going his or her separate way.

Too much separateness may, of course, be detrimental to the relationship. There are also times when accommodation is not possible. If the conflict issue is whether to buy or not buy a new home, there can be no accommodation.[46]

References

1. PATTERSON, GERALD R.; HYMAN HOPS; and ROBERT L. WEISS. "Interpersonal Skills Training for Couples in Early Stages of Conflict." *Journal of Marriage and the Family*, vol. 37, 1975, pp. 295–393.
2. KIEREN, DIANNE; JUNE HENTON; and RAMONA MAROTZ. *Hers and His: A Problem Solving Approach to Marriage.* Hinsdale, Ill.: Dryden Press, 1975.
3. LANTZ, HERMAN R., and ELOISE C. SNYDER. *Marriage: An Examination of the Man-Woman Relationship.* New York: Wiley, 1969.

4. Ibid.
5. Ibid.
6. Beck, Dorothy F. "Marital Conflict: Its Cause and Treatment as Seen by Caseworkers." *Social Casework*, vol. 47, 1966, pp. 211–221.
7. Ibid.
8. Ibid.
9. Ibid.
10. Ibid.
11. Ibid.
12. Ibid.
13. Ibid.
14. Lantz and Snyder, op. cit.
15. Ibid.
16. Ibid.
17. Ibid.
18. Ibid.
19. Ibid.
20. Chapman, A. H. *Marital Brinkmanship*. New York: Putnam, 1974.
21. Ibid.
22. Blood, Robert O. *Marriage*. New York: Free Press, 1969*a*.
23. Ibid.
24. Ibid.
25. Schmidt, Stuart M., and Thomas A. Kochan. "Conflict: Toward Conceptual Clarity." *Administrative Science Quarterly*, vol. 17, 1972, pp. 359–370.
26. Landis, Paul. *Making the Most of Marriage*. Englewood Cliffs, N.J.: Prentice-Hall, 1975.
27. Ibid.
28. Ibid.
29. Blood, 1969*a*, op. cit.
30. Buerkle, Jack V.; Theodore R. Anderson; and Robin F. Badgley. "Altruism, Role Conflict, and Marital Adjustment: A Factor Analysis of Marital Interaction." *Marriage and Family Living*, vol. 23, 1961, pp. 20–26.
31. Barry, William A. "Marriage Research and Conflict: An Integrative Review." *Psychological Bulletin*, vol. 73, 1970, pp. 41–54.
32. Epstein, Nathan B., and Jack Santa-Barbara. "Conflict Behavior in Clinical Couples: Interpersonal Perceptions and Stable Outcomes." *Family Process*, vol. 14, 1975, pp. 51–66.
33. Blood, 1969*a*, op. cit.
34. Ibid.
35. Kieren, Dianne, and Irving Tallman. "Spousal Adaptability: An Assessment of Marital Competence." *Journal of Marriage and the Family*, vol. 34, 1972, pp. 247–256.
36. Barry, op. cit.
37. Raush, Harold L.; William A. Barry; Richard K. Hertel; and Mary Ann Swain. *Communication, Conflict, and Marriage*. San Francisco: Jossey-Bass Publishers, 1974.
38. Morrison, E. S. "Family Peace at Any Price?" *International Journal of Religious Education*, vol. 43, 1967, pp. 8–9.
39. Satir, Virginia. *Conjoint Family Therapy*. Palo Alto, Calif.: Science and Behavior Books, 1967.

40. Blood, 1969*a*, op. cit.
41. Morrison, op. cit., pp. 8–9.
42. Bach, George R., and Ronald M. Deutsch. *Pairing.* New York: Avon Books, 1971, pp. 202–204.
43. Blood, Robert. "Resolving Family Conflicts." In *Marriage and Family in the Modern World,* Ruth Cavan, ed. New York: Crowell, 1969*b*, pp. 421–433.
44. Ibid.
45. Ibid.
46. Ibid.

9 Family Financial Management

Photo by Nancy Stinnett

Decision-making is the most important factor in management, and most decisions involve money.

Jerome D. Folkman and Nancy M. K. Clatworthy

Where Are Families Today Economically?

The recession of the 1970s has had a profound impact on American family life. Families are worried about the state of the economy. Over half are concerned about their own future financial security. For many families this is a time of watching, but for some it is already a period of serious economic stress. These are the findings of a study based on a national sample of 55 million families in the United States.[1]

Interviews with over 150 experts who deal with the American family indicated that there was little doubt in their minds that money can be a major source of stress and breakdown in families.[2] There is little doubt that *how* we learn to manage our resources will greatly affect the quality of our family life and the happiness that we will attain.

Because we are a people who have—in the last generation—become accustomed to affluence, many of us have not learned to save, to shop wisely, to use credit properly, or to conserve the materials we have. We have operated on the philosophy that if we want it, we should have it. The economic indicators suggest, however, that we will need to learn to be less wasteful, become better shoppers and managers, and become satisfied with less. We have grown up with the expectation that economically things should get better for us *each* year and that the party in power—whether it be the Democrats or the Republicans—has the responsibility to see to it that things get better. If they do not it is their fault, not ours. Increasingly, families assume that their future well-being is determined not by their own actions, but by what happens to the nation.[3]

The concern about our economy outweighs concern with crime, urban blight, or quality of education. A national survey indicates that economic fears include fear of unemployment (28 per cent), savings diminishing in value as a result of inflation (35 per cent), debt (16 per cent), and using savings to meet current living expenses (22 per cent).[4]

Managing Finances

Most couples can increase their enjoyment of life by learning to utilize financial resources more effectively. Money management is an important aspect of marriage and, if effective, can assist a couple in achieving many of their goals. Although the accumulation of money itself is rarely cited as a goal in life, the realization of many goals depends on money; for instance, travel, or establishment of a home, or college education. Because money is closely tied to the actualization of goals, lack of skill in handling money or disagreement on how to handle it can be a source of conflict.

Who will make financial decisions? Apparently some agreement exists between the sexes as to who is making decisions, as is illustrated in Table 9–1.

In most families both the husband and the wife share in making financial decisions. In the remaining families the husband is much more likely to assume the responsibility than the wife.[5]

Regardless of who makes decisions, the utilization of money has been found by researchers to be a major problem area in marriage adjustment (see Table 9–2). This is even more understandable when one considers the fact that the income of most young couples is more limited than their choices of ways to spend it.[6]

It is clear that many families have to forego luxuries in order to maintain economic stability within the family. But what do today's families consider to be luxuries? Table 9–3 presents some evidence.[7]

Over half of the families in the United States consider having a new car, paying someone to do housework, and taking a vacation each year to be luxuries. And 20 per cent or more consider the following to be luxuries: going to movies, smoking cigarettes, drinking liquor, playing golf or tennis, having a color television, belonging to clubs, going to a hairdresser regularly, going on weekend trips with the family, having a second car, and going to eat in a nice restaurant.

Table 9–1 The Main Financial Decision Maker in the Family

	Men Say: %	Women Say: %
Husband	39	38
Wife	16	21
Both	42	39
Not sure	3	2

SOURCE: From *The General Mills American Family Report: 1974–75.* Reprinted with permission from General Mills, Inc.

Table 9–2 Argument About Money *

Subject	%
Money in general	59
Need for family to economize	47
Wasting money	42
Unpaid bills	38
Keeping track of where money goes	33
Saving for future	25
Borrowing money	17
Bad investment	10
Lending money	8

* Based on those who say they argue about money.

SOURCE: From *The General Mills American Family Report: 1974–75.* Reprinted with permission from General Mills, Inc.

Table 9–3 The Definition of a Luxury

Defined as a Luxury	Total %
Having a new car	72
Paying someone to do housework	59
Taking a vacation each year	55
Going out to eat in a nice restaurant	45
Having a second car	33
Going on weekend trips with family	31
Going to a hairdresser regularly	29
Belonging to clubs	26
Having a color television	24
Drinking liquor	23
Playing golf/tennis	21
Smoking cigarettes	20
Going to the movies	20
Giving money to charity	18
Buying a winter coat	15
Having meat with meals	14
Subscribing to magazines	11
Having company for dinner	11
Having a baby-sitter	10
Taking a Sunday drive	8
Having a telephone	7

SOURCE: From *The General Mills American Family Report: 1974–75.* Reprinted with permission from General Mills, Inc.

Some of the luxury items noted in the General Mills study would not have been considered a luxury a few years ago. Thus, it is easier to understand why financial decisions create problems for families. Of the fourteen main problems families are facing, eight are related to finances either directly or indirectly. Table 9–4 presents a summary of the problems in relation to the standard of living compared to a year ago.[8]

Since few families have enough money to pay for everything they want, it is important to learn to establish priorities early in the family life cycle to determine what things and what experiences are most important. No one can tell you what to purchase or what experiences to save for in order to achieve the greatest satisfaction because family goals vary tremendously. In considering a purchase, it is far more important to ask oneself, "Can I live *without* it?" rather than, "Can I live with it?" Such questions tend to inhibit impulse buying, one of the chief reasons for wrecked budgets.

One of the most important principles to remember in handling money is that *errors cost money.*

People do make errors in money management. A total of 63 per cent of the respondents in the General Mills study [9] admitted to making some unwise financial decisions in the previous year. These are reported in Table 9–5.

Table 9–4 Main Problems Families Are Facing

	Standard of Living Compared to a Year Ago			
	Total %	*Better* %	*Same* %	*Worse* %
Investments/savings losing value due to inflation	35	26	34	40
Not as well off financially now as expected	32	15	23	51
Health problems	28	25	29	29
Fear of unemployment	28	21	17	43
Can't make ends meet	26	19	14	44
Fear of being robbed/mugged	23	22	21	27
Having to draw on savings for current expenses	22	10	17	32
Not enough time with family	20	27	20	18
Sense of personal stress/anxiety	17	16	14	22
Being too far in debt	16	17	9	26
Seeing neighborhood deteriorate	11	5	11	13
Not knowing how to manage money wisely	10	13	7	13
Family problems—husband/wife/children	9	10	9	8
Difficulty in getting credit	5	3	4	8

SOURCE: From *The General Mills American Family Report: 1974–75.* Reprinted with permission from General Mills, Inc.

Table 9–5 Financial Mistakes Made in Last Year *

	Total %
Had to draw on savings or investments to meet current bills	38
Overdrew on checking account	24
Didn't repair the car until too late	16
Ran up too big a bill on credit cards or charge accounts	14
Used savings for some kind of luxury or trip	13
Got behind in mortgage or rent payments	8
Made a major purchase you couldn't afford	8
Borrowed more than you can afford to pay back	6
Borrowed money from a loan company which charged an unusually high interest rate	6
Made a bad loan to someone	6
Got cheated by a store/company who overcharged	6
Made a bad investment	5
Got behind in taxes	5
Had to borrow on insurance	5
Sold stock or other investments you should have kept	3
Took out second mortgage on house	2

* Based on those making these mistakes.

SOURCE: From *The General Mills American Family Report: 1974–75.* Reprinted with permission from General Mills, Inc.

The most common mistakes included using savings too freely to meet expenses, purchasing things they could not afford, waiting too long to have cars repaired, and using savings for luxuries.

By eliminating errors in spending, families can save more money and achieve greater satisfaction during the course of a lifetime. All of us have grown up as consumers and have learned dozens of sound principles, such as, the least expensive article is not always the best value. It is important to re-evaluate many of these principles periodically to keep ourselves from making decisions based on a momentary impulse that will result in dissatisfaction.

In a grocery store, for example, there are many items from which to choose, and dozens of sales techniques designed to create demand. Items that are higher priced are often placed on the shelves at eye level, whereas similar kinds of goods of lesser price are placed on the bottom shelves where they may be overlooked in favor of the article that will yield greater profit.[10]

Often overstocked items display a large sign marked SALE! The consumer may assume that the price marked on the item reflects a reduction in price, and this is not necessarily true.[11] Also, purchasing a coat "marked down" from $50 to $39 is no bargain if it can be purchased elsewhere for $29. Many consumers assume, however, that if an item is "marked down," they are obtaining a bargain.

Most people who have shopped at different grocery stores have observed variations in the prices of articles they use regularly, and they are delighted if they save 20 cents by purchasing ten cans of soup that normally sell for 2 cents a can more than the sale price. These same people, however, in purchasing an automobile, may fail to check differences in interest rates and may end up paying several hundred dollars more. For the "error" they made on one day, the purchase of literally thousands of grocery items on sale may be required to make up the difference.

In order to reduce the effects of impulse buying, a period of cooling off before buying a desirable item is practiced by many persons. A day or two later, the buyer's perspective may change. This reflects a sound principle of money management: If a substantial amount of money is involved, plan carefully. Too often the *child* in us demands compulsive action and really does not give the *adult* in us a chance to reason things out.[12]

Planning a Budget

Few activities are dreaded more than planning a budget. Most people try to budget and most experience some frustration.[13] However, planning how money will be used can draw a couple closer together. As husbands and wives begin to understand why they each spend money as they do, they gain further insight into each other and the nature of their relationship.

It is necessary for couples to recognize that marriage does not relieve the sensitivity most people feel regarding their personal use of money. It seems a bit unrealistic for husbands and wives to assume that this area of living together will be conflict-free. Nevertheless, openness and careful resolution of differences of opinion will make it easier to enjoy using money together and may contribute to appreciation of the marriage relationship.

Views of budgeting, of course, are related to whether one budgets or not. Table 9–6 indicates differences between budgeters and nonbudgeters with respect to their opinions.

As might be expected, those who budget reflect more positive opinions about the process than those who do not. A sizable percentage of both groups (46 per cent) believe that inflation makes it impossible. More of the nonbudgeters believe they can do as well without a budget.[14]

Because life is so unpredictable, it is difficult to see how a plan for expendi-

Table 9–6 Views of Budgeting

	Budgeters %	Nonbudgeters %
Only way to keep track of money	53	18
Inflation makes it impossible	46	46
Keeps me from overspending	45	16
Only way to get ahead financially	42	17
Best way to build up savings account	36	15
Doesn't work in emergencies	23	37
Can do as well without it	12	37
More trouble than it's worth	10	34
Not enough willpower	9	20
Have so little money, won't help	9	17
Creates too many arguments	5	9
Have enough money, not necessary	3	14
Don't know how to keep	3	10

SOURCE: From *The General Mills American Family Report: 1974–75.* Reprinted with permission from General Mills, Inc.

tures will work all the time. Those who find budgets helpful admit to going through a period of trial and error. Initially, an attempt may be made to keep account of every penny spent in order to determine exactly where the money is going. Although this procedure is recommended for a short period of time, most people eventually discard it. Figure 9–1 presents a form for recording daily expenditures.[15]

The fact that in different months expenditures vary within a given category is troublesome to some families. The $15 allowed each month for gifts simply does not work right before Christmas. Getting bogged down in categories misses the point. Budgets are to help people utilize their resources in ways that will enable them to achieve their goals; budgets are not to enslave people.

There are a few things that remain fairly constant throughout the year, and these can be planned more accurately, such as house payments, automobile payments, and insurance that is paid monthly. Other items may vary slightly, such as food and clothing expenditures (September is normally an expensive month in terms of clothing expenditures because growing children must be dressed for school). There are still other expenditures that may come just once or twice a year. For example, big items can be spaced throughout the year as follows:

January: Dad's insurance payment
February: Dad's professional meeting
March: Income tax fund

Figure 9–1 Record of Your Expenses

Date	Item (or Service) Bought	Food and Beverages	Household Operation and Maintenance	Furnishings and Equipment	Clothing	Personal	Trans-portation	Medical care	Recreation and Education	Gifts and Contribu-tions
		$	$	$	$	$	$	$	$	$
Total		$ ____	$ ____	$ ____	$ ____	$ ____	$ ____	$ ____	$ ____	$ ____

SOURCE: Reprinted from "A Guide to Budgeting for the Family," *Home and Garden Bulletin* No. 108, 1972. U.S. Department of Agriculture Washington, D.C.

April: Mother's insurance payment
May: Car tune-up and car emergency fund
June: Vacation fund
July: Dad's insurance payment
August: Taxes on the house
September: Children's school clothes
October: Mother's insurance payment
November: Christmas gifts
December: Christmas gifts

In the foregoing example, large insurance premiums are paid for the father and mother semiannually, and are spaced to avoid times when other expenses are normally heavy, such as at Christmas, or vacation time, or when taxes are due on the house. Figure 9–2 presents a form that will help families plan expenses.[16]

Every family will need to develop its own spending plan; because of differing goals, each family functions differently. It is important for families to approach the expenditure of money with a sense of flexibility. However, it is necessary to determine which areas are more pliant and the way in which flexibility is best achieved. For instance, some families contribute an established monthly amount to their synagogue or church, others make larger contributions during those months when expenses are lighter than usual.

COPING WITH INFLATION

In the development of a spending plan, one factor with which all families must cope is inflation. Some ways in which families are currently responding to inflation are as follows:

1. Leisure activities reflect important changes: eating in restaurants, expensive hobbies, entertaining friends, and "going out" are less common.
2. Vacations are regarded differently, with nearly two out of three families regarding them as a real luxury.
3. Families are reducing their use of electricity.
4. One in four families is not serving meat regularly, and 45 per cent of American families report that they are spending less on sweets than a year ago.
5. Families are looking for sales before they spend.
6. Families are postponing dental and medical checkups.
7. Charitable contributions are being reduced, and fewer gifts are being given.
8. Families are purchasing fewer clothes and repairing rather than purchasing new home appliances and equipment.
9. Families are attempting to put off car repairs. Unfortunately, this may be an unwise choice because it frequently leads to a disabled car or an accident.
10. Women who are wives are gainfully employed in increasing numbers.[17]

SAVINGS

Savings should be a part of every family's plan if possible. A savings account that grows over the years can provide a real sense of security, and it helps families to avoid paying high interest rates when they want a new color television or have an opportunity to purchase a stereo at a good price.

The advantage in saving money is fairly apparent to most people; the difficulty is in knowing how. The old adage, "a penny saved is a penny earned," has little value. Suppose, however, a young family of moderate income could learn to save a dollar a day—every day—over a period of years. This would be the same as obtaining a raise in salary of over $400 a year if the family were in the 20 per cent tax bracket—enough to purchase a color television set.

Obviously, many young families cannot save a dollar *every day* without significantly affecting their level of living. However, for many families, saving an *average* of $30 a month is not unreasonable.

Keep in mind that the people with the most limited resources need to be those who are best able to utilize resources effectively. Poor people cannot afford to make mistakes because they usually have the least amount in reserve to tide them over when emergency situations arise. It is important to remember that emergencies arise for everyone, and those who suffer the least are those who are best prepared.

PLAN FOR SPENDING

A budget is a specific plan for spending the family's income at a future time period of a few months or a year; [18] it is a method of financial planning. The budget is designed to assist families in utilizing financial resources in such a way that their goals and needs are best fulfilled with the income available.

A couple should consider the following in making a budget:

1. The Major Family Goals. Each family has its own goals that may vary with income, number of children, interest of family members, and stage of the family life cycle. An important step in effective financial management is to identify what the goals of family members are. Couples need to ask themselves the question, "What is *most* important to us in life?" Long-range as well as short-term goals need to be identified so that couples will have a better idea how financial resources can best be utilized. Long-term goals for a couple may include the purchase of a home or a college education for their children. Short-range goals may include a vacation or the purchase of a new car. If a budget is to assist a couple in the attainment of their goals, it must be realistically based on level of in-

Figure 9–2 Spending Plan *

	Last Year	Budget for This Year	Jan.	Feb.	March	Apri
Income:						
Fixed Expenses:						
Mortgage or Rent						
Insurance—Auto and other property						
Insurance—Life						
Taxes						
Licenses, Fees and Dues						
Installment payments						
Emergency Fund						
Day-to-Day Expenses:						
Food						
Clothing						
Personal Items						
Furnishings & Equipment						
Operating Expenses						
Auto and Transportation						
Medical and Dental						
Education						
Recreation						
Contributions						
Gifts and Miscellany						
Regular Savings or Plans for Special Events:						
TOTALS						

SOURCE: "Planning Family Spending." Publ. No. 199, 1973. Extension Service of Virginia Polytechnic Institute and University, Blacksburg, Va.

May	June	July	Aug.	Sept.	Oct.	Nov.	Dec.

come, and it must be checked periodically and adjusted to meet changing conditions.[19]

2. Estimated Expenditures. It is important for a couple to estimate approximately how much money they will be spending each month. One efficient way of doing this is to establish expense categories: (a) money set aside for long-term goals and emergency fund, (b) fixed or regular expenses, such as car payments, insurance premiums, rent or house payments, (c) variable or irregular expenses, such as clothing expenditures, automobile upkeep, food, and recreation. It is helpful to examine past expenditures for items under each of these categories.[20]

It is also necessary to include emergencies in financial planning. In the General Mills study[21] a fourth of the families reported that a serious illness had occurred during the previous year. Table 9–7 presents the percentages of families who faced emergencies or unexpected expenses during the previous year.

One may surmise from an examination of this table that few families will live through a given year without unexpected expenses. In any event, the evidence clearly supports the need for a reserve fund to take care of unforeseen expenditures. How do most families handle these unexpected expenses? Results are presented in Table 9–8.

3. Balance of Income and Expenses. Many couples annually spend more than their income. One purpose of the budget is to help couples avoid overspending in order to live within their income. Another advantage in examining past expenditures is improvement of ability to determine where current expenses can be reduced, thus aiding the task of making income and expenses balance. Until ad-

Table 9–7 Percentages of Families who Faced Emergencies or Unexpected Expenses Last Year

	Faced Last Year %
Serious illness	25
Major car repairs	23
Replaced major appliance	23
Vacations	23
New car	18
Moving	13
Wedding expenses	6
Divorce	2

SOURCE: From *The General Mills American Family Report: 1974–75.* Reprinted with permission from General Mills, Inc.

Table 9–8 How Families Met Emergencies and Unexpected Expenses *

	Income %	Credit %	Savings %	Debt %	Insurance %	Other %
Serious illness	19	6	14	10	65	9
Major car repairs	50	15	20	8	6	5
Replace major appliance	34	33	20	7	2	5
Moving	53	6	21	15	—	13
Vacations	47	12	40	1	1	4
New car	15	49	24	13	2	3
Wedding expenses	54	3	34	4	—	6
Divorce	11	2	42	21	—	19

* Based on those who faced these expenses in last year.

SOURCE: From *The General Mills American Family Report: 1974–75.* Reprinted with permission from General Mills, Inc.

justments and changes have been made to balance expenses and income, the budget process is incomplete.[22]

Irma Gross, Elizabeth Crandall, and Marjorie Knoll in *Management for Modern Families* [23] suggest that when the goals and needs of a family total more than the expected income, which is not unusual, the family can deal with the situation in one of two basic ways or a combination of the two.

1. The couple may increase their income. The wife may become employed or the husband or wife may take on additional part-time work. Investments or savings may be withdrawn. Credit may also be used.
2. The couple may decrease expenditures. Often it is not possible to increase income; in such instances the only alternative is to reduce expenses.

Expenses can be reduced in different ways. It may be possible to make small cuts in the amount of money spent for several items. By cutting a little in several places, a couple may retain all of their expense items but significantly reduce the *amount* of expenses. For example, if a family can save 10 cents per person each day on food, the annual saving for a family of four would be $146. The clothing budget may be reduced by buying less expensive brands or buying at discount houses or manufacturing outlets.

A second way expenses may be decreased is by eliminating purchases or expenses that are not absolutely necessary. The couple may decide that they really do not have to maintain two cars, so one set of car payments can be eliminated, or they may decide to repair their present automobile instead of purchasing a new one.

A third way expenditures may be decreased is by acquiring services and commodities through some means other than money. A vegetable garden may reduce food expenses. The husband and wife may take their lunches to work. Someone in the family may provide such services as giving haircuts. Couples can exchange baby-sitting services.

4. **Budget Review.** Making a budget is not a once-a-year undertaking. Some goals may be eliminated or modified and new ones adopted. Major changes may occur with the birth of a child or a substantial increase in salary. The family may wish to respond to such changes by reviewing the budget and making needed modifications.[24]

COMMITMENT TO A BUDGET

Before committing themselves to a budget, a couple should review it with the following questions in mind: (a) Is the budget realistic? (b) Does it meet the needs of family members reasonably well? (c) Does it provide for major long-range and short-range family goals? (d) Does the budget allow for the possibility of emergencies? (e) Does it permit the family to live within its income?

Two helpful budget guides have been prepared by the Consumer and Food Economic Research Division of the U.S. Department of Agriculture. One is a bulletin for beginning families entitled, "A Guide to Budgeting for the Young Couple." [25] The other is for families more advanced in the family life cycle entitled, "A Guide to Budgeting for the Family." [26] Single copies of these guides may be obtained free by writing to the Office of Information, U.S. Department of Agriculture, Washington, D.C. 20250.

Overspending

Many families are hopelessly in debt, yet continue to purchase things they cannot afford. Interestingly enough, many people find that by purchasing lots of *things*, they really do not feel a lot better about themselves, their spouses, or life. Like the child who feels blue and eats a candy bar to feel good, a bag full of candy—once it is owned—isn't nearly as satisfying as was imagined. Some people overspend for psychological reasons to compensate for feelings of inadequacy or depression. On the other hand, some families overspend because they simply do not have a sufficient income to meet their daily needs.

Everyone has heard, "You get what you pay for." This rationalization is used when we want to justify what we want but believe we cannot afford. The *child* in us gives us permission to behave foolishly economically even when our *adult* tells us to be prudent and thrifty.

On the other hand, inferior merchandise may cost less and give less than adequate performance. The performance, of course, depends on what we expect of it. Shoes worn only a few times to formal dances do not require the quality construction of shoes worn daily to school. Teen-agers who live in jeans except at church may actually require a "dress-up outfit" that costs only a fraction of the outfits their parents wear for work over a period of five years.

It is clear that the misuse of credit leads families into financial difficulty and has led many people into bankruptcy. In the year ending June 30, 1971, nearly 183,000 personal bankruptcies were filed in United States courts.[27] Personal bankruptcies have dramatically increased in the last decade. One study of families who were overextended indicated that they had committed 54 per cent of their next year's income to debt obligations.[28]

Few things facilitate misuse faster than the indiscriminate use of credit cards. In the General Mills study [29] it was found that two out of three families use credit to pay for many everyday expenses. Table 9–9 presents a list of items the respondents indicated they used credit cards for.

Over 50 per cent of the respondents used credit cards for the purchase of clothes for adults and for gasoline. Over a third used credit cards in purchasing major ap-

Table 9–9 Things Credit Cards Are Used For *

Base: Use Credit Cards (66%)	%
Clothes for adults	57
Gasoline	54
Major appliances	39
Children's clothing	39
Christmas expenses	36
Gifts	29
Household goods	27
Vacations	18
Drugs and medicines	17
Eating out in restaurants for pleasure	12
Food and groceries	11
Toys	8

* Adds to more than 100% because of multiple response.

SOURCE: From *The General Mills American Family Report: 1974–75.* Reprinted with permission from General Mills, Inc.

pliances and children's clothing, and for Christmas expenses. Fifty per cent of those with incomes $10,000 or under and 91 per cent of those with incomes $20,000 or over made use of credit.[30]

Views of the use of credit cards are presented in Figure 9–3. As shown, 42 per cent indicated that having credit cards provided them with a "horrible temptation to spend money," whereas 36 per cent described them as "handy"; 25 per cent perceived credit cards as "something to lean on when short of funds" and "good source in emergency"; only 17 per cent reported that they were a useful way to systemize spending. Of those who had owned credit cards, 24 per cent quit using the cards because of high interest rates (see Figure 9–4).[31]

However, of those who quit only 16 per cent reported that their standard of living was better as a result, whereas 29 per cent reported it was worse. By overspending, many families *quickly* find themselves in debt. What can a couple do to remedy the situation? Perhaps the most important first step is to review fixed expenses and obligations to obtain a realistic picture of how much money is left after these expenses are met. The couple may then decide that some of them can be eliminated or reduced. Some alternative ways to reduce expenses were discussed in the section on balance of income and expenses.

Another helpful step in reducing debt is to decide to contract no new debt that can be avoided until a significant reduction has been achieved in the debt level. Some families may need to turn to a family service agency or a nonprofit consumer credit counseling service for guidance.[32]

If the couple owes money to several different creditors, it may be desirable to take out a new loan for the purpose of consolidating the debts. The advantages of this are that the couple then owes only one creditor and gains needed time to repay the money. It may also reduce the monthly payments to a level the couple

Figure 9–3 Views of Credit Cards and Plans

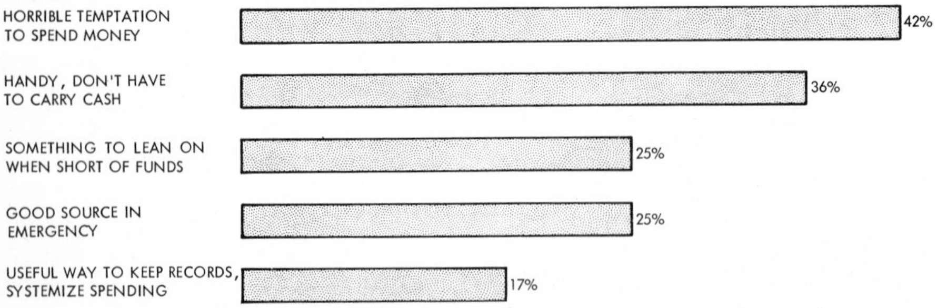

SOURCE: From *The General Mills American Family Report: 1974–75.* Reprinted with permission from General Mills, Inc.

Figure 9–4 Quit Using Credit Cards Because of High Interest Rates

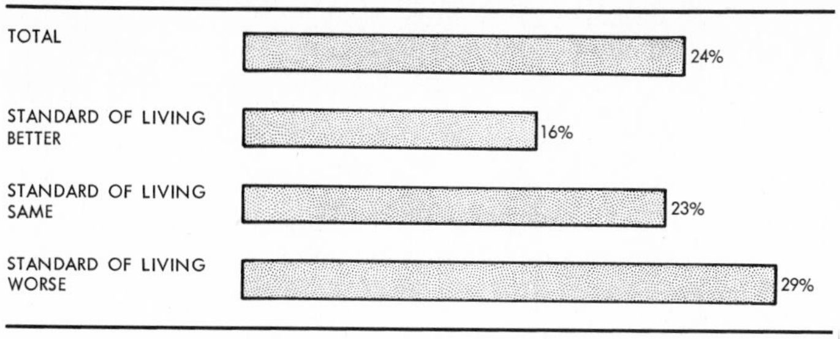

Source: From *The General Mills American Family Report: 1974–75.* Reprinted with permission from General Mills, Inc.

can handle. When a consolidation loan is considered, great care should be exercised in the selection of a loan agency. All the costs of credit must be examined and compared. In any event, the consolidation loan increases the cost of credit because the repayment is extended over a longer period of time.

Some people who have sought to consolidate their debts have fallen prey to debt-consolidation agencies whose operations are less than satisfactory. Abuses have been of such a nature that in 26 states commercial debt adjusters are not permitted to provide services. The Legal Aid Society provides information to persons whose debts are of such a magnitude that they are unable to handle them. Some professional unions, credit unions, and other organizations also offer this service. The National Foundation for Consumer Credit has been instrumental in the establishment of over 120 consumer credit counseling services in 35 states and Canada.[33]

Families who are overextended financially will probably have to be willing to commit themselves to a lower standard of living until a significant reduction in the debt level has been achieved. This adjustment is easier if the couple recognize that this sacrifice is temporary and that they are making progress toward the goal of solvency.

Cost of Credit

Few people realized how much they were paying for credit until in 1968 the United States Congress passed the Consumer Credit Protection Act that made it mandatory for the lender to indicate to the borrower the finance charge and the annual percentage rate of the loan. The finance charge is the cost the customer pays to obtain the credit. Many of the credit cards available involve an annual percentage rate of 18 per cent, or 1.5 per cent per month.

If people always saved up money before making a purchase, they would not have to pay this interest. However, few families have enough money in reserve to avoid paying interest. There are many occasions when a consumer finds exactly what he is looking for and could not purchase the article if credit were not available. Occasionally, a person may stumble onto such a bargain that it would not make sense to pass it up simply because there is not enough money in one's checking account.

Like a child selecting food in a cafeteria line, however, it is easy to overconsume. Usually, we can find all sorts of reasons for making certain decisions, even though we may regret them later. It is a wise consumer who keeps some money in reserve to be able to take advantage of unusual opportunities when they present themselves.

The advantage of the Consumer Credit Protection Act is that it makes it virtually impossible for a consumer not to know how much he is paying for credit, which enables him to weigh alternatives. In many instances the consumer may recognize that the savings effected by a sale item may not compensate for the interest he will have to pay if he must carry the loan over an extended period.

Intelligent consumers quickly learn that the cost of credit varies with the lending agency. Life insurance loans—for those who have owned life insurance for several years and have built up significant loan values—are normally one of the better values with their low interest rates. Also, persons who are members of credit unions should explore the cost of credit there as well as at other lending agencies.

There is merit in adding the cost of the interest to the purchase price of an article as a matter of routine to determine its true cost. A $5,500 automobile, for example, may end up costing well over $6,000 if the payments are extended over a period of years.

Life Insurance

Life insurance is one type of savings plan most families recognize as necessary. The need for life insurance varies with the number and ages of family members. Studies have shown that—considering the amount of income lost when wives leave employment to have children—it costs, on the average, between $90,000 to $100,000 to support a child from conception through college.

Obviously, if a wife loses her husband through death when her children are very young, she faces an economic burden she may not be able to carry alone. Many spouses are mindful of the costs of child rearing and seek to provide maximum protection at minimum cost during years when demands for protection from economic disaster are greatest. After considering various alternatives, many couples decide on term insurance.

Term insurance provides protection for a specified period, such as twenty years, and is less expensive than ordinary life insurance. However, if death does not occur within the specified term, the holder receives neither the money paid into the plan nor interest on money paid. The purchase of life insurance should be made after consideration of many factors. Family financial counselors and many life insurance agents can provide individuals with the necessary information to assist in making decisions. The view that "nothing bad is ever going to happen to you" is hardly realistic because death is not limited to the aged. It is wise to discuss needs with several representatives to be sure that the facts are understood correctly. If resources are limited, planning must be executed even more carefully. Many young couples are relatively inexperienced in long-term financial planning and are unaware of the many factors to be considered.

Because of competition among companies, their success in management, their willingness to insure high risks, and numerous other factors, considerable variation exists in the amount each individual pays for insurance. One cannot assume that everyone pays about the same amount, regardless of the company.

In order to encourage sales, a variety of plans have been developed by companies and the options should be considered individually. For example, some term insurance policies are convertible in that, without proving insurability, a person may convert term insurance to ordinary life insurance within a specified period. The conversion will, of course, require higher premiums, but it is an extremely attractive feature if, for example, one develops a disability that would prevent obtaining life insurance.

Over the years the cost of term insurance increases because the probability that death will occur in a given year increases with age. In most families, income increases during the early years of marriage. On the average, couples have a greater income at thirty-five than they do at twenty-five. As soon as couples can afford it, there is merit in obtaining ordinary life insurance that provides protection throughout the entire life of an individual. Most people *do* live past middle age and will need life insurance—although normally not so much—after their children become economically independent.

Another type of insurance policy is called *straight life insurance.* The amount of money a person pays in premiums with this type of policy is the same throughout his life. The amount of premiums the individual pays on the straight life-insurance policy depends upon the age at which the policy is purchased. The younger the person is at the time, the less the death risk and consequently lower premiums are paid each year. The person pays more for straight life-insurance premiums than is actually required for protection during the younger years in order to maintain lower premiums during the later years.

An *endowment policy* is essentially life insurance that is paid in full within a specified period of time. Money paid into the policy accrues interest, and all the money, including interest, can be withdrawn at the end of the specified period. Therefore, this type of plan is often used by parents to provide educational funds for their children. It is also frequently used for retirement benefits. A $5,000 endowment policy to mature when a child is eighteen provides money for college in the amount of $5,000 when the child reaches that age. If death of a parent occurs before the child reaches eighteen, he collects $5,000 as a beneficiary.

Other Forms of Insurance Protection

There is little doubt that the quality of family life can be improved if families protect themselves from financial disaster through adequate insurance protection. For this reason, it is important that couples with limited resources have medical and hospitalization insurance; major medical insurance for serious, extended illnesses; and income protection insurance to assure that income will be available in the event it is curtailed due to illness. Although income protection insurance may be considered by some to be too expensive for benefits that begin with the onset of illness, there are programs available that begin payment after an extended period, such as ninety days of illness, and these programs are inexpensive. Whereas some couples could endure three months without income, few could endure indefinitely without some support. Such programs are essential for couples who cannot rely on family or friends during periods of illness when there is no income.

A young couple with extremely limited resources may put off the purchase of such protection until they are better able to afford it. Often, however, they drive relatively new cars, own stereos and television sets, and go on vacations. One of the reasons that we do not always perceive financial solidarity accurately is that our understanding of current status is partially based on assumptions regarding future economic conditions. A summary of the perceptions of families concerning their finances and their feelings about the future are presented in Table 9–10.[34]

Insurance programs designed to protect individuals and families with limited resources make good economic sense. Families not covered by such programs frequently find themselves faced with economic problems that cannot be readily solved and regret the fact that they failed to plan for such emergencies.

Table 9–10 The Balance Sheet

83% of families doing very/fairly well personally.	**17%** of families doing badly personally.
73% don't owe more money than a year ago.	**27%** do owe more money than a year ago.
71% optimistic about achieving own goals next year.	**28%** not optimistic about achieving own goals next year.
62% have better/same standard of living as a year ago.	**37%** have worse standard of living than a year ago.
46% feel that families can work out own problems.	**45%** believe solving their own problems depends on what happens to the country.
46% don't argue about money.	**54%** argue about money.
45% have begun to accept the idea that each year may not be better financially.	**53%** believe that they have *the right* to a better standard of living each year.
44% feel secure about own long-range economic future.	**56%** feel insecure about own long-range economic future.
34% say inflation is not having an impact on their family.	**65%** say inflation is having a very/fairly serious impact on their family.
28% say country is not heading for a depression.	**52%** say country is heading for a depression.

SOURCE: From *The General Mills American Family Report: 1974–75.* Reprinted with permission from General Mills, Inc.

Cost of Children

Tremendous variation exists in the cost of rearing children. The costs involved in having a baby normally vary between $300 and $3,000, depending upon physicians' fees, hospital rates, and the difficulty encountered. Premature babies, for example, require longer periods of hospitalization and special services that are costly.

Couples with annual incomes under $3,000 obviously are not spending a great deal in rearing their children, although, proportionally, they may be spending a greater amount than couples with ten times as much income. Estimates of the total cost of child rearing may range from $10,000 per child for low-income families in the United States to much larger amounts for children who attend college. There is little doubt, however, that the most expensive period for parents is the time when their children are adolescents. College costs have soared during the last generation and, increasingly, families are assisting their adolescents with the purchase of automobiles. Parents who prefer to have their children buy their own cars may help them by purchasing auto licenses, insurance, and gasoline occasionally. More affluent parents may provide the down payment on an automobile or may purchase cars as gifts for their children. This is but one example of the fact that social change has brought with it increased costs of child rearing. During the early years of their children's lives, many middle-class families require at least an additional $1,000 per child per year to maintain the quality of life they had before the arrival of their children.

That perceptions of problems are related to whether one has children eighteen years of age or younger is clearly evidenced in Figure 9–5.

Families with children under the age of eighteen are less able to meet everyday expenses and are more fearful of unemployment and of being too far in debt.[35]

Because of the costs of rearing children, many people have decided to limit the number they will have and to postpone having a child until they feel better able to provide him with a reasonable amount of economic security. To provide the kind of security that will enable children to achieve their potential requires substantial economic support. If adults are to be effective in their roles as parents, they must assume responsibility for the economic well-being of their children; to do less is to do their children a disservice.

Buying a Car

The expense of a car involves more than the purchase price. For the person who has never owned a car, major considerations usually are: "How much does one cost?" and "What are the monthly payments?" There are other questions to be asked: (a) Is service readily available? (b) Are the parts standardized? (c) Will the car be satisfactory as family needs change? (d) Is it comfortable for daily use?

Prospective buyers can obtain an indication of repair costs for certain au-

Figure 9–5 Main Kinds of Problems by Family Status

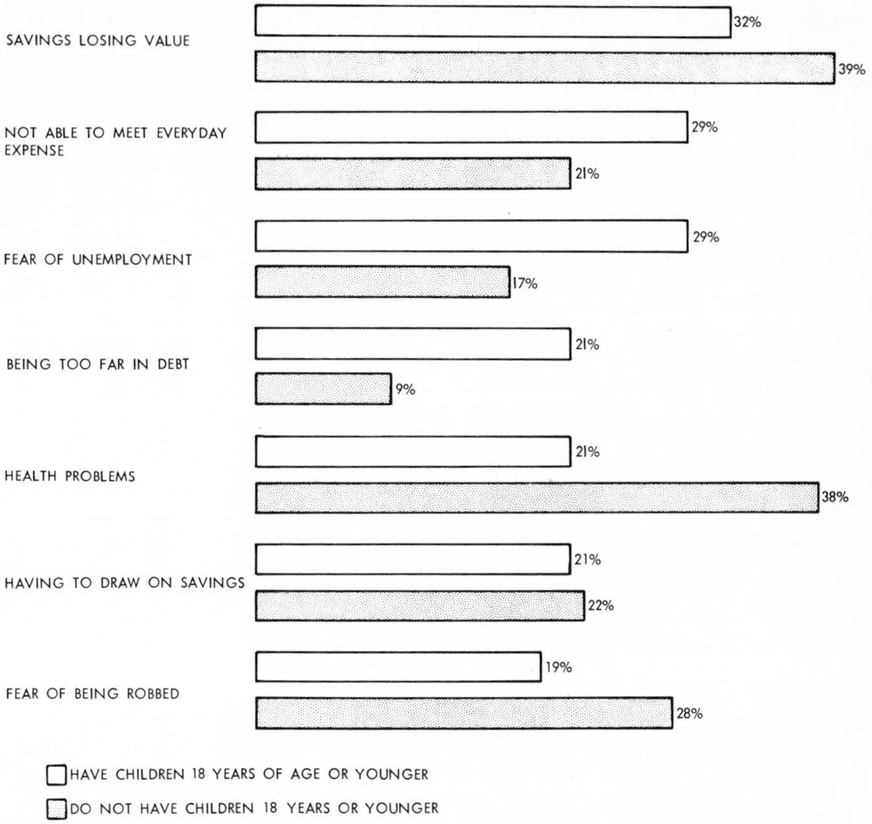

SOURCE: From *The General Mills American Family Report: 1974–75.* Reprinted with permission from General Mills, Inc.

tomobiles that others have owned by reviewing *Consumer Reports*, a periodical available in most libraries. Each year the editors poll its readers to obtain repair ratings of the major makes of automobiles. Of course, such ratings can only serve as a guide and may not necessarily apply to a particular car.

Because cars are increasingly considered a necessity, most people will eventually be faced with making a decision that involves a good portion of their income. As with other decisions involving large amounts of money, it is unwise not to seek professional help. Personnel in lending institutions can often provide useful information concerning costs of different makes of automobiles in the current market. Here, again, useful information is to be found in *Consumer Reports*, but it is best to rely on an experienced mechanic to tell you about the condition of a particular car. It is frequently assumed that used cars are cheaper to own than new cars. This may not necessarily be true. Due to maintenance costs, many older automobiles are actually more costly to own. If a seller is reluctant to have a used automobile inspected by a mechanic of your choice, it is best to go elsewhere. Even an experienced mechanic can make errors in judgment concerning the condition of an automobile; however, he should be able to keep you from making some of the more obvious errors.

Purchasing a House

One of the major purchases a family makes is a house. There are many subtle points that must be taken into account before a house is purchased. If one has not lived in a house with sewage problems it is hard to fully appreciate the importance of an adequate sewage-disposal system. Although not an exhaustive list, the following considerations may prove helpful when evaluating a house:

1. Is the price reasonable?
2. Is it in a location convenient to schools and work?
3. Is it attractive?
4. Is it functional for the family?
5. Is it well constructed?
6. Is it in a neighborhood the family enjoys?
7. Is it on a city sewer system or does it have an adequate sewage-disposal system?
8. Is the house free from termites?
9. Does it have an adequate heating system?
10. What are the taxes on the property?
11. What is the cost of the utilities per month?
12. Are repairs required?
13. Does the house fit the life-style of the family?
14. What are the upkeep costs on the house?
15. Will the owner provide a title that is free and clear?
16. Is there adequate storage?
17. Is it a house that all members of the family will enjoy?
18. Does the house require repainting?
19. What is the interest rate of the mortgage?
20. Can the family afford the down payment?

Few families can afford everything they want in a house. Compromises must be made and the amount of satisfaction achieved is often a reflection of the care exercised in making a decision. Since the purchase of a home normally involves a considerable expenditure of the available monthly income, it warrants careful consideration.

A home that may seem expensive in terms of the cost of square feet may be a real bargain in terms of the psychological satisfaction it will provide. Similarly, a home that may appear to be a bargain in terms of its price may actually be costly in that, for the money involved, it may have little value to the couple who own it. It is important to remember that price alone is a poor index of the value a house may have for a family. However, price must be considered realistically in relation to what a family can afford and to the resalability of the house.

Few purchases are equal to the amount one invests in a home. It involves one of the most important economic decisions a person will ever make. Unfortunately, most people are simply not qualified to evaluate the structural qualities of a house, nor are they specialists in evaluating the contract, which is legally binding whether they understand what it means or not.

In an excellent book, A. M. Watkins outlines *How to Avoid the 10 Biggest Home-Buying Traps.*[36] The book explains such considerations as the following:

THE OVERPRICED HOUSE

A seller can deliberately overprice a house, recognizing that he will get much less than he asks for but hoping to obtain more than the house is worth. The selection of a house is often not done rationally. A buyer may think he has obtained quite a bargain if he gets a $40,000 house for $41,000 after he has talked the seller down from an initial asking price of $48,500. For this reason, it is always wise to have the house appraised by a specialist who can give an objective appraisal of the market value of the house. Such an appraisal normally costs from $50 to $75 but may save the buyer thousands of dollars.

THE HIDDEN COSTS OF HOME OWNERSHIP

A frequently overlooked cost is the distance the house is from work, schools, shopping centers, and church. For example, let us assume that a buyer finds two houses he likes very much. One is three miles from work and the other fifteen miles. To make the calculation easy, let us assume his car gets twelve miles to the gallon, so he uses two additional gallons of gas a day, twenty days a month. At 60 cents a gallon, he is spending an additional $24 a month for gas. With other automobile expenses, he is spending an additional $300 a year for a house he likes no better than the one closer to his work. Although this amount may seem small in itself, there are many other small hidden costs that, considered totally, can boost the cost of a house substantially. The moral is clear: before purchasing a home, careful study should be made of many factors to insure the best buy.

THE MORTGAGE

Many people talk as if interest paid on a mortgage is of little significance because they can deduct the amount on their income taxes. Let us assume a buyer is paying 10 per cent on a $30,000 mortgage and is in a 25 per cent tax bracket. Roughly, this means that he is paying $3,000 a year in interest, only 25 per cent of which will be saved on his income tax. That leaves $2,250, or nearly $200 a month he is paying in interest. Over a thirty-year period he may find that he has actually paid in interest more than the house cost him.

During periods of inflation, it is always wise to consider attempting to assume the mortgage that the present owner holds. If the present owner has owned the house for several years, he may have a lower interest rate, 8 per cent as compared to 10 per cent, for example. On a $30,000 mortgage, this would amount to $600 a year, or $50 a month. During periods of inflation, however, his house may have appreciated in value, and the house for which he paid $30,000 may now be worth $35,000. This means that his equity may be worth more than you can afford. Buyers anxious to sell their house so that they can buy another sometimes are willing to take a second mortgage if the buyer is an excellent credit risk. When this is done, it is important to consult an attorney who will make the terms of the agreement very clear to both the buyer and the seller. Of course, the lending agency, such as a savings and loan association, will need to agree that your credit rating is of such a nature that they will approve your picking up the seller's loan. In such transactions, it is wise not to assume anything in order to be sure that you have all the facts straight. Clear communication in selling and purchasing a house is exceedingly important.

Most people when cashing checks in stores have noted little signs that read, "$3.00 for all returned checks." Such signs would not appear if people kept their financial affairs in order and did not write checks for which there were insufficient funds in their banks. There is no better financial advice than to manage your financial affairs responsibly and rationally. Your credit rating becomes exceedingly important when you wish to secure a loan for a substantial amount of money in order to purchase a home. Irresponsible management of your financial affairs may mean that you will be unable to secure a loan.

THE VANISHING BUILDER

Be certain that in purchasing a home you check out the reputation of the builder. In most communities there is considerable variation in the quality of construction. There are few things more disheartening than to move into a new home to find the roof leaks and huge cracks appear in the walls or foundation. In many communities builders will stand back of the quality of their construction. If you obtain a warranty on a new house from a builder, make sure you understand its provisions clearly, and check with others who have purchased homes from the builder to see if he has provided the services promised. Legal action against builders is costly. Many buyers find it costs more than it is worth and end up paying for the cost of the needed repairs themselves.

Builders who come into communities, develop an area, and then are gone may be less likely to please buyers than builders who live within the community and whose future business is dependent upon your comments as a satisfied customer. Such builders are likely to skimp on details that provide satisfaction. Closets, for example, are likely to be big enough to hold just half of what they should. Empty closets look adequate when purchasing a house; but when filled, where does one put the rest of the clothes?

GOOD DESIGN IS NOT ALWAYS COSTLY

Everyone who has shopped for a wedding gift in a department store by asking to see the patterns of china, silver, and crystal selected by the prospective bride has concluded that cost is not a reliable index to excellence in design. The same is true of houses, household furnishings, clothing, and many other things that are a part of our daily lives. Many houses of excellent design actually cost less than houses of poor design.

The relationship of the rooms to each other is important. Some parents, for example, may not wish to have their bedrooms adjacent to their children's rooms. Kitchens, of course, should be adjacent to dining areas. Most people prefer that bathrooms do not open directly into living rooms, and that garages or carports be attached to their house.

Studies of the dissatisfactions that homeowners experience frequently indicate that they are most dissatisfied with the size of the rooms. When buyers go through a new house, they may wander from room to room, impressed with the deep shag carpeting. But after they get their furniture in the rooms, they cannot see the carpeting because it is covered with furniture. The house that was beautiful unfurnished becomes a nightmare to live in. The scale of the furniture is wrong and there is not enough space between the bed and the dresser to permit safe passage without risk to shins. Tiny kitchens, tiny bedrooms, and tiny bathrooms prove to be a constant source of irritation.

PURCHASING OLDER HOMES

One of the advantages in purchasing older homes is that you may get more floor space for the money. On the other hand, you may find lending institutions willing to loan you only 80 per cent instead of 90 or 95 per cent. You may enjoy being in a home with a well-established lawn, garden, and trees. However, you may be buying a house with a roof and a heating system that already have twenty years of wear. And, of course, you may be purchasing a home with twenty years of termite destruction.

You may find an architectural style available that would be virtually impossible to reproduce today because of the increase of building costs since World War II. Although there are many exceptions, older homes are more difficult to resell unless they are truly distinguished in terms of their design and value.

Older houses are likely to have very small closets, reflecting a period when people did not have the kinds of wardrobes they have today. Other storage areas, such as kitchen cabinets, may be inadequate. High ceilings—in very old houses—may make heating more expensive, also the walls may not have been insulated. This is particularly important now with the shortage of fuel. Although houses already built can easily be insulated, this cost should be considered as part of the total purchase price of the house.

THE GIMMICK HOUSE

Some houses may be filled with gimmicks in order to lure the unsuspecting buyer. A gimmick is anything that "dresses the house up." Watkins discusses how a housing builder installed distinctive, Japanese-styled light screens in bathrooms with recessed lights above.[37] Numerous people in the area were influenced by this feature, which cost the builder $65 per bathroom.

Distinctive features—perhaps a beautiful view from a dining room or family-room window—will stimulate people to throw reason aside and make a purchase that will affect their lives daily for years. If a couple is not well informed about housing, it is important to take someone along who is.

The simple truth is you are not likely to find everything you wish in a house you can afford. But choices *are* available, and the better able you are to verbalize the things you value, the greater the chances that you will be satisfied with the choices you make.

THE TOTAL COST OF HOUSING

An important thing to remember is that when you reach a point in life when you can make a choice, it is necessary to get as many of the facts as possible to make an intelligent decision. When many young couples ask the question, "What is the down payment on this house?" they actually mean, "How much money do we need to get into the house?" To the first question, however, they may obtain an answer that will not include the closing cost—a substantial amount involving hundreds of dollars—which is required at the time of the sale.

Housing gets mixed up with people's dreams, and it is easy to launch on an adventure that you basically cannot afford. Remember to allow about 25 per cent of the total cost for furnishings. That means on a $20,000 house you can expect to spend another $5,000 for furniture, draperies, and accessories. If this figure sounds high, sit down with a furniture catalog and add up the cost of beds, a washing machine, living-room furniture, carpeting, a refrigerator. It is an exercise that will be long remembered.

Many young couples are inventive and build some of their own furniture, receive gifts from family members, shop at garage sales and auctions, and have a great time putting a home together. It *is* fun, but it *is* also costly. The glamour of purchasing a home must be tempered *with costs that may be added to the purchase price of your house,* including title examination, title insurance, survey cost, appraisal fees, credit reports, and attorney fees. These fees are normally paid when the transaction is completed and are often called closing costs.

RENTING VS. OWNING A HOME

The cost of renting a house versus owning one can be estimated, although accurate estimates are difficult because of such unknown factors as cost of required repairs. It is more difficult to estimate the value that ownership may have for a family. To some families, owning a house of their own means a great deal. In a home of your own you can paint a wall black if you want to. This is not always possible in a house that is rented.

Most people believe that because they can deduct interest payments on federal income tax, ownership of a home actually means big savings. However, comparisons of the actual amount paid for rent and the actual amount paid for ownership reflect a smaller difference than many consumers think. If the house is owned for only a few years, renting may be less expensive.

Retirement Planning

Retirement is a very important part of a couple's financial planning, even though it seems so far in the future. Couples in the early stages of the family cycle also find saving for retirement difficult due to the expenses of buying a home, furnishing a home, child rearing, and getting established in a profession. Even if it is difficult, it is nevertheless important to establish some type of financial planning for retirement, however minimal, relatively early in the family life cycle.

Income during the later years of life is for most people much lower than during preretirement years. This is substantiated by the fact that about 50 per cent of older persons have incomes below the poverty level.

There are a variety of ways that a couple may plan for retirement. Social Security is the one source of income with which people are most familiar. However, many people do not realize that maximum use of Social Security requires early planning. In addition, the benefits as a sole source of income, though helpful, are not adequate for most people to live on. Pamphlets, counseling service, and other information concerning requirements for eligibility and schedules of benefits are available from local Social Security administration offices.

Retirement programs and pension plans are offered through many businesses and professions. These programs vary widely. Couples should become familiar with programs available through employers. It might be an important consideration before accepting a job.

Most people will have income from Social Security and retirement and pension plans. This income may not be sufficient to maintain the life-style to which the couple has been accustomed. Therefore, there is merit in planning to supplement income from other sources during retirement. Examples of such additional sources of income are the following:

1. Regular savings accounts and tax-sheltered annuities. Such savings should ideally be started relatively early in the marriage.
2. Income from investments such as stocks, bonds, and mutual funds.
3. Income from other investments such as rental property or sale of real estate.
4. Earned income during retirement from part- or full-time work. A person can only earn a certain amount of money without losing Social Security benefits. In contrast, income from annuities, rents, sale of property, pensions, dividends, and interest, or any form of unearned income, does not influence Social Security benefits.

Utilizing Available Resources

One learns through experience—often bitter experience—to stop making economic mistakes and seek professional assistance. The information in this chapter is a brief introduction to a variety of areas that require economic decisions. These decisions are not infrequent and are faced by individuals in the course of daily living.

No one can be competent in everything, yet families become involved in decisions for which they are ill prepared. The economic society in which we live is complex, and errors cost money. For instance, everyone must pay income tax, yet few people understand tax regulations well enough to avoid costly mistakes. Occasionally, individuals decide to purchase mutual funds, and they may invest in "load" funds that require a purchase cost without realizing that "load" funds often have a poorer performance record than funds that do not require a purchase cost. People frequently sign contracts, purchase insurance, and obtain warranties they do not understand.

As the complexity of economic life increases, it becomes important to acquire a more complete understanding of the factors that contribute to economic welfare. Many available publications support the intelligent use of our resources. *Sylvia Porter's Money Book,*[38] a recent publication by a distinguished journalist who keeps a watchful eye on the American economy, discusses in detail many of the practical problems faced by families. U.S. News and World Report, Inc., has published an excellent *Money Management Library* to assist families in planning their financial future. The series is written in nontechnical language and, among others, includes these volumes: *Planning Your Financial Future: Investments, Insurance, Wills,*[39] *Stocks, Bonds, and Mutual Funds,*[40] and *How to Buy Real Estate.*[41]

The existence of these and other similar publications suggests that concern for the economic welfare of individuals and families is growing. Evidence points to the fact that the quality of married life is affected by the couple's skill in managing money and their willingness to discuss money openly. It seems reasonable for families to acknowledge the complexity of our economic society and to take advantage of the available resources to understand and improve their own financial status.

References

1. *The General Mills American Family Report 1974–75, A Study of the American Family and Money.* Minneapolis: General Mills, 1975.
2. Ibid.

3. Ibid.
4. Ibid.
5. Ibid.
6. Ibid.
7. Ibid.
8. Ibid.
9. Ibid.
10. PACKARD, VANCE. *The Hidden Persuaders.* New York: McKay, 1957.
11. Ibid.
12. BERNE, ERIC. *Games People Play.* New York: Grove Press, 1964.
13. "A Guide to Budgeting for the Family." *Home and Garden Bulletin,* no. 108. Washington, D.C.: U.S. Department of Agriculture.
14. General Mills, op. cit.
15. "A Guide to Budgeting for the Family," op. cit.
16. "Planning Family Spending." Publ. No. 199, 1973. Blacksburg, Va.: Extension Service of Virginia Polytechnic Institute and State University.
17. General Mills, op. cit.
18. GROSS, IRMA H.; ELIZABETH W. CRANDALL; and MARJORIE M. KNOLL. *Management for Modern Families.* New York: Appleton-Century-Crofts, 1973.
19. Ibid.
20. Ibid.
21. General Mills, op. cit.
22. GROSS, CRANDALL, and KNOLL, op. cit.
23. Ibid.
24. Ibid.
25. "A Guide to Budgeting for the Young Couple," *Home and Garden Bulletin.* Washington, D.C.: U.S. Department of Agriculture.
26. "A Guide to Budgeting for the Family," op. cit.
27. "Who's Going Bankrupt and Why." *U.S. News and World Report,* vol. 71, 1971, p. 83.
28. MARGOLIUS, SIDNEY. "Why Families Get in Debt." *The Machinist,* 1965, p. 10.
29. General Mills, op. cit.
30. Ibid.
31. Ibid.
32. Ibid.
33. *Summary of State Laws Prohibiting or Regulating the Business of Debt Pooling.* Washington, D.C.: Bureau of Labor Standards, U.S. Department of Labor, 1967.
34. General Mills, op. cit.
35. Ibid.
36. WATKINS, A. M. *How to Avoid the 10 Biggest Home-Buying Traps.* New York: Meredith, 1968.
37. Ibid.
38. PORTER, SYLVIA. *Sylvia Porter's Money Book.* New York: Doubleday, 1975.
39. NEWMAN, JOSEPH, ed. *Planning Your Financial Future: Investments, Insurance, Wills.* Washington, D.C.: U.S. News and World Report, 1974.
40. NEWMAN, JOSEPH, ed. *Stocks, Bonds, and Mutual Funds.* Washington, D.C.: U.S. News and World Report, 1974.
41. NEWMAN, JOSEPH, ed. *How to Buy Real Estate.* Washington, D.C.: U.S. News and World Report, 1975.

10 Relationships with Relatives and In-laws

Photo by Walker Montgomery

The assertion, "I'm marrying him (her) and not his (her) family," would seem to be a debatable one.

Rose M. Somerville

Importance of Relatives

Our family life extends beyond our spouse and children. Interaction with our relatives can constitute an important part of our life and may have many beneficial aspects. Relatives may provide a sense of belonging, emotional support, financial assistance, and help with household tasks or child rearing. However, problems with relatives were among the most common problems identified during the first five years of marriage by 544 couples.[1]

That the establishment of harmonious, positive relationships with relatives is important to a marriage relationship [2] was made clear in a study by Judson Landis who found a positive association between marriage happiness and the development of good relationships with in-laws and other relatives.[3]

Involvement with Relatives

It has been observed that many families today are isolated from relatives; consequently many experience a sense of loneliness and alienation because of less face-to-face contact with relatives than in the past. A higher proportion of individuals today probably do experience loneliness and alienation as a result of this increased isolation.

GEOGRAPHICAL CLOSENESS TO RELATIVES

Most individuals are geographically close to their relatives; geographical isolation and separation is the exception and is characteristic of only a small portion of the population.[4] There is evidence that an individual living in an urban area is likely to be a second or third generation resident of that city and also is likely to have a network of relatives living there.[5] One study found that 60 per cent of the respondents lived within a hundred miles of their parents and most of the remaining 40 per cent had other relatives living within a hundred miles of them.[6]

Approximately 62 per cent of the 2,567 older persons in a study by Ethel Shanas [7] reported that they had a son or daughter within walking distance. Mirra Komarovsky [8] found among working-class couples that 68 per cent reported their parents lived in the same community. Only 7 per cent lived further than "two hours by car" from their parents.

Many individuals within certain ethnic groups live very close to their relatives. One study found that 86 per cent of Jewish families living in New York City had sixteen or more relatives living in the area.[9]

AMOUNT OF CONTACT WITH RELATIVES

Young adults and couples have more frequent contact with parents than with siblings or other relatives.[10] In one study, 26 per cent of the young adult males and 43 per cent of the young adult females had contact with their parents once or more a week, and 54 per cent of the males and 38 per cent of the females reported having contact with their parents several times monthly. Only 13 per cent of the males and 5 per cent of the females visited their parents once a year or less.[11]

Couples spend more time with relatives than is commonly assumed. In fact, evidence indicates they spend more time with relatives than with friends or neighbors. One study found that the typical married couple in Detroit saw at least one relative each week.[12] Most of the visits between relatives are between parents and children. Undoubtedly, some visits to parents reflect merely a sense of obligation, but most of the contact is voluntary. In fact, a great many couples prefer to visit with parents and siblings rather than with other companions. Research by Robert Blood and Morris Axelrod indicates the frequency with which Detroit couples had contact with relatives.[13]

Parents do tend to expect visits from their married children. If both sets of parents are equally accessible, an equal amount of contact is normally expected. If one set of parents lives close and the other set far away, the young couple may be expected to balance the frequent weekend visits with the close parents by vacation visits to the distant parents. Visits with parents are often not equal, of course, for various reasons. The couple may be more compatible with one set of parents than with another, or distance may prohibit frequent visits with one set of parents. Some parents expect and need visits more than others, such as a parent who is widowed or ill. Parents of an only child may need more visits than parents with several children.[14]

However, many individuals have limited face-to-face contact with relatives because they live far apart. Two ways that these individuals manage to maintain

Table 10–1 Contact with Relatives, Neighbors, Coworkers, and Other Friends

Frequency of Contact	Group Contacted			
	Relatives	*Neighbors*	*Coworkers*	*Other Friends*
Every day or almost every day	29%	20%	1%	3%
Once or twice a week	38%	25%	8%	22%
Once or twice a month	20%	17%	20%	43%
Less often	13%	14%	30%	24%
Never	0	24%	41%	8%
Total	100%	100%	100%	100%
Number of Families	728	723	723	726

SOURCE: Representative sample of Detroit metropolitan area married women, 1955. Adapted from Detroit Area Study, 1956.

contact are by letter writing and telephone. Also, vacations and holidays can become a happy time of reunion for these parents.[15]

NUMBER OF CLOSE RELATIVES

How close do people today feel to their relatives? How many relatives does an individual regard as good friends? One study indicated that 15 per cent of the people named as friends were relatives. Other evidence indicates that husbands and wives maintain close relationships with four relatives.[16] Such findings suggest that many families are not completely isolated from relatives.

People have closer relationships with their parents and siblings than with other relatives, as might be expected. Young adults particularly are more apt to be closer to their parents, both geographically and emotionally, than to other relatives.[17]

Some interesting differences have been observed between middle-class and working-class individuals concerning which relatives are most closely associated to each other. Middle-class persons are more oriented toward parents. Working-class individuals, in contrast, tend to be more oriented toward siblings or same-generation relatives,[18] live closer to their relatives, and interact with them more frequently than do middle-class persons.[19]

RELATIVES AND MUTUAL AID

When crises or disasters occur, many people who believe that they should be independent and make it on their own turn to their relatives for help.[20] It is not uncommon to receive aid from relatives long after the time people believe they are supposed to be independent.[21] Many couples find themselves involved in a network of mutual assistance with relatives, particularly with parents, which may include services, gifts, advice, emotional support, as well as financial assistance.[22]

Although the mutual aid is most often between parents and children, when three generations are involved, the assistance usually flows from the middle generation to the other two. Aged grandparents often do reciprocate in various ways. Young adults frequently provide help to their parents, though more often parents provide assistance to their young adult children.[23] There is a substantial amount of assistance among relatives. A study by Marvin B. Sussman [24] provides a view of the frequency with which such mutual help is given (see Table 10–2.)

Relatives may provide more needed services and assume more importance for those who are alone, single, widowed, or disabled than is commonly believed. Single, divorced, and widowed persons are more involved with relatives than are married persons.[25]

In a study of persons (486 disability applicants) likely to need assistance from relatives, it was found that 38 per cent of the available relatives lived in the same community. Fifty-one per cent of these relatives were seen at least monthly and 17 per cent provided help.[26]

Table 10–2 Direction of Service Network of Respondent's Family and Related Kin by Major Forms of Help

	Direction of Service Network				
Major Forms of Help and Service	*Between Respondent's Family and Related Kin Per cent*	*From Respondents to Parents Per cent*	*From Respondents to Siblings Per cent*	*From Parents to Respondents Per cent*	*From Siblings to Respondents Per cent*
Any form of help	93.3	56.3	47.6	79.6	44.8
Help during illness	76.0	47.0	42.0	46.4	39.0
Financial aid	53.0	14.6	10.3	46.8	6.4
Care of children	46.8	4.0	29.5	20.5	10.8
Advice (personal and business)	31.0	2.0	3.0	26.5	4.5
Valuable gifts	22.0	3.4	2.3	17.6	3.4

SOURCE: Marvin B. Sussman, "The Isolated Nuclear Family: Fact or Fiction," *Social Problems,* 6:4 (Spring, 1959), p. 336. Reprinted by permission of The Society for the Study of Social Problems and the author.

GENEALOGICAL KNOWLEDGE

One indication of how strongly people are oriented toward relatives or their extended family is how much they know about the genealogy of the family. Many Americans know very little about their family background and history. For example, some evidence indicates that one third do not know what their grandfathers' occupations were.[27] It seems that younger adults know less about their family backgrounds than the older generation.

Some people, of course, have a substantial amount of genealogical knowledge, and there is evidence that we, in the United States, have more knowledge of our family backgrounds than do people in several other industrial societies.[28] One study, for example, investigated 1,556 soldiers' knowledge of their grandfathers' occupations and found that sons of native-born Americans were more likely than sons of immigrants to know how their grandfathers earned a living.[29] Another study indicated that older Americans had a greater genealogical knowledge than did older English persons.[30]

The evidence concerning geographical closeness to relatives, amount of contact, number of close relationships, mutual aid, and genealogical knowledge suggests that there is a substantial involvement with relatives today and that interaction with relatives represents an important aspect of our lives.

Women Are Closer to Relatives

Women are closer to their relatives than are men; they identify and have more contact with them than do men; they know more relatives, consider them more important, and are generally more involved in obligations and activities with relatives. Women more frequently represent the family in contacts with relatives and assume responsibility for relaying to their husbands what goes on with relatives.[31]

Usually, women tend to be closer emotionally to their parents than men. This closer emotional tie is expressed by the fact that when aging parents move in with an offspring, it is usually with a daughter. Also, when aging parents face a crisis, they are more likely to look to a daughter for help.[32]

The greater closeness of women to their parents and other relatives results in a tendency for couples to have more family contacts with the wife's relatives than with the husband's kin.[33] Both husbands and wives expect to be more involved with the wife's relatives.

This expectation and the actual greater involvement with the wife's kin often results in problems and conflict with the husband's relatives. The husband's relatives, particularly his parents, often feel rejected or ignored. Such feelings breed resentment. That couples tend to be more involved with the wife's relatives may be one major reason why research shows that conflict with relatives that leads to conflict in the marriage more often involves relatives on the husband's side of the family.[34]

Importance of In-law Relations

In-law relationships have long been a common theme for jokes and are associated with trouble and conflict in the minds of millions. Couples often enter marriage fully expecting problems and conflict with their in-laws, and thus attempt to ignore their in-laws both before and after marriage. A woman may have the attitude, "I am marrying Bill, not his family." In a very real sense she *is* marrying Bill's family. Why is it very important for her to cultivate positive relationships with Bill's family?

SPOUSE IS PRODUCT OF IN-LAWS

The kind of person Bill is today is primarily a result of the influence of his family, and his family probably will continue to be a major influence in his life. The kind of foods he likes; his views of the world, himself, and others; his religious attitudes; his views of sex, marriage, and the roles of men and women; and the way he relates to others—all have been largely influenced by his family. Similarly, a husband can better understand his wife and why she is the type of person she is by getting to know her parents and family both before and after marriage.

A man married for fifteen years states:

> I have a very close relationship with Jill's parents. I think one reason why we get along so well is that I have always realized how important they are to her. I didn't expect her to stop seeing them or stop being close to them just because we married. Most of the good qualities that I love about Jill came from her parents. I became aware of this during our third year of marriage when financial problems forced us to live with them. I got to know them on an everyday basis. Jill's marvelous wit comes from her dad; her optimism and enthusiasm from her mother.

IN-LAWS AND MARRIAGE SUCCESS

In-law relationships are important to the success of a marriage.[35] Good relationships with in-laws provide a source of emotional and social support, whereas conflict produces strain that often damages a marriage.

Most people would probably find it psychologically difficult to accept that they did not have a good relationship with their parents because normally parents are an important part of a person's life. This does not change with marriage. Perhaps the major reason in-law relationships are important is because of the potential for expanding one's network of loving family members. Instead of two parents, a person can literally come to have four parents with whom he or she can enjoy emotionally supportive relationships.

Myths About In-laws

Some common myths prevail about in-law relationships. Practically all of them communicate negative messages. Such myths, in turn, influence us to develop negative attitudes about our in-laws before we ever meet them. It can be beneficial to examine these myths objectively.

IN-LAW MYTH 1: NOTHING CAN BE DONE ABOUT IN-LAW RELATIONSHIP PROBLEMS

Many people believe that in-law problems are inevitable and there is little that can be done to improve them. If a person has problems with in-law relationships, he or she does not need to feel helpless about it because much can be done to make the relationships satisfactory. Often problems can be eliminated or improved through the application of a few simple human relationship principles such as respect, understanding, listening, and emphasizing the positive qualities in another person.

IN-LAW MYTH 2: THE MOTHER-IN-LAW MYTH

Probably no one has been more the subject of disparaging comments and jokes than mothers-in-law. A common stereotype of a mother-in-law is a mean, meddling battle-ax.

We have all heard hostile jokes such as the following:

"Do you know what conflicting emotions are? It's when you see your mother-in-law driving over a cliff in your new Cadillac." [36]

"The Court must have evidence that none dare dispute," says the judge sternly.

"That's what I'm giving, Your Honor," replies the witness humbly. "It was my mother-in-law who told me." [37]

People have made comments such as these:

Mother-in-law—a foreign body of doubtful origin, species recognized instantly by a large opening in the middle of face, ruddered by flopping tongue. Natural habitat—your home! Occupation—your business! [38]

A mother rocks the cradle, but a mother-in-law rocks the boat.[39]

Mother-in-law problems are frequent but not as frequent as is commonly believed. Research by Judson Landis indicates that when in-law relationships are a source of conflict, the mother-in-law is most often mentioned by the husband and wife as being the cause of friction.[40] Evelyn Duvall analyzed the case-history documents of over 1,800 in-law relationships and found the mother-in-law to be the major source of conflict.[41]

However, the research does not support the myth that the mother-in-law is always a curse, nor the view that everyone has mother-in-law problems. Some investigations have shown that 75 per cent of the wives studied rate their relationships with their mothers-in-law as very good or good.[42] One in two men and women indicate that they love their mothers-in-law as a mother or as the best friend they ever had,[43] and there are many couples who have no in-law problems at all. Many mothers-in-law provide services that are greatly appreciated, such as assistance in getting a home established, baby-sitting, and help during illness or when children are born. As one Oklahoma wife stated:

My mother-in-law has been a big help to us in several situations where we really needed help, particularly when the children were born. I have learned a lot from her about cooking for which I am grateful—she is a wonderful cook. I am very lucky. She is like a mother to me—not a mother-in-law. I really feel that I have two mothers.

IN-LAW MYTH 3: IT IS IMPOSSIBLE TO LIVE WITH OR NEAR IN-LAWS

Bureau of Census statistics show that approximately 20 per cent of the married couples in which the husband is under age twenty live with relatives. For many couples this results in problems. For others it works out fine. Contrary to this myth, many couples do live with or near their in-laws and many enjoy it.

IN-LAW MYTH 4: PARENTS ARE THE GREATEST CRITICS

The idea that parents are supercritics and particularly that parents are more critical than their children are is a very common myth. It is actually the younger generation that is more critical of parents and parents-in-law.[44]

Patterns of In-law Conflict

Research analyzing the frequency of conflict that couples report with specific in-laws indicates that the mother-in-law heads the list followed by the sister-in-law. Most in-law conflict involves women.[45]

Most of the in-law conflict takes place between mother-in-law and daughter-in-law. What are the major reasons for this?

HUSBAND'S PARENTS MAY FEEL NEGLECTED

The fact that mother-in-law and daughter-in-law conflict is the most frequent form of in-law friction is, in part, due to the tendency of couples to visit the wife's

Table 10–3 Percentages of 116 Husbands and 160 Wives Reporting Various In-law Relationships That Were Causing Conflict in Marriages

In-law	Husband per cent	Wife per cent	Both per cent
Mother-in-law	42	50	46.7
Sister-in-law	16	13	13.8
Father-in-law	15	11	12.3
Brother-in-law	3	6	5.0

SOURCE: Judson T. Landis and Mary G. Landis, *Building a Successful Marriage*, 6th ed. (Englewood Cliffs, N.J.: Prentice-Hall, 1973), p. 296. Reprinted by permission.

parents and other relatives more often than the husband's parents and relatives. This is particularly important since it may cause the husband's mother to have a more difficult time in "letting go" of her son than does the wife's mother.[46] The husband's mother may interpret the more frequent visit to her daughter-in-law's parents as a form of rejection.

Since our son has married he doesn't see us much anymore. They prefer to visit her folks. I raised him and gave everything I could. Now I hardly ever see him because of her and her parents. It gets hard to take sometimes.

This type of situation can result in the husband's mother coming to resent her daughter-in-law.

ROLES ARE SIMILAR

Perhaps the most important reason for conflict between mother-in-law and daughter-in-law is that their roles are similar. The husband's mother identifies her daughter-in-law's role with her own and tends to compare the daughter-in-law's performance in certain areas.[47] Many of these roles are openly and consistently available for inspection and comparison. Managing the home, rearing children, and preparing food can very easily be evaluated and compared by the mother-in-law and daughter-in-law. Furthermore, they may be compared when they visit each other. In contrast, there are fewer roles openly available for inspection and comparison among men in the family. How one fulfills his occupational role is usually not easily observed by the other. This is a major reason why there is less conflict between father-in-law and son-in-law.[48]

The wife and her mother-in-law perform many of the same roles, but they may have learned to perform the roles very differently. The daughter-in-law brings to the marriage the family-life education she received from her mother.[49] It is understandable that the daughter-in-law and mother-in-law often do things very differently.

Personal immaturity can contribute to these differences becoming sources of conflict. For example, different methods may be considered inferior just because they are different, or a constructive suggestion may be rejected and wrongly interpreted as an attempt to control one's behavior. Such reactions can, in turn, result in negative responses starting a cycle of conflict.

In-law Problems and Complaints

Much can be learned about avoiding conflict and developing positive in-law relationships by looking at the most common complaints that have been expressed toward in-laws in general and toward the mother-in-law, daughter-in-law, and son-in-law, specifically.

COMPLAINTS AGAINST IN-LAWS

A large study by Evelyn Duvall [50] examined the complaints and problems with in-laws as reported by 1,337 persons. The most common complaints were being meddlesome, nagging and criticizing, possessive, aloof, and thoughtless. All of these complaints involve behavior that would produce problems in any human relationship.

It is interesting that aloofness and indifference were frequently mentioned as a problem with in-laws. Instead of thinking that their in-laws are too meddlesome and interfering, some people obviously feel they do not receive enough attention from them.

Table 10–4 Problems with In-laws Reported by 1,337 Persons

Complaint	Number	Per cent
Meddlesome, interfering, dominating	589	22.6
Nagging, criticizing, and ridiculing	276	10.5
Possessiveness	252	9.6
Indifferentness, aloofness, and being uninterested	232	8.9
Thoughtlessness, and unappreciativeness	206	7.9
Too dependent, immature	183	7.2
Does not agree on traditions, has different standards, intolerant	163	6.2
Superior attitude, self righteousness	113	4.3
Has favorites and takes sides in disagreements of others	103	3.9
Gossiping, misrepresenting facts, deceitfulness	101	3.9
Incompetent	97	3.7
Is envious, jealous, and rivalrous	95	3.6
Abusing hospitality, coming without invitations, not reciprocating	91	3.5
Talking too much, not listening	87	3.3
Unconventional behavior	23	0.9

SOURCE: Evelyn Duvall, *In-laws: Pro and Con* (New York: Association Press, 1954), p. 287. Reprinted with permission.

Table 10–5 Complaints Against Mothers-in-law Reported by 1,369 Persons

Complaint	Number	Per cent
Meddlesome	383	28.0
Possessive	193	14.1
Nags	150	10.9
Indifferent	99	7.2
Immature	93	6.8
Uncongenial	84	6.2
Thoughtless	76	5.6
Pampers	72	5.3
Intrudes	58	4.2
Self-righteous	41	3.0
Talkative	39	2.8
Gossips	34	2.5
Jealous	33	2.4
Ineffective	12	0.9
Unconventional	2	0.1

SOURCE: Evelyn Duvall, *In-laws: Pro and Con* (New York: Association Press, 1954), p. 191. Reprinted with permission.

COMPLAINTS AGAINST MOTHERS-IN-LAW

Since the majority of in-law conflict involves mothers-in-law, it is interesting to observe that more than half of all complaints against mothers-in-law involve the syndrome of meddlesomeness, possessiveness, and nagging.[51]

COMPLAINTS AGAINST DAUGHTERS-IN-LAW AND SONS-IN-LAW

Very few parents-in-law, when given the opportunity, state that the children-in-law are difficult.[52] This seems to suggest that either parents-in-law are much more difficult or are more tolerant and less critical than children-in-law. In either event, in-law conflict is not a one-way street. Many daughters-in-law and sons-in-law cause friction. When parents-in-law level criticisms against their children-in-law, what are the most common complaints?

My daughter-in-law doesn't mind asking me to do anything for her. She acts as if she's entitled to my help. It doesn't matter how tired I am or how busy. What really gets me though is that when I need help she refuses and acts as if I'm taking advantage of her.

Table 10–6 Complaints Against Daughters-in-law and Sons-in-law

Criticism	Daughter-in-law Rank	Daughter-in-law Number	Daughter-in-law Per cent	Son-in-law Rank	Son-in-law Number	Son-in-law Per cent
Indifferent	1	19	22.1	2	5	20.8
Thoughtless	2	14	16.3	1	6	25.0
Incompetent	3	11	12.8	6	2	8.3
Rivalrousness	4	7	8.2	—	0	0.0
Critical	5	6	7.0	7	1	4.2
Interferes	6	5	5.8	3	3	12.5
Uncongenial	7	5	5.8	5	3	12.5
Talkative	8	4	4.6	—	0	0.0
Partial	9	3	3.5	—	0	0.0
Self-righteous	10	3	3.5	—	0	0.0
Misrepresentation	11	3	3.5	—	0	0.0
Possessive	12	2	2.3	4	3	12.5
Immature	13	2	2.3	8	1	4.2
Intrudes	14	2	2.3	—	0	0.0
Unconventional	15	0	0.0	—	0	0.0
Total		86	100.0		24	100.0

SOURCE: Evelyn Duvall, *In-laws: Pro and Con* (New York: Association Press, 1954), p. 163. Reprinted with permission.

Our daughter-in-law is really like a stranger to us. She's not very friendly and acts more like she is just tolerating us when we are together.

These comments reflect what research has shown to be the most common criticisms of children-in-law. The major complaints against daughters-in-law and sons-in-law are that they are indifferent or distant and that they are thoughtless and inconsiderate.[53] Parents often feel that the young couple is too busy living their own lives to be interested in or sensitive to the parents' needs.[54]

A Major Source of In-law Conflict

Perhaps the major source of in-law conflict is that parents tend to center their lives around their children and are expected to drop this absorbing interest after the children are married. Parents normally are closely involved with their children for about twenty years. When their children marry, this close involvement stops. We put extreme emphasis upon independence and autonomy of children in our culture, and this cultural prescription may add to the problem. In subtle ways we encourage young married couples to ignore their parents. However, it is difficult for parents to change twenty years of habit, to stop advising, helping, and directing their children. To parents, their children do not stop being their children just because they marry.

Sometimes the potential for conflict and hurt feelings is increased by young couples acting immaturely by demanding that parents drop the interest they have had in their children for twenty years. Perhaps this is one reason why the younger the couple, the more difficulty they tend to have with in-laws. Other possible reasons are that the very young more often marry against parental advice or for reasons of pregnancy.[55]

Building Successful In-law Relationships

Harmonious and satisfying in-law relationships can be developed in many ways. If an individual decides to build positive in-law relationships, he or she has every right to expect happiness and satisfaction from these relationships and that they will be a source of strength to the marriage. What are some important ways that good relationships can be developed?

ADOPT AN OPTIMISTIC VIEW OF IN-LAW RELATIONSHIPS

Perhaps the basic step in building good relationships is to adopt an optimistic, positive view toward in-laws.[56] Most of us have a self-fulfilling prophecy operating in our lives. This means that we expect certain things to happen or conditions to develop, and then we do things—often unconsciously—that actually make our expectations, or "prophecies," come true.

When a young couple enters marriage expecting problems with the in-laws, they may reflect negative attitudes from the beginning without a real basis except that they have decided that in-law relationships inevitably are bad. Both partners may stereotype their in-laws as being selfish and meddlesome. Because they are looking for the worst from their in-laws and expecting problems, the young couple may cause problems. In-laws, sensing a negative and critical attitude toward them, may feel threatened and hurt. As a means of self-defense, they may, in turn, become critical or intolerant.

In contrast, a couple with an optimistic attitude and expecting the best from in-law relationships, tends to concentrate upon the strengths and positive characteristics of those relationships. They are much more likely to experience satisfying in-law relationships. If in-laws believe that they are perceived as being OK, they will be more likely to reflect OK messages in return by giving friendly and supportive responses. Thus, a positive "I'm OK—You're OK" cycle of interaction is established.

VIEW IN-LAWS AS YOUR OWN FAMILY

One important way that an individual can build good in-law relationships is to think of and treat in-laws as family, not as remote in-laws of whom one must be wary.[57] If you think of your parents-in-law as your own family and relate to them as you do to your own parents, they will feel accepted, valued, and loved by you. There will be little reason for them to feel defensive.

When you "join a family," rather than thinking of yourself as an outsider, becoming as committed and helpful to your partner's family as to your own, it will be difficult for your in-law relationships not to be happy and positive.

AVOID IGNORING IN-LAWS

The most common complaint parents have against their daughters-in-law and sons-in-law is that they are indifferent, uninterested, aloof, or distant. This makes many parents-in-law feel hurt, rejected, and resentful and the potential for developing close relationships becomes impaired. Lower divorce rates occur among spouses who develop mutual ties to *both* families. Divorce rates are highest in those societies where spouses maintain separate ties to their respective families of origin.[58]

ACCEPTANCE AND RESPECT

"We accept and respect each other" is a frequent answer people give for the reason they experience positive in-law relationships. People who have good, harmonious relationships with others most often cite acceptance and respect as the major factors contributing to their positive relationships.[59]

> We got along just great from the beginning. Sue's family took me in and accepted me as if I were one of the family. This has meant a great deal to me. I have the highest respect for them. They don't make a big deal out of any differences we have.

We all like to be around people who accept and respect us as we are. They make us feel OK about ourselves. Much in-law conflict is due to a lack of acceptance and respect. People who encounter difficulty in relationships are often intolerant of differentness and are possessive and dominating.

Often in-law conflict results from trivial differences that should be of little real importance to the persons involved, yet hurt feelings and hostility that result from the process of conflict *are* important. Couples can do much to build harmonious, positive relationships by using good judgment in avoiding conflicts over things that cannot be changed or are unimportant.[60]

References

1. LANDIS, JUDSON T. "Length of Time Required to Achieve Adjustment in Marriage." *American Sociological Review*, vol. 11, 1946, pp. 666–677.
2. FOLKMAN, JEROME D. and NANCY M. K. CLATWORTHY. *Marriage Has Many Faces.* Columbus, Ohio: Merrill, 1970.
3. LANDIS, JUDSON T. "On the Campus." *Survey Midmonthly*, vol. 84, 1948, p. 19.
4. ADAMS, BERT N. "Isolation, Function, and Beyond: American Kinship in the 1960's." *Journal of Marriage and the Family*, vol. 32, 1970, pp. 575–598.
5. HALLER, A. O. "The Urban Family." *American Journal of Sociology*, vol. 66, 1961, pp. 621–622.
6. ADAMS, BERT N. *Kinship in an Urban Setting.* Chicago: Markham, 1968.
7. SHANAS, ETHEL. *Family Relationships of Older People.* New York: Health Information Foundation, 1961.
8. KOMAROVSKY, MIRRA. *Blue-Collar Marriage.* New York: Random House, 1964.
9. LEICHTER, HOPE J., and WILLIAM E. MITCHELL. *Kinship and Casework.* New York: Russell Sage Foundation, 1967.
10. ADAMS, 1970, op. cit.
11. ADAMS, 1968, op. cit.
12. BLOOD, ROBERT O. and MORRIS AXELROD. Detroit Area Study data reported in *Marriage* by Robert O. Blood. New York: Free Press, 1969.
13. Ibid.
14. BLOOD, ROBERT O. *Marriage.* New York: Free Press, 1969.
15. ADAMS, 1970, op. cit.
16. LAUMANN, EDWARD. *Prestige and Association in an Urban Community.* Indianapolis: Bobbs-Merrill, 1966.
    BABCHUK, NICHOLAS, and JOHN BALLWEG. "Primary Extended Kin Relations of Negro Couples." *The Sociological Quarterly*, vol. 12, 1971, pp. 66–77.
17. ADAMS, 1970, op. cit.
18. Ibid.
19. STRAUS, MURRAY A. "Social Class and Farm-City Differences in Interaction with Kin in Relation to Societal Modernization." *Rural Sociology*, vol. 34, 1969, pp. 476–495.

20. DRABEK, THOMAS E., and KEITH S. BOGGS. "Families in Disaster: Reactions and Relatives." *Journal of Marriage and the Family*, vol. 30, 1968, pp. 443–451.
ADAMS, 1970, op. cit.
21. SUSSMAN, MARVIN B., and LEE BURCHINAL. "Kin Family Network, Unheralded Structure in Current Conceptualization of Family Functioning." *Marriage and Family Living*, vol. 24, 1962, pp. 231–240.
22. Ibid.
23. ADAMS, 1970, op. cit.
24. SUSSMAN, MARVIN B. "The Isolated Nuclear Family: Fact or Fiction." *Social Problems*, vol. 6, 1959, pp. 333–340.
25. GIBSON, GEOFFREY. "Kin Family Network: Overheralded Structure in Past Conceptualizations of Family Functioning." *Journal of Marriage and the Family*, vol. 34, 1972, pp. 13–23.
26. Ibid.
27. CROOG, SIDNEY H., and PETER KONG-MING NEW. "Knowledge of Grandfather's Occupation—A Clue to American Kinship Structure." *Journal of Marriage and the Family*, vol. 27, 1965, pp. 66–77.
28. ADAMS, 1970, op. cit.
29. CROOG and NEW, op. cit.
30. YOUNG, MICHAEL, and HILDA GEERTZ. "Old Age in London and San Francisco: Some Families Compared." *British Journal of Sociology*, vol. 12, 1961, pp. 124–141.
31. ADAMS, 1968, 1970, op. cit.
LEICHTER and MITCHELL, op. cit.
ROBBINS, LEE N., and MIRODA TOMANEC. "Closeness to Blood Relatives Outside the Immediate Family." *Marriage and Family Living*, vol. 24, 1962, pp. 340–346.
32. KOMAROVSKY, op. cit.
BABCHUK and BALLWEG, op. cit.
ADAMS, 1970, op. cit.
33. ADAMS, 1970, op. cit.
34. Ibid.
35. LANDIS, JUDSON, 1948, op. cit.
36. SHLEIN, JOHN M. "Mother-in-law: A Problem of Kinship Terminology." In *Marriage, Family, and Society*, edited by Hyman Rodman. New York: Random House, 1965, p. 199.
37. DUVALL, EVELYN. *In-laws: Pro and Con.* New York: Association Press, 1954, p. 25.
38. Ibid., p. 27.
39. Ibid.
40. LANDIS, JUDSON, 1946, op. cit.
41. DUVALL, op. cit.
42. BELL, ROBERT R. *Marriage and Family Interaction.* Homewood, Ill.: Dorsey Press, 1971.
43. DUVALL, op. cit.
44. Ibid.
45. LANDIS, JUDSON T., and MARY G. LANDIS. *Building a Successful Marriage.* 6th ed. Englewood Cliffs, N.J.: Prentice-Hall, 1973.
46. LANDIS, PAUL. *Making the Most of Marriage.* Englewood Cliffs, N.J.: Prentice-Hall, 1975.
47. Ibid.

48. BELL, op. cit.
49. Ibid.
50. DUVALL, op. cit.
51. Ibid.
52. Ibid.
53. Ibid.
54. KELLEY, ROBERT K. *Courtship, Marriage, and the Family.* New York: Harcourt Brace Jovanovich, 1974.
55. LANDIS, PAUL, op. cit.
56. KELLEY, op. cit.
57. ADAMS, 1970, op. cit.
58. BARRY, WILLIAM A. "Marriage Research and Conflict: An Integrative Review." *Psychological Bulletin*, vol. 73, 1970, pp. 41–54.
59. DUVALL, op. cit.
60. KELLEY, op. cit.

11 Sexual Encounter

Photo by Larry White

To learn about sexuality is to deal . . . with a kind of personal knowledge about oneself.

Eleanor S. Morrison

Sexuality

We usually think of sex as involving a physical attraction to another person. We also associate sex with a variety of physical activities such as kissing, hugging, caressing, stroking, and sexual intercourse. However, sexuality, in contrast with sex, is much more than physical attraction and contact. Sexuality begins at conception when maleness or femaleness of the fertilized ovum is determined by the chromosome content of the fertilizing sperm cell. Sexuality even involves such factors as traditional cultural expectations that baby girls are dressed in pink and baby boys in blue as well as the sex-appropriate toys and education each receives. Sexuality involves all that it means to be a man or a woman; it is part of a person's total being. Our sexuality includes emotions, values, moral and ethical makeup, social relations, ability to use good judgment and make decisions, physical desires and fulfillment. Sexuality cannot be separated from a person's total life. It is not a separate, exclusive component of an individual. It interrelates with every other part of life.

Most of us have difficulty being objective about such a personal area of our lives. Each of us has definite ideas about what is desirable and undesirable sexual behavior. As we grow up, we internalize from parents, church, and others a set of rules and standards about "proper" and "improper" sexual behavior. Problems such as guilt and other negative feelings may arise when personal behavior violates these rules and standards that have been internalized. Many people experience a feeling of confusion concerning what is a desirable standard of sexual behavior due to the fact that there are an increasing number of different philosophies and teachings about sexual behavior. Each of us decides whether to espouse a hedonistic philosophy toward sexual behavior or a "sex is excusable only for procreation" philosophy, or something in between these two extreme views. Most of us adopt an "in between" view, but even in this middle range there is a wide variety of opinion regarding proper sexual conduct.

This chapter naturally reflects the philosophy of the authors. It will be too conservative for some; too liberal for others. The research evidence concerning the factors that contribute to a happy, satisfying sexual relationship as well as those that serve as a barrier to achieving a satisfying sexual relationship are presented with the intent that it will provoke an examination of the readers' values. In the final analysis, no one can tell you how you should behave. This is a decision each of us must make based on the ethical and moral values we have learned.

Sexual Relationships

Just as sexuality is integrated with every other part of our lives, sexual relationships are integrated with every other aspect of the total man-woman relationship. It is recognized that sexual interaction occurs in a variety of contexts. However, because a successful sexual relationship contributes importantly to marriage, reference is made throughout the chapter to *husbands* and *wives.* This emphasis should not be interpreted as reflecting a lack of understanding that sexual encounter occurs outside of marriage and for some people between members of the same sex. It should be remembered that many of the principles important to satisfying sexual relationships apply regardless of the context. The sexual relationship is influenced by the quality of the total interpersonal relationship. A good sexual relationship contributes greatly to a high degree of satisfaction in the total marriage relationship. However, a good sexual relationship is more likely to be a result of a satisfying interpersonal relationship rather than the cause.[1]

Couples who depend upon sex as the *only* bond holding their relationship together may soon discover that it is not enough. A sexual relationship that reflects a husband's and wife's concern, love, respect, and responsibility for each other increases marriage happiness and mental health.[2]

Sexuality and Self-actualization

We can learn much about sexual relationships by examining the role of sex in the lives of persons who have healthy and wholesome personalities, a high degree of happiness, a high degree of control over their lives, and who have achieved a great deal of their human potential. Abraham Maslow has completed such a study.[3] He has termed such individuals "self-actualizing" persons. Maslow's concept of a self-actualizing person is similar to a very mature person.

Maslow's study found that:

1. For self-actualizing persons, love and affection must be present before establishing a sexual relationship. The self-actualizing person would prefer to do without sex than to have a sexual relationship that lacked love and affection.
2. The intensity of sexual relationships among self-actualizing persons is great and appears to be more intense than among persons who are less self-actualizing.
3. The self-actualizing person does not use sex to prove anything or to manipulate another. Sex is a source of mutual enjoyment that reflects the positive quality of a total relationship.
4. The self-actualizing man is confident of his masculinity and the self-actualizing woman is confident of her femininity.
5. Self-actualizing persons view sexuality as being integrated with their total selves and the sexual relationship as being integrated with their total relationship. The total self and personality are involved in the sexual relationship.
6. Self-actualizing persons are completely involved with their sexual partners as persons. This involvement requires that the needs of both husband and wife merge. Each partner must care and have great concern for the other and be responsive to the other's needs in order to achieve a complete union in the sexual as well as in the total marriage relationship.[4]

Sexual Attractiveness

A quality many persons strive for is sexual attractiveness. Professionals in the area of advertising capitalize on this to sell products. A leading toothpaste company, for example, has advertised toothpaste "with sex appeal." Several advertisements on television and in popular magazines communicate the message, "If you buy our product, you will be more sexually attractive."

What makes a person sexually attractive? It is interesting that a quality so widely talked about and so deeply desired is very difficult to define. Few people can explain what sex appeal means to them. Little research has been conducted on this topic.

However, one research study, conducted by Nancy Clatworthy,[5] found the following characteristics associated with a high degree of sex appeal:

1. The ability to respond warmly to another.
2. The quality of expressing sincere appreciation to others and helping others to feel good about themselves.
3. The quality of being fully alive and aware of others and the environment; being involved with life as a participant rather than as a spectator.
4. Enthusiasm, vitality, and happiness.
5. The appearance of wholeness and completeness.

6. The awareness of sexuality and the ability to be comfortable with it.
7. Self-confidence.
8. Personal magnetism—a type of electrical or chemical attraction.
9. Adventuresomeness.
10. A certain degree of mysteriousness.
11. Physical appearance and dress; many people associate sex appeal with beauty in women but not to the extent that it detracts from the impact of her personality.

Clatworthy's research suggests that a vital element of sex appeal is enthusiasm for and interest in people and life in general. Also important is the ability to respond warmly and positively to others and to make them feel good about themselves.

Barriers to Sexual Happiness

Sexual satisfaction and happiness is an important goal of husbands and wives. Many enjoy the achievement of this goal. Yet, there are also many who experience major problems in their sexual relationship. Why? A general answer is that because an individual functions sexually as a total person, "anything which is capable of undermining him/her personally is capable of undermining his/her sexual response." [6] The following factors contribute to sexual dissatisfaction:

1. A negative, nonsupportive interpersonal relationship between a couple can do more to harm the sexual relationship than anything else. When a husband and wife develop a threatening pattern of interaction in which they consistently give each other negative psychological strokes and reinforce each other's "I'm not OK" position, they minimize their chances of achieving sexual happiness with each other.
2. Simple boredom with the daily routine of life and the marriage relationship can be a major barrier to a satisfying sexual relationship. Couples can allow themselves to become indifferent to each other and, in turn, allow their sexual relationship to become so monotonous that they actually replace their sexual activities with work, television, or other leisure-time activities.[7] When a cable-television strike shut down all broadcasts in a West Virginia city in 1968, the birth rate nine months later was three times the usual rate.[8]
3. Anxiety and depression are detrimental to the desire and ability to function sexually.[9] Husbands and wives who find their sexual relationship suddenly decreasing in satisfaction often discover that one or both partners are worried, anxious, or depressed about something. An understanding, supportive hus-

band or wife who helps the other partner come to terms with his or her anxiety or depression often can help the partner to deal effectively with the source of stress and at the same time help to restore their satisfying sexual relationship. Outside sources of stress, such as loss of a job or business pressure, can be temporarily detrimental by causing a person to become preoccupied to the extent of not being able to concentrate upon the sexual relationship.

4. Lack of basic knowledge concerning the psychological and biological aspects of sex can cause great problems and dissatisfaction. For example, most males can achieve orgasm a few minutes after intromission. Most females, however, normally do not achieve orgasm until after ten minutes of intercourse. Failure to understand this physiological difference can serve to damage the sexual relationship.
5. The internalization of negative attitudes and perceptions from early childhood concerning sex is a major barrier to the achievement of a satisfying sexual relationship. Examples of such attitudes are that sex is a wife's *duty* or that respectable people do not really enjoy sex.
6. Fatigue often interferes with sexual satisfaction and is a major barrier to sexual responsiveness.[10] Couples can eliminate or minimize this problem by purposely planning for sexual interaction at a time of day or night when they are least likely to be fatigued.
7. Much sexual dissatisfaction is due to the fact that husbands and wives do not talk to each other about their sexual likes and dislikes. Many husbands and wives erroneously expect that their partners know intuitively what pleases and displeases them sexually.
8. Physical problems sometimes hinder sexual functioning and contribute to decreased sexual satisfaction. Some physical illnesses and diseases interfere with sexual responsiveness.

   There are also physical problems caused by aging that may make sexual intercourse painful. These problems occur primarily in older women. The vaginal walls of older women tend to become thinner and less flexible and less lubricating secretions are produced. These changes often result in sexual intercourse being painful. However, such problems can be remedied medically and through the use of sterile, water-soluble lubricants.[11] There are also women, young and older, who have vaginas small enough to experience pain during sexual intercourse if insertion of the penis takes place before they achieve a high degree of sexual excitement with a corresponding dilation of the vagina.[12]
9. Interpersonal conflict between husband and wife can result in decreased satisfaction in the sexual relationship. Intense conflict, hostility, and resentment can cause loss of sexual interest and general dissatisfaction in a marriage. Destructive interactions, such as insults and ridicule, are deadly to a sexual relationship.
10. Becoming overly concerned with sexual response often serves as a barrier to full sexual satisfaction among both men and women. For example, one cause

of many women's inability to respond sexually is an overconcern with orgasm. These women approach sexual behavior with a grim determination to succeed that is likely to be self-defeating. When husbands and wives begin to enjoy sexual intercourse for *the pleasure it gives them and their partner*, it is more likely that their sexual relationship will be happy and satisfying.[13]

Developing a Satisfying Sexual Relationship

The success of a sexual relationship is not just a matter of physiological factors. Because it is integrated with the total interpersonal relationship, the satisfaction of the sexual relationship is strongly influenced by various aspects of the total marriage relationship. The following are among the major factors contributing to satisfying sexual relationships.

1. Probably nothing is more important than a positive, loving, total interpersonal environment characterized by genuine mutual care and concern, respect, a sense of being responsive to each other's needs, understanding, trust, and commitment.
2. The quality of feeling comfortable with each other is a major factor. Comfort is an important but largely ignored quality of successful interpersonal relationships. Surprisingly, many husbands and wives do not feel comfortable with each other. Being uncomfortable with a partner can make it difficult for either to respond sexually. A person is most likely to feel comfortable with a partner when that partner expresses genuine concern, care, and respect, is not threatening but emotionally supportive, and expresses a strong sense of commitment.
3. Recent research has shown the importance of commitment to sexual responsiveness. William Masters and Virginia Johnson, on the basis of their laboratory research and clinical experience, conclude that commitment is one of the most important factors contributing to satisfaction in a sexual relationship.[14] Both men and women tend to be more sexually responsive when they know their partner has a high degree of commitment toward them. Commitment encourages trust, which in turn allows a person to give himself or herself freely in a sexual relationship. Research by Norman Lobsenz [15] indicates that women who have difficulty in experiencing orgasm tend to feel that there is a lack of commitment from others close to them.
4. Cultivating a *relaxed, enjoyable attitude* and approach to sexual interaction is extremely important in contributing to a happy and satisfying sexual relationship. A couple should concentrate on simply enjoying the experience and the pleasure they bring to themselves and each other. They should not place too much emphasis on performance, how they are measuring up, or upon

achieving orgasm. To do so creates tension and anxiety and tends to remove sexual interaction from its pleasurable context.

5. Communication can help a couple avoid many problems and promote satisfaction. When a husband and wife can communicate the types of sexual behavior that please and displease them, they increase their probability of experiencing a good sexual relationship.
6. Possessing basic knowledge concerning the psychological and physical aspects of sex contributes to a more satisfying sexual relationship.
7. Many couples find that avoiding routine in their sexual behavior with each other keeps their sexual relationship interesting and fresh.[16] Some couples achieve this by varying their sexual activities in such a way as to maximize their enjoyment.
8. The likelihood of enjoying a satisfying sexual relationship is greatly increased by getting plenty of sleep and rest, adequate exercise, and good nutrition.
9. The development of positive, healthy attitudes toward sex from early childhood is conducive to the establishment of a satisfying sexual relationship.

Sexual Myths

Human sexuality is one of many aspects of life that has been shrouded in misinformation. Some common myths are in existence that perpetuate this misinformation.

SEX MYTH 1: THERE HAS BEEN A GREAT REVOLUTION IN SEXUAL BEHAVIOR DURING RECENT YEARS

The notion prevails, often expressed in the mass media, that America is in the midst of a sexual revolution. The assumption is expressed that most youth are sexually very permissive and the proportion of single young women who are no longer virgins has increased greatly during the last twenty-five years. These widespread discussions concerning the great sexual revolution have undoubtedly induced much anxiety among many people who are not personally experiencing a sexual revolution. Many young persons may ask themselves, "What's wrong with me?"

The popular discussions of the current sexual revolution are out of touch with reality according to the research evidence.[17] Recent research indicates there has been little change in sexual attitudes and behavior during the last thirty years.[18] One recent study found that compared with the change in rates of premarital sexual intercourse at the beginning of the century, the rates since the 1960s have increased only one fourth as much.[19] A study by Jon Alston and Francis Tucker [20] indicates that 80 per cent of American adults believe it is wrong to have sexual relations before marriage.

Research by Alfred Kinsey, Wardell Pomeroy, Clyde Martin, and Paul Gebhard showed that the big change in female nonvirginity occurred between those born before and after 1900.[21] There has been little change recently in female nonvirginity. The research evidence currently suggests that there has been no change in the proportion of nonvirginity during the past four or five decades equal to that which occurred during the 1920s.[22] This evidence contradicts the myth that there is widespread sexual promiscuity among youth.[23]

The biggest change is that there is much more open discussion of sexual behavior today. This openness has increased public awareness and has resulted in an increased acceptance of sexuality.[24]

Attitudes toward sexual behavior should not be confused with actual behavior. An interesting example of the difference between attitudes and behavior is the research evidence indicating that 75 per cent of college females believe their classmates are engaging in sexual intercourse whereas research studies consistently indicate that actually only 20 per cent of college females experience premarital sexual intercourse.[25]

SEX MYTH 2: NOTHING CAN BE DONE TO HELP COUPLES WHO HAVE SEXUAL PROBLEMS

Much can be done to assist persons who have sexual problems. Masters and Johnson [26] report achieving approximately 80 per cent success in the treatment of all kinds of unsatisfactory sexual functioning. Their success seems to be enduring. One year following treatment, the success rate is reduced by only 5 or 6 per cent.

The likelihood of successfully treating sexual problems, of course, depends upon the particular problem. Masters and Johnson [27] report 100 per cent success in treating women who suffer from vaginismus, a painful contraction of vaginal muscles that makes intercourse exceedingly difficult. This condition responds very well to the gradual dilation of the vaginal orifice.[28] Correction of this condition is often accomplished in as little as five days.[29]

Premature ejaculation is one of the more common sexual problems of men. Masters and Johnson [30] report that 97 per cent of the men who experience premature ejaculation are successfully treated. Most men are inclined to have a premature ejaculation if they are inexperienced, extremely excited, have maintained an erection for a prolonged period of time before engaging in sexual intercourse, or have been sexually abstinate for a long period of time.[31] Most men seem to ejaculate soon after intercourse begins. Kinsey's research indicated that 75 per cent of the men reported ejaculations within two minutes of intercourse.[32]

Many men can prevent premature ejaculation by using a condom, which decreases the sensitivity of the glans, hence slowing sexual excitement and orgasm. A more effective method is to apply a local anesthetic ointment to the glans approximately thirty minutes before sexual intercourse.

Masters and Johnson report that their success rate drops to 59 per cent in treating men who experience *primary impotence,* that is, the male has never maintained an erection firm enough to make sexual intercourse possible. Fear and anxiety are major factors contributing to primary impotence. A man who experiences impotence over a prolonged period of time approaches sexual intercourse in an increasingly anxious and fearful state of mind and attempts to achieve erection through will power. This takes sexual interaction completely out of a pleasurable context and makes it even more difficult to achieve an erection. However, treatment of *secondary impotence,* that is, the male has succeeded in intercourse previously but is unable to achieve an intravaginal erection, is highly successful.

Successful treatment of impotence in husbands and frigidity in wives focuses upon removing the individual's fear of failure and extreme concern with performance and successfully passing the "test" of sexual interaction. They are encouraged to relax and enjoy sexual activity without any concern about performance, ejaculation, or orgasm.[33]

In the therapy of Masters and Johnson [34] both the husband and wife are encouraged to engage in sexual play not intended to result in sexual intercourse. Once the husband is able to relax and enjoy noncoital sexual play, he is probably capable of proceeding to successful sexual intercourse because the pattern of failure has been broken and a pattern of relaxing and enjoying sexual behavior has been initiated.[35]

SEX MYTH 3: SEXUAL INTERCOURSE IS DANGEROUS DURING MENSTRUATION

The origin of this very old myth is closely related to the shame associated with menstruation in the past. For example, the Roman historian Pliny in 60 A.D. stated that merely the presence of a menstruating woman would cause "new wine to become sour . . . and garden plants to become parched." [36] The association of bleeding with sickness led to a limiting of physical activities during the menstrual period in many societies. Sexual intercourse was one of them.

Some women may find it somewhat painful to engage in sexual intercourse during menstruation because there may be reduced vaginal lubrication during this time. However, this problem can be eliminated by using a sterile water-soluble lubricant.

The menstrual blood is absolutely harmless to both the man and the woman and no damage of tissue occurs from the penetration of the penis. Also, a woman's sexual desire does not usually decrease during the menstrual period. If a husband and wife both desire to have sexual intercourse during menstruation, there is ordinarily no reason why they should not do so.[37]

There are even some advantages to a couple having sexual intercourse during the menstrual period. One possible advantage is that intercourse which culminates in orgasm for the woman can relieve discomfort of menstrual cramps. A second advantage is that the menstrual period is a period of peak sexual desire for some women. A third advantage is that the possibility of pregnancy is virtually eliminated during this time.

SEX MYTH 4: SEXUAL INTERCOURSE SHOULD BE AVOIDED DURING PREGNANCY

Generally, there is no reason why sexual intercourse should be avoided until late in the third trimester of a pregnancy. There is little change in the woman's sexual interest during the first three months of pregnancy. Most women experience an increase in erotic feelings during the second three months. A decrease in sexual desire is characteristic during the last three months of a pregnancy.[38]

Research indicates that unless there are certain complications, couples may engage in sexual intercourse with safety until approximately four weeks before delivery. The strong contractions of the uterus during the woman's orgasmic response can cause labor contractions to begin if the woman is within three weeks of delivery.[39] Also, because there is increased danger of infections at this time, many physicians advise the cessation of intercourse because of the possibility of the penis introducing infections into the vagina.

Three complications that may make it inadvisable to continue sexual intercourse during pregnancy are (a) if there is pain during sexual intercourse; (b) if there is bleeding or spotting; (c) if the fetal membrane is not intact. If a couple has any doubt about the safety of intercourse during any phase of the pregnancy, a physician should be consulted.

SEX MYTH 5: OLDER MEN DO NOT PERFORM AS WELL AS DO YOUNGER MEN

This rather widespread belief is incorrect. Most older men attain erection more slowly than younger men do and orgasm may not last quite as long; however, this is compensated for by the fact that men between ages fifty and seventy have much better control of ejaculation than younger men. An older man is also usually able to prolong sexual intercourse for a considerably longer period of time than a young man can.[40]

SEX MYTH 6: MENOPAUSE OR HYSTERECTOMY TERMINATES THE SEXUAL DESIRE AND BEHAVIOR OF A WOMAN

The research shows that the sexual desire of a woman ordinarily continues undiminished long after menopause, until sixty years of age or over. Many women remain sexually active well into their later years.[41] The removal of the uterus is referred to as a total hysterectomy. No physical reasons exist for a decrease in a woman's sexual desire or behavior as a result of a hysterectomy. There may be a loss of desire caused by psychological factors; however, if she is informed of the effects of the operation by her surgeon or other reliable sources, there should be no loss of sex drive because of psychological factors. Instead, some women report an increase in sexual desire largely because the fear of pregnancy is eliminated.[42]

SEX MYTH 7: LARGE SEXUAL ORGANS CONTRIBUTE TO GREATER SEXUAL SATISFACTION

The size of the sexual organs of either men or women has no physical relationship to the sexual satisfaction experienced. Of course, if a woman or a man believes that physical characteristics make a difference, then sexual satisfaction may be psychologically influenced. If, however, differences in sizes of anatomical structures are of such a nature to cause discomfort in intercourse, then special consideration must be exercised to achieve a satisfying sexual relationship. In some very few instances medical attention should be sought.

Aphrodisiacs

Erotic potions designed to increase sexual desire are described in the medical literature from ancient Egypt. From the early beginnings of civilization, people have searched for methods to increase sexual desire. These methods include a variety of foods, drugs, physical activities, and mechanical devices. Erotic pictures, movies, records, and literature are also employed by some as methods of stimulating sexual desire and excitement.[43]

FOOD

Certain foods have long been thought to possess sexually stimulating powers. Fish, oysters, honey, artichokes, asparagus, even bananas are among the foods commonly considered to be aphrodisiacs.

Food has no aphrodisiac quality according to our present medical knowledge except in the sense that food contributes to good nutrition and promotes the general health and vitality of the body. Poor nutrition results in low energy, fatigue, and poor health and thus can be responsible for sexual indifference.

ALCOHOL

One of the most famous of alleged aphrodisiacs is alcohol. In reality it does not serve as a sexual stimulant except that in some individuals the moderate consumption of alcohol temporarily removes certain inhibitions, fear, and guilt concerning sexual behavior, thereby enabling them to interact sexually in a more relaxed manner.

Actually alcohol is a depressant. When taken in considerable quantity, alcohol deadens the nerves, narcotizes the brain, retards reflexes, dilates blood vessels, and interferes with the ability to achieve an erection.[44] Many individuals after consuming large amounts of alcohol and then being unable to achieve erection have become very anxious about their sexual potency and have visited a physician to see what is wrong.

OTHER DRUGS

Drugs other than alcohol have been publicized erroneously as being aphrodisiacs. Some users believe that various drugs, such as marijuana, amphetamines, and heroin, increase sexual awareness and intensify and prolong orgasm.[45]

Some marijuana users maintain that the use of it heightens sexual pleasure. However, marijuana is not an aphrodisiac. There is evidence that continual use of marijuana, such as on a daily basis, actually leads to decreased sexual desire and behavior and may replace the physical expression of sexual behavior altogether. For such individuals the physical expression of sex takes more initiative than they feel like expending.[46]

The use of heroin also can lead to decreased sexual desire and activity.[47] In fact, the research indicates that approximately 95 per cent of heroin addicts are sexually impotent.[48]

Addiction to most drugs, including alcohol, leads to a decrease in sexual desire and behavior and eventually to sexual impotence. Evidence by Hardin Jones,[49] a research physiologist at the University of California in Berkeley, and by Thaddeus Mann, psychiatrist at the University of Cambridge in England, indicates that the major way drugs work is to activate the sensual or pleasure centers in the body. These pleasure centers are primarily sexual in nature. For example, individuals who use heroin intravenously describe the experience as similar to having an orgasm and being hit on the head simultaneously. Stimulation of the pleasure centers by drugs can soon replace normal sexual experiences as well as other forms of pleasure, such as eating. Drug addicts have very little sex life because they have cultivated other types of sensual stimulation.[50]

Some heavy drug users will take amphetamines to maintain a pre-orgasmic phase of sensual pleasure for perhaps ten to twelve hours, then use drugs intravenously for the orgasm and letdown. The entire experience is nongenital and is an example of how drugs may completely substitute for the physical expression of sexual pleasure among drug addicts.[51] Donald Cooper, director of the Oklahoma State University Hospital, stated,

> The real tragedy, once this route of drug taking gets into full swing, is that apparently these chemicals do permanent damage to the pleasure centers, making it very difficult for an addict ever to register pleasure from normal genital sex again. Even after the individual has gone through withdrawal and returned to society and his job, his ability to feel pleasure in anything, including sex, is very limited.[52]

One of the most widely used drugs for increasing sexual desire is yohimbine, which is taken from the yohimbé tree in Africa. This drug is used to increase the excitement in the lower areas of the spine where erection and ejaculation centers are located. It stimulates the nervous system and is dangerous in large doses. Yohimbine should be used under the direction of a physician. There is much doubt about its true effectiveness.[53]

In summary, drugs in general do not act as true aphrodisiacs. Any changes that occur in sexual desire seem to be because of psychological rather than physical factors. Any of the drugs are potentially dangerous if used without medical supervision, and constant use of most drugs to the point of addiction acts to decrease sexual desire and behavior.

When all the evidence is considered, the best aphrodisiacs seem to be good nutrition, good health, and adequate degree of exercise, freedom from emotional stress and anxiety, and enough rest and sleep.[54] As James McCary states concerning the specific potions that supposedly act as aphrodisiacs:

> Aphrodisiacs are not likely to increase sex drive unless a psychological component of suggestion is present that might whet the sexual appetite and increase the drive momentarily; or unless the individual is physically debilitated, in which case such treatment as hormonal therapy might be of benefit.[55]

Sexual Arousal

Sexual arousal in both men and women comes from psychological as well as physical sources. A person becomes aroused in innumerable ways.

Although most of us recognize the importance of music, perfume, movies, and literature as stimulants, many times we fail to recognize that a powerful source of sexual arousal for men and women is the expression of admiration, affection, and appreciation whereby each partner's "I'm OK" position is reinforced. Words of endearment, compliments of one's attractiveness, and expressions of admiration and appreciation increase an individual's feelings of being sexually attractive and desirable. Most of us hunger to be sincerely appreciated and loved. The verbal expression of affection and admiration not only contributes to a more satisfying sexual relationship, it also adds to a more positive total marriage relationship.

The physical touch can be an effective way of communicating warmth, emotional support, or understanding; it is an important way of providing positive psychological strokes. Physical touch is necessary to the positive emotional, physical, and social development of people. Touching symbolizes the overcoming of human separateness. It is not surprising, then, that the sense of touch is such a powerful medium of communication in the sexual relationship. Touching in the form of stroking, caressing, and kissing is one of the most effective sources of sexual arousal.

Foreplay

Physical touching, or foreplay, has a very important role, particularly for the wife, in contributing to a more pleasurable sexual relationship. Research suggests that a woman's ability to experience orgasm is closely related to the *length* of foreplay before intercourse occurs.[56]

Paul Gebhard [57] reports that three fifths of the women in his study almost always experienced orgasm if foreplay lasted longer than twenty minutes; half, after fifteen to twenty minutes; and two fifths, when the foreplay lasted one to ten minutes. Only 7 per cent never reached orgasm when the foreplay continued for more than twenty minutes.

The importance of foreplay is further substantiated by findings of Kinsey [58] that three out of every four men reach orgasm in less than two minutes after intercourse begins. Many men obtain orgasm within ten to twenty seconds. This is too brief a period of time to bring most women to the peak of sexual enjoyment and to orgasm unless there has been sufficient foreplay. It is a powerful method of sexual stimulation for both men and women.

About Orgasm

So much has been written about orgasm in fiction and nonfiction that some anxiety and unrealistic expectations have been created. Some couples actually become so concerned with achieving orgasm that their sexual satisfaction is decreased.

Orgasm has been memorialized, particularly in fiction, as extremely explosive, and it is this type of experience for many people. Unfortunately, some husbands are disappointed and feel they have failed to arouse their wives sufficiently, or their wives are not sexually responsive if they do not respond in an explosive manner. Some women feel sexually inadequate because they do not respond as intensely as they think they should. Such concern is often unnecessary, as the research indicates that orgasm is for women more often a quieter and less intense experience than described in some fictional works.[59]

ORGASM AND SEXUAL SATISFACTION OF THE WOMAN

Because of the emphasis on orgasm, the impression is often given that the sexual encounter cannot really be satisfying for a woman unless she achieves orgasm. This is false. Many women and men experience a high degree of sexual satisfaction without achieving an orgasm.[60]

Many women do not achieve orgasm every time they have sexual intercourse. Studies show approximately 40 per cent achieve it virtually every time and approximately 10 to 15 per cent never experience orgasm.[61]

MULTIPLE ORGASM

The research of Masters and Johnson indicates that with a sufficient amount and type of stimulation the average woman can experience multiple orgasms.[62] Some women experience as many as twenty consecutive orgasms; however, this is unusual and quite exhausting.

Hopefully, multiple orgasms will not be enshrined, like simultaneous orgasms have been as the "proper goal of all enlightened husbands and wives." [63] Feelings of inadequacy, disappointment, and resentment will inevitably arise if multiple orgasms are considered by the husband and wife as a right or duty. It should be kept in mind that fewer than 15 per cent of all women experience multiple orgasms.[64]

During the adolescent years the male is capable of renewed intercourse and a second orgasm after only a short time following the initial one. The period of time required to achieve a second ejaculation increases as a man grows older. For example, the average man of age thirty-eight will not usually find it quite as easy to have sexual intercourse twice in one night as would an eighteen-year-old.

Only about 6 to 8 per cent of men are able to experience more than one orgasm during a particular sexual encounter. Those men who do have a second orgasm shortly after the first report that the first orgasm is more pleasurable than the second.[65] A man's ability to experience multiple orgasms depends much upon the degree of stimulation his wife provides.

Although the ability to have repeated intercourse decreases as a man ages, this is compensated for in that he has increased ability to control his sexual response. Increased control makes the sexual experience more pleasurable to both the man and the woman.[66]

How Important Is Technique?

Many books concerned with human sexual response emphasize the importance of various techniques in sexual encounter; however, there has been some criticism of an emphasis upon technique. The criticism stems from the belief that an extreme emphasis upon sexual *techniques* actually tends to inhibit spontaneity and results in a mechanical approach to the sexual relationship. A mechanized approach may tend to destroy the romantic element and decrease sexual pleasure. Focusing upon techniques of sexual behavior can lead to a distorted view of sex and sexual relationships. For example, it can result in a couple overlooking the importance of commitment, which—Masters, Johnson and Levin report in *The Pleasure Bond* [67]—is one of the most important factors contributing to a satisfying sexual relationship. A preoccupation with techniques can also lead to the erroneous conclusion that learning the proper techniques will insure a satisfying sexual encounter; but it involves far more than that. Mere sexual technique does not automatically produce a satisfying sexual life.

The quality of the sexual relationship between two individuals is influenced by the quality of their entire interpersonal relationship. The quality of their sexual responses depends upon the degree of mutual commitment, how secure they feel with one another, the degree of emotional support they provide each other, the degree of mutual understanding, empathy, and respect, and even the compatibility of their personalities, values, and cultural backgrounds. The sexual relationship between two persons is, in essence, influenced by the totality of the two individuals.

Sexual technique comprises only a small part of the sexual relationship. However, basic knowledge of various methods of sexual behavior is helpful, and some couples have improved their sexual relationship by learning more effective techniques.

There is no "right" or "normal" way for couples to enjoy each other sexually. There has been an increasing acceptance of the view that whatever provides pleasure and enjoyment to both partners without offending either is satisfactory. Many couples find that experimenting makes their sexual relationships more enjoyable and interesting.

FACTORS INFLUENCING THE CHOICE OF A PARTICULAR SEXUAL LIFE-STYLE

In choosing methods of sexual interaction, such as coital positions, use of oral sexual stimulation, use of erotic clothing, and so on, a couple can use the following criteria:

1. **Psychological Acceptance.** An individual or a couple may find certain forms of sexual interaction unacceptable because of past cultural conditioning. A couple should respond sexually in ways that are psychologically acceptable to both. One partner should not coerce another into an activity about which the other has very strong, negative feelings.

2. **Sexual Pleasure.** Certain sexual activities bring more pleasure to some couples than to others. Some may find the use of erotic literature to be simulating, whereas others may find the same literature repugnant.

3. **Physical Comfort.** Differing body sizes of the partners or special circumstances may make some coital positions impractical or uncomfortable. For example, the male superior position may be uncomfortable late in a pregnancy.

Sexual Behavior and Responsibility

In transactional-analysis terms, it is the *child* in us that often operates in sexual encounters. This is to be expected since the *child* is our fun-loving, pleasure-seeking ego state. Sometimes we have problems because our *parent* ego state fails to give us permission to respond sexually even after marriage. A large number of couples are sexually dysfunctional, not because of physiological problems, but because of psychological barriers. Other problems arise when the *child* dominates the sexual relationship to the extent of being irresponsible and unconcerned with the feelings of others.

As in other aspects of an interpersonal relationship, the *adult* ego state is needed to balance the situation so that each person relates responsibly toward self and others in the sexual relationship. We have tended to think of sex in terms of human plumbing rather than human loving. Most of our sex education has been reproductive education rather than education for sexual responsibility. Relationships are facilitated when persons approach one another with a loving, responsible attitude. Such couples will find that they can bring joy to each other.

References

1. CROSBY, JOHN F. *Illusion and Disillusion: The Self in Love and Marriage.* Belmont, Calif.: Wadsworth, 1973.
2. FOLKMAN, JEROME D., and NANCY M. K. CLATWORTHY. *Marriage Has Many Faces.* Columbus, Ohio: Merrill, 1970.
3. MASLOW, ABRAHAM H. *Motivation and Personality.* New York: Harper & Row, 1954.
4. FOLKMAN and CLATWORTHY, op. cit.
5. Ibid.
6. American Medical Association. *Human Sexuality.* Chicago: American Medical Association, 1972, p. 89.
7. Ibid.
8. AUERBACK, A. "Sex Versus the Late Late Show." *Medical Aspects of Human Sexuality,* vol. 2, 1970, p. 38.
9. KATCHADOURIAN, HERANT A., and DONALD T. LUNDE. *Fundamentals of Human Sexuality.* New York: Holt, Rinehart and Winston, 1972.
10. MASTERS, WILLIAM H., and VIRGINIA E. JOHNSON. *Human Sexual Inadequacy.* Boston: Little, Brown, 1970.
11. KATCHADOURIAN and LUNDE, op. cit.
12. MASTERS, WILLIAM H., and VIRGINIA E. JOHNSON. *Human Sexual Response.* Boston: Little, Brown, 1966.
13. McCARY, JAMES L. *Human Sexuality* (2nd ed.). New York: D. Van Nostrand, 1973.
14. MASTERS, WILLIAM H., and VIRGINIA E. JOHNSON in association with ROBERT J.

LEVIN. *The Pleasure Bond: A New Look at Sexuality and Commitment.* Boston: Little, Brown, 1974.
15. LOBSENZ, NORMAN. "Why Some Women Respond Sexually and Others Don't." *McCall's*, October 1972, p. 86.
16. FOLKMAN and CLATWORTHY, op. cit.
17. SIMON, WILLIAM; ALAN BERGER; and JOHN H. GAGNON. "Beyond Anxiety and Fantasy: The Coital Experiences of College Youth." *Journal of Youth and Adolescence*, vol. I, 1972, pp. 203–222.
18. OFFER, DANIEL. "Attitudes Toward Sexuality in a Group of 1,500 Middle-Class Teen-Agers." *Journal of Youth and Adolescence*, vol. I, 1972, pp. 81–90.
19. SIMON, BERGER, and GAGNON, op. cit.
20. ALSTON, JON P., and FRANCIS TUCKER. "The Myth of Sexual Permissiveness." *Journal of Sex Research*, vol. 9, 1973, pp. 34–40.
21. KINSEY, ALFRED C.; WARDELL POMEROY; CLYDE E. MARTIN; and PAUL H. GEBHARD. *Sexual Behavior in the Human Female.* Philadelphia: Saunders, 1953.
22. Sex Information and Education Council of the United States. *Sexuality and Man.* New York: Scribners, 1970.
23. WEINER, IRVING B. "Perspectives on the Modern Adolescent." *Psychiatry*, vol. 35, 1972, pp. 20–31.
24. Sex Information and Education Council of the United States, op. cit.
25. MCCARY, op. cit.
26. MASTERS and JOHNSON, 1970, op. cit.
27. Ibid.
28. KATCHADOURIAN and LUNDE, op. cit.
29. American Medical Association, op. cit.
30. MASTERS and JOHNSON, 1970, op. cit.
31. MCCARY, op. cit.
32. KINSEY, POMEROY, MARTIN, and GEBHARD, op. cit.
33. American Medical Association, op. cit.
34. MASTERS and JOHNSON, 1970, op. cit.
35. American Medical Association, op. cit.
36. MCCARY, op. cit.
37. Ibid.
38. Ibid.
39. Ibid.
40. "The Chemistry of Love." *Man and Woman: The Encyclopedia of Adult Relationships*, vol. II. New York: Greystone Press, 1970, pp. 189–197.
41. MASTERS and JOHNSON, 1966, op. cit.
42. MCCARY, op. cit.
43. Ibid.
44. "The Chemistry of Love," op. cit.
45. EVERETT, GUY M. "Effects of Amyl Nitrate ("Poppers") on Sexual Experience." *Medical Aspects of Human Sexuality*, vol. 6, 1972, pp. 146–151.
46. COOPER, DONALD L. "Understanding the Drug Menace." *The Bulletin of the Association of Secondary School Principals*, vol. 56, 1972, pp. 53–60.
47. DELEON, GEORGE, and HARRY K. WEXLER. "Heroin Addiction: Its Relation to Sexual Behavior and Sexual Experience." *Journal of Abnormal Psychology*, vol. 81, 1973, pp. 36–38.

48. JONES, HARDIN. "The Deception of Drugs IV." *Clinical Toxocology*, 1971, pp. 129–136.
COOPER, op. cit.
49. JONES, op. cit.
50. COOPER, op. cit.
51. Ibid.
52. Ibid., p. 55.
53. KATCHADOURIAN and LUNDE, op. cit.
54. MCCARY, op. cit.
55. MCCARY, JAMES L. *Human Sexuality.* New York: Van Nostrand, 1967, p. 310.
56. American Medical Association, op. cit.
57. GEBHARD, PAUL H. "Factors in Marital Orgasm." *Medical Aspects of Human Sexuality*, vol. 2, 1968, pp. 22–25.
58. KINSEY, ALFRED C.; WARDELL POMEROY; and CLYDE E. MARTIN. *Sexual Behavior in the Human Male.* Philadelphia: Saunders, 1948.
59. American Medical Association, op. cit.
60. Ibid.
61. Ibid.
62. MASTERS and JOHNSON, 1966, op. cit.
63. American Medical Association, op. cit., p. 99.
64. Ibid.
65. MCCARY, 1973, op. cit.
66. "The Chemistry of Love," op. cit.
67. MASTERS, JOHNSON, and LEVIN, op. cit.

12 Family Planning

Photo by David Tomlinson

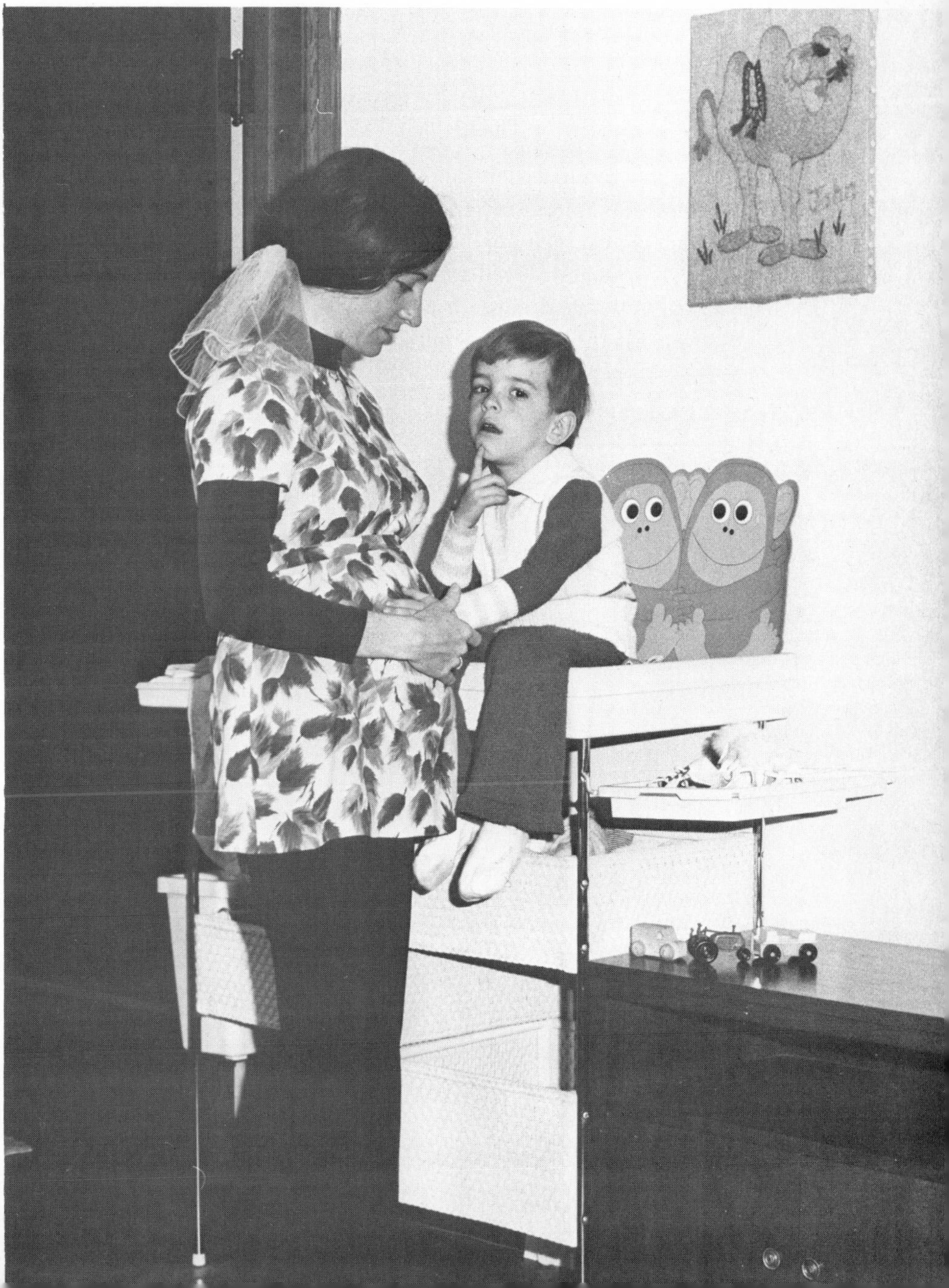

Bringing another into the world is a serious act and once done sets the stage for life's most important work—the nurturance and molding of a life.

Jonathan Bach

Smaller Families

Few issues have received more emphasis during recent years than family planning. This emphasis has been because of concern about world population and the desire that couples plan their families in a manner that maximizes their chances for happiness. The result has been a reduction in the number of children per family. The annual birth rate declined from over seven children per woman in 1800 to slightly over two in 1975. The number of births per 1,000 population has

Figure 12-1 Crude Birth Rate Since 1940

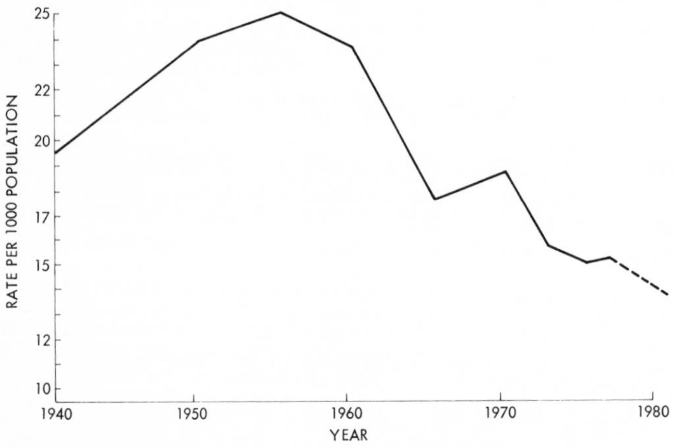

BIRTH RATE PROJECTION TO 1980 BASED ON DATA FROM 1970–1975.

From *Statistical Abstract of the United States, 1975,* 96th ed. (Washington, D.C.: U.S. Bureau of Census, 1975); Births, Marriages, Divorces, and Deaths for March 1975 in *Monthly Vital Statistics Report,* Vol. 24, No. 3 (Rockville, Md.: Division of Vital Statistics, National Center for Health Statistics, Public Health Service, May 27, 1975).

decreased from 19.4 in 1940 to 15 in 1975.[1] The expectation now is for small families. Approximately 73 percent of young wives in the United States (ages eighteen to twenty-four) in 1974 expected to have no more than two children.[2]

Family planning involves several important decisions: when to have a child, how many children to have, how far apart to space the children, what form of contraception to use, and even whether or not to have children. These decisions have enormous impact upon a couple's family life.

Voluntary Childlessness

A large number of couples in the United States are voluntarily choosing not to have children.[3] Why do couples decide to remain childless?

CONCERN ABOUT THE POPULATION PROBLEM

A growing number of couples who choose not to have children are concerned about the world population problem. This concern has removed much of the negative stigma from childlessness that formerly existed. Couples feel freer now to make this choice and are convinced it is the best way they can help the population problem.

CONCERN WITH OTHER WORLD PROBLEMS

Some couples are distressed about world conditions. One young husband stated:

> The world is in such a mess. There is the constant threat of wars and famines. We seem to be moving more toward a "dog-eat-dog" and "hurry up" type of society. Everybody's looking out for number one and not concerned about the welfare of others. I just can't see bringing a child into this type of world. I don't think it would be fair to the child.

OCCUPATIONAL INVOLVEMENT

Some couples become so involved in their jobs, they have little time for anything else. They attach top priority to their careers and decide against having children because they are not willing to give them the time and attention they need.

> Look, what kind of life could we give a child? My wife and I both spend eight hours a day on the job. Then, we bring work home in the evenings and average about two hours each evening on the take-home work. It's very important to us that we advance in our work. To achieve success, we have to spend this kind of time. I don't think we would change much if we had a child and that would be a lousy deal for a kid.

DESIRE TO MAINTAIN THE CHILDLESS LIFE-STYLE

Some couples enjoy their interaction with each other so much, they do not wish to make any major changes in their life-style. They prize freedom and mobility. They enjoy being able to take a trip at a moment's notice or being able to devote their full attention to each other. In short, they value highly their life together as a couple and do not wish to have their life-style changed by the birth of a child.

WISH TO AVOID THE RESPONSIBILITY OF HAVING CHILDREN

There are a few couples who look upon having children as an awesome responsibility. They do not feel adequate to meet it or simply do not wish to assume such a responsibility. One wife has stated:

> When I think about bringing another human life into the world and having a great influence on the way that life develops, it scares me. I just don't think I'm ready for that kind of responsibility. I feel like I have a lot of personal problems to work out and a lot of maturing to do before I would be ready to take on the responsibility of rearing a child. I may never be ready for it.

Much of the fear of assuming the responsibility for children may be caused by an overemphasis in the mass media on the influence of parents upon children and all the wrong things parents do to them. Obviously, parents exert great influence upon children, but they are not the only influence. Too much emphasis on what parents do wrong has resulted in some couples' being reluctant to become parents.

UNSUITED TEMPERAMENTALLY

There are individuals unsuited temperamentally to have children. They may become easily irritated and tense in their presence; therefore, some couples decide to remain childless.

Involuntary Childlessness

Many couples are childless but not by choice. An estimated half to two thirds of childless marriages are because of sterility. Each year approximately 150,000 newly married couples face sterility.[4]

Usually, the cause of infertility is not found entirely in the husband or wife. Medical research indicates that in most infertile, or sterile, marriages, some evidence of infertility is shown by both husband and wife. At least one third of the causative factors are in the husband. For example, approximately 50 per cent of the wives who sought assistance at Wister Institute in Philadelphia became pregnant upon receiving artificial insemination by a donor other than the husband.[5]

Causes of Involuntary Childlessness

Approximately 10 per cent of all couples are unable to have children.[6] Involuntary childlessness may have a number of causes, some of which can be remedied.

Tension and Anxiety. Conception can sometimes be prevented by a woman's excessive anxiety and tension, which may cause spasms that block the Fallopian tubes. This may explain why some women who have been unable to conceive for years and who adopt a child become pregnant later. It is possible that by becoming involved with the adopted child the woman relaxes. The relaxation may open the Fallopian tubes previously blocked by spasms.[7]

Blocking of Fallopian Tubes. Besides tension, the Fallopian tubes may be blocked because of disease, infection, or injury. When the Fallopian tubes are closed, sperm are unable to meet the ovum and, as a result, fertilization does not take place.

Glandular Malfunctioning. Some failures in glandular functioning can cause infertility. Although fertilization has occurred, implantation of the embryo in the uterine wall may be hindered by glandular malfunctioning.[8]

Failure to Ovulate. A woman's failure to ovulate is a basic cause of inability to conceive. If ova are not produced, then conception cannot take place. Some research indicates that many women who have difficulty conceiving normally ovulate in less than half of their menstrual cycles. Some of these women ovulate only three or four times during a period of one year. Women who are normally fertile ovulate during approximately eight out of ten menstrual cycles.[9]

Inadequate Production of Sperm. Failure to conceive may be caused by a man's insufficient production of sperm. Many men do not produce sperm either in sufficient amount or of vigorous enough quality. Extreme lack of vitamin A is frequently associated with poor quality of sperm. Lack of vitamin E can result in sperm not being produced at all. If vitamin E deficiency is prolonged, the testes can permanently lose their ability to produce sperm.[10]

Genetic Incompatibility. Sometimes a particular couple may have sex cells (ova and sperm) that are incompatible; therefore, the sex cells destroy each other and prevent conception.

Extreme Acidity of the Woman's Genital Tract. A woman's genital tract may be too acid for sperm to survive. Although the genital tract is normally acid, when the level is particularly high and if the sperm are not very vigorous, conception can be prevented.[11]

Environmental Factors. Certain environmental factors may contribute to infertility. High altitudes and very warm temperatures sometimes cause infertility among persons who are not accustomed to the climate.[12]

Gonorrhea. Gonorrhea can cause sterility. The Fallopian tubes are frequently scarred and sealed by untreated gonorrhea. When this happens, conception can never occur because no remedy for sterility resulting from the disease is known.

Other Causes of Infertility. Any condition that impairs healthy functioning of the body may decrease fertility. Several such conditions include poor nutrition, insufficient rest, obesity, insufficient exercise, constitutional diseases, infections, blood incompatibilities, anemia, tuberculosis, syphilis, irritating contraceptives, excessive use of tobacco, drugs or alcohol, overwork, improper development of sex organs, and hormonal disturbances.[13]

Treating Infertility

Approximately 50 per cent of all couples accomplish pregnancy within one month of regular sexual intercourse without using any contraceptive practices, and more than 75 per cent within six months of regular sexual intercourse without contraception.[14] Couples who fail to achieve pregnancy may be subject to primary or secondary infertility. Primary infertility is involved when conception has never occurred. Secondary infertility is when conception takes place followed by stillbirth or miscarriage that leaves the couple childless.

A couple, desiring children, who have engaged in sexual intercourse without any form of contraception for one year and have not achieved a pregnancy should seek professional help.[15] Fortunately, almost 75 per cent of the couples experiencing infertility today are probably able to have children through professional assistance.[16] There are some effective methods of helping childless couples achieve pregnancy.

INTRODUCING SEMEN DIRECTLY INTO THE UTERUS

Research has shown that in some couples infertility is caused by the husband's sperm being inactivated through some lethal factor when introduced in the wife's vagina.[17] This is the case when a woman's genital tract is more acid than normal. Treatment involves introducing the husband's semen through the cervix directly into the uterus. Many women receiving this treatment have become pregnant. This procedure is referred to as AIH, or artificial insemination where the husband serves as the donor. AID refers to the procedure where semen from a donor other than the husband is used. Several thousand babies have been born in the United States by means of artificial insemination.[18]

STORING UP THE HUSBAND'S SUPPLY OF SPERM

The physician, after completing a sperm count, may find that a major reason for a woman's difficulty in conceiving is an insufficient supply of sperm from the husband. A count of 100,000,000 sperm per cubic centimeter of semen represents the average count; a count of less than 60,000,000 is generally considered inadequate for fertilization.[19]

If the sperm count is insufficient, the physician may recommend that the husband abstain from sexual activity for at least three days before the wife's fertile period begins. By abstaining, the husband's supply of sperm is stored up and the probability of having a sufficient count during the fertile period is increased.

HORMONE THERAPY

The woman's pituitary gland governs the production of ova and determines her fertile period. Hormones from the pituitary gland stimulate the ovaries to release ova. Infertility can be caused by a lack of pituitary hormones, which results in the ovaries not being stimulated to release ova. Such cases have been successfully treated by hormone therapy. Chemicals are prescribed by the physician to stimulate the pituitary gland to produce the needed hormones. Sometimes, after such treatment multiple births result; some women have had as many as seven births from one pregnancy. The survival rate of the infants in such cases is very low. Researchers anticipate that hormone therapy can be regulated in the future so that multiple births will be minimized or eliminated.[20]

The use of oral contraceptives (the pill), besides helping couples avoid pregnancy, has also made a contribution in overcoming infertility. Research with oral contraceptives and the use of steroid hormones reveals that women who stop taking the pill are more likely to become pregnant. The use of the pill or steroid hormones helps women achieve pregnancy by stimulating the ovaries and increasing ovulation. It also helps achieve pregnancy by identifying the expected time of ovulation. The primary purpose of research with steroid hormones had been to stabilize the menstrual flow more closely to the twenty-eight-day cycle in order to assist couples who wanted to use the rhythm method of birth control.[21]

IDENTIFYING THE PERIOD OF OVULATION

Conception is most likely to occur if the husband and wife have sexual intercourse during the fertile period. This is the time during the woman's menstrual cycle shortly before ovulation, during ovulation when the ovum starts its way through the Fallopian tubes toward the uterus, and shortly after ovulation. Generally, the ovum lives only approximately twenty-four hours after ovulation unless fertilization occurs. Because the sperm usually lose their potency after about forty-eight hours, fertilization is most likely to occur if sexual intercourse takes place within the period from two days before ovulation to one day following ovulation. The fertile period lasts only about three or four days.

The difficulty in identifying a woman's fertile period lies in pinpointing the time of ovulation. Most women ovulate fourteen to sixteen days before their next menstrual period is due. Thus a woman with a twenty-eight day menstrual cycle usually ovulates on about the thirteenth to fifteenth days (the day that menstruation begins is counted as the first day of the cycle). However, many women have menstrual cycles of lengths other than twenty-eight days. The woman with a thirty-day cycle would most likely ovulate between the fifteenth to seventeenth days of her cycle.

Because the exact day of ovulation is difficult to determine, a couple wishing to increase their chances of conception by sexual intercourse during the fertile period should allow several days before and after the most likely time of ovulation.

Figure 12-2 Menstrual Cycles of Varying Lengths Showing Most Probable Times of Conception

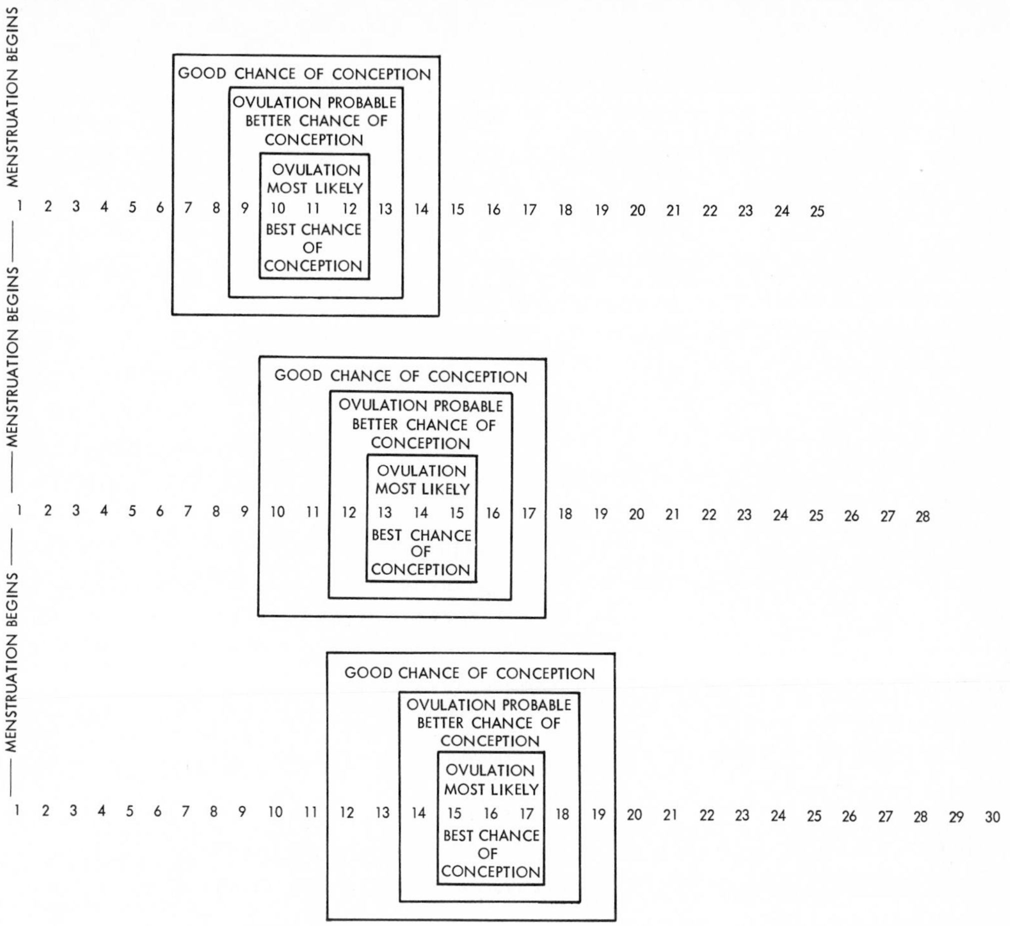

Although this entire time would not be the fertile period, it would be a more probable time for conception.

Several medical methods that help couples identify a woman's particular time of ovulation are great aids in achieving pregnancy. One method a woman may determine the day of ovulation is by taking a daily temperature reading because body temperature tends to rise at the time of ovulation. This is not completely reliable, however, as an increase in temperature may not always indicate that ovulation has begun. Another more accurate method is a urine test by which the exact day of ovulation can be identified.

The physician can also identify the day that ovulation begins for a particular woman by doing a vaginal smear. This involves taking small samples of skin cells from the wall of the vagina or the uterus each day and observing the changes in the cells as the month progresses. Within about two months, the physician can identify the day that ovulation begins.[22]

REMOVAL OF FALLOPIAN TUBE OBSTRUCTION

Pregnancy is sometimes prevented because a woman's Fallopian tubes are blocked due to a physical reason. After conducting medical tests to determine if the tubes are blocked, surgery may be performed to remove the tubal obstruction. For many couples this has resulted in pregnancy.

Birth-Control Methods

The only effective way to control family size is to practice some form of contraception. The search for the ideal birth-control method continues, because the perfect method has not yet been found. The ideal method would be 100 per cent effective and reliable, have no side effects, be easy and convenient to use, would not interfere with sexual enjoyment, and be inexpensive. Presently, there are ten major ways of controlling unwanted births.

STERILIZATION

Surgical sterilization is the surest and most effective form of birth control and is relatively inexpensive. In fact, it is, in the long run, the least expensive method. And it does not interfere with sexual enjoyment or desire.

It has one disadvantage that accounts for the fact it is not used more often. Reversal of sterilization is very difficult and uncertain. For this reason, a person considering surgical sterilization should think of it as practically an irreversible operation. Individuals considering this form of birth control usually give the question much serious thought before making the final decision.

There are two types of sterilization. Sterilization of the man is called a vasectomy and sterilization of the woman is called a tubal ligation.

Vasectomy. A vasectomy requires an incision into the scrotum, then the vas deferens (the tubes that carry seminal fluid from the testes to the urethra) are cut on each side. As a result of cutting these tubes, the sperm are prevented from being ejaculated. The operation is very simple and involves little discomfort. It is performed under local anesthesia and takes only from seven to fifteen minutes. There is no need for hospitalization and the man does not normally have to lose any time from his job. It is a relatively inexpensive operation, costing approximately $100 to $200 to perform.

A vasectomy does not interfere with sexual pleasure or desire. The man continues to ejaculate fluid during intercourse after the operation just as he did before. The amount of semen produced is not noticeably changed. The only difference is that there are no sperm in the fluid.

Vasectomies are becoming more accepted as a form of birth control. Of the more than 1,000,000 sterilization operations now performed annually, most are vasectomies.

The major disadvantage is that reversing the operation may not be possible. Some successful reversal operations have been accomplished, but the success rate is low. The search continues for more effective ways that the vasectomy can be reversed.

Many doctors are reluctant to perform the vasectomy because of the possibility that a man may later change his mind and wish to have children. To deal with this possibility, some cities have established sperm banks in which the husband may store his sperm before the operation. This serves as a precaution in case he should later change his mind and desire to father another child. His wife could then be given his sperm through artificial insemination.[23]

There is a small possibility that the vasectomy will fail to prevent conception. (Failures are more frequent for vasectomies than for female sterilization). Failure is usually because the man is unaware that for approximately *one month* after the vasectomy he should assume he is fertile and practice some form of contraception, which should not be discontinued until a physician has examined the semen a few weeks later and found that it contains no sperm. The reason for this is that when the vas deferens are cut, they already contain some sperm, which is later released during sexual intercourse. There may be enough of these sperm to impregnate someone during sexual intercourse for several weeks after the vasectomy.[24]

One study of 330 couples, in which the husband had undergone a vasectomy, found that most of the couples felt the vasectomy had been beneficial to their sexual relationship and to their marriage adjustment. Most of the couples reported a greater frequency of sexual intercourse. Major reasons for the improved sexual relationships seemed to be elimination of the fear of pregnancy and decrease in conflict and tension concerning the use of unsatisfactory contraceptives.[25]

A similar study was conducted in Japan with couples in which one partner had been sterilized some years previous to the study. The majority of the couples indicated that their sexual activity had not decreased. In fact, a large proportion reported that their sexual activity had increased since the operation.[26]

Tubal Ligation. A tubal ligation is a more serious and complicated operation than the vasectomy. The tubal ligation requires hospitalization and is considerably more expensive because it involves opening the abdominal cavity of the woman in order to tie and then cut each of the Fallopian tubes. By cutting the Fallopian tubes, the woman becomes unable to conceive because the ova no longer reach the uterus.

Laparascopy. Laparascopy is a rather new method of sterilizing the woman that does not require hospitalization. Under general anesthesia, an incision of about one half inch is made approximately two inches below the navel and a second incision approximately six inches below the first. Thus, women who are concerned about scars need not fear this surgical procedure. A flexible instrument is introduced into each of the Fallopian tubes. The instrument electrically cauterizes (mildly damages by heat) the interior of the tubes. In response to the electrical cauterization, the tubes form scar tissue and seal themselves. In this manner passage of ova down the tubes is prevented.[27]

Female sterilization is very effective and failure is extremely rare. It has no effect upon a woman's sexual activity or enjoyment; neither are the production of female hormones changed in any way. The disadvantages of female sterilization are that it is a relatively serious operation and there is presently no way to reverse it.

THE PILL

Oral contraceptives have become a popular form of birth control in a relatively short period of time. More than twelve million women now use them. With the exception of sterilization, this is the most effective method of birth control. When taken properly, oral contraceptives are almost 100 per cent effective in preventing pregnancy. The effectiveness lies in giving doses of the female hormones that would be present during pregnancy, thus preventing ovulation. Two major types of oral contraceptives are manufactured: these are the combined pill and the sequential pill.

The *combined pill* contains two female hormones, estrogen and progesterone, combined in synthetic form. The pattern for taking this pill is that the woman takes the first one on the fifth day following the onset of menstruation, then takes one pill each day for twenty successive days. The next menstrual period begins about three days after the last pill is taken. After menstruation, the pattern is repeated.

The *sequential pill* involves taking estrogen and progesterone separately in sequence. Again, the woman begins taking the pill on the fifth day of the menstrual cycle. Estrogen is taken for fifteen successive days followed by five days of taking progesterone. The woman taking the sequential pill is not protected against pregnancy during the first seven days of the *first* cycle, but fewer side effects are experienced than with the combined pill.[28]

Birth-control pills continue to be improved. More recent pills contain less hormones and, therefore, cause fewer side effects. One of these is the "minipill," which is taken every day without a break and contains only a small amount of progesterone. However, the minipill is not as effective as the other birth-control pills described.

Another oral contraceptive developed in recent years is called the "morning after" pill. It should be used only for emergency situations when other methods have been neglected. The first "morning after" pill should be taken within forty-eight hours after sexual intercourse. These pills are taken twice a day for five days in order to prevent a pregnancy.

The effectiveness of birth-control pills depends upon the routine of taking them, which should not be broken. If a woman forgets to take the pill one day, she should use some other form of contraception *for the rest of the month* to insure the prevention of pregnancy.

Although oral contraceptives are a very effective method of birth control, they do have certain undesirable side effects anyone considering their use should be aware of. These side effects have been greatly reduced since birth-control pills were first introduced; however, many women still experience side effects even with the improved pills. Some of the symptoms are nausea, breast tenderness, cramps, weight increase (generally from water retention), "break-through" bleeding, and an increased tendency to get vaginal infections. Some women also experience migraine headaches and severe emotional depression. The pill may cause visual disorders, strokes, and sometimes can stop bone growth if taken before the woman is physically mature.

Birth-control pills offer no protection against venereal disease. The evidence indicates that women taking the pill are more likely to contract venereal disease when exposed than are women not taking the pill. One reason is that oral contraceptives reduce the acid level in the genital tract and, as a result, create a more favorable environment for venereal infection. The current epidemic of venereal disease is partially because the pill is now used more often than the condom, which provides the best protection against venereal infection.[29]

One of the most serious side effects of the pill is that it may cause blood clots. Pill users are about four to seven times more likely to develop blood clots and about eight times more likely to die as a result of a blood clot lodging in a vital organ than are women not taking the pill.

The question still remains as to whether oral contraceptives increase the incidence of cancer in women who are predisposed to cancer. Some researchers believe that the hormones in birth-control pills speed the growth of an existing cancer in some women, whereas in others they actually inhibit the growth of an existing tumor. Much is still unknown about the relationship of the pill to cancer.

Women with the trait for sickle-cell anemia have been warned not to use the pill because it might increase the chance of developing blood disorders. Approximately ten per cent of all black persons have the sickle-cell trait.[30]

The pill's potential for causing such a variety of side effects is that use of it involves a woman's entire hormone balance. The pill prevents ovulation each month by suppressing the pituitary gland. The hormones in the pill influence the endocrine system in a similar manner as a pregnancy does. In some ways, taking the pill simulates a perpetual state of pregnancy. It is not surprising, then, that some of the minor side effects are similar to symptoms experienced during the first three months of pregnancy. These symptoms disappear for most women within a few months after starting the use of oral contraceptives.

The majority of women, approximately 80 per cent, experience little or no side effects. In fact, some women seem to feel better emotionally and physically as a result of using the pill. However, about 20 per cent of the women who take birth-control pills experience side effects in such intensity, they do not continue their use.

After evaluating all of the available research on the pill, the Pure Food and Drug Administration in 1970 required that all manufacturers of oral contraceptives include this warning on each box of pills:

> The oral contraceptives are powerful, effective drugs. Do not take these drugs without your doctor's continued supervision. As with all effective drugs, they may cause side effects in some cases and should not be taken at all by some. Rare instances of abnormal blood clotting are the most important known complications of oral contraceptives. These points were discussed with you when you chose this method of contraception. While you are taking these drugs, you should have periodic examinations at intervals set by your doctor. Tell your doctor if you notice any of the following: 1. Severe headache; 2. Blurred vision; 3. Pain in the legs; 4. Pain in the chest or unexplained cough; 5. Irregular or missed period.

The pill will continue to be a popular form of birth control because it is effective, does not interfere with sexual intercourse in any way, and most women experience no serious side effects. Researchers continue to work on the development of a birth-control pill that will have no side effects for anyone.

INTRAUTERINE DEVICES

The intrauterine device, although not quite as successful as the pill, is an effective method of contraception and in recent years is increasing in popularity.

Failure rates reported for the IUD range from 0.50 per cent to a high of only 2 per cent. In other words, it is 98 per cent effective.[31]

The IUD is a small device made of plastic or metal, or a combination of the two. A physician inserts it into the woman's uterus. It usually does not need to be removed for a year or more unless the woman wishes to become pregnant.

Many people believe that the IUD approaches being the perfect form of contraception. In addition to being very effective, it is simple to use, inexpensive, and once successfully inserted, it may remain in the uterus for an indefinite period of time.

The IUD does have some disadvantages. Some women experience side effects, such as cramps, bacterial infection, and excessive bleeding. Bleeding occurs among approximately 6 per cent of IUD users. Another disadvantage is that the IUD sometimes falls out or is expelled; and it can be expelled without a woman being aware of it. This primarily occurs among younger women who have not yet given birth to a child. Therefore, many physicians advise against the use of the IUD by women who have not yet had a child.

If pregnancy does happen to occur, the IUD cannot be removed without causing an abortion. This normally presents no problem, however, as the IUD is usually expelled from the uterus at the same time as the placenta. If it is not spontaneously expelled, the device is removed manually.[32]

One of the most serious disadvantages of the IUD is that it sometimes pierces or perforates the uterine wall at the time of insertion. This is relatively rare, but when it does happen it is serious. Great care by the physician to be certain the IUD is properly inserted, and inserting the device during menstruation, minimize the possibility of perforating the uterine wall.[33]

The IUD is not a contraceptive method that all women can use. Some do not wish to use it because they object to having a foreign object placed in their bodies. Generally, the IUD is not recommended for women who:

1. May already be pregnant.
2. Have a pelvic infection or disease.
3. Have an abnormality of the uterus.
4. Have a history of very painful or very heavy menstrual periods.
5. Have cancer of the uterus or cervix.
6. Have never been pregnant.

Research continues to perfect the IUD and eliminate its side effects and disadvantages. New IUD's are being developed that do not expel as easily as the earlier ones. This form of contraception will probably continue to become more widely accepted in the future as a growing number of women are reluctant to use the pill.[34]

THE DIAPHRAGM

The diaphragm is a flexible rubber dome about two inches in diameter. The specific size of the diaphragm is determined through a fitting by a physician. It is inserted at the upper end of the vagina and fitted over the cervical opening to prevent semen from entering the uterus. The most effect diaphragms are coated with a spermicidal cream, foam, or jelly to provide additional protection. The diaphragm is inserted before intercourse and removed several hours after.

The diaphragm is a relatively effective method of birth control. It is successful approximately 95 per cent of the time. Other advantages are that it is inexpensive, does not interfere with sexual intercourse, and has few side effects.

There are certain disadvantages associated with the diaphragm. Among them are as follows:

1. The diaphragm may become displaced from its proper position during sexual intercourse.
2. The internal anatomy of some women is not suitable to holding the diaphragm in proper position.
3. The woman must learn how to insert the diaphragm, and sometimes both she and her husband doubt her efficiency in this respect.[35] The entire responsibility for preventing pregnancy is placed upon the woman.
4. Many women dislike placing any foreign object in their bodies.
5. Some women have allergic reactions to the rubber dome or the spermicidal cream used with the diaphragm.

CONTRACEPTIVE CHEMICALS

Chemicals are also used as a means of contraception. Contraceptive chemicals include spermicidal jellies, creams, foaming tablets, aerosol foams, and suppositories. All of these are available without prescription in drugstores. Contraceptive chemicals prevent conception by killing the sperm before they can penetrate the cervix to the uterus. The chemicals must be inserted into the vagina before each act of sexual intercourse.

Suppositories are the least effective of the contraceptive chemicals, whereas aerosol foams are reported to be the most effective. Foams lose their effectiveness after a certain period of time. Therefore, if sexual intercourse is repeated several hours after the application of foam, another application would be needed. Failure to take such precautions contributes to some of the failures of this method.[36]

Jellies, creams, foaming tablets, and suppositories have the disadvantage of uneven distribution within the vagina and external dripping that many couples find annoying. There are a few side effects with contraceptive chemicals. Many women as well as men find the particular chemical they are using to be irritating. In such cases a burning sensation may be experienced during and after sexual intercourse.

Perhaps the major disadvantage of contraceptive chemicals is that even the most effective of them cannot be expected to be 100 per cent successful. The reason for this is the difficulty of getting the chemicals in contact with all of the sperm before the sperm enter the cervix and swim into the uterus where there are no spermicidal chemicals. Because of this disadvantage, it is a good practice to combine the use of a contraceptive chemical with a mechanical device such as a diaphragm, which covers the neck of the uterus and prevents the entrance of any sperm not killed by the chemical.[37]

THE RHYTHM METHOD

The rhythm method involves determining the time during the menstrual cycle when conception is most likely and then avoiding sexual intercourse during that time. Ovulation occurs once in each menstrual cycle, and for the majority of women there is a period of about three days at the time of ovulation during which the ovum can be fertilized.[38]

As mentioned earlier in the section on treating infertility, there is considerable variation in the time when ovulation may occur and in the length of menstrual periods. Because of this variability, women using the rhythm method are urged to keep accurate records of their menstrual cycles for twelve consecutive months. They may then determine the time when they are most likely to conceive in the following way: subtract nineteen from the number of days in the shortest menstrual cycle to obtain the number of safe days in the first half of the menstrual cycle; then subtract eleven from the number of days in the longest menstrual cycle to get the number of safe days in the last half of the cycle. For example, Mary's records indicate that during one year, her longest menstrual cycle was thirty days and her shortest was twenty-six days. She calculates this way: $26-19=7$; thus from the first day of her menstrual cycle to the seventh day is considered a safe time. She then calculates this way: $30-11=19$; this indicates that from the nineteenth day of her menstrual cycle until the next menstruation begins is a safe time. From the seventh day of her cycle to the nineteenth day is the time when conception is most likely to occur. Sexual intercourse is avoided during this time.[39]

To be more certain about their time of ovulation, women using the rhythm method are often advised to take their temperatures daily and to keep a temperature chart to identify when their period of ovulation begins. However, one difficulty is that an increase in temperature may be caused by other factors, such as an infection. There is some evidence that the temperature method is reliable about 50 per cent of the time.

Major disadvantages of the rhythm method are

1. It is very difficult if not impossible to be absolutely certain when ovulation begins. Irregularities in ovulation can be caused by illness or emotional stress. Sexual intercourse sometimes stimulates ovulation.[40]
2. It is an extremely unreliable method for women who have irregular periods.
3. It has a higher than desirable failure rate (15 per cent) among women who have regular periods.[41]
4. For all women, with both regular and irregular periods, the rhythm method has a very high failure rate (30 per cent).[42]
5. The rhythm method is practically useless for a long period of time following childbirth. There may be no menstruation at all for a few months, and when menstruation does start again, the cycle may be irregular for a time. The cycle may also be different from the earlier one. Irregular menstrual cycles may also be caused by emotional excitement, travel, or illness.[43]
6. It places all of the responsibility for birth control upon the woman.

DOUCHING

The douche has long been used as a way of preventing pregnancy. Its popularity has greatly declined since the 1930s, and it is now used by only about 15 per cent of women.[44] Douching involves washing sperm from the vagina immediately following sexual intercourse. A mildly acidic solution such as three tablespoons of vinegar per quart of water is used for the washing and is designed to kill any remaining sperm. Douching solutions are also available in drugstores without prescription.

It is among the least reliable contraceptive methods. It is usually used too late and is, in general, ineffective. The cervix is not reached, and by the time the woman douches, sperm may easily have entered the cervical opening.

Douching also has a psychological disadvantage in that it must be done immediately after sexual intercourse. This tends to interrupt the emotional relationship following sexual intercourse. Another disadvantage of douching is that the natural fluids of the vagina may be destroyed if it is done too often or if a harsh solution is used.

Douching is not a desirable contraceptive method. However, it may be helpful as an emergency measure when a woman has reason to believe that another method has failed, such as the tearing of a condom. Douching is also used by some women for hygiene purposes.

WITHDRAWAL

Withdrawal is one of the oldest methods of contraception and is practiced today by many couples. The man simply withdraws just before ejaculation takes place so that no sperm are released into the vagina. It has the advantage of not requiring any chemicals, gadgets, or advance preparation.

The major disadvantage of withdrawal is that it is very unreliable because a man cannot always accurately anticipate when he will ejaculate and, therefore, frequently does not withdraw soon enough. Another reason for the ineffectiveness of this method is that often there is a leakage of semen before ejaculation, particularly when intercourse is prolonged, which may result in impregnation.[45]

Withdrawal before ejaculation requires much will power by the man and is not conducive to complete relaxation and pleasure. It has the added disadvantage of being psychologically unsatisfying for many couples.

CONDOM

The condom is a widely practiced and effective method of contraception. When good quality condoms are properly used, they are approximately 99 per cent effective.[46]

The condom is a thin sheath made of rubber or animal membrane that fits over the erect penis. Condoms may be purchased without prescription in drugstores. When ejaculation occurs, the sperm is retained in the condom and prevented from entering the vagina.

The condom is not acceptable to some because it disrupts the spontaneity of foreplay and reduces sensitivity in the man. However, many men who wish to delay ejaculation find the dulled sensitivity to be an advantage. Also, condoms are the only method of birth control that provides any protection against venereal disease.

ABORTION

Abortion has been increasingly used during the last ten years as a method of preventing the birth of an unwanted child. The demand for abortions has increased as a result of the ruling by the United States Supreme Court, on January 22, 1973, which granted women the right to have medical abortions during the first six months of pregnancy. Abortion is not a contraceptive method and is not desirable as a *regular* form of birth control. Contraceptive methods prevent conception, whereas abortion eliminates a life that has already begun. It is expensive and there is evidence that a woman's health may be endangered by repeated abortions.

If an abortion is performed, it is best when done as soon as possible after conception. It becomes far more dangerous to perform after the first three months of pregnancy. Twice as many mothers die from legal abortions as from childbirth, even when the abortion is performed during the first three months of pregnancy.

Spontaneous abortion, or miscarriage, is a natural type of abortion that usually occurs to eliminate an embryo which is not developing as it should. Some reasons for the inadequate development of the embryo may be improper implantation in the uterine wall or defective sperm or ovum.

Abortions induced by a physician may be performed in order to protect the health and life of the mother, because there are indications that the fetus is defective, or because the woman does not wish to have the child for personal reasons. The reason most often given is the woman's mental health.[47] The typical abortion patient is unmarried, pregnant for the first time, and under twenty-five years of age.[48] Abortion as a method of birth control is, of course, effective in that it prevents the birth of the child.

There are many women for whom abortion is an unacceptable alternative. Many choose to give birth to an unplanned child rather than have an abortion. As one woman who was pregnant by a man she was not going to marry said:

> I thought about it a lot. People have told me "It's your body. You have a right to get an abortion if you wish." But I've decided it's really not my body. It's the baby's body that would be killed. I feel I don't have a right to take away that life. I wouldn't take away a child's life after it's born. To me, the child is no less alive while it's still in the womb. I'm not sure what I will do with my baby after it's born. But I do know that giving birth to my child is the only alternative for me.

There are four basic methods of abortion: suction, D and C, saline injection, and a hysterotomy.

Suction Method. The majority of abortions in the United States and Canada are performed by this method. The suction method is done under local anesthetic injected around the uterine cervix. A vacurette, or sterile tube, is then inserted through the vagina into the uterus until it touches the amniotic sac, at which point the fetus is sucked away from the uterine wall into the tube. The suction method may be used up to twelve weeks after conception. This method is the most desirable to use if possible because the danger, complications, and expense are minimized.

D and C Method. This method is used between twelve and fourteen weeks after conception and involves the dilation of the cervix and the use of a curette (a spoon-shaped instrument) to scrape the uterine lining. The fetal material is then removed by suction. There is more danger of perforation of the uterine wall and hemorrhage with this than with the suction method and an overnight hospital stay is customary.

Saline-Injection Method. The saline-injection method, sometimes referred to as "salting out," is usually performed between fourteen and sixteen weeks after conception. It involves injecting a salt solution into the amniotic sac. The fetus is poisoned by the salt and dies. The salt solution induces labor and the fetus is usually expelled within twenty-four to thirty-six hours.[49] This method usually requires more than an overnight stay in the hospital.

Hysterotomy. A hysterotomy is actually a Caesarean section abortion and is major surgery. An incision is made in the lower abdomen and then in the uterine wall, after which the fetus and placenta are removed.

A hysterotomy is the most dangerous of the four methods of abortion that have been discussed and requires a hospital stay of several days. It is also the most expensive. A major disadvantage is that sometimes future deliveries must be done by Caesarean section because the hysterotomy leaves a weakened area in the uterine wall that will not withstand the stress of labor.

NEW CONTRACEPTIVE METHODS

Some promising new contraceptive methods are now being researched and introduced on a limited basis. The Food and Drug Administration, for example, has approved a drug for limited use as an injectable contraceptive. But it is not available to the general public and is primarily being used with women who have difficulty using other contraceptives successfully. The injection remains effective for three months. Research is being done concerning the relationship of this drug to infertility. The evidence to date suggests that most women can become pregnant after terminating use of the injectable contraceptive, but only after several months have elapsed.[50]

Research is also being conducted on a new contraceptive for men. This new method consists of taking a pill daily combined with a monthly injection. The research evidence indicates that the sperm count does not return to normal until several months after the injection is discontinued.

Spacing of Children

One important aspect of family planning that has received much less attention than limiting the number of children born is the spacing of children. Many couples believe that it is best to have children within a one- to two-year period of each other. Others believe that it is better to have wider spacing of children. There are no absolutely right or wrong ways to space children, but there are certain advantages and disadvantages to consider.

Many couples believe that an advantage of having their children within a one- to two-year period is that the children will have greater companionship and do more things together as they grow up because they are closer together in age. Another perceived advantage is that the parents complete their child-rearing roles in a shorter period of time if the children are spaced close together.

There are some major disadvantages of close spacing of children (within a one- to two-year period). Close spacing is associated with higher rates of infant mortality, prematurity, and brain damage to the child.[51] Medical reports indicate that it takes a woman approximately two years to fully recover after the birth of a child. If a second child is born within this time period, it may place a strain upon the mother's physical health. In addition, a pregnant woman's health may be taxed by having to lift, carry, bathe, and chase a toddler.

Close spacing also has some disadvantages for the children. Although they have the advantage of being playmates, the chances of sibling rivalry are greater. Close spacing also makes it more difficult for each child to receive all the necessary attention.

There are also possible disadvantages to spacing children very far apart. When children are spaced as far apart as eight years, the youngest child may actually assume the role of an only child. In such an instance where there are only two children, both the younger child and the older sibling are deprived almost completely of any sibling companionship.

It is impossible to state the optimal time between children. However, many family-life specialists believe that an interval of approximately three years seems to be most advantageous. The children are still close enough in age to be able to enjoy doing several things together. And sibling rivalry is reduced in that the older child may be better able to understand and accept a new family member. Also, the age differences mean fewer demands on the time of parents, allowing them to give each child more attention. For example, a two-year-old and an infant would *both* be in diapers. This would be avoided by an age difference of three or more years.

References

1. U.S. Bureau of Census. *Statistical Abstract of the United States, 1975*. 96th ed. Washington, D.C., 1975.
   Division of Vital Statistics, National Center for Health Statistics. "Births, Marriages, Divorces, and Deaths for March 1975." *Monthly Vital Statistics Report*, vol. 24, no. 3, May 27, 1975. Rockville, Md.: Public Health Service.
2. U.S. Department of Commerce. "Fertility Expectations of American Women: June 1974." *Current Population Reports*. Series P-20, no. 277, February 1975. Washington, D.C.: U.S. Government Printing Office.
3. U.S. Bureau of Labor Statistics. *Special Labor Force Report*, no. 153. Washington, D.C.: U.S. Government Printing Office, 1973.
4. LANDIS, JUDSON T., and MARY G. LANDIS. *Building a Successful Marriage*. Englewood Cliffs, N.J.: Prentice-Hall, 1973.
5. MURPHY, DOUGLAS P. "Donor Insemination—A Study of 511 Prospective Donors." *Fertility and Sterility*, vol. 15, 1964, pp. 528–533.
   LANDIS and LANDIS, op. cit.
6. American Medical Association. *Human Sexuality*. Chicago: American Medical Association, 1972.
7. GREENBLATT, BERNARD R. A *Doctor's Marital Guide for Patients*. Chicago: Budlong Press, 1964.
   FOLKMAN, JEROME D., and NANCY M. K. CLATWORTHY. *Marriage Has Many Faces*. Columbus, Ohio: Merrill, 1970.
8. LANDIS and LANDIS, op. cit.
9. Ibid.
10. FOLKMAN and CLATWORTHY, op. cit.
11. LANDIS and LANDIS, op. cit.
12. FOLKMAN and CLATWORTHY, op. cit.
13. BASSETT, WILLIAM T. *Counseling the Childless Couple*. Englewood Cliffs, N.J.: Prentice-Hall, 1963.
14. American Medical Association, op. cit.
15. Ibid.
16. LANDIS and LANDIS, op. cit.
17. BRECHER, RUTH, and EDWARD M. BRECHER. *An Analysis of Human Sexual Response*. New York: Signet Books, New American Library, 1966.
18. American Medical Association, op. cit.
19. FOLKMAN and CLATWORTHY, op. cit.
20. LANDIS and LANDIS, op. cit.
21. Ibid.
22. GREENBLATT, op. cit.
23. LANDIS and LANDIS, op. cit.
24. HARDIN, GARRETT. *Birth Control*. Indianapolis: Pegasus, 1970.
25. LANDIS, JUDSON T., and THOMAS POFFENBERGER. "The Marital and Sexual Adjustment of 330 Couples Who Chose Vasectomy as a Form of Birth Control." *Journal of Marriage and the Family*, vol. 27, 1965, pp. 57–58.
26. HARDIN, op. cit.
27. Ibid.

28. Folkman and Clatworthy, op. cit.
29. Landis and Landis, op. cit.
30. Ibid.
31. American Medical Association, op. cit.
32. Ibid.
33. Ibid.
34. Landis and Landis, op. cit.
35. Blood, Robert O. *Marriage.* New York: Free Press, 1969.
36. Rossman, Isadore. *Two Children by Choice.* New York: Parents' Magazine Press, 1970.
37. Hardin, op. cit.
38. Pierson, Elaine C. *Sex Is Never an Emergency.* Philadelphia: Lippincott, 1973.
39. McCary, James L. *Human Sexuality* (2nd ed.). New York: Van Nostrand, 1973.
40. Pierson, op. cit.
Folkman and Clatworthy, op. cit.
41. Hardin, op. cit.
42. Ibid.
43. Ibid.
Folkman and Clatworthy, op. cit.
44. Williamson, Robert C. *Marriage and Family Relations.* New York: Wiley, 1972.
45. Pierson, op. cit.
46. Hardin, op. cit.
47. Duffy, Edward A. *Effects of Changes in State Abortion Laws.* U.S. Department of Health Service Publication, no. 2165, February 1971, pp. 1–28.
48. Tietze, Christopher, and Sarah Lewit. "Early Medical Complications of Legal Abortion." *Population Council: Studies in Family Planning,* vol. 3, 1972, p. 97.
49. Pierson, op. cit.
50. "Injectable Contraceptive Approved for Limited Use." *What's New,* April 1974.
51. Ramos, Suzanne. "Planning Ahead." *New York Times Magazine,* November 14, 1971.

13 Pregnancy and Birth

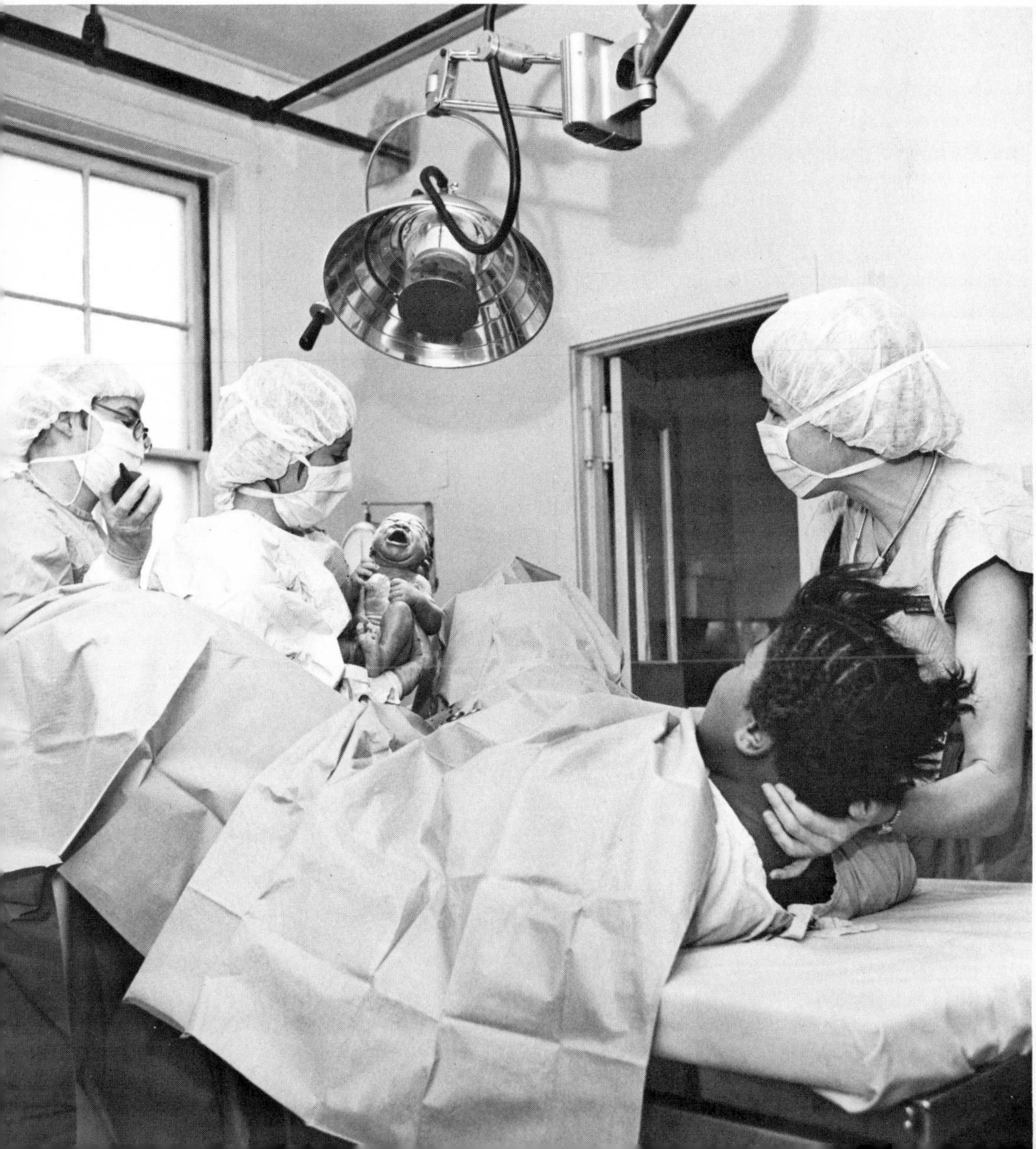

Photo courtesy of The National Foundation/March of Dimes

It sometimes happens, even in the best of families, that a baby is born. This is not necessarily cause for alarm. The important thing is to keep your wits about you and borrow some money.

Elinor Goulding Smith

An Important Decision

One of the most important decisions that a woman or a couple can make in life is to have a baby. Most of us wish to have children because they bring us happiness. However, not all people desire children. But even with improved methods of birth control, all pregnancies are not planned. A single woman, for example, who has an unwanted pregnancy has several options available. She may choose to terminate the pregnancy by abortion. She may also choose to continue the pregnancy. After birth of the child, she may keep the child or allow the child to be adopted.

Generally, the same alternatives are available for a couple with an unwanted pregnancy. However, very few couples choose to allow their child to be adopted. Most couples with an unwanted pregnancy seem inclined to choose abortion or to go through with the pregnancy and keep the child. Quite a few couples come to terms with their objections to having a child and accept their new family situation. Some even change their minds completely and want the child very much by the time the baby is born.

No greater responsibility can be assumed than to conceive and bring a new life into the world. Although having a child is a great responsibility, it can also be one of the greatest pleasures in life if the child is wanted and if the parents are prepared physically, financially, and emotionally.

Why Do Couples Wish to Have Children?

Many pregnancies are believed to be unplanned; however, a common view among psychiatrists is that pregnancy is seldom accidental.[1] It can be very important and helpful for a couple to ask themselves, "Do we truly want to have children?" and "*Why* do we want children?" Among the common reasons are the following:

1. *To love, nurture, and guide another human being to adulthood.*
2. *To have someone who will love the parent.*
3. *To have someone who will be dependent upon the parent.* As a result of this dependency, the parent becomes important to the child. Each one of us has a strong psychological need to be important to someone. Parenthood fulfills this need for many.
4. *To fulfill the expectation of society.* There have been in the past, and still are today, such strong pressures for married couples to have children that few question whether they will have children or not. Pressures influence the decision to have children to a greater extent than most of us realize. Because of societal expectations, many couples who do not want children and who are not emotionally suited for parenthood literally drift into it.
5. *To prove virility or femininity.* Many people view having children as a manifestation of their sexuality. Parenthood for them becomes a symbol of prestige.
6. *To provide grandchildren for the couple's parents.* Some couples feel they must have children so that their parents can enjoy grandchildren. Even in the absence of overt pressure, couples may, nevertheless, perceive that their parents desire grandchildren and begin to feel guilty about being childless. Although this influences many couples to have children, it is an unsound reason for parenthood if it is the only reason.
7. *To carry on the family.* Some people want to have children so that their family will not end with their death, believing strongly that if they do not continue the family by giving birth to children, they are "letting down" their ancestors. They may also derive a sense of immortality, feeling that they continue to live through the lives of their children. Children become their passport to the future.
8. *To provide a playmate and companion for an only child or for themselves.*
9. *To compensate for an unsatisfying marriage.* Some individuals have a baby in order to fill an empty marriage, believing that the baby will provide them the opportunity to give and receive affection, love, and companionship that they lack in marriage. Others have a child hoping that the child will cure an ailing marriage and bring the husband and wife closer together. Sometimes a marriage experiencing major problems is brought closer together with the coming of a child. However, more often the advent of a child only further complicates a troubled marriage.
10. *To create a human life.* We all have a strong need to be creative and to see the result of our creation. Having a baby is one way of expressing this need to create. For many individuals, the miracle of pregnancy and birth is a most satisfying form of creation.

11. *To obtain attention and care.* Some women enjoy being pregnant as a time when they are dependent upon others and when others provide them with extra attention. Some women who are not receiving enough attention and whose dependency needs are not being met may choose pregnancy as a way of fulfilling these needs. Although these women wish to be pregnant, they may not actually wish to have and rear a child.[2]

The Best Time to Have a Child

With improved birth control methods, a couple can choose the time and circumstances in which to have a child. Certain conditions increase the probability that the development of the child will be positive:

1. *When the health of both husband and wife is good.* Good physical health, of course, helps to insure that the parents have the necessary strength, endurance, and energy to rear a child.
2. *When there are few or no genetic problems in the family histories of both husband and wife.* This helps to insure that the child will be born with no birth defects.
3. *When both husband and wife are prepared emotionally, financially, and intellectually for the child.* Periods of great emotional stress are not the best times for pregnancy and can adversely affect the unborn child. A couple with adequate financial resources and occupational stability before having a child will find their situation easier.[3]
4. *When the mother is between the ages of twenty-five and thirty-five.* Maternal age is related to some birth defects and mental retardation in the child. Generally, very young women (under twenty) and older women (over forty) have greater chances of bearing retarded or defective children. The highest proportion of mentally retarded children are born to teen-age mothers. The danger of mental retardation increases with each successive birth during the teen years. A mother who gives birth to two children before the age of twenty is six times more likely to have a child with a defect than a mother whose second child is born when she is at least halfway through the third decade of life. A forty-year-old woman is ten times more likely to have a mongoloid baby than a twenty-five-year-old woman.[4]
5. *When the child is wanted by both husband and wife.* It is tragic for the child and the parents when a child is unwanted. Every child who is born has a right to be wanted. A wanted child has a much greater chance of receiving the love, care, and attention that every child needs. Also, when the child is wanted, the parents are much more likely to be happy and well adjusted than when they have an unwanted one.

Symptoms of Pregnancy

When a woman conceives, it is important that she know she is pregnant as soon as possible. Being aware of the pregnancy very early allows the woman, her husband, and the physician to provide the best possible prenatal care. A woman who knows or suspects she is pregnant should always inform any physician treating her for any illness, as it may influence the kind of treatment she receives. For example, certain antibiotics should not be used during pregnancy and dental or chest X rays can damage the fetus.

There are several symptoms of pregnancy. The signs are of two types: presumptive and positive. Presumptive symptoms are those signs of pregnancy exhibited by the mother. However, presumptive symptoms are not definite indications of pregnancy and can be symptoms of other conditions. Usually, however, a combination of presumptive symptoms represents a strong indication of pregnancy. Positive symptoms of pregnancy are those exhibited by the baby and represent definite evidence of pregnancy.

PRESUMPTIVE SYMPTOMS

Missing a Menstrual Period. Failure to menstruate is generally the first indication of pregnancy. A woman who is usually regular in her menstruation period may consider a delay of ten or more days to be rather strong evidence that she is pregnant. It should be remembered, however, that failure to menstruate can also be caused by various other factors, such as emotional upsets, or excitement, illness, thyroid disturbances, severe anemia, malnutrition, and climatic changes. Some women continue to menstruate a few times after conception, although the flow is usually less than normal.

Breast Changes. Pregnancy may be indicated by certain changes in the breasts, such as enlargement of the breasts, increased size of nipples, increased tenderness, and a tingling sensation. Also, an increased blood supply to the mammary glands may make the blood vessels more visible.

Nausea. Many women experience nausea when their first period is overdue. Research shows that approximately 50 per cent of pregnant women experience some nausea.[5] This nausea is usually due to biochemical changes in the body. The common pattern appears to be the experencing of nausea during the morning, hence the term *morning sickness.* Most of the nausea is mild. Medication usually relieves it, and most often it disappears in approximately eight weeks.

Fatigue and Need for Extra Sleep. Because of the many physical changes taking place, a woman may very often exhibit fatigue and a need for extra sleep during pregnancy.

Increased Frequency of Urination. Pregnancy may be signaled by a greater frequency of urination. The enlarged uterus increases pressure upon the bladder and produces the sensation of needing to urinate more often.

Increased Size of Abdomen. One of the more obvious signs of pregnancy is an increase in the size of the abdomen. The expanding uterus causes a slight bulge in the lower portion of the abdomen, which is noticeable late in the third month or early in the fourth month.

Increase in Basal Body Temperature. The body temperature of a person upon waking in the morning is referred to as basal body temperature. Basal body temperature increases during pregnancy. A temperature level of 98.8 to 99.9 degrees that is maintained for a period of more than sixteen days is highly indicative of pregnancy. Diagnosis of pregnancy based on body temperature is accurate 97 per cent of the time.[6]

Changes in the Vagina and Cervix. Certain changes in both the vagina and cervix suggest pregnancy. Vaginal secretions increase and the vaginal lining becomes congested and bluish in color. The cervix is firm in the nonpregnant state. There is a softening of the cervix during pregnancy.

POSITIVE SYMPTOMS

Movement of the Fetus. A positive and dramatic sign of pregnancy is when the mother can feel the fetus move within her. Fetal movements usually become noticeable during the fourth or fifth month of pregnancy.

The Fetal Heartbeat. Another positive sign of pregnancy is the fetal heartbeat. It can be detected as early as the tenth to the twelfth week after the last menstrual period. The heartbeat of the fetus varies from 120 to 160 beats per minute, which is approximately twice the mother's normal heartbeat.[7]

Seeing the Fetus by X Ray. The pregnancy may be positively confirmed by taking an X ray of the fetus. The X ray is used relatively late in the pregnancy after other symptoms have appeared and is, therefore, usually unnecessary. However, X rays are sometimes made in order to assist in the diagnosis of multiple births or to determine the size of the fetus's head in comparison to the opening in the mother's pelvis.[8]

Feeling the Shape of the Fetus. The shape of the fetus can be felt through the abdominal wall by a physician at about the fifth month.

Laboratory Tests. Very early diagnosis of pregnancy can be made with great accuracy through the use of various laboratory tests. Some chemical tests diagnose pregnancy as early as ten to fourteen days following the first missed menstrual period. These laboratory tests have a high degree of accuracy, although each does involve a small margin of error.

Stages of Prenatal Development

The creation of a new life is a miraculous phenomenon. The development of this new life is characterized by three stages: the fertilization-implantation period, the embryo period, and the fetal period.

THE FERTILIZATION-IMPLANTATION PERIOD

The fertilization-implantation period begins with conception and extends through the second week of life when implantation has occurred. Conception happens the moment the sperm of the man unites with the ovum of the woman. This meeting usually takes place in one of the Fallopian tubes. At the time of ovulation, the mature ovum travels to the uterus through the Fallopian tube. For most women ovulation occurs fourteen to sixteen days before the next menstrual period is due. (See Figure 12-2 on page 251.) The sperm that unites with the ovum is one of approximately 500 million contributed by the father. Conception must occur within approximately twenty-four hours of ovulation or the ovum will not be capable of being fertilized.[9]

After fertilization has occurred, the ovum begins to grow by cell division. It is now called a zygote. The zygote continues down the Fallopian tube to the uterus. It is approximately the size of a pin head by the time it reaches the uterus.

The zygote is unattached and moves freely during the first week of life. Implantation occurs on about the tenth day after fertilization. Implantation is the important process in which the zygote attaches itself to the wall of the uterus. By attaching itself in this manner, the developing zygote can obtain nourishment from the mother through the blood vessels in the uterine wall.

THE EMBRYO PERIOD

The embryo period extends from the end of the second week to the end of the second month. The embryo, as the unborn baby is called during this period, undergoes extremely rapid development and growth. All of the important external and internal features of a human being appear by the end of the embryo stage. For example, fingers and toes are well formed and all facial features are present by the end of this period. By the end of the third week, the heart begins to function.

There is an increase in size of approximately 2,000,000 per cent from the time of fertilization to the end of the embryo period. The body of the embryo is about 1½ to 2 inches long and weighs approximately two thirds of an ounce by the end of the embryo period.[10]

In addition to the embryo itself, special structures designed to protect and nourish the baby until it is born also develop during the embryo period. These important structures include the placenta, the umbilical cord, and the amniotic sac.

The placenta develops from the mass of threadlike structures the zygote sent into the uterine wall to obtain nourishment. The placenta is the organ that transports nutrients from the mother to the embryo and wastes from the embryo to the mother. It also serves as an endocrine gland that produces hormones essential to the maintenance of pregnancy, such as progesterone and estrogen. The placenta reduces its production of progesterone and estrogen just before delivery and thus plays a role in initiating labor.[11]

The umbilical cord is the connecting link between the placenta and the embryo. The umbilical cord attaches to the placenta at one end and to the embryo's abdominal wall at the other. The cord eventually grows to a length of 10 to 20 inches, which makes fetal activity and freedom of movement possible.

The amniotic sac is a water jacket, or bag, within which the embryo develops. In addition to containing the embryo, it also contains a watery fluid called amniotic fluid. The amniotic sac serves the important function of protecting the embryo from injury.

THE FETAL PERIOD

The fetal period is the longest of the three prenatal periods. It extends from the end of the second month to birth. Much growth and development occur during this period but no new features appear. At four months, the fetus has gained half of what its length will be at the time of birth. Internal organs are well developed by the fifth month.

The fetus reaches the age of viability by the sixth or seventh month, which means that it has a chance to survive if born at this time. By the sixth or seventh month, the nervous system of the fetus has developed sufficiently to be able to function independently of the mother.[12]

Influences upon Prenatal Development

The best way parents can help to insure successful prenatal development of the child is to provide the best possible environment in which the child lives before birth. The most critical period of prenatal development is the first three months because it is during this period that all the structures of the body are formed. This is why *early* diagnosis of pregnancy and prenatal care by a physician are urged. The prenatal environment is extremely important to the development of the child. The genes a child inherits are substantially affected by the prenatal environment with respect to what the given set of genes will produce. Whether a child comes into the world well prepared to make satisfactory adjustments determines to some extent whether the child matures into an emotionally and socially well-adjusted person. Certain factors have been identified as having the greatest influence upon prenatal development.

MATERNAL EMOTIONS

The emotional state of the mother during pregnancy can influence the developing baby in various ways. Emotional disturbances in the mother are associated with increased fetal activity. Very active fetuses tend to weigh less at birth than do less active fetuses. More active fetuses tend to have greater than average postnatal adjustment difficulties. It is interesting that two-and-a-half-year-old children who were hyperactive fetuses express conspicuous shyness, greater anxiety in response to aggression, and apprehensiveness in social contacts.[13] Mothers who have experienced prolonged, strong emotional upsets during pregnancy are likely to have infants with gastrointestinal disturbances such as diarrhea and regurgitation, excessive crying, and frequent irritability.[14]

Mothers experiencing severe emotional stress during pregnancy from such sources as marriage conflict or death of a loved one are more likely to have a mongoloid or mentally retarded child.[15] Extremely high degrees of emotional tension and stress during pregnancy increase the possibility of deformity or infant death.[16]

Emotional disturbance among pregnant women has been found to be associated with pregnancy and birth complications. For example, there is a higher frequency of premature births, stillbirths, and miscarriages among women who experience severe emotional stress during pregnancy.[17] Prolonged pregnancy and labor are more often experienced by mothers with a high degree of anxiety.[18] Women who have delivery-room difficulties are more likely to have experienced anxiety during pregnancy.[19]

The research evidence clearly indicates the importance of a woman avoiding prolonged periods of emotional disturbances, such as depression or anxiety, during pregnancy. A happy, contented, relaxed pregnancy may contribute immeasurably to the physical and mental health of the baby. It is very desirable that the husband and other family members be considerate, understanding, and affectionate toward the expectant mother and do everything possible to contribute to her happiness and well-being, not only for her sake, but for the baby's health as well.[20]

NUTRITION

Few things are more important to the development of the unborn child than the mother's nutrition. Nourishment for the unborn child must come from the maternal bloodstream, and it is, therefore, essential that the mother's diet contain the necessary nutritional elements.

A woman in good nutritional condition before she becomes pregnant is very fortunate since she is in a position to provide the best possible environment for her baby from the very beginning. Nutritional deficiencies are difficult to correct during pregnancy as the demands upon the body are increased in order to nourish the baby as well as the mother.[21] A lifetime of bad nutrition cannot be remedied overnight; however, a woman who is pregnant or is planning a pregnancy can develop good eating habits that will benefit her and the baby.

What are some of the effects of inadequate nutrition during pregnancy upon the child? Research evidence indicates that extreme malnutrition of the mother during pregnancy results in the child's developing such physical problems as rickets, general physical weakness, cerebral palsy, epilepsy, and extreme nervousness.[22] One of the most common causes of fetal death is prolonged malnutrition during pregnancy.[23] Severe malnutrition has been found to be associated with premature births, stillbirths, miscarriages, congenital defects, illness during infancy, and small size.[24]

Malnutrition can seriously affect the growth and size of the fetal brain as well as other organs.[25] Various research studies show that extreme malnutrition during pregnancy is associated with a reduction in the intelligence of the child. For example, a study of mothers with extreme protein deficiencies during pregnancy revealed that their children at four years of age had significantly lower IQ scores than did children whose mothers had normal amounts of protein.[26] A deficiency of vitamin B in the mother's diet during pregnancy is associated with lower levels of intelligence during the early years of life. Many children who have difficulties in school have experienced unfavorable prenatal environments largely as a result of maternal malnutrition.[27]

The probability of malnutrition during pregnancy is highest among teen-age mothers. The reason is that adolescent girls tend to have the poorest diet of any age group in America. Their desire to be slim and the popularity of snacks such as potato chips and soft drinks are possible explanations.

Many women are quite concerned about weight gain during pregnancy. The average optimal gain during pregnancy is eighteen to twenty-four pounds. This can be analyzed in the following way:

Weight of:	
Average baby	7 lbs.
Placenta	1 lb.
Amniotic fluid	2 lbs.
Increased weight of uterus	2 lbs.
Increased breast tissue	2 lbs.
Excess water	6 lbs.
Total	20 lbs.

Much depends upon the weight of the woman before pregnancy. Thin women and younger women tend to gain more, whereas heavier women tend to gain less in pregnancy. This is certainly not a time for women to try to lose weight. Extreme restriction of calories can be harmful to both the baby and the mother.[28]

When vitamin deficiencies occur, they can have adverse effects on either the baby or the mother, or both. A sufficient nutritional intake is very important during pregnancy. A well-balanced diet should include protein from lean meats or fish; milk, cheese, and eggs; whole grains or cereals; fresh fruits and vegetables. Women concerned about weight gain may select lower-calorie protein sources such as fish and poultry, use skim milk, and substitute fresh fruits for high-calorie desserts or snacks. Most physicians prescribe iron and/or calcium supplements.

INFECTIOUS DISEASES

Infectious diseases such as German measles (rubella), syphilis, or gonorrhea if contracted during the early months of pregnancy are particularly damaging to the unborn baby. These diseases can cause mental deficiency, stillbirths, miscarriages, blindness, or deafness. For example, studies of German measles in the Baltimore-Washington area indicated that over 50 per cent of the women who contracted German measles during the first three months of pregnancy had either handicapped infants, miscarriages, or stillbirths.[29]

RH BLOOD INCOMPATIBILITY

Incompatibility between the Rh blood types of the mother and baby has been found to cause stillbirths, miscarriages, brain damage, and anemia. The difficulty arises when the mother's blood is Rh negative and the fetus's blood Rh positive. When this incompatibility occurs there is one chance in ten that some of the fetus's red blood cells will be destroyed. If some of the red blood cells are destroyed, the fetus responds by producing antigens that pass through the placenta into the mother's bloodstream. The mother's body then produces antibodies that pass back through the placenta to the fetus's blood. This results in the problems already mentioned: anemia, miscarriage, or stillbirth.[30] Usually there is no problem with the first pregnancy because time and exposure to fetal antigens are required for the mother to build up a sufficient level of antibodies to damage the fetus.

Couples in which the wife has an Rh negative and the husband an Rh positive blood type are the only couples for which the Rh blood incompatibility is a concern. The Rh blood factor is genetically controlled by one pair of genes. Rh positive is a dominant trait and Rh negative is recessive. Proper prenatal care requires blood typing for the mother and would detect an Rh negative blood type. If the mother is Rh negative, then the father's blood type must be determined to ascertain the probability of Rh blood incompatibility between the mother and the baby.[31]

Medical science has greatly reduced the problems of Rh incompatibility. Following the birth of an Rh positive baby, it is possible to give the mother an injection of a special gamma globulin that prevents her from developing her own permanent antibodies. This reduces the risk of damage to future babies. This injection must be given after the birth of each Rh incompatible baby and is *not* effective for mothers who have already developed antibodies in a previous pregnancy. It is possible for the physician to check periodically the antibody level in the mother's bloodstream during pregnancy. If the antibody level begins to get high late in the pregnancy, labor may be induced to prevent or minimize damage to the unborn child. Babies suffering from Rh difficulties can also be protected by intrauterine transfusions and complete blood exchange at birth.

X-RAY EXPOSURE

The expectant mother should avoid being exposed to X rays early in the pregnancy. The fetus is not likely to be affected by X rays when they are used lightly at the end of pregnancy. However, when a woman is exposed to X rays of great strength early in the pregnancy, the effects on the fetus are likely to be severe. Among the most common adverse effects on the fetus are microcephaly, which is a form of mental deficiency accompanied by a small pointed head, malformations, stillbirths, miscarriages, and decrease in birth weight.[32]

DRUGS

The expectant mother should only take drugs or medication prescribed by her physician. Several drugs are, of course, harmless, but many drugs can be very damaging to the unborn baby.

Extensive use of barbiturates during pregnancy may interfere with the oxygen supply to the brain of the fetus and result in brain damage. Barbiturates may also produce asphyxiation. The tranquilizer thalidomide, which was used to treat morning sickness during the early stages of pregnancy, caused thousands of tragic birth defects in England, Germany, and Canada. It produced malformations of the baby's arms and legs. Large doses of quinine during pregnancy can cause deafness.

Babies of heroin-addicted mothers who have heroin withdrawn from them shortly before birth are themselves born with withdrawal symptoms. The central nervous systems of these babies are affected. They lack quiet-sleep patterns. They have greater variability in their heart rates and also have more rapid eye movements. These babies usually recover from their withdrawal symptoms within three days.[33]

Other drugs that can cause congenital abnormalities are:

> Oral progestrogens, androgens, estrogens, cortisone acetate (cortogen acetate), potassium iodide, propylthiouracil, methinaxole (tapazole), lophenonixic acid (teridos), sodium aminopterin, methotrexate (amethopterin), chlorambucil (leukeran), bishydroxycoumarih (dicumerol), ethyl bicoumacetate (tromexam ethyl acetate), sodium warfarin (coumadin sodium, panwarfin, prothromadin), salicylate (large amounts of aspirin), streptomycin, sulfonamides, chloramphenicol (chloromyctin), sodium novobiocin (albamycin sodium, cathomycin sodium), erthromycin (ilosone), nitrofuratoin (furadentin), tetracyclines, Vitamin K (in excess), ammonium chloride, intravenous fluids (in excess), peserpine (ranloydin, raurine, rau-sed, recerpoid, saudil, serfin, serpasil, serpate, vio-serpine), hexamethonium bromide . . . morphine . . . sulphonylurea derivatives, Phanformin hydrochloride (DBI), phenothiazines, meprobiamate (Equanil, Meprospan, Meporotabs, Miltown), Chloroquine phosphate (aralen phosphate), Vaccination (smallpox or influenza), antihistamines, Thiazide diuretics.[34]

SMOKING

There is evidence that smoking tobacco—which contains a powerful narcotic poison—during pregnancy increases the possibility of having a premature birth or a baby of low birth weight.[35] The prematurity rate for women who smoke is about twice as high as for women who do not smoke. Women who are heavy smokers (more than ten cigarettes each day) show the highest rate of premature births, women who are light smokers (one to ten cigarettes each day) have a lower rate of premature births, and nonsmokers show the lowest rate of all. Smoking by the mother during the last six months of pregnancy is followed by an increase in the heart rate of the fetus.[36]

Ashley Montagu notes it is possible that

> . . . the products of tobacco entering the embryonic and fetal circulation adversely affect not only the heart and circulatory system, but also many other organs. The increase in cardiac and circulatory disorders in recent years may not be unconnected, in part at least, with the smoking of pregnant mothers.[37]

ALCOHOL

The consumption of alcohol during pregnancy, even a moderate amount, results in decreased quantities of milk secretion by the mother.[38] With the introduction of any chemical, such as alcohol, into the mother's bloodstream, accommodation by her biological mechanisms also imposes a burden upon the fetus because it depends upon the mother's bloodstream for nourishment. When the burden becomes too great, there are certain danger signs, such as irregular heart action, wakefulness, and nervousness. If the mother's body is adversely affected by alcohol or any other chemical, the fetus is also likely to be damaged. Alcohol can adversely affect the fetus if the father drinks, even though the mother may not. Alcohol consumed by the father tends to weaken the sperm.[39]

ENDOCRINE DISORDERS

Certain endocrine disorders during pregnancy can have negative effects on the fetus. An extreme endocrine imbalance can cause mongolism and microcephaly. Extreme thyroid deficiency during pregnancy can result in cretinism in which the cartilage and bones of the fetus fail to develop, the stomach becomes large and protrudes, and the intellectual development is severely impaired.[40] It is very important for a woman to obtain a thorough physical examination as soon as she suspects that she is pregnant so that any such endocrine disorders may be detected and corrected as early as possible.

AGE OF THE MOTHER

As was noted earlier in the chapter, the age of the mother can be an important influence upon the development of the unborn child. The optimum age for pregnancy generally seems to be between the ages of twenty-five and thirty-five. There is a higher frequency of birth defects, miscarriages, stillbirths, and premature births among mothers below the age of twenty and over the age of thirty-five. Before the age of twenty the woman's reproductive system is not yet fully matured and the production of hormones necessary for reproduction has not yet reached optimum levels. Women past the age of thirty-five are more likely to experience endocrine imbalance and as a result are more likely to produce a damaged child.[41] The highest frequency of mongoloid chilren are born to mothers past the age of forty. The probability of having a mongoloid baby before the age of thirty is one in 1,000, whereas at the age of forty, the probability is one in 100.[42]

Labor and Birth

Pregnancy and the prenatal development of the child culminate with birth approximately 266 days after conception. Certain changes take place in the mother a few weeks before birth in preparation for delivery. One of these changes is that the fetus drops to a lower position in the mother's abdomen approximately three or four weeks before delivery. Another change in the mother that prepares her for delivery is the dilation and softening of the cervix. Just before labor begins, there is usually a small, slightly bloody discharge caused by the expelling of the plug of mucus that has been blocking the opening of the cervix. The amniotic membranes enclosing the fetus break during labor in order to make the delivery possible. However, in approximately 10 per cent of pregnant women these membranes burst before labor begins. This is signaled by a flow of amniotic fluid from the vagina. Labor usually starts within twenty-four hours after these membranes have ruptured. If labor does not begin approximately within this period of time, there is a risk of infection and the mother needs to be hospitalized for observation.[43]

STAGES OF LABOR

The work the mother does in giving birth to the child is called labor. True labor starts with regular uterine contractions that dilate the cervix. There are three stages of labor.

First Stage of Labor. The first stage of labor is the longest and involves the mouth of the uterus (cervix) opening until it is wide enough for the baby to pass through. The diameter of the opening is approximately four inches when the cervix is completely dilated.

The cervix is composed of a band of circular muscles that are potentially elastic and capable of stretching when the head of the baby is ready to pass through. If the mother is extremely tense and fearful, these circular muscles tighten and block the passage of the baby, which, in turn, causes more pain for the mother.

Relaxation is helpful during this stage of labor, as it enables the muscles of the cervix to relax. In addition to general relaxation, slow and deep breathing can help the baby rotate into position for delivery through the pelvic opening.[44]

The first stage of labor averages about fifteen hours in the first pregnancy, and only about eight hours in later pregnancies. After the first pregnancy, subsequent deliveries are generally easier in all respects.[45]

Uterine contractions during the first stage begin at time intervals as far apart as fifteen or twenty minutes. Usually, the initial contractions are not strong enough to be painful. The time intervals get closer as delivery approaches and the uterine contractions occur with greater frequency, regularity, and intensity. At her physician's direction, the woman usually goes to the hospital where she will be admitted to a labor room for the duration of this first stage of labor.[46] Medication can be given to relieve discomfort as the contractions intensify.

Second Stage of Labor. During the second stage of labor the woman is brought to the delivery room. Her husband may be allowed to be present in the delivery room, depending upon the judgment of the physician, wishes of the couple, policy of the hospital, and laws of the state.

The second stage continues from the time that the cervix is completely dilated until the baby is delivered. This stage may last a few minutes or a few hours. The average length of time for the second stage is an hour and a half for the first baby. The time is only half as long for the second baby.[47]

Any anesthetic to be used for the actual birth is given as the second stage begins. General anesthesia for childbirth is less widely used than in years past. General anesthesia has the disadvantage of depressing the baby's activity, particularly the respiration rate; it also slows the labor process. Another disadvantage is that because the mother is unconscious, she cannot assist in the delivery.

Using a spinal anesthetic for childbirth is currently considered very desirable by physicians. The anesthetic is injected with a small needle into the spinal canal and produces a temporary loss of sensation below the waist. A desirable advantage of the spinal anesthetic is that the baby is free from anesthetic effects; also, the mother is conscious and can assist in the delivery.[48]

Rhythmic contractions of the uterus during the second stage of labor gradually bring the baby out, a push at a time. The mother can assist by gently bearing down and pushing with her diaphragm, thereby reinforcing the uterine contraction. This type of cooperation speeds the delivery. The baby emerges wide awake if the mother has not had too much anesthesia, and the infant's spontaneous crying enables the breathing process to begin.[49]

Third Stage of Labor. The third stage of labor takes place after the baby has been delivered and is called the afterbirth. This stage involves the necessary expelling of the placenta and membranes. It usually occurs five to fifteen minutes after the baby is delivered and continues for about an hour.

During this stage the physician examines both the mother and baby very carefully. At this time the physician repairs any tears of the perineum (the skin and deeper tissues between the anal and vaginal orifices) that may have occurred during delivery. In order to prevent such tears of the perineum, an episiotomy is routinely performed by many physicians. An episiotomy is a surgical incision of the perineum that is made to facilitate the passage of the infant's head. If an episiotomy has been performed, the physician sews up the incision during this stage. For several days following delivery, these stitches cause discomfort and itching. However, episiotomy incisions usually heal more quickly and with fewer complications than do tears of the perineum.[50]

Natural Childbirth

Natural childbirth, or childbirth with a minimum of drugs, has become increasingly popular in recent years. An effort is made to minimize the discomfort in childbirth by breath control and the use of prescribed exercises that enable the woman to relax her abdominal muscles voluntarily. Natural childbirth is based on the philosophy that a pregnant woman who is well informed concerning what is happening in childbirth can relax, and because of her reduced muscular tension, she can better assist the physician during delivery.

One unfortunate aspect of it is that the term *natural childbirth* may imply that other methods of childbirth are not natural and are not desirable.[51] Some women who choose natural-childbirth techniques feel they have failed if they receive medication to relieve pain. We all have different pain thresholds. Many women respond to natural childbirth very positively; others do not. Some women are better suited emotionally and physically for natural childbirth than others. Any woman considering natural childbirth should carefully consider the advice of her physician.

The Hospital Stay After Delivery

Within twenty-four hours after delivery, the mother is encouraged to get out of bed and obtain a little physical exercise by walking. This revitalizes muscle tone. The mother and baby usually stay in the hospital for three to five days after delivery.[52]

In the past, hospitals customarily have assigned the infant and the mother to separate rooms. Under this procedure the infant stays in a central nursery where only the nursing staff may enter. This has the advantage of relieving the fatigued mother of the responsibility of caring for the baby. However, many mothers strongly wish to have their babies with them. Also, first-time mothers who assume responsibility for much of the child's care from the beginning, with needed assistance from the nurses, gain skill in becoming sensitive in administering to the child's needs.[53]

As an alternative to isolating mother and infant, many hospitals have started rooming-in arrangements. This arrangement places the infant where the mother can observe her baby and have easy access to it at any time. Some hospitals may provide a small nursery next to the mother's room; in other hospitals the baby may be placed beside the mother's bed in a bassinet. The rooming-in arrangement gives the mother the opportunity to give her baby physical affection, cuddling, and nestling. This is important and may lay the foundation for a more secure and happy personality and more positive physical development of the child.[54]

Babies need close physical contact early. There is evidence that the rhythmic sound of the mother's heartbeat is an important influence on the emotional security of the baby. Dr. Lee Salk, a clinical psychologist, used recorded heartbeats with infants in a hospital that required separation of mother and baby. He found that babies who had the heartbeats transmitted to them showed greater regularity and depth in breathing, less restlessness, and cried less than the control babies who were not exposed to the recorded heartbeats. Babies who had difficulty going to sleep were helped by the recorded heartbeats. Babies exposed to the recorded heartbeats also had less feeding difficulties and gained weight better than did the control group.[55]

Feeding the Baby

"Should I breast-feed or bottle-feed my baby?" Numerous women ask this question. Some are undecided even after delivery. How to feed babies has been an issue of much controversy. Only 18 per cent of mothers in the United States are completely breast-feeding their babies. This is a 20 per cent decrease in twenty years.[56]

Many women cannot breast-feed their babies because of physical reasons. Some women do not produce enough milk and some find nursing too painful because of sore nipples. Some do not wish to breast-feed because of psychological reasons. Others prefer to bottle-feed because they feel it is easier and more convenient. Also, bottle-feeding is widely adopted in the United States because of our technological sophistication in producing formulas that are very similar to human milk, and because these formulas can be administered under sanitary conditions.[57]

Research studies indicate that breast-feeding has some advantages. Babies who breast-feed are more resistant and immune to diseases. Before the flow of milk, the mother's breast contains colostrum, which helps to provide the infant with resistance to disease. Cow's milk contains only one thirteenth to one fifteenth as much fortification against disease as human milk. Breast-fed babies tend to exhibit more positive patterns of weight gain, physiological reactions, and body composition. And breast-feeding benefits the baby in that it will have close physical contact with the mother.[58] Also, the biting and sucking motions required by breast-feeding result in the baby's jaw becoming better developed. The more passive movements involved in bottle-feeding do not promote jaw development as effectively.[59]

Breast-feeding has advantages for the mother, too. The mother who nurses her baby after delivery frequently does not suffer as severe after pains (menstrual-like cramps as the uterus contracts to expell blood and debris) and returns more rapidly to her nonpregnant condition.[60] The baby's sucking during the first weeks stimulates the uterus to contract and thus helps to speed its return to normal size. Several months of nursing seems to improve the firmness and shape of breasts among women whose breasts tend to have too much fatty tissue. There is also evidence that breast-feeding decreases a woman's chances of developing breast cancer.[61]

Many women enjoy both physical and psychological benefits resulting from breast-feeding. However, no woman who has strong feelings against beast-feeding, or for whom it is physically painful should be pressured to do so.

It has been pointed out by the leading child-development specialists, Mollie and Russell Smart,[62] that women who choose to bottle-feed their babies can and should imitate the psychological as well as the nutritional context of breast-feeding by holding and cuddling their babies during feeding. Frequent holding and cuddling of the baby is just as important as getting the formula correct.

Adjustments to Birth of a Child

Pregnancy is a rather lengthy, gradual process in which the husband and wife prepare for the arrival of a baby. Once the baby is born, however, the husband and wife find themselves abruptly assuming the role of parenthood. This new role is a twenty-four-hour endeavor from which there is little retreat. The transition to parenthood brings many changes in the lives of the husband and wife and many couples do not adequately prepare themselves for some of these changes. Adjustments can be made more smoothly if the couple is aware of some of the major changes brought about by the arrival of children.

CHANGES IN RELATIONSHIPS

The birth of a child brings about a change in the marriage relationship by the simple fact that a third person is introduced into the family. Before the advent of a child, husband and wife normally give their full attention to each other, considering themselves, their desires, and their needs in everyday living. With the birth of a baby, the couple can no longer enjoy each other's *undivided* attention exclusively because a child demands much of their attention, and a child's needs and interests often conflict with those of the parents. Parents must administer to a baby's needs almost constantly because babies are so dependent.

PHYSICAL DEMANDS

The physical demands of a newborn are considerable. Most parents, particularly mothers, experience a great degree of fatigue and loss of sleep, especially during the early months. Some research indicates that tiredness, exhaustion, and loss of sleep are widespread problems of new mothers.[63] There is additional laundry to be done. Feeding a baby is very time consuming, and the time required for housekeeping almost doubles during infancy.

DISRUPTION OF DAILY ROUTINES

General disruption of daily routines in the life of the couple occurs with the coming of a child. Babies sleep and feed when they feel like it. It takes time for the baby to adjust to the routines of parents. Because at the beginning, the parents almost completely adjust to the baby's schedule, couples consistently find their sleep disrupted and their meals disturbed.

CURTAILMENT OF SOCIAL LIFE

One change many couples find difficult to adjust to is that with the arrival of the baby their social life is curtailed. The new baby cannot be left alone, and since few young parents can afford a good baby-sitter very often, this means that the parents must be with the baby almost continuously. However, many couples enjoy their baby so much, they want to go out less and enjoy staying home. Grandparents and baby-sitting cooperative arrangements with other couples provide possibilities for free baby-sitting services.

DECREASE IN ADULT COMPANIONSHIP

Some women find it difficult to stay home all the time with little contact with other adults. Outside stimulation and adult companionship are soon missed, even though they enjoy the baby very much. This adjustment can be more easily made by inviting friends over, having the husband take care of the baby to give the wife an opportunity to go out, or by taking the baby out periodically.[64]

FINANCIAL STRAIN

The arrival of a baby brings added pressure to the financial resources of a couple because a child demands additional expenditures. And if the wife was employed before the pregnancy, the loss of her income can be felt sharply.

THE POSITIVE CHANGES

The arrival of a child brings many changes that parents may find difficult. However, many are only temporary and most parents do eventually adjust to the more enduring changes. Although many parents feel the transition to parenthood is uncomfortable in many respects, most of them feel that having a child is well worth the adjustments required.[65]

Having a child also brings pleasant changes into the lives of many couples. Loving and nurturing a youngster can be one of the most fulfilling experiences in life. As one new mother said concerning her baby:

> I think this baby is the most happy experience in my life. To me it's wonderful just to hold it, to love it, to see it grow. I enjoyed having a baby far more than I thought I would and I really wanted a baby to begin with.

One of the largest studies done on the effects of the arrival of a child on parents is one which was conducted by Daniel Hobbs, who found that 91 per cent of the men and 70 per cent of the women rated their marriages happier following the birth of their baby than it had been before.[66] Clearly, children bring much joy to the lives of many couples in spite of the work they create for their parents.

References

1. "A Pregnant Choice." *Time*, May, 29, 1972.
2. ANTHONY, E. JAMES, and THERESE BENEDEK, eds. *Parenthood: Its Psychology and Psychopathology*. Boston: Little, Brown, 1970.
3. FOLKMAN, JEROME D., and NANCY M. K. CLATWORTHY. *Marriage Has Many Faces*. Columbus, Ohio: Merrill, 1970.
4. FRIEDMANN, THEODORE. "Prenatal Diagnosis of Genetic Disease." *Scientific American*, November 1971, pp. 34–42.
5. SMART, MOLLIE S., and RUSSELL C. SMART. *Children: Development and Relationships*. New York: Macmillan, 1972.
6. BOWMAN, HENRY A. *Marriage for Moderns*. New York: McGraw-Hill, 1974.
7. Ibid.
8. Ibid.
9. KATCHADOURIAN, HERANT A., and DONALD T. LUNDE. *Fundamentals of Human Sexuality*. New York: Holt, Rinehart and Winston, 1972.
10. HURLOCK, ELIZABETH B. *Child Development*. New York: McGraw-Hill, 1972.
11. KATCHADOURIAN and LUNDE, op. cit.
12. HURLOCK, op. cit.
13. SONTAG, L. W. "Fetal Behavior as a Predictor of Behavior in Childhood." Paper presented at Annual Meeting of the American Psychiatric Association, May 1962, in Toronto, Ontario.

14. SMART and SMART, op. cit.
15. STOTT, D. H. "Mongolism Related to Emotional Shock in Early Pregnancy." *Vita Human*, 1961, pp. 57–76.
16. GRIMM, ELAINE R. "Psychological Tension in Pregnancy." *Psychosomatic Medicine*, 1961, pp. 520–527.
17. WORTISS, HELEN, and A. M. FREEDMAN. "Maternal Stress and Premature Delivery." *Bulletin: WHO*, 1962, pp. 285–291.
JAMES, WILLIAM H. "The Effect of Maternal Psychological Stress on the Fetus." *British Journal of Psychiatry*, 1969, pp. 811–825.
18. CERUTTI, G. B. "Importance des lacteurs Psychiques, dans la grossesse prolongée," rev. *Medicine Psychosomatique*, 1962, pp. 11–12.
19. MCDONALD, R. L.; M. GYNTHER; and A. CHRISTOKOS. "Relation Between Maternal Anxiety and Obstetric Complications." *Psychosomatic Medicine*, 1963, pp. 357–363.
20. SMART and SMART, op. cit.
21. Ibid.
22. HEPNER, R. "Maternal Nutrition and the Fetus." *Journal of the American Medical Association*, vol. 168, 1958, pp. 1774–1777.
KNOBLOCH, H., and B. PASAMANICK. "Seasonal Variations in the Births of the Mentally Deficient." *American Journal of Public Health*, vol. 48, 1958, pp. 1202–1208.
23. STEARNS, G. "Nutritional State of the Mother Prior to Conception." *Journal of the American Medical Association*, vol. 168, 1958, pp. 1655–1659.
24. SMART and SMART, op. cit.
25. BEADLE, MURIEL. *A Child's Mind*. New York: Doubleday, 1970.
26. "It Really May Be Food for Thought." Interview with John Churchill. *The New York Times*, July 28, 1968.
27. HURLOCK, op. cit.
28. SMART and SMART, op. cit.
29. HARDY, J. B. "Rubella and Its Aftermath." *Children*, vol. 16, 1969, pp. 91–96.
30. SMART and SMART, op. cit.
31. Ibid.
32. HURLOCK, op. cit.
33. SCHULMAN, C. A. "Sleep Patterns in Newborn Infants as a Function of Suspected Neurological Impairment of Maternal Heroin Addiction." Paper presented at the Meeting of the Society for Research in Child Development, March 27, 1969, in Santa Monica, California.
34. List compiled by Department of Pediatrics at Ohio State University. Reported in Folkman and Clatworthy, op. cit., p. 191.
35. PASAMANICK, B., and H. KNOBLOCH. "Retrospective Studies on the Epidemiology of Reproductive Causality: Old and New." *Merrill-Palmer Quarterly*, vol. 12, 1966, pp. 7–26.
36. HURLOCK, op. cit.
37. MONTAGU, ASHLEY. *Human Heredity*. New York: Harcourt Brace Jovanovich, 1959.
38. Ibid.
39. HURLOCK, op. cit.
40. Ibid.
41. Ibid.
42. EASTMAN, N. J., and L. M. HELLMAN. *Williams Obstetrics*. 13th ed. New York: Appleton-Century-Crofts, 1966.
43. KATCHADOURIAN and LUNDE, op. cit.

44. BLOOD, ROBERT O. *Marriage.* New York: Free Press, 1969.
45. KATCHADOURIAN and LUNDE, op. cit.
46. Ibid.
47. SMART and SMART, op. cit.
48. KATCHADOURIAN and LUNDE, op. cit.
49. BLOOD, op. cit.
    SMART and SMART, op. cit.
50. KATCHADOURIAN and LUNDE, op. cit.
51. Ibid.
52. BLOOD, op. cit.
53. Ibid.
54. LANDIS, PAUL. *Making the Most of Marriage.* Englewood Cliffs, N.J.: Prentice-Hall, 1975.
55. POPENOE, PAUL. "Close to the Mother's Heart." *Family Life,* vol. 21, 1961, pp. 1–2.
56. MEYER, H. F. "Breast Feeding in the United States." *Clinical Pediatrics,* vol. 7, 1968, pp. 708–715.
57. SMART and SMART, op. cit.
58. BAKWIN, H. "Current Feeding Practices for Infants." *Nutrition News,* vol. 28, 1965, p. 3.
59. BERLAND, T., and A. SEYLER. *Your Children's Teeth.* New York: Meredith, 1968.
60. SMART and SMART, op. cit.
61. PRYOR, K. *Nursing Your Baby.* New York: Harper & Row, 1963.
62. SMART and SMART, op. cit.
63. DYER, EVERETT D. "Parenthood as Crisis: A Restudy." *Marriage and Family Living,* vol. 25, 1963, pp. 196–201.
64. BLOOD, op. cit.
65. LEMASTERS, E. E. "Parenthood as a Crisis." *Marriage and Family Living,* vol. 19, 1957, pp. 352–355.
66. HOBBS, DANIEL F. "Parenthood as Crisis: A Third Study." *Journal of Marriage and the Family,* vol. 27, 1965, pp. 367–372.

14 Parent-Child Relationships

Photo by Walker Montgomery

Children aren't happy
With nothing to ignore
And that's what parents
Were created for.

Ogden Nash

Rearing Children

One of the greatest challenges in life is to provide a child with the type of parental guidance that will help that child develop an "I'm OK—You're OK" position in his or her relationships with others.

The rearing of children can be a most satisfying achievement, and it can be a most frustrating experience. The difference is not simply due to the kind of children we have, *but depends upon the competence we attain in guiding children.*

Human growth and development follows an orderly, predictable pattern. Parents who become knowledgeable of the sequences of these patterns, and understand the limits of children in each of the developmental stages, can learn to adapt their responses in ways that contribute to the healthy development of their children. Many unsuccessful parents, however, fail to understand the genetic limitations of their children, or fail to appreciate the immaturity of their development, and pursue goals in child rearing, which, if not unattainable, require too much of a child too soon. Any benefits they attain are offset by residual "sleeper" effects that have devastating, long-range consequences.

Parents may be "successful" in getting their children to read before the children enter first grade by exerting psychological pressure to succeed, for example, but in the process the parents may generate so much anxiety about learning that they actually set the stage for failure in school. Many years ago, children were required to memorize all sorts of things on the assumption that it trained their minds. There are still many well-meaning parents who naïvely believe that fast growth enables children to achieve more in the long run. Parenthood becomes a chore when parents attempt to get children to respond in ways they will not accept. Parenthood is a pleasure when both parents and children work together to attain common goals. This requires patience, understanding, thoughtfulness, skill, and an appreciation of a child's lack of maturity.

Although not all "problem children" have "problem parents," a great many have. Rearing children is not a matter of evoking responses that parents find satisfying. It involves the preparation of people for over fifty years of living after they leave their parents' home. The major goal of guidance, then, should be the preparation of children for increasing self-direction. Guidance that focuses on children learning to please others *exclusively* often results in children either rejecting their parents or conforming to others to compensate for their failure to please parents.

In *How to Be Your Own Best Friend*, Mildred Newman and Bernard Berkowitz [1] discuss the futility of rearing children in a way so that they become entirely "other directed." If everyone is reared so that he subordinates his own motivations to meet the expectations of others, no one ends up satisfied with life.

One important task parents must learn is to focus their attention on their *own* behavior to discover ways they can help their children achieve their potential. Too often, parents focus attention on their children's behavior with little regard for the messages they communicate. Children of parents who are very punitive frequently interiorize messages such as "My parents don't love me," "I'm no good," "I can't do anything right." To protect themselves from the psychological pressure such messages stimulate, they frequently retaliate with messages of their own: "I hate you," "You can't make me do it," "I don't like school anyway," "I'll quit and get a job." Those messages can have long-range effects and can be self-destructive.

Research demonstrates that one of the best predictors of success in the future is present success. There is an important lesson to be learned from this: children who are guided to enjoy life for today, to learn the skills for dealing with their present problems, to relate to others in an open manner without being self-conscious about criticism, and to value themselves and others, have a head start to becoming winners. An important difference between a winner and a loser is that the winner does not let defeats destroy him. As Eric Berne [2] has indicated, parents provide the foundation for their children's scripts—life plans that are formulated in childhood. Many times the scripts that parents impose on their children are not the ones parents would choose but are the results of messages they communicate indirectly. Often the scripts are unverbalized but serve as important determiners of behavior that may persist throughout life.

Apprehension and Confusion About Child Rearing

An enormous amount of material has been written in the last few decades concerning child rearing. The popular media abound with information focusing upon problems and techniques, and this abundance of literature has done much good. However, many parents have become confused over which particular child-rearing technique they should employ and many feel overwhelmed at the responsibility of rearing children.

Apprehension and confusion about rearing of children can be greatly reduced if certain points are kept in mind.

1. *Parents are not the only influence upon children.* Many parents are inclined to feel that they are the only influence upon their children. As a result, they assume responsibility for everything that happens to their children. If a child is happy in school, experiences positive social adjustment and achieves well, many parents believe it is primarily because of *their* influence. Similarly, if a child has problems with social adjustment and does not achieve well, many parents tend to believe it is primarily because of something they have done and feel guilty. "What have I done wrong?" they ask themselves.

   Certainly, parents exert a great influence upon children. However, when they believe they are the *only* significant influence, they create an unrealistic burden for themselves. Many other persons influence children profoundly, including peers, siblings, teachers, and even television personalities. The older children become, the more they are influenced by these other sources.
2. *There is no one-and-only correct way to rear children.* Some parents experience confusion and anxiety over whether they are using the correct method of child rearing. Although research studies show that a certain child-rearing method may be associated with more positive social and emotional adjustment in children than another method, it should be remembered that such an association applies to groups of people studied, and may not apply to a specific parent and child and their special circumstances. Child-rearing methods should be individualized to the specific parent and the specific child. A method that is successful with one parent and child may not necessarily be successful with another.[3]
3. *Parents should have confidence in their ability to guide their children successfully.* Research over the last few decades has pointed to the importance of children developing positive concepts about themselves. As Thomas Harris has indicated in his best seller, *I'm OK—You're OK,*[4] the development of an OK position in children is dependent upon their parents to a great degree. Parents who enjoy their children focus their attention on the relationship. Such parents reflect to their children that they are indeed OK.

   On the other hand, parents who constantly focus their attention on building skills, having their children achieve, making their children "do right," soon will question their confidence concerning their ability to guide their children successfully. Few children turn out exactly as their parents wish because children are guided by their own goals, motivations, and aspirations. Confidence comes to parents who value individuality and respect the right of children to make some of their own choices. This does not mean the child should not learn regard for the rights and feelings of others.

   Some couples who are inexperienced in living with children quite naturally feel a little uncomfortable when their first child is born. Parents who remember that the greatest gift they can give a child is to enjoy that child soon develop confidence because of the child's responses to warm, loving, caring attention.

Some children are much easier to rear than others because they are more placid, less aggressive, and are simply more fun. All parents encounter difficulties in rearing children and, at times, experience frustration. Children can be one of life's greatest joys, but parenthood involves much work, much money, and much patience. The realities of parenthood are enough to shake the confidence of anyone, but keep in mind that most people, though not all, find parenthood worth the effort required.

Many parents, unfortunately, who are confident in their abilities as parents manage to do a poor job in terms of rearing a child to become productive, happy, and fun to be with. In recent years we have come to understand, as Bruno Bettelheim has described in *Love Is Not Enough*,[5] that child rearing involves considerably more than loving children. Many parents who love their children may beat them to make them behave, threaten them, ridicule them, and make them feel ashamed. If, in self-defense, a child has the courage to retaliate, such parents rebound with increased amounts of pressure. The result often leaves a child either physically or psychologically "whipped" and, what is worse, convinced that he or she cannot cope with the world without defeat. Mental institutions are filled with defeated people. Productive people, for the most part, are winners in life, persons of all ages who continue to believe that they still have the capacity for winning. Good parents consider the long-range effects of their guidance and concentrate on structuring the environment of their children to insure the production of winners.

All parents make some mistakes in rearing their children. Therefore, it should be emphasized that serious emotional problems in children are not generally produced by occasional parental mistakes that occur within a healthy parent-child relationship. In order to develop serious emotional and psychological problems, a child usually must be subjected to destructive or unhealthy responses over a long period of time.

Importance of Parent-Child Relationships

The adage, "the child is father to the man," is especially true in the area of interpersonal relationships. What a person learns and experiences with respect to interpersonal relationships as a child influences his or her attitudes and behavior later in adult relationships. The attitudes a child develops toward interpersonal relationships are influenced by the quality of relationships with the parents and the degree to which the parent-child relationship fulfills or thwarts basic emotional needs.

Basic Needs of the Child

LOVE

One of the most important needs a child has is to be loved. The child hungers for affectionate relations with others. Parents are, of course, very influential in satisfying this need as they provide the child with the first experiences that either satisfy or thwart this desire for love. Children who receive genuine affection and know that adults truly care for them tend to see themselves as persons of worth and as loveable. Children who are genuinely loved for themselves without any conditions attached develop strong, positive self-concepts and have little need to try to obtain love and attention from others in an immature, exploitative manner. The child who is loved is better able to love others. Not satisfying the need for love is a basic factor involved in emotional maladjustment and psychopathology.

SECURITY

Basic to the emotional health of children is their need for security. Children must feel safe and protected; they must feel that their parents consistently love and support them and care for them. They need to see the world as reliable, safe, and nonthreatening. Parental behavior which is unjust and inconsistent appears to make the child feel anxious and that the world is unsafe and unreliable. An important factor in the development of a sense of security is that children perceive themselves as having the inner resources to deal successfully with the world. Parental behavior which promotes these perceptions in children greatly contributes to their sense of security.

ACCEPTANCE

Another factor in emotional health and in the development of a positive self-concept is the need to be accepted completely and unconditionally. When children are truly accepted as unique individuals of worth, then self-concepts are validated. Thus, children adopt an "I'm OK—You're OK" approach to human relationships. Children who are genuinely accepted develop a sense of belonging, stability, and security. On the other hand, children who are not accepted are likely to feel rejected and undesirable, and frequently develop a negative self-concept and a fear of intimate relationships with others because of a fear of being rejected. Such persons may also find it difficult to accept others because they perceive they have not been accepted. In this situation a child has learned, "I'm not OK—You're not OK."

TRUST

Of vital importance to establishing a secure foundation for later development and happy interpersonal relationships is satisfaction of the need for trust. When their physical and emotional needs are satisfied, children learn a sense of trust, perceiving the world as good and reliable. However, if these needs are not satisfied, they are prone to develop mistrust and feel that the world is hostile and unreliable. When they consistently receive love, care, and support from their parents, children are more apt to develop an attitude of trust toward interpersonal relationships.

SELF-ESTEEM

Children have strong needs to value themselves and their contributions and to feel that they are OK persons. They need to respect their potential, worth, and achievement. Emotional health and development of a positive self-concept demand that they esteem themselves highly. Children must receive esteem from others as their self-esteem is largely dependent upon the recognition, attention, and appreciation they receive from others. When their needs for self-esteem are not met, children experience feelings of inferiority, inadequacy, and helplessness, which, in turn, can lead to neurotic behavior. Fulfillment of the need for self-esteem contributes to feelings of worth, usefulness, competence, and self-confidence. Also, persons with self-esteem are better able to respond to the worth and potential of others. This ability contributes to more satisfying interpersonal relationships.

LIMITS

The establishment of limits and boundaries is essential to the sense of security of children. The problem behavior of children who have been given free rein and have never been told "No" is often a plea for parents or teachers to set limits and to show enough concern to give them guidance. Children require guidance because they lack the insight and experience to be completely self-directive. In order to experience the most positive and rewarding interpersonal relationships during childhood and later in adulthood, children must learn to respect the rights and feelings of others. The setting of limits requires a sensible balance. Limitations and direction that are severe or unfair may contribute to the child's becoming passive and dependent or extremely aggressive.

FREEDOM

Children have a basic desire for freedom within reasonable limits to explore, to be independent, to make decisions, and to learn. They benefit from the freedom to develop their potential and interests at their own pace. When this freedom is not given or children are pushed to develop according to the pace of other children, when their interests are ignored and someone else's interests are pushed upon them, they cannot develop naturally to be themselves. If the child is forced to remain dependent upon either parents or peers, the development of independence and the ability to make decisions is impaired. Important characteristics of satisfying human relationships are the mutual granting of freedom to be one's self, and to be different. Children need this freedom so that they will be able to grant others freedom in future interpersonal relationships.

Goals of Child Rearing

Although an important part of child rearing is satisfying children's emotional needs, there are also other goals. A clearer perspective is gained concerning parent-child relationships if parents and prospective parents ask themselves, "What are my goals of child rearing? What are the qualities that I wish my child to develop?" University students were recently asked this question, and among the most common qualities they wanted their children to develop were the following:

1. Sensitivity to the needs of others; to be thoughtful and considerate of others.
2. A positive self-concept.
3. Ability to accept differentness in others.
4. Empathy, the ability to see the viewpoints of others even though they differ from the individual's own viewpoints.

5. Emotional security and adjustment.
6. Social adjustment; ability to get along well with others.
7. Independence.
8. The ability to assume responsibility for the consequences of one's own behavior.
9. The freedom to be oneself.[6]

In a research study by Nick Stinnett and Carroll Kreps,[7] a sample of college students were asked to indicate the values they believed were most important for parents to help their children learn to develop. The values listed most frequently by the students were the following:

1. Honesty and integrity.
2. Spiritual development.
3. Seeing each person as having dignity and worth.
4. Self-respect.
5. Moral courage (courage to stand by one's inner convictions).

These qualities are all desirable goals of child rearing. Others could be mentioned. An important question is, "What type of parental attitudes and behavior is most likely to achieve these child-rearing goals?"

Parental Supportiveness, Warmth, and Acceptance

The most important factor in promoting favorable emotional, social, and intellectual development of children is the presence of parental supportiveness, warmth, and acceptance. This conclusion is indicated by a review of approximately two hundred research studies in the area of parent-child relationships.[8] Parental commitment, love, and acceptance represent major influences in the development of children. Specific rearing techniques, such as bottle- or breast-feeding, early or delayed toilet training, whether or not the child has home chores, are of much less importance.[9]

There is evidence that children who are rejected by their parents are likely to express such problems as emotional instability, quarrelsomeness, resentment of authority, and restlessness. It seems that rejecting children has the effect of encouraging them to reject those with whom they live. In contrast, children who perceive themselves to be accepted by their parents tend to be emotionally stable, happy, cooperative, and friendly.[10] On the other hand, negative parent-child relationships are commonly found in the background of nonnormative groups, such as homosexuals. Homosexual persons, when matched with heterosexual persons, describe their parents as more rejecting, less loving, and less supportive.[11]

Poor parent-child relationships and lack of parental support have been found to be associated with drug problems. For example, heroin addicts when matched with nonusers are more likeiy to have had an unhappy childhood and to have lacked parental support and concern in the areas of school, career guidance, friends, and sexual conduct.[12]

The importance of parental support and warmth to the development of the child is illustrated in a study by Diana Baumrind,[13] which compared parents of preschool children who exhibited positive behavior with parents of children who were discontent, distrustful, withdrawing, and who had little self-control or self-reliance. The parents of the preschool children exhibiting positive behaviors were markedly more supportive and loving toward their children. Parents of the children expressing negative behaviors were much less supportive and used withdrawal of love and ridicule as incentives for their children, thereby communicating to them that they could not depend upon the support of parents. Learning that parental love and commitment are conditional frustrates the child's need for security.

Discipline

Few topics of child rearing are more frequently discussed than which method should be used to discipline or guide children. Most parents think of discipline as punishment for undesirable behavior and rewards for desirable behavior. They believe that responses will increase in frequency and in intensity when children are rewarded and that those responses which are punished will become extinguished. If the process were this simple, rearing children might well be considerably easier. In reality, the impact of the discipline parents provide is dependent upon the relationship between parents and children. Children who dislike their parents may persist in responding in ways that parents punish because of the satisfaction derived in defying the parents. The "reward" they receive from seeing their parents distressed at being unable to regulate their behavior is often greater than the distress they experience as a result of their parents' punishment.

Also, many children would rather receive negative strokes from their parents than be ignored. In families where parents fail to assure their children that they are important, children may behave in ways that parents consider displeasing to establish that they are persons with whom to be reckoned. Not infrequently, these children grow up and pose serious problems for the larger society when they continue to attain recognition by being destructive.

Discipline may be thought of in terms of punishing undesirable behavior or rewarding desirable behavior. Discipline may be thought of as a way in which parents control the behavior of children. However, it is difficult for anyone to control the behavior of another over a prolonged period of time; attempting to do so is conducive to conflict between parents and children, which leads to adjustment problems for both children and parents. Ideally, discipline should assist children in learning to (a) control their own behavior and develop self-discipline; (b) accept responsibility for the consequences of their own behavior; (c) become sensitive to and respect the needs and feelings of others.

Discipline is a necessary part of the parents' role. Society demands that children learn and accept social requirements. If children do not learn discipline from parents, they are apt to learn it later, often at a higher cost, from other areas of society. The question of discipline is a matter of type and degree. How permissive should discipline be? Where should the line be drawn between arbitrary discipline by the parents and free experimentation by the child? Philosophies on discipline move in both directions. The extremes are represented by the overdisciplined child who lacks security or spontaneity and the child who has never been told "No." Some parents are reluctant to discipline their children fearing that they will lose their children's love or possibly damage them psychologically.

Children need security and independence, yet to obtain these qualities, they must have limits and boundaries set for them before they can control and discipline themselves. The following is a brief discussion of some of the more common methods of discipline used by parents and some of their effects upon the child.

WITHDRAWAL OF LOVE

The method of withdrawing love to control a child's behavior is used most frequently among middle-class parents. Various psychiatrists maintain that withdrawing love can have a devastating effect, psychologically and emotionally, upon the child. This manner of discipline puts love on a conditional basis and causes insecurity in the child, often creating a situation far more harmful to the child than the behavior that led to the discipline.

EXTREME AUTHORITARIANISM

Although authoritarianism is considered a successful method by parents who are concerned with immediate conformity rather than long-range consequences, in its more extreme degree it tends to have negative effects on the child. Authoritarianism is usually reflected in discipline that is punitive, either psychologically or physically, and is given with the attitude of, "Do this because I say so and if you don't, I will punish you," with very little attempt to explain to the child the reasons for the request. Children who are disciplined in this way tend to learn that the primary reason for controlling their behavior is so that they will not be punished by someone else. They may feel that if they can "get away" with a certain act, they will do it. They may not learn to consider their behavior in terms of its effects upon others or upon themselves. Such children frequently fail to develop inner discipline.

The evidence suggests that where power is exercised entirely by parents, the children experience responsibility as being external to themselves; [14] whereas in families where the power is shared by parents and children, the children experience responsibility as being within themselves and also tend to be more responsive to the needs of others.[15] Extreme punitiveness by parents frequently results in passivity or hyperaggression on the part of the child.[16] There is also evidence that mothers who use physical punishment often and rarely reason with their children tend to have children who do not achieve well in school.[17]

We often assume that parental authoritarianism and restrictiveness automatically have negative effects upon children. This is not necessarily true because authoritarianism is largely a matter of degree. Extreme restrictiveness often does have adverse effects upon children; however, many authoritarian parents have children who reflect positive social and emotional adjustment. Some children respond quite positively to authoritarian methods. It should be remembered, however, that those children frequently lack spontaneity in their social relationships.

Whether authoritarianism has positive or negative effects upon the child depends upon several conditions. Perhaps the most important is whether the parent communicates love, acceptance, and supportiveness to the child. A negative self-concept and negative emotional and social adjustment of children seem to be the result of extreme parental authoritarianism, restrictiveness, and punitiveness *when there is an absence of parental acceptance, love, and supportiveness.*[18]

PERMISSIVE-INDULGENT

The permissive-indulgent method is characterized by a "hands off" policy. Few, if any, limits or boundaries are set for the child. He has difficulty making social adjustments and is prone to be selfish, demanding, and often expects constant attention. Such children may respond to discipline and denial of their requests with impatience, temper tantrums, or assaults. Children reared in a permissive-indulgent atmosphere often do not learn to control themselves, which jeopardizes their potential for healthy development.[19]

Another adverse effect of indulgent atmospheres on children is that they do not encourage the development of habits involving regularity or fastidiousness. The evidence indicates that extreme indulgence may contribute to psychiatric disorders because low habit regularity and low fastidiousness are predictive of later psychiatric disorders among children.[20] In some families, children exercise most of the power and control the parents. Such children are preoccupied with their own needs and tend to remain indifferent or insensitive to the needs of others.[21]

One study measuring the degree of readiness of college students to perform the roles involved in meeting the basic emotional needs of a future marriage partner found that those reared in very permissive families had significantly lower degrees of readiness to perform such roles than did those reared in either an authoritarian or democratic atmosphere.[22] It seems that children reared in an indulgent atmosphere are often not well prepared to establish positive, fulfilling, interpersonal relationships.

DEMOCRATIC

The democratic form of discipline is characterized by warmth and acceptance and involves providing children with a reasonable degree of freedom but also providing firm guidance. Reasons are given to children why they should do or not do certain things. They are helped to see the consequences of behavior for themselves and other people. Children from democratic homes are found to be cooperative, self-reliant, and well adjusted in social situations. They assume responsibilities well and demonstrate perseverance.[23] Such qualities provide a good foundation for later establishing satisfying marriage and family relationships. A study by Nick Stinnett [24] found that those college students reared in a democratic atmosphere indicated a significantly greater degree of readiness to perform the roles involved in marital competence than did either those reared by authoritarian or indulgent parents.

Behavior Modification

Discipline involves modification of behavior. As mentioned earlier, behavior may be changed in a negative manner by punishing the child for undesirable behavior, or it may be changed by rewarding or reinforcing desirable behavior. Those methods are referred to as behavior modification, and it is the thesis of behavior modification researchers that by the use of social reinforcement, such as reward, recognition, and praise, children can develop more desirable and positive forms of social behavior.

Most of us tend to continue behavior for which we are rewarded. Parents often unintentionally reward their children for problem behavior. One reason for this is that parents frequently give more attention to their children when they are engaged in problem behavior than at any other time. For example, a child may persist in hitting her brother because she has found that when she hits him, her parents focus complete attention upon her rather than on her brother. Children may get into a pattern of habitually disrupting the household because they have learned that disruptive behavior results in the parents' focusing attention upon them.[25]

One way of modifying behavior to achieve a desired result is for parents of a child who persists in problem behavior to praise and recognize the child for responding positively so that greater attention is obtained for manifesting nonproblem behavior. Giving the child positive attention for positive behavior tends to eliminate the child's motivation to respond negatively, especially if the parents work hard to stop reinforcing negative behavior.

Behavior modification may also include the use of material rewards. For example, parents who experience difficulty getting their son to pick up his toys from the sidewalk in front of the house every day might use a contract system in which he earns a few points every time he does pick up his toys. After he earns a certain number of points, he is given a tangible reward. He may receive five points every day that he picks up the toys. After he accumulates twenty-five points, he is permitted to decide the kind of dessert the family will have for dinner.[26]

Parents find that behavior modification is successful in some situations but not in others. Like any other technique, it can be overused and misused. One criticism of behavior modification is that rewards could become bribes and children could lose their motivation to respond positively unless they were rewarded in some tangible way. Whether this happens or not depends upon the manner in which parents apply behavior modification and upon many other factors as well.[27] The majority of families in one study who had professional supervision in applying behavior modification techniques reported a marked decrease in the problem behavior of their children.[28]

David Shaw [29] outlines some principles for the use of behavior modification procedures with children.

1. *Identify specifically the desired behavior change.* Parents should pinpoint these in terms like "my son whines to get his way" or "my daughter throws her clothes on the floor." A good approach is to count the behaviors and keep a record of them. This way parents will be able to observe small changes in the

child's behavior and reinforce him for his efforts. If there is no change, they will also be able to see this and alter their behavior change program so that it is more effective.

2. *Be consistent.* Many problems with children's behavior are the result of parental inconsistency since many inappropriate behaviors are made worse by parents' *inconsistent* attempts either to punish misbehavior or reward good behavior. Consistency is essential until new patterns of behavior are established.
3. *Be contingent.* When children behave in the way that parents desire, it is important to reward them as quickly as possible. Rewards can range from material objects such as food and money to such things as a smile or a nod of approval. Conversely, behaviors which parents want children to eliminate should receive contingent consequences that make those behaviors less likely to occur again. The difficulty that most parents have is not really following these obvious rules. Parents often reward misbehavior by giving much attention to that behavior by pleading with, screaming, or nagging at the child. This has the effect of increasing misbehavior. It is fine for parents to show children attention and affection noncontingently, but parents must be especially careful not to reward inappropriate behavior. Also, it is desirable to save the most powerful rewards for those behaviors in children which parents most want to encourage.
4. *Provide immediate rewards.* Providing immediate rewards is most important in the earliest stages of helping a child learn a new behavior. Reinforcement should be given *immediately* after the behavior whenever possible. The simple statement, "that's right," is a reinforcer and takes very little time to say. Waiting several minutes before rewarding the child can reduce the effectiveness of the reward to half what it would be if it were immediate.
5. *Break the desired behavior which the child is to learn into small steps and initially reward each small step. Then gradually require larger amounts of appropriate behavior before giving the reward.* For example, in helping children learn to pick up their room, parents may start with rewards for each item they pick up, then reward them only after they have picked up all of their room, and finally the parents can require a week of neat rooms before the reward is given. In this case it is desirable to mark down the points for a clean room daily. The reward for a week of cleaning needs to be larger than that for picking up one item; so parents should start with small rewards. If the child stops the desired behavior, parents must either change the reward, go back to smaller steps required for the reward, or both.
6. *With older children, these programs go more smoothly if parents set them up on a contractual basis.* If a contract system is used, parents and children should discuss what behaviors it is reasonable to change and the reinforcers to be used. Desired reinforcers are more effective than those which are only slightly interesting. When a contract system is used, children can see the similarity between behaviors required of them and the rewards they receive and the requirements of adults' jobs and their salaries.

Communication is a part of every aspect of the parent-child relationship. The quality of the relationship between parent and child is largely determined by the messages that are communicated and *how* they are communicated. Today, parents are probably more interested than ever before in learning how to communicate more effectively with their children. It is recommended that it is also important that children learn to communicate with parents in a positive manner. Children learn many of their communication patterns from their parents; this further emphasizes the importance of parents serving as a model.

There are some guidelines for communicating with children:

Treat the Child as a Person. This does not mean treating the child as an adult but simply as a *person* with feelings and needs. Some anthropologists have observed that American parents often do not talk with their children as though they are persons. For example, when parents turn from conversation with another adult and begin talking to their child, their manner of communication may change completely. Their voice tone frequently becomes condescending, or they may speak much more loudly and crisply. Sometimes parental communication is so artificial, the child easily senses it is not genuine. Frequently, parents will pretend interest or excitement about something the child is doing in an extremely superficial manner, carrying on dialogues with their children that they would not dream of doing with other adults.

Be an Active Listener. Many older children and adolescents do not like to talk with their parents because their parents never really listened to them when they were younger. Perhaps nothing establishes good communication patterns better with children than being a good listener. This also teaches the child to be a good listener.

Thomas Gordon in *Parent Effectiveness Training* [30] has suggested active listening by the parent is a vital element in promoting good parent-child communication. Active listening is defined as listening not only to the words the child says, but also to the child's feelings. When we talk about something that concerns us, it is usually the feelings we have about that issue that matter most to us; the words are merely a way of trying to communicate those feelings.

Active listening requires that parents want to listen and take the time to listen. Identifying the feelings that underlie children's words necessitates that parents give complete attention to what children say and the way they say it. Active listening also requires empathy. Parents must develop the ability to put themselves in their children's position, to think and feel from their point of view. Children respond very positively when parents provide acceptance, empathy, and sincere interest and attention; such parental behavior assists children in clarifying their feelings and encourages them to share their feelings and concerns.

An important part of active listening—in addition to listening and trying to understand the child's message—is the practice of feeding back to the child what the parent thinks the child's message meant. This type of feedback can help children clarify their feelings and encourages them to communicate these feelings more specifically. Children can often free themselves of bad feelings by being encouraged to express them openly. They are also helped to become less afraid of negative feelings. Thomas Gordon [31] gives the following example of feedback in active listening.

Child: Daddy, when you were a boy, what did you like in a girl? What made you really like a girl?
Parent: Sounds like you're wondering what you need to get boys to like you, is that right?
Child: Yeah. For some reason they don't seem to like me and I don't know why.

Giving feedback minimizes the possibility of misunderstanding the child. It provides a method of verifying whether the message the parent received is the message the child intended. As with all ways of responding, feedback is more effective if it is not overused.

Avoid Sending Conflicting Messages. Parents sometimes give a child a verbal message that says one thing and at the same time send a nonverbal message that says just the opposite. A father may tell his son, "I don't want you to play football. It's too rough," yet he talks constantly to his son about the football exploits of his old friends. A mother may inform her daughter that she should learn to cook but always insists on cooking everything herself without the assistance of her daughter.

Conflicting messages are confusing and can decrease children's security and certainty as to what is expected of them. Sending conflicting messages can place the child in a double-bind situation so that regardless of what the child does, it is not acceptable. When parents avoid sending conflicting messages, the child understands the parents better and has a clearer idea of what is expected.

Minimize Put-down Messages. Many parents get into a pattern of frequently sending put-down messages to their children. These messages have the effect of decreasing children's self-esteem, depreciating them as persons, and emphasizing their inadequacies. Put-down messages may include ridicule, sarcasm, and criticism. Perhaps the most severe put-down message is to deny the child attention and interest. Such messages make children feel badly about themselves and also about the relationship with the parent. As a consequence, children respond by decreasing communication with the parent. A study by Millard Bienvenu,[32] for example, found that parental sarcasm and criticism were associated with a lower degree of parent-child communication.

It is difficult for parents to avoid completely sending put-down messages to their children. However, many parents allow themselves to get in a pattern of interaction in which put-down messages constitute the majority of their communication with the child. Most parents could probably significantly reduce the number of put-down messages they send and thus markedly improve their relationship.

The Generation Gap

In discussing relationships between parents and teen-age children, a generation gap is frequently mentioned. Although the generation gap has probably been overemphasized, a serious gap does indeed exist in many families between parents and adolescents. This gap is found in many families, and has existed to some degree for generations as both Plato and St. Augustine severely criticized the unconventional and "undesirable" behavior of youth during their respective periods in history. Slogans have emerged to symbolize the gap, such as, "You can't trust anyone over thirty." Undoubtedly, the effectiveness of the mass media draws much attention to the problem.

CAUSES OF THE GENERATION GAP

Duane Angel [33] and others have suggested the following possible causes for the generation gap.

The Education Gap. Because of greater affluence, more formal education has been possible for the younger generation. Many of the younger generation take a college education for granted, whereas for many of the older generation it was financially impossible or, at least, very difficult. In 1946 less than 20,000 television sets existed, whereas today approximately nineteen out of every twenty households own a television. Today's youth grow up seeing history taking place around the world through the television set. Because of this type of exposure, youth of today tend to grow up with a greater awareness of world happenings than did previous generations. Also, paperback books, children's books, and magazines have become much more common so that today a child enters school better prepared and progresses faster and further than did the earlier generations. Unfortunately, this difference in amount and type of education between the generations can often contribute to a gap in understanding and communication.

Isolation of Youth from Adults. There is a tendency in our society to isolate children and youth from adults. From an early age, children are encouraged to involve themselves with their peer group. Increasing numbers of parents send their children to nursery school. Organized sports and other activities, such as little league baseball, occupy the time of children. As a result, they come to derive their sense of self-worth from their peer group. This is encouraged by many parents in various ways by such messages as, "You should be out playing with other children instead of staying around the house with us," or "We know you and your teen-age friends would be bored talking with us and the other parents here, so if you would like to go down to the game room . . ." The message the children are receiving is that they should not desire, nor enjoy, interacting with adults or members of the older generation.

The Affluence Gap. There is quite a difference between the older and the younger generation concerning financial experiences. Persons over fifty years of age experienced the Great Depression with its very limited amount of money, jobs, and food, and many also had few luxuries during World War II. From the time of the Great Depression, the older generation set about creating an increasingly affluent society; this was an important endeavor because the depression was a terrible reminder of financial insecurity.

The experience of the younger generation from the middle-class has been quite different. Unfamiliar with a depression or the hardships of a world war, many members of the younger generation have not known real hardships and some have come to take affluence for granted.

The Value Gap. As economic security is attained and taken for granted, more time is available to emphasize less materialistic values, such as building satisfying human relationships. More attention is given to the social problems of the larger society, which the older generation, busily involved in establishing financial security for themselves, could only give fleeting attention.

Although it is fortunate that the older generation has established a foundation that makes it possible for the younger generation to give their attention to problems too long ignored by society, it is unfortunate that this difference in experience has created a gap in understanding and communication between the generations.

CLOSING THE GENERATION GAP

How can the generation gap be closed? Since there is probably as much of a lack of understanding and a gap between people of the same generation as there is between people of different generations, perhaps the question should be, "How can the *communication* gap be closed?"

Better Communication. The basic factor contributing to the generation gap problem is simply a lack of communication. Often parents and children appear too occupied in their own individual interests to listen to each other. It is not surprising that in a study in which over 2,000 adolescents were asked what they would most like to change in their home life, one of the three most frequently given answers was, "Better communication." [34]

As one adolescent said, "It's really a frustrating and depressing feeling when you are talking to your parents about something that you are very excited about and eager to share and all you get is a nod of the head, a blank look, and a disinterested 'uh-huh.' You know then that they haven't heard a word you have said and they couldn't care less." Another adolescent stated, "I need someone I can talk with about my problems and dreams . . . It's nice to have someone who is really interested in you and who will listen."

Spending More Time Together as a Family. It is easy for parents and children to become so busy with their own individual activities that they have little time to spend together as a family. Before there can be meaningful communication between parents and children, they must spend time together. It is significant that "spending more time together as a family" was one of the three most frequently given answers to the question, "What would you most like to have changed in your home life?" in Bienvenu's survey.[35]

Less Age Segregation. Much of the lack of understanding between generations is caused by the high degree of age segregation in our society. We tend to understand those with whom we have a great deal of social interaction. Increased understanding and better communication patterns between the generations and specifically between parents and children could be obtained if there were more age integration in social activities and in opportunities to work and play together. Each family can help to decrease age segregation by increasing the number of age-integrated activities within the family.

Differences in Parental Influences According to Sex

I can remember that my sister always seemed to get more affection and compliments from my parents than my brother and I did. We were a little jealous, but we didn't think too much about it. We decided it was because she was a girl and girls were supposed to get more attention than boys.

The relationships between parents and children are often influenced by the sex of the parent and the sex of the child. The above experience of a male college student has been shared by many. Parents frequently treat their male children differently from their female children. Research evidence indicates that girls are given more affection and praise than boys. Boys also tend to receive more stern discipline.[36] A study by Urie Bronfenbrenner [37] found that girls are much more likely to be overprotected, whereas boys are more likely to be negatively affected by stern discipline. Although boys receive more stern discipline, they are also less responsive to discipline.

Differences in parental responses to male and female children are the result of cultural sex-role expectations. Society has in the past valued initiative, independence, toughness, achievement, and self-sufficiency for boys. It has been assumed that to develop such qualities in boys, it is required that they be treated less affectionately and more sternly than girls. In contrast, girls have been expected to develop different qualities, such as nurturance, which parents believe requires more affection from them. Girls do not have as rigid a set of sex-role expectations to fulfill as do boys and, as a consequence, are not subjected to as much restrictive parental action, such as discipline.[38]

Fathers often place great importance on the early sex-role identification of their sons and exert pressure upon them to incorporate desired sex-role behaviors. Normally, sons experience greater pressure to meet certain sex-role expectations than do daughters.

Parental behavior toward the child is also a function of the sex of the parent. Children tend to see their fathers as less warm, less nurturant, and less understanding than their mothers.[39] The behavior of mothers toward children tends to be more nurturant and warmer than that of fathers.[40] This, again, reflects cultural expectations; we *expect* mothers to be more nurturant and warm than fathers. Traditional father-son relationships are often characterized by pressure and rigid expectations that prevent the development of relaxed and positive interaction which often exists within the father-daughter relationship.[41]

Parents are more permissive toward their opposite-sex children. Mothers are more permissive toward sons, whereas fathers are more permissive toward daughters.[42] Mary Rothbart and Eleanor Maccoby [43] examined differential responses of parents to sons and daughters in which parents were requested to respond to a child's voice in a hypothetical situation. A child's voice, which could not be identified as to sex, had been recorded and was the stimulus material for the parents. In the experiment, some parents were informed that it was a girl's voice, whereas others were told that it was a boy's voice, and differences in the parents' responses were then observed. The results showed that mothers responded more permissively when told it was a boy's voice, and fathers responded more permissively when informed it was a girl's voice.

Several research studies suggest that boys are more sensitive and susceptible than girls to the influence of parents. For example:

1. Having positive or negative perceptions of parents seems to have greater influence on the adjustment of adolescent males than females; the more positive the perceptions of the parents, the more positive is the adjustment.[44]
2. The responses of the mother to the child are more strongly related to the intelligence level of boys than of girls. The effects of maternal behavior on intelligence seems to be more persistent over time for male children than for female children.[45]

The indications that boys are more susceptible than girls to the influence of parents may help explain why boys have a higher frequency of stuttering, delinquency, schizophrenia, and reading and behavior problems.[46]

Why would male children be more susceptible than female children to the influence of their parents? Perhaps it is partially because boys experience less positive and supportive parent-child relationships. This possibility is suggested by research, which shows that when parents communicate a great deal of supportive behavior toward their children, it tends to generate satiation effects and the children become less influenced by their parents in the performance of certain tasks. It is possible that because girls receive more positive and supportive behavior from their parents, they also experience more satiation effects of this behavior and, as a consequence, become less susceptible than boys to parental influence.[47]

Social Class and Parent-Child Relationships

Parent-child relationships are influenced by social class. For example, children in lower socioeconomic families, much more often than middle-class children, develop an attitude that life is unpredictable and that one's affairs are the result of fate; there is little that one can do to determine one's own success or destiny. They also lack long-range goal planning and put emphasis upon the present instead of the future or past, seeking immediate pleasures. Middle-class parents communicate verbally more often with their children than lower-class parents. This difference is observed as early as the first year in the life of the child. There is, in fact, less verbal communication among *all* family members in the lower socioeconomic groups.[48] Middle-class parents also have more expectations and higher educational and occupational aspirations for their children than do parents in the lower socioeconomic groups. Middle-class parents give their children more encouragement to achieve in school and to attend college.

There are basic differences in child-rearing practices between middle-class parents and parents in the lower socioeconomic groups:

1. Middle-class parents allow their children more autonomy and independence.[49]
2. Middle-class parents are less restrictive and authoritarian and discipline their children more in terms of the intent of the child's behavior, whereas lower-class parents are more likely to discipline their children in terms of the consequences of the behavior. Middle-class parents less often use physical punishment and are more inclined to use reasoning with their children. Parents in the lower socioeconomic groups are more inconsistent in their discipline.[50]

Most of the research concerning social class and parent-child relationships has focused upon the problems of parent-child relationships in the lower class and has indicated the advantages of parent-child relationships in the middle class. However, some conditions in the lower socioeconomic class may provide advantages for parent-child relationships. For example, many lower-class parents have more time to be with their children than middle-class parents because they do not become as involved in community activities or civic or professional organizations.[51]

Individuals in the lower socioeconomic group are less apt to be exposed to an extreme degree of competitiveness and pressure to achieve. Lower-income persons also enjoy the cooperativeness and mutual assistance of the extended family to a great degree.[52]

References

1. Newman, Mildred, and Bernard Berkowitz. *How to Be Your Own Best Friend.* New York: Random House, 1971.
2. Berne, Eric. *What Do You Say After You Say Hello?* New York: Bantam Books, 1972.
3. Bowman, Henry A. *Marriage for Moderns.* New York: McGraw-Hill, 1974.
4. Harris, Thomas. *I'm OK—You're OK.* New York: Harper & Row, 1969.
5. Bettelheim, Bruno. *Love Is Not Enough.* New York: Free Press, 1950.

6. STINNETT, NICK. "Child-Rearing Goals." Unpublished study, 1975.
7. STINNETT, NICK, and CARROLL A. KREPS. "Values Relating to the Development of Character." *Journal of Home Economics*, vol. 64, 1972, pp. 53–57.
8. WALTERS, JAMES, and NICK STINNETT. "Parent-Child Relationships: A Decade Review of Research." *Journal of Marriage and the Family*, vol. 33, 1971, pp. 70–111.
9. WILLIAMS, JOYCE WOLFGANG, and MARJORIE STITH. *Middle Childhood: Behavior and Development.* New York: Macmillan, 1974.
10. Ibid.
11. SIEGELMAN, MARVIN. "Parental Background of Male Homosexuals and Heterosexuals." *Archives of Sexual Behavior*, vol. 3, 1974, pp. 3–18.
12. BAER, DANIEL J., and JAMES J. CORRADO. "Heroin Addict Relationships with Parents During Childhood and Early Adolescent Years." *Journal of Genetic Psychology*, vol. 124, 1974, pp. 99–103.
13. BAUMRIND, DIANA. "Child Care Practices Anteceding Three Patterns of Preschool Behavior." *Genetic Psychology Monographs*, vol. 75, 1967, pp. 345–388.
14. LEVENSON, HANNA. "Perceived Parental Antecedents of Internal Powerful Others and Chance Locus of Control Orientations." *Developmental Psychology*, vol. 9, 1973, pp. 260–265.
15. LAND, LAWRENCE H. "Responsibility as a Function of Authority in Family Relations." *Dissertation Abstracts*, vol. 29, 1969, pp. 3668–3669.
16. WALTERS and STINNETT, op. cit.
17. BARTON, K.; T. E. DIELMAN; and R. B. CATTELL. "Child Rearing Practices and Achievement in School." *Journal of Genetic Psychology*, vol. 124, 1974, pp. 155–165.
18. WALTERS and STINNETT, op. cit.
19. ELIASBERG, ANN P. "How to Make the Most of Your Parent Power." *Parents' Magazine and Better Homemaking*, vol. 49, March 1974, p. 40.
20. GRAHAM, PHILIP; MICHAEL RUTTER; and SANDRA GEORGE. "Temperamental Characteristics as Predictors of Behavior Disorders in Children." *American Journal of Orthopsychiatry*, vol. 43, 1973, pp. 328–339.
21. LAND, op. cit.
22. STINNETT, NICK. "Readiness for Marital Competence and Family, Dating, and Personality Factors." *Journal of Home Economics*, vol. 61, 1969, pp. 683–686.
23. HURLOCK, ELIZABETH B. *Child Development.* New York: McGraw-Hill, 1972.
24. STINNETT, 1969, op. cit.
25. LANG, JOYCE. "Behavior Modification Research: Family Involvement." *Focus on the Family*, vol. 2, September 1971, pp. 1, 3–5.
    PATTERSON, GERALD; J. A. COBB; and R. S. RAY. "A Social Learning Technology for Retraining Aggressive Boys." In *Georgia Symposium in Experimental Clinical Psychology*, vol. 2, edited by H. ADAMS and L. UNIKEL. Springfield, Ill.: Thomas, 1972.
26. LANG, op. cit.
27. WILLIAMS and STITH, op. cit.
28. LANG, op. cit.
29. SHAW, DAVID. "Vest Pocket Refresher Course for Parents Using Behavior Modification Procedures." Reprogramming Project, Oregon Research Institute.
30. GORDON, THOMAS. *Parent Effectiveness Training.* New York: Wyden, 1970.
31. Ibid., p. 53.
32. BIENVENU, MILLARD. "Why They Can't Talk to Us." *New York Times Magazine*, September 14, 1969, pp. 87–90.

33. ANGEL, D. DUANE. "Gaposis: The New Social Disease," *Vital Speeches*, 1968, pp. 671–672.
34. BIENVENU, op. cit.
35. Ibid.
36. STINNETT, NICK, JOE ANN FARRIS, and JAMES WALTERS. "Parent-Child Relationships of Male and Female High School Students." *The Journal of Genetic Psychology*, vol. 125, 1974, pp. 99–106.
    WALTERS and STINNETT, op. cit.
37. BRONFENBRENNER, URIE. "Toward a Theoretical Model for the Analysis of Parent-Child Relationships in a Social Context." In *Parental Attitudes and Child Behavior*, edited by John Glidewell. Conference on Community Mental Health Research, Washington University, St. Louis, pp. 90–109.
38. STINNETT, FARRIS, AND WALTERS, op. cit.
39. Ibid.
40. EMMERICK, WALTER. "Variations in the Parents' Parent Role as a Function of Sex and the Child's Sex and Age." *Merrill-Palmer Quarterly of Development and Behavior*, vol. 8, 1962, pp. 3–11.
41. STINNETT, FARRIS, AND WALTERS, op. cit.
42. WALTERS AND STINNETT, op. cit.
43. ROTHBART, MARY K., AND ELEANOR E. MACCOBY. "Parents' Differential Reactions to Sons and Daughters." *Journal of Personality and Social Psychology*, vol. 4, 1966, pp. 237–243.
44. MEDINNUS, GENE R. "Adolescents' Self Acceptance and Perceptions of Their Parents." *Journal of Consulting Psychology*, vol. 29, 1965, pp. 150–154.
45. BAYLEY, NANCY. "Research in Child Development: A Longitudinal Perspective." *Merrill-Palmer Quarterly of Development and Behavior*, vol. 11, 1965, pp. 183–208.
    SCHAEFER, E. S., AND NANCY BAYLEY. "Maternal Behavior, Child Behavior and Their Intercorrelations from Infancy Through Adolescence." *Monographs of the Society for Research in Child Development*, vol. 28, 1963, p. 127.
46. MEDINNUS, GENE R. *Readings in the Psychology of Parent-Child Relations*. New York: Wiley, 1967.
48. STINNETT, FARRIS, and WALTERS, op. cit.
48. WALTERS, JAMES; RUTH CONNOR; and MICHAEL ZUNICH. "Interaction of Mothers from Lower-Class Families." *Child Development*, vol. 35, 1964, pp. 433–440.
    TULKIN, STEVEN R., and JEROME KAGAN. "Mother-Child Interaction in the First Year of Life." *Child Development*, vol. 43, 1972, pp. 31–41.
49. BUSSE, THOMAS V., and PAULINE BUSSE. "Negro Parental Behavior and Social Class Variables." *Journal of Genetic Psychology*, vol. 120, 1972, pp. 287–294.
50. CHILMAN, CATHERINE S. "Child-Rearing and Family Relationships Patterns of the Very Poor." *Welfare in Review*, January, 1965.
51. LEMASTERS, E. E. *Parents in Modern America*. Homewood, Ill.: Dorsey Press, 1974.
52. Ibid.

15 The Later Years

Photo by Walker Montgomery

To be seventy years young is sometimes far more cheerful and hopeful than to be forty years old.

Oliver Wendell Holmes

What Is an Old Person?

Each of us is in the process of aging from the time we are born, in fact, from the time we are conceived. Aging continues throughout life: it is not something that begins at age forty. Since aging is a continuous process, it is not possible to identify a particular time in life and say, "Beginning today you are an old person." People are *not* old just because they are at a certain age. All we can say is that a sixty-five-year-old person has had more birthdays than a fifty-year-old.

Biological Aspects of Aging

Aging is most often discussed in terms of biological changes. In fact, we usually associate aging with physical deterioration. We have been told many times from our childhood that as people grow older, the digestive and nervous systems, lungs, heart, kidneys, and liver begin losing the ability to function properly. We observe that the skin of older persons becomes wrinkled and is sometimes characterized by dark pigments.

The association of aging with biological decline is a major reason for our fear of aging and our negative attitudes toward it. Yet, people age physically at varying rates. Some people look remarkably young at the age of seventy; others at seventy look much older. What accounts for such individual variation? What are the explanations for the physical changes that take place during aging? Surprisingly, we do not really know why. We know that we do age, but there are no really adequate explanations of the aging process. Several major theories provide interesting possible explanations, although none has been completely supported by research.

RATE-OF-LIVING THEORY

A popular theory of aging is that the faster a person's rate of living, the sooner life will end for that person. This theory implies that those who live vigorous lives should die young. However, this theory is contradicted by evidence that regular, sensible exercise prolongs life.[1]

WEAR-AND-TEAR THEORY

One of the most frequently proposed theories is the wear-and-tear theory, which maintains that the body is like a machine, and just as the parts to a machine eventually wear out, so the parts of the body wear out.

Many organs perform specific functions in the body, and in the later years of life these organs may not function properly. For example, some forms of heart disease result from calcification of the heart valves. However, this theory has serious weaknesses. One difficulty lies in determining the exact cause of organ deterioration. Is the malfunctioning of the organs due to their wearing out or to certain nutritional deficiencies? Nutrition often plays a major role in the malfunctioning of organs.

Another serious weakness of this theory is that no specific organ or organ system of the body consistently deteriorates in all older persons.[2] Why do the organs and body systems of some older people deteriorate, yet function perfectly in other older individuals? Why should one organ in a person's body wear out while the other organs continue to function? This theory also ignores the fact that the body can repair itself; that cells renew themselves. No evidence supports the common assumption that the body automatically and inevitably wears out in all older people.

WASTE-PRODUCT THEORY

The waste-product theory proposes that accumulated waste products in the body play a major role in the process of aging. According to this theory, chemical wastes collect in the tissues and interfere with cell functioning. Chemical wastes do collect in some tissues; however, there is no evidence that these chemical wastes interfere with cell functioning in any crucial way.[3]

COLLAGEN THEORY

The collagen theory has promising possibilities. Collagen is a substance associated with connective tissue and is present in most organs, skin, blood vessels, and tendons. As a person ages, the tissues containing collagen lose elasticity because collagen becomes increasingly stiffer with age. The increased stiffness is a result of changes over a period of time in the cross-linkages between the strands of the collagen molecules. The loss of elasticity may cause a deterioration in the functioning of the organs that are affected and may result in certain symptoms of aging.[4] An excess amount of collagen in tissues is associated with aging; however, it apparently is not a primary cause.[5]

AUTOIMMUNITY THEORY

The autoimmunity theory maintains that as a person grows older, mutations occur that cause some body cells to produce proteins that are not recognizable and are, therefore, responded to as if they were foreign substances. Antibodies are produced in the body to neutralize the effect of a foreign substance. This production of antibodies is called an immune reaction.[6]

Evidence suggests that increased longevity is associated with a "slowdown" in the immune reaction. For example, one experiment that supports the autoimmunity theory of aging involved rats that were severely underfed during the first half of their lives. This underfeeding increased their longevity greatly. The organs of the rats that showed the greatest weight loss were those which produced antibodies.[7]

The autoimmunity theory is also supported by the fact that rheumatoid arthritis and several other diseases common to older persons are caused by autoimmune reactions. However, the autoimmunity theory does not explain all aging because many aging diseases, such as diabetes, are not related to autoimmune reactions.[8]

MUTATION THEORY

The mutation theory has received the greatest support from research. This theory recognizes that the functioning of our body cells is controlled by the genetic material DNA. When mutations in DNA take place, all resulting cell divisions perpetuate the mutations. As there is an increase in cells with mutation, a large proportion of cells of a particular organ may become mutated. Such organs may malfunction because most mutated cells function less efficiently.[9]

This is a very promising theory as evidence exists that rates of genetic mutation increase steadily with age. However, this theory cannot be completely accepted as an explanation of aging as there is evidence that in some cases genetic mutations increase greatly with only a small reduction in life expectancy. This suggests that some other factor minimizes the effects of genetic mutations.[10]

ERROR THEORY

The error theory is similar to the mutation theory in that it deals with the effects of mutations in DNA. In addition, the error theory takes into account the cumulative influence of mistakes in RNA synthesis, protein synthesis, and enzymatic reactions. These errors, according to this theory, contribute to the aging process. Research evidence on the error theory is limited.[11]

We have theories that offer possible explanations of why people age. However, the actual research evidence indicates that the question is still largely unanswered. The research has found no conditions that always occur in older persons but not in younger people.

Attitudes Toward Aging

Although each of us is in the process of growing older, many people hold negative attitudes toward aging. They fear old age and associate the later years of life with sickness, disability, and death. We are prone to think of older persons as not able to perform adequately and not really able to contribute significantly to society. A common belief is that older persons are much less happy and satisfied than they were in their younger days. Some social scientists have even promoted the notion that marriage satisfaction inevitably declines in the later years.

Largely because of the idea that older people do not contribute significantly to society, we often think of them as burdens. As a result, little respect or prestige is attributed to older persons. This is not true worldwide, because in many societies older persons are treated with reverence and respect and are considered sources of wisdom. In such societies, people actually look forward to the later years. In our society, however, we are youth oriented. Middle-aged persons get face-lifts and wear clothes associated with youth. Many people celebrate their thirty-ninth birthday year after year.

We are also very work oriented in our society, admiring and valuing productiveness. The later years of life are usually not economically productive because most people are forced to retire at age sixty-five. Largely because of this lack of economic productivity, there is less respect for the later years than for the younger, more economically productive years.

Young people tend to look upon the later years as a period of life characterized by loneliness, poor health, deteriorating mental powers, economic insecurity, and resistance to change. These attitudes reflect our cultural expectations of what old age is like. Such negative cultural expectations create a social climate that is not conducive to feelings of usefulness, adequacy, security, nor to good adjustment in the later years. The major twentieth-century stumbling blocks with respect to enriched living during the later years are negative, fatalistic attitudes and stereotypes.[12]

Negative attitudes and stereotypes create a complex set of problems for older persons. As James E. Montgomery has stated, "Like the evil spells of fairy tales, we effectively turn once useful princes and princesses into frogs of society." [13] We do many things as a society to reinforce an "I'm not OK" position in older persons, and we do little to reinforce an "I'm OK" position.

Myths of the Later Years

It is doubtful that any period of life has been more distorted by myths than the later years because our society has concentrated upon the problems and negative aspects of old age, ignoring its positive, rewarding aspects. Understanding of the later years can be increased by examining what the research evidence reveals about some of these more common myths.

MYTH 1: MOST OLDER PERSONS ARE UNHAPPY AND DISSATISFIED

That most older persons are unhappy and dissatisfied is perhaps the most common myth of the later years. There seems to be a cultural expectation that life satisfaction inevitably declines with age. However, a massive study recently conducted by the Gerontology Center at the University of Southern California [14] investigated the attitudes and living conditions of 70,000 older persons throughout the nation. This study found that 87 per cent of them reported that they were pleased with their present life-style and situation. Similar results were obtained in a study by Nick Stinnett, Linda M. Carter, and James E. Montgomery,[15] who found that over 50 per cent of the older persons felt they were in the happiest period of their lives.

MYTH 2: MARRIAGE SATISFACTION DECLINES DURING THE LATER YEARS

A very prevalent myth is that marriage satisfaction inevitably declines during the later years of life. Associated with this notion is the belief that most older couples are not happy in their marriages. However, one study [16] showed that approximately 95 per cent of the older husbands and wives rated their marriages as happy or very happy. The majority of them also reported that their marriage relationships had become better over time.

MYTH 3: OLDER PERSONS CAN NO LONGER FUNCTION SEXUALLY

Another common misconception is that older persons have little sexual interest and cannot function adequately. On the contrary, many older persons remain sexually active. Research indicates that one of the most important factors associated with the continuation of sexual behavior in the later years is a regular outlet for sexual expression. Older men and women who had active sexual lives in their youth and throughout adulthood tend to continue this active pattern during the later years.[17]

Sexual activity does decline during the later years. Several physical changes contribute to this decline, among them a general slowing and attenuation of body responses in both older males and females. Older males achieve erection more slowly and ejaculation is not as vigorous as it was in younger years. However, once erection is achieved, it can be maintained longer.

As mentioned in Chapter 11, among older females there is a tendency toward vaginal walls becoming thinner, loss of tissue flexibility, and delayed or inadequate vaginal lubrication. These changes may result in sexual intercourse being painful for some older women. This problem can be solved medically and/or by the use of sterile, water-soluble lubricants.[18]

Except in extreme cases of physical infirmity, the greatest cause for the decline in sexual activity during the later years, particularly among men, is social/psychological rather than biological in nature. Mental and physical fatigue, fear of failure, overindulgence in eating, boredom with a partner, preoccupation with work, and physical and mental infirmities seem to be more important in contributing to a decline in sexual activity than is aging in and of itself.[19]

MYTH 4: MOST OLDER PERSONS ARE DISSATISFIED WITH THEIR HOUSING

Many older persons have inadequate housing. However, the belief that *most* older persons are dissatisfied with their housing is not supported by the evidence. In one study, 89 per cent of the older persons responding reported satisfaction with their housing arrangements. Those with incomes over $8,000 a year tended to be more satisfied with their housing and general environment. However, 80 per cent of those with annual incomes below $3,000 indicated contentment with their housing. Approximately 11 per cent were unhappy with their housing situations.[20]

MYTH 5: MOST OLDER PERSONS SUFFER FROM TOO MUCH LEISURE TIME

Many people believe that older persons are unhappy because they have too much leisure time and can find nothing to do. The fact is, however, that many older persons are quite happy being at the stage of life when they have the time and opportunity to pursue interests, hobbies, travel, and other activities they never had time for before. Many go back to school, start a second career, volunteer in community activities, and are extremely happy with their independence and freedom from the responsibility of employment. One survey of 70,000 older persons found that a majority from all income levels reported satisfaction with their independence and freedom from responsibility.[21]

MYTH 6: OLDER PERSONS CAN NO LONGER DO ACCEPTABLE WORK

The idea that ability to do good work inevitably declines during the later years is obviously very prevalent. Our system of mandatory retirement at age sixty-five in many areas of work reflects this belief. However, many older persons are able to do high-quality work, as is reflected in the performance of some of the members of the Supreme Court of the United States and in the United States Senate and House of Representatives. Yet our society consistently discards the skills and knowledge that older persons have acquired over a period of forty or fifty years. Older persons are told, in effect, that they have little to contribute and that they have limited capacities or potential to develop.[22] They are given the message, "You're not OK."

Physical strength declines during the later years and the capacity for heavy labor is less than it was at the age of forty. However, in jobs that are not physically demanding, older persons often perform as well or better than young people. The quality of work done declines very slowly after the age of forty-five. Also, the age at which many eminent individuals do their best work does not coincide with the period at which they reach their peak physically. For example, many famous scientists, writers, and philosophers have done their best work when they were over sixty years old.

In a productivity study of 6,000 office workers, the U.S. Bureau of Labor Statistics found that older workers had a productivity record comparable to that of younger workers and even had a more steady weekly productivity rate.[23] Because older workers are steadier in their jobs, they have to be replaced less frequently. They are also more careful with equipment and waste less materials than the younger workers.

The Bureau of Labor Statistics reports that workers aged forty-five and over have better safety records than younger workers. The rate of disabling injuries declines with age and reaches its lowest point in the seventy to seventy-four age category. Older workers also have a better absenteeism record than younger workers.[24]

Many changes that occur with an increase in age are not in the direction of decline or deterioration. For example, speed in learning decreases during the later years; however, *accuracy* of learning increases during the later years.

Later Years Becoming More Significant

The later period of life, usually defined as sixty-five years of age and over, is becoming a more significant part of our living experience because people are increasingly enjoying better health during their later years.

In 1900 there were 3 million older persons, which constituted about 4 per cent of our society's population. Today there are over 20 million older persons, making up approximately 10 per cent of our total population. This represents approximately a sixfold increase since 1900.[25]

The increase in the proportion of older people has largely been due to advances in medicine, improved nutrition, better health, and a high level of living. For example, the death rate in the seventy-five-and-over age category was reduced by about one fifth in the first half of this century. Life expectancy in the United States has risen from fifty-four years in 1920 to about seventy-two years in 1974. There will be additional medical and health advances in the future, and the length of life will probably continue to increase slightly.

The later years will be increasingly healthy and vigorous because:

1. Positive health concepts will encourage improved habits of nutrition, exercise, activity, and periodic checkups.
2. Research will gain greater knowledge of aging and perhaps of ways to slow . . . the aging process.
3. Treatment and diagnostic centers will use new restorative techniques focusing upon the total person.

4. Most suffering and premature death due to cancer, heart disease, and circulatory diseases will be eliminated. Arthritis and rheumatism will be greatly reduced.
5. Custodial care of older persons will be replaced by home service programs, active home care, rehabilitative services associated with community hospitals, and health maintenance activities in congregate living centers.[26]

People who are young now can expect to live a rather large proportion of their life after age sixty-five and enjoy relatively good health. Because of this, it is important that young people gain greater understanding, empathy, and preparation for the later years of life.

Problems

Because there *are* common problems experienced during the later years of life, and because we have, in the past, associated aging primarily with problems, we have negative attitudes toward it. However, understanding of the major problems experienced during the later years can provide a foundation leading to the discovery of ways in which those years may be enriched.

HEALTH

Physical illness is the most obvious problem among older persons. Many have one or more chronic health conditions (long-term health problems that are permanent or require a long period of treatment), the most common of which are high blood pressure, heart disease, arthritis, and rheumatism.[27]

The duration of health problems increases with age; older people take longer to recover from illness. For example, older persons report twice as much time restricted because of illness than report people in the age category of forty-five to sixty-four.[28] On the positive side it is interesting that older people are *less* often afflicted with acute health problems, such as colds or infectious diseases, than are younger persons.[29]

Physical health is a major influence upon the older person's life because it determines how much he or she participates in activities in the family and the community. Severe chronic health problems can contribute to an older person becoming socially isolated and can, in turn, result in loneliness and depression. Health problems can also be a great drain upon a person's income.

NUTRITION

Nutrition is a major problem among the elderly. Many live alone, and there is a tendency for such persons not to consume well-balanced meals because they believe that preparing meals for one person is too much trouble. Low income is another reason that malnutrition is common among older individuals. Intestinal disorders and poor teeth often are responsible for older persons not eating sufficient raw vegetables and fibrous foods.

Among the most notable nutritional deficiencies of older persons are vitamins A and C and calcium. These deficiencies contribute to many health problems. The 1971 White House Conference on Aging reported that from one third to one half of the health problems of older people are related to inadequate nutrition.[30]

INCOME

When people retire, their income generally decreases by 50 per cent or more. More than 50 per cent of the 20 million older people in America have incomes below the poverty level. The median income for people sixty-five and over was $2,785 in 1974.[31]

The limited income is normally devastated by any major expense or emergency, and more than one out of every ten older persons is hospitalized in any given year. The average length of stay is fourteen days. This expense involves over $1,000 for the hospital alone, which would shatter an annual income of $3,000. Only about half of the older population has hospitalization insurance. Even if an older person is insured and even if Medicare pays part of the cost, the individual still must assume approximately 50 per cent of the health-care cost.[32]

Many older persons, regardless of Medicaid and Medicare, are unable to pay for needed medical services. And a high proportion suffer from malnutrition because they cannot afford the type of food they need. Limited income coupled with the high cost of food means that many consume foods high in carbohydrates and low in vitamins and protein. A vicious cycle is set in motion with limited income contributing to poor nutrition, which, in turn, contributes to health problems.[33]

The great majority of the aged in America are not employed in the labor force, but have Social Security as their major source of income.[34] Social Security now pays a median monthly amount of $200 to retired individuals, a very limited amount of income. The periodic increases in Social Security payments, which are designed to offset inflation, often lag behind the inflation. Only 5 per cent of the aggregate income of older persons comes from private pensions. Assets such as homes, cars, stocks, and savings provide help, of course. However, equity in a home is the most common asset among older persons and more than 50 per cent own no equity in a home. Not counting home equity, the majority of older persons have less than $1,000 in assets.[35]

Income is important to older persons, as it determines the range of alternatives they have in adjusting to the later years. Older people with adequate income can afford to travel, entertain friends, maintain an attractive wardrobe and household, pursue hobbies, and engage in various recreational activities. For these persons, the later years can be a most pleasant period of life. However, older persons without adequate incomes can do very few of these things. Inadequate income is for many one of the major problems preventing the later years from being a satisfying period of life.[36]

ISOLATION AND LONELINESS

A psychologically devastating problem for older persons is that of isolation and loneliness. As people grow older, in our society there is a tendency to become more isolated, with fewer contacts with peers and companions with whom to share the past. Increasing isolation is the result of many factors. Forced retirement at age sixty-five and chronic health problems remove older persons from the mainstream of life. Because there has been some decline in the extended family system, many older persons do not live with their children, as they often did in the past. Emphasis upon children being autonomous and independent of their parents has led older parents to be concerned about being burdensome, which has contributed to their isolation. Anthropologist Margaret Mead has stated,

> We are beginning to see the tremendous price we've paid for independence and autonomy. We have isolated old people and we've cut them off from their children and young people from their grandparents. We have made older people feel they have to devote their energies to "not being a burden."[37]

The increased isolation of many older persons leads to increased feelings of loneliness, which is one of the most painful problems during the later years. Research indicates that as many as 50 per cent of older women and 25 per cent of older men are abnormally anxious and worried. The admission rate of older persons to public mental hospitals is approximately 2.5 times the rate for younger persons.[38] Psychoses, in particular, seem to be more prevalent among older persons. For example, the incidence of psychoses is 40 cases per 1,000 persons aged sixty-five and over, as compared to 3.5 cases per 1,000 persons aged fifteen to thirty-four.[39] Other types of mental illness, such as neuroses, do not increase with age.

HOUSING

Housing constitutes a major problem for many senior citizens. In fact, some research indicates that many consider housing to be the major problem during the later years of life.[40]

Suitable housing conditions are important for anyone regardless of age. However, desirable housing conditions are even more important for older persons, because they spend a proportionately greater amount of time at home.[41] The United States Senate's Special Committee on Aging has stated,

> Few factors have as much potential for promoting the well-being of the elderly as housing of appropriate size which offers safety, comfort, and the opportunity of choice between privacy and contact with the community.[42]

Personal satisfaction with housing arrangements is positively associated with physical health and personal adjustment in the later years. Yet, many older persons live in houses that are too big or spacious for them to manage comfortably, are frequently dilapidated, and often of lower value than is true for the average housing unit.[43] The presence of stairs or steps in a house can be a serious hazard for older persons, and many live in isolated conditions far from medical services, shopping centers, churches, or recreational facilities.

The extent of possible isolation in living arrangements can be seen in the fact that 75 per cent of the older people live in their independent households; only 5 per cent live in some form of group housing; and only a small proportion live with their children.[44]

Other common housing problems include inadequate temperature control, inadequate sources of both sunlight and artificial light, inadequate sound control, and a house design that does not minimize the necessity for lifting, bending, pulling, climbing, and reaching.[45]

FEELINGS OF USELESSNESS AND NOT BELONGING

Another psychological problem of older persons is feeling useless. As one seventy-three-year-old man said:

> I don't really know what I'm supposed to be doing. You have to retire at sixty-five. Then it's like your forty-five years of work didn't really happen. Few people are interested in your ideas or what you can do anymore. In a way I feel like I'm not a part of the mainstream of life anymore.

The fact that many older persons find themselves in situations in which they feel as though they do not belong is, perhaps, an important factor contributing to the increased incidence of mental disturbances mentioned earlier.

In a society that puts as much emphasis upon work and productivity as ours, it is understandable why retirement is often more difficult for men to adjust to than for women. A man's masculinity, identity, and feelings of importance are strongly associated with work and job performance. When this is taken away, his sources of identity are removed. Women are more apt to be involved with children and home, even when they have careers as well. Retired men tend to feel more useless than their wives, and it is believed that this may be one important factor contributing to the higher rate of suicide among older men than among older women.[46]

A Minority Group

Are the aged a minority group? Increasingly older persons may be considered a minority group because of:

1. Negative stereotypes about the aged.
2. Discrimination in employment.
3. Segregation of the aged from younger persons in housing.
4. The growth of a subculture among older persons.[47]

Recent evidence indicates a trend over the last thirty years toward increasing gaps between older and younger people in economic, social, and residential aspects of life. One third to one half of older persons are poorer, employed less, employed in lower-status occupations, have less education, and poorer health than the younger generation. They are also similar to certain minority groups in that they are concentrated in either rural areas or in the central city, and tend to be underrepresented in the suburbs.[48]

Despite recent benefits and programs designed to assist the elderly, the gaps are widening between them and the young in many ways. Numerous social scientists believe that older persons could be assisted to a much greater degree. The income gap could be narrowed by larger Social Security payments, greater opportunities for employment, increased pensions, and guaranteed income. The employment gap could be decreased by increasing the jobs designed to be compatible with the skills and abilities of older persons. Leisure time could also be increased among younger persons through shorter work weeks, more time spent on education, and more extended vacations, and in this way provide employment opportunities for older persons. The education gap could also be narrowed by encouraging and making adult education more accessible during the middle and later years.[49]

Those Who Live Long

Many people live very long lives and greatly enjoy the later years of life. Consider the following case:

The oldest living American as of 1976 was 134 years old! His name is Charlie Smith of Bartow, Florida. He was born in 1842. He was 21 when the Emancipation Proclamation was signed by President Abraham Lincoln. Charlie was 113 years old when he retired from his work in a Florida citrus grove. His employer at that point felt that Charlie was getting too old to climb trees. In 1972, at the age of 130, Charlie was running a small candy shop in Bartow.

You are probably thinking this is interesting but a very rare exception. Charlie's situation is rather rare in America. However, in some other cultures around the world he would be a rather common case. For example, a cross-cultural study has been completed and reported in *National Geographic,*[50] and later in *Reader's Digest,* of three cultures in Ecuador, Pakistan, and Russia where it is not uncommon for people to be over a hundred years old. Most of the younger people in these three cultures reported that they expected to live to be over the age of one hundred.

As might be expected, the concept of youth in these three cultures is quite different from what prevails in America. When one 117-year-old man was asked, "To what age do you think youth extends?" his answer was, "Youth normally extends to the age of eighty. I was young then." [51] This was the typical answer given by the elders in these three cultures. There were indications that most of them greatly enjoyed the later years of life.

Why do these people live so long? No one really knows. However, some common characteristics were discovered in the three cultures that may provide possible answers. These characteristics also give us greater insight into the important needs of older persons. The following characteristics are shared by the old people in all three cultures:

1. They maintain a high degree of physical activity through the later years of life. The older persons weed the fields, milk the cows, do the laundry, and take care of children on a daily basis.
2. They feel useful and needed. They continue to contribute in their cultures and they know they are needed. That they feel useful is hardly surprising since they perform important chores on a daily basis.
3. The older person has a high social status in all three cultures. Older persons are highly respected, valued, and looked to as sources of wisdom and knowledge.[52]
4. All three cultures are relatively free from stress and competition. Living in

such an environment means that the older persons have experienced a minimum amount of worry and tension.

5. They have a very simple diet of less than 2,000 calories a day. They eat very little meat and dairy products. Their diet is composed largely of nuts, fruits, and vegetables.
6. All three cultures are located in mountainous, high-altitude regions.

A survey by the American Medical Association has found 7,000 persons aged one hundred and over in the United States. What are the characteristics of these individuals? This survey indicates that they tend to have an easygoing disposition, a good sense of humor, a desire to stay active, and a firm belief in God.

Needs of Older Persons

The characteristics of persons who live beyond the age of one hundred that have been indicated by research studies identify some of the most important needs of older persons. If these needs were better met in the lives of more people, perhaps a much greater proportion of persons would live longer and would enjoy their later years more. Among the most important psychological needs of older persons are the following:

1. *Need to feel important to someone.* Robert Louis Stevenson once said, "So long as we are loved by others, I would almost say we are indispensable." We all need to feel important to someone. Many older persons feel they are no longer of use and that they are not important to anyone.

   Everyone, including older persons, needs to be reassured by family members and friends that he or she is loved, valued, and respected. The need to feel necessary to someone was successfully fulfilled in the lives of older persons living in the cultures of Ecuador, Pakistan, and Russia.
2. *Need for a clear, respected social role.* Older persons in the United States do not really have a clear social role. They are not expected to make contributions. In fact, a rather prevalent attitude is that they have little to contribute.

   A social role for older persons is necessary. Part-time and full-time employment could be profitably utilized on a much wider scope both on a volunteer and paid basis. Activities such as retired teachers tutoring students, retired business executives providing consultation for business organizations, and older persons serving as foster grandparents could be expanded.
3. *Need for self-esteem.* Self-esteem is important to the health of anyone. Yet, in a society where a person's worth is judged primarily in terms of a job, a title, and salary, older people often have a decreased sense of self-esteem after retire-

ment. Many view their later years as being primarily a burden upon others. Older individuals need to be respected and valued as *persons*. They need to have their strengths and past accomplishments recognized by others. They need to have their OK position reinforced.

4. *Need for companionship.* We are all social beings who need to be with others who care for us, respect us, and enjoy our company. Many people feel this need more strongly during the later years of life than at other periods because this is the time when they are more likely to be isolated from others.

   Age segregation in our society causes older persons to be gradually separated from younger age groups. Many older individuals are frequently confined to their homes because of chronic health problems. They depend upon people visiting them for their contacts. Unfortunately, many have very few visitors.

5. *Need to continue to grow.* Everyone needs to continue to develop skills, acquire new interests, make friends, and take up new hobbies. Many persons do this successfully. One outstanding example of such a person is Jacques Hans Gallrein, a distinguished landscape artist who was named Oklahoma's Environmental Artist for his preservation of the beauty of Oklahoma through his canvas. He received this honor in 1974 at the age of 86. He continues to paint, teach his art classes, and write poetry. He shares some of his life philosophy:

> My love and reverence for all life leads me to be involved with the conservation of the earth. To me all things in nature are beautiful, and that is why I paint them. By watching animals at play my sense of humor is stimulated, and I have preserved my childlike delight in their happiness. Trials and tribulations did not keep me from the thing I always wanted to do—paint. I feel no insecurity because painting has given me the awareness to see nature's creation with absolute assurance of my faith in the cosmic universe. My philosophy is very simple—I should leave this world better than I found it.

   Too often older people are expected to stop growing, to become inactive. Their talents, skills, and wisdom are not used. Providing older persons with opportunities to teach skills they have developed over a lifetime would benefit others and also provide the older person with a sense of usefulness and respect.

The psychological needs just mentioned are perhaps most important to the older person's morale. However, physical needs, too, greatly influence morale. Among the more important physical needs are sufficient nutrition, comfortable housing arrangements, adequate income, and good transportation services.

A physical need that is very important to older persons is the need to maintain a regular system of exercise, which provides the following benefits:

1. Helps circulation and respiration, which are two of the major physical problems experienced by older persons.
2. Stimulates the digestive system, resulting in better digestion.

3. Often prevents back pains.
4. The exercise of joints helps slow the onset of arthritis.
5. Helps to prevent becoming overweight.
6. Provides better muscle tone.
7. Stimulates the brain.
8. Provides more oxygen for the body.
9. Counteracts nervous tension and worry.

Older persons tend to experience most of the physical problems that exercise tends to prevent. Of course, exercise should be sensible, on a regular basis, and adapted to the individual's pace and physical condition. Regular exercise ideally should be started early in life and continued through the later years. Most medical experts believe the most convenient and effective exercise for older persons is vigorous walking on a daily basis. It is interesting that many physicians believe that the exercise of housework is one of the major reasons why fewer women than men experience hardening of the arteries.

Preparing for the Later Years

A review of some of the evidence presented in this chapter may lead one to the conclusion that the later years are, indeed, one of the least desirable periods in life. However, Abraham Lincoln once observed that each of us is going to have about as much happiness in life as we make up our minds to have. There is little doubt that the person who prepares himself to enjoy life is going to reap greater rewards than the person who views himself as a victim of a life over which he has no control.

Many people who lead satisfying lives in the later years planned them that way. Their happiness is no accident. Although we do not have absolute control over our lives, much can be done during the early and middle years to contribute to health, to build desirable skills, and to develop attitudes that will serve us to advantage in the later years. The person who views retirement with the attitude, "They're making me retire at sixty-five and I'll have nothing to do," lives in a different psychological world than the person who concludes, "I'll get to retire at sixty-five and then I'll have time to do the things I've always wanted!" The psychological worlds we create are largely of our own choosing, and they determine, to a large extent, the happiness we feel at every stage of development.

References

1. ATCHLEY, ROBERT C. *The Social Forces in Later Life.* Belmont, Calif.: Wadsworth, 1972.
2. Ibid.
3. Ibid.
4. CURTIS, HOWARD J. "A Composite Theory of Aging." *The Gerontologist,* vol. 6, 1966, pp. 143–149.
5. ATCHLEY, op. cit.
6. Ibid.
7. WALFORD, ROY. "The Immunologic Theory of Aging." *The Gerontologist,* vol. 4, 1964, pp. 195–197.
8. ATCHLEY, op. cit.
9. Ibid.
10. Ibid.
11. Ibid.
12. STINNETT, NICK, and JAMES E. MONTGOMERY. "Youth's Perceptions of Marriages of Older Persons." *Journal of Marriage and the Family,* vol. 30, 1968, pp. 392–396.
13. MONTGOMERY, JAMES E. "Magna Carta of the Aged." *Journal of Home Economics,* vol. 65, 1973, p. 8.
14. PETERSON, JAMES A., as told to JERRY LEBLANE. "Myths of the Golden Years." *Orbit Magazine. The Sunday Oklahoman,* September 23, 1973, pp. 6–7.
15. STINNETT, NICK; LINDA M. CARTER; and JAMES E. MONTGOMERY. "Older Persons' Perceptions of Their Marriages." *Journal of Marriage and the Family,* vol. 34, 1972, pp. 665–670.
16. Ibid.
17. MASTERS, WILLIAM H., and VIRGINIA E. JOHNSON. *Human Sexual Response.* Boston: Little, Brown, 1966.
    PETERSON, JAMES A. and BARBARA PAYNE. *Love in the Later Years.* New York: Association Press, 1975.
    KATCHADOURIAN, HERANT A., and DONALD T. LUNDE. *Fundamentals of Human Sexuality.* New York: Holt, Rinehart and Winston, 1972.
18. Ibid.
19. ATCHLEY, op. cit.
    MASTERS and JOHNSON, op. cit.
    KATCHADOURIAN and LUNDE, op. cit.
20. PETERSON, op. cit.
21. Ibid.
22. MONTGOMERY, op. cit.
23. LOETHER, HERMAN J. *Problems of Aging: Sociological and Social Psychological Perspectives.* Encino, Calif.: Dickenson, 1967.
24. Ibid.
25. U.S. Bureau of Census. *Statistical Abstract of the United States, 1975.* 96th ed. Washington, D.C., 1975.
26. STROUP, ATLEE L. *Marriage and Family,* A *Developmental Approach.* New York: Appleton-Century-Crofts, 1966, p. 521.
27. ATCHLEY, op. cit.

28. Ibid.
29. Ibid.
30. MONTGOMERY, op. cit., pp. 6–13.
31. U.S. Bureau of Census, op. cit.
32. ATCHLEY, op. cit.
33. MONTGOMERY, op. cit.
34. KALISH, RICHARD A. *Late Adulthood: Perspectives on Human Development.* Monterey, Calif.: Brooks/Cole, 1975.
35. Ibid.
36. Ibid.
37. MEAD, MARGARET. "A New Style of Aging." *Current*, vol. 136, January 1972, p. 44.
38. LOETHER, op. cit.
39. RILEY, MATILDA W., and ANN FONER. "Aging in Society." *An Inventory of Research Findings*, vol. I. New York: Russell Sage Foundation, 1968.
40. STINNETT, CARTER, and MONTGOMERY, op. cit.
41. LOETHER, op. cit.
42. *Developments in Aging: 1963 and 1964*. Report no. 124. Washington, D.C.: U.S. Government Printing Office, 1965, p. 29.
43. ATCHLEY, op. cit.
44. Ibid.
45. LOETHER, op. cit.
46. ATCHLEY, op. cit.
47. PALMORE, ERDMAN. "Sociological Aspects of Aging." In *Behavior and Adaptation in Late Life*, edited by Ewald W. Busse and Eric Pfeiffer. Boston: Little, Brown, 1969. PALMORE, ERDMAN, and FRANK WHITTINGTON. "Trends in the Relative Status of the Aged." *Social Forces*, vol. 50, 1971, pp. 84–91.
48. Ibid.
49. Ibid.
50. LEAF, ALEXANDER, and JOHN LAUNOIS. "Search for the Oldest People." *National Geographic*, vol. 143, 1973, pp. 93–118.
51. Ibid., p. 112.
52. Ibid.

16 Family Relationships in the Later Years

Photo by Jane Carroll

When grace is joined with wrinkles, it is adorable. There is an unspeakable dawn in happy old age.

Victor Hugo

Marriage Relationships

Numerous older persons are married and living with their spouses. Both the proportion of older people who are married and the duration of the marriage in the later years will continue to increase in the future as the life-span is extended.

The marriage relationship is particularly important to the psychological and emotional well-being of the older person. In certain respects, the marriage relationship may be of greater consequence to a person in the later years of life than in the younger years. The older person often depends more upon the marriage partner than anyone else to fulfill critical emotional needs, such as the need for affection, respect, and meaning in life. An older person increasingly relies upon a spouse for the satisfaction of basic emotional needs largely because interaction with institutions in society and with children tends to decline in the later years.[1] Older individuals gradually withdraw from the activities that previously demanded their time, such as work and child rearing, and find themselves spending more time with their marriage partner.

Being married is positively related to adjustment in the later years. Older persons living with their spouses are better adjusted socially and emotionally, experience less loneliness, have a higher morale, and enjoy better health than those who are unmarried.[2] The mortality and suicide rates are also much lower among older married than unmarried persons.[3]

HOW HAPPY ARE OLDER MARRIAGES?

Marriage relationships during the later years have the potential for being very satisfying. The older couple has more time to be with each other and to engage in interests and activities they both enjoy. They are unencumbered by career pressures. In a sense, they have a freedom to enjoy life they did not have when they were younger. Knowing each other for a long time has given them the opportunity to achieve understanding and empathy for one another and the chance to develop communication patterns that are satisfactory to both.

How well is this potential achieved? How happy and satisfying are marriage relationships during the later years? As with most aspects of aging, attitudes toward marriage relationships in the later years have been negative. The idea has prevailed even among some social scientists that marriage satisfaction inevitably declines during the later years. Yet, the evidence indicates that older persons consider their marriage relationships to be as happy *if not more happy* than when they were younger.[4] In fact, older persons are less likely than young persons to report that their marriages are characterized by recurrent problems or inadequacy feelings.[5]

Perhaps the most important factor involved in marriage satisfaction during the later years is whether the marriage was satisfactory at the beginning. Marriages that were satisfactory in the early years tend to be as satisfactory or more during the later years. In contrast, those marriages that were unsatisfactory in the beginning are likely to be unsatisfactory in the later years.[6]

The marriage relationships of 408 older husbands and wives were investigated in a research project conducted by Nick Stinnett, Linda M. Carter, and James E. Montgomery,[7] and the results indicated that

1. Approximately 95 per cent of the older husbands and wives rated their marriages as being either *very happy* or *happy*.
2. Over 53 per cent of the older husbands and wives indicated that their marriage had become better over time.
3. The later years were reported to be the happiest period of marriage by *most* of the older husbands and wives.

These results, presented in detail in Table 16–1, indicate that the husbands and wives in this study had very positive marriage relationships. This research clearly contradicts the view that marriage satisfaction inevitably declines during the later years.

For many husbands and wives, marriage during the later years does achieve the potential of being the most satisfying period of marriage.

REWARDING ASPECTS OF MARRIAGE DURING LATER YEARS

What do husbands and wives find most rewarding and pleasing about marriage relationships during the later years? Many of them indicate satisfaction with the increased freedom they experience in their marriage interaction. As Stinnett, Carter, and Montgomery [8] have stated,

> Perhaps with the children launched and the husband no longer employed, the older husband and wife have greater freedom to do what they desire, can go at their own pace,

Table 16–1 Perceptions of 408 Older Husbands and Wives Concerning Their Marriage Relationships

Perceptions	%
Own marriage happiness	
Very happy	45.4
Happy	49.5
Unhappy	2.8
Undecided	2.3
Whether own marriage has improved or worsened over time	
Better	53.3
Worse	3.8
About the same	40.9
Undecided	2.0
Happiest period of own marriage	
Present time (later years)	54.9
Middle years	27.2
Young adult years	17.9

SOURCE: Nick Stinnett, Linda M. Carter, and James E. Montgomery, "Older Persons' Perceptions of Their Marriages," *Journal of Marriage and the Family,* November 1972, p. 667. Copyright 1972 by National Council on Family Relations. Reprinted by permission.

Table 16–2 Perceptions of 408 Older Husbands and Wives Concerning Most Rewarding Aspects of Marriage Relationships During the Later Years

Perceptions	%
Companionship	18.4
Mutual expression of true feelings	17.8
Economic security	16.2
Being needed by mate	12.0
Affectionate relationship with mate	11.2
Sharing of common interests	9.3
Having physical needs cared for	7.6
Standing in the community	7.0

SOURCE: Nick Stinnett, Linda M. Carter, and James E. Montgomery, "Older Persons' Perceptions of Their Marriages," *Journal of Marriage and the Family,* November 1972, p. 667. Copyright 1972 by National Council on Family Relations. Reprinted by permission.

can spend more time together and enjoy each other's companionship more than in the past.

The two most rewarding aspects of marriage relationships during the later years as reported by older husbands and wives are companionship and being able to express true feelings to each other.[9] These findings are consistent with other research, which indicates that expressive qualities such as companionship and understanding are seen by older couples as the most important things they can give to each other during the later years of life.[10]

PROBLEMS OF MARRIAGE DURING LATER YEARS

What do husbands and wives see as the most troublesome aspects of marriage during the later years? One study [11] found that the two aspects of marriage relationships during the later years most often reported as troublesome were having different values and philosophies of life and lack of mutual interests. These two particular marital problems seem to reflect personality incompatibility, which is, of course, a major problem among younger couples too. A very high proportion of the older husbands and wives in this study reported that there was no major problem in their marriage relationship.

Table 16–3. Perceptions of 408 Older Husbands and Wives Concerning the Most Troublesome Aspects of Marriage Relationships During the Later Years

Perceptions	%
Different values and life philosophies	13.8
Lack of mutual interests	12.5
Mutual inability to express true feelings	8.6
Unsatisfactory affectional relationships	8.5
Frequent disagreements	8.5
Lack of companionship	7.7
Other	8.5
Nothing is troublesome	36.2

SOURCE: Nick Stinnett, Linda M. Carter, and James E. Montgomery, "Older Persons' Perceptions of Their Marriages," *Journal of Marriage and the Family,* November 1972, p. 667. Copyright 1972 by National Council on Family Relations. Reprinted by permission.

Retirement and Marriage

One event with a strong impact upon marriage in the later years as well as upon the older couple's adjustment to aging is retirement. When a couple retires, the career roles that have occupied so large a portion of their lives are abandoned. The husband no longer bases his identity upon the instrumental functions of providing money and status.

Retirement tends to reduce the differences between the roles of husband and wife.[12] Husbands and wives move toward a common identity in role activities when they retire. This shared area of identity centers upon expressive or psychological and emotional aspects of the marriage relationship, such as providing love, understanding, affection, and companionship for each other. Research has indicated that retired husbands and wives see these expressive qualities, such as companionship and understanding, as the most important benefits a couple could give each other.[13]

The happiest older marriages are those in which fewer role differences exist between husband and wife and in which the expressive aspects of the relationship are emphasized.[14] Difficulty in adjustment arises if either partner insists upon adhering to a preretirement role pattern that stressed work activity. Men generally show greater reluctance in relinquishing their preretirement role pattern than women because male identity and sense of masculinity is more exclusively associated with an occupational role. Women with careers are more likely to derive identity from their home and family related roles as well as occupational roles.

There is also evidence indicating that older wives who stress the instrumental aspects of the marriage relationship, such as housework, rather than the expressive aspects, such as love, understanding, and companionship, have a much lower degree of morale than those wives who emphasize expressive aspects of the relationship.[15] Two thirds of the older wives who indicated instrumental roles as being the most important role for the wife during the later years of marriage expressed a decrease in morale since retirement.[16]

Retirement seems generally beneficial to marriage relationships. The majority of husbands and wives feel that their marriage becomes more satisfactory and happier after they retire.[17] Retirement tends to benefit marriage because:

1. It contributes to the equalitarian nature of the relationship by promoting cooperation in many of the same roles. This is important because older couples who are happily married are characterized by greater equality between partners than is true of unhappily married older couples.[18]
2. It encourages a common identity that results from sharing many of the same roles.[19]
3. It encourages the couple to dwell upon the psychological and emotional

aspects of the marriage relationship rather than upon the instrumental, preretirement role patterns. Husbands and wives who approach retirement focusing upon the expressive aspects of their relationship have a better chance of experiencing a satisfying marriage relationship and a successful adjustment to retirement than those who emphasize the instrumental, preretirement roles.[20]

Widowhood

It is emotionally devastating when a person loses a spouse of many years through death. It is as though a large part of the surviving spouse also dies. Most people are able to cope with widowhood. However, studies show that older widows and widowers are preoccupied with grief, express more unhappiness and worry, have a lower degree of morale, and have a greater fear of death than do older persons whose spouses are still with them.[21] The mortality and suicide rates are higher among widowed older persons than among those still married.[22]

How do older persons respond to widowhood? Some try to keep occupied. They may plunge into volunteer work or projects around the home, develop new hobbies, travel, or become involved in recreational activities. Financial resources limit many persons in the kinds of activities they can pursue, particularly if the spouse had a long, financially taxing, illness preceeding death.[23] Some respond to widowhood by going to live with children or other relatives. Some associate with other widows and widowers to find companionship with people who understand their situation. Some, after a period of time, begin to date. And some eventually remarry. Remarriage has become a response to widowhood for an increasing number of older persons.

December Marriages

> They say old people shouldn't marry but I say differently. I lost my first husband when he was seventy and I was nearly sixty-five. We were happy together at that age. In fact, we were happier those last few years after he retired than ever before. My present husband is about my age and we're happy, so I say marriage is good for old folks.[24]

These words are from an older woman who had made the decision to marry during the later years and found it good. Today, an increasing number of senior citizens feel that marriage is good for older persons. The following case is another example.

Ella, age seventy, had devoted her life to teaching school and had never married. She entered a retirement community but made few friends. One gentleman, a widower, persisted in joining her in the dining hall for meals. Soon they were taking walks in the evening and had joined a bridge group. In a few months they married. Both say they feel better, are more optimistic, and are happier than they have been in years.

The need for companionship is perhaps greater during the later years than at any other time primarily because an individual often is isolated during this period. More and more, older persons are satisfying this need through December marriages. December marriage refers to a marriage entered by two people who are sixty-five years of age or over. Most December marriages are remarriages. The men have the advantage of having a larger field of eligibles to choose from than the women, as they are outnumbered because women generally have a longer lifespan than men. Also, some older men marry younger women. There are approximately seventy-five males per one hundred females in the sixty-five-and-over age category. A much lower proportion of older males remains unmarried. Only 29 per cent of older males are unmarried, whereas 62 per cent of older females are unmarried.[25]

PRESSURES AGAINST DECEMBER MARRIAGES

Stanley R. Dean, speaking at a meeting of the World Federation of Mental Health, stated,

> We know the old do not cease to be human just because they are old; they have many of the desires of the young, and their need for companionship is even greater.[26]

Unfortunately, many of our attitudes suggest that we believe older persons do not have the same emotional needs as younger persons. For example, our society strongly supports courtship and marriage of young couples. However, attitudes toward the courtship activities and marriages of older couples are much less positive. Older persons with good health and financial security who decide to marry often find children, friends, and the community condemning the marriage. They are often ridiculed, criticized, and faced with the attitude, "There is no fool like an old fool."

Although there has been an increase in December marriages, the number and rate of such marriages would be higher if it were not for societal pressure that prevents many older persons from entering marriage or from courting. Some older couples cope with this pressure by simply not discussing their marriage plans with anyone.

"It was embarrassing," one woman stated. "My friends had all known my late husband, George. And my new husband, Mac, isn't like George was at all. Some of these friends just insisted on telling me how foolish I was and how Mac and I wouldn't get along. It hurt worst, when they would say, 'How can you forget George so soon?' "

Another woman declared:

I told my children and friends that I was old enough to make my own decisions. After all, I got married once before some forty years ago without their helpful advice; I could do it again.

A sixty-nine-year-old widow wrote to Abigail Van Buren for advice about marrying in secret.

Is there any state near Iowa where a couple can go to be married in a hurry? We would like to get married as soon as possible as his children want to put him in a rest home.[27]

When friends and family strongly disapprove of the December marriage, it is less likely to be successful. However, evidence indicates that when friends are told of the wedding plans, most of them approve. Walter McKain in his research of December marriages found that two thirds of the friends approved of the marriage and less than one fifth were opposed.[28]

REASONS FOR DECEMBER MARRIAGES

What are the major reasons that older couples get married? They are similar to the reasons that young couples marry. An important study [29] of one hundred older couples has identified the following reasons for marrying during the later years.

Companionship. A desire for companionship was the most frequently given reason. Approximately three fourths of the men and two thirds of the women in McKain's study reported that the need for companionship was the major reason for their December marriages. Other research also indicated that older husbands and wives see companionship as the major reason for December marriages.[30]

Many of these persons prior to their remarriages had feelings of uselessness, of being isolated, and of missing out on experiences that had formerly constituted a large part of their lives. They wanted to be cherished by someone. They wanted to be necessary and useful. As one man reported:

I had nothing or no one to fill my days. I ate alone; went for days without a good conversation with someone. I finally decided that I had to find someone or else I'd die. Life was just too empty otherwise.

For many older persons, marriage is the best way of adequately fulfilling their need for companionship.

Romantic Love. Very few of the couples in McKain's research reported romantic love as a major reason for their marriage. However, some did marry because of romantic love. One older woman reported, "It was love at first sight. I couldn't resist him." [31]

Sexual Expression. Few of the couples in McKain's research directly mentioned sex as a major factor in their marriage. However, many gave subtle indications that sex was an influence in their marriage and that the role of sex in their lives extended far beyond sexual intercourse and lovemaking. As McKain states,

> A woman's gentle touch, the perfume on her hair, a word of endearment—all these and many more reminders that he is married help to satisfy a man's urge for the opposite sex. The same is true for the older wife. One woman had this comment on her marriage: "I like the little things; the smell of his pipe, the sound of steps on the back porch, his shaving mug—even his muddy shoes." The sex life of older marriage couples is not confined to the bedroom.[32]

Poor Health. A few couples reported that they married for health reasons. Some of the older persons had such health problems as poor vision, hearing problems, lameness, or some other handicap, and wanted someone to live with them. Some required a special diet and needed someone who could prepare the proper food for them. These older persons married primarily to reduce anxiety about their poor health.

Financial Reasons. Some of the December marriages were primarily for financial reasons. In these instances the older person had inadequate income to pay taxes and maintain a home independently. As one man bluntly stated, "It was either get married or lose my home." [33] This man indicated, however, that marriage had brought other advantages as well. Couples that married primarily for financial reasons believed that a second income, usually from Social Security, would help them meet the daily expenses of living more easily.

To Avoid Being Dependent on Children. Some persons in McKain's study married so they would not have to be dependent upon their children. In some cases the children did not want to care for their aged parent, and for these persons a December marriage was one of the remaining alternatives. One seventy-year-old woman who had recently married stated, "I will not stay where I am considered a pest. We are all happier this way." In other instances the children welcomed the parent living with them but the parent refused because of a desire to remain independent.

HOW SUCCESSFUL ARE DECEMBER MARRIAGES?

> Our marriage is like the sugar in the bottom of the coffee cup—the best of all.[34]

> Both of us knew how nice a good marriage can be. That's why we got married and it turned out just as we thought it would—simply wonderful.[35]

These are some typical comments of older husbands and wives. Seventy-four of the one hundred couples in McKain's study were found to have successful marriages. The success was judged by criteria such as the couple expressing affection, respect, consideration toward each other, enjoying each other's company, pride in their marriage, and absence of complaints about each other.

FACTORS ASSOCIATED WITH SUCCESS OF DECEMBER MARRIAGES

What are some of the most important factors in contributing to the success of a December marriage? McKain reported several factors.

1. Couples who had known each other well over a period of years before being married were more likely to be successfully married. A surprisingly large number of the couples had known each other several years before being married. For example, some had grown up in the same community, whereas others had met as young adults and then drifted apart before marrying each other in later life. A large number of the couples had been related to each other through their previous marriages and had become well acquainted with each other as relatives. Many met each other and became good friends during the previous marriage. One older man reported,

   > When Ethel (his first wife) died, Marie was only a friend. I never even thought of marrying her until a year later when I suddenly realized how much she meant to me. Up until then I always thought of her as Ethel's friend. Now it seems that I've always been married to her.[36]

   An older woman who had known her second husband long before their marriage said, "I have known Alvin since long before his wife and my husband passed away. He was a good husband before, so I knew he would be now. Marrying just seemed the natural thing to do."

Knowing each other a long time before marriage provided the older couple with a greater understanding of each other and a sound basis by which to judge their compatibility. Therefore, a long friendship before marriage contributed to the success of December marriages.

2. Couples who had common interests and enjoyed the same activities tended to be happily married. Couples who did not share interests were less likely to be happy. The importance of common recreational interests was indicated by the large number of couples who greatly enjoyed fishing together or playing cards "all night."
3. Approval by children and friends was quite important to the success of the December marriage because those marriages that were approved by children and friends were more likely to be successful than those that were not approved. Older persons are sensitive to the societal pressure against December marriages. As a result, they depend upon their children and friends in overcoming this problem.[37] Approval by family and friends is important to the success of marriage at any age but may be particularly important to the success of December marriages.

   If the marriage has not been approved by the children and friends, the older person may feel alienated from them. This could eventually contribute to resentment toward the marriage partner. The practical everyday problems of marriage adjustment are more difficult without the support of children and friends. Also, the morale of older persons may be lowered if they perceive that children and those close to them feel they lack wisdom and good judgment in their decision to marry.
4. Those older persons who easily adjusted to the reduced involvement with society and reduced life space that occurred in various aspects of their lives, whether these were the result of personal choice or forced upon them by society, tended to be happily married. Those who had difficulty in adjusting to this reduced involvement also had difficulty in adjusting to marriage. Adaptability is important in successfully meeting life changes in general, and influences the ability to adjust to a December marriage in particular.
5. Those individuals who were well adjusted personally and had a high degree of morale were more likely to be happily married than those who were unhappy. McKain's research indicated that unless both the husband and wife were reasonably well adjusted, their December marriage was not likely to be successful. Couples tended to be happily married when both the husband and wife were satisfied with their lives, content and happy with the later years of life, optimistic and cheerful, and did not feel that luck had been against them.
6. Adequate financial resources are positively related to successful December marriages. If both husband and wife owned homes prior to the marriage, they were much more likely to be happily married than if only one or neither owned a home.

The importance of dual home ownership probably is a reflection of the couple's relative affluence. Dual home ownership also may have symbolized an equality in the relationship and indicated that both partners brought something concrete to the marriage relationship. In those cases where only one partner owned a home, there was a tendency for the partner who did not own one to feel at a disadvantage and that something of the spouse's former marriage remained in their December marriage. As one older wife stated, "This will always be Millie's (his first wife) home. Everything in it reflects her taste and personality. I feel like a houseguest. I don't think I'll ever be comfortable here."

If both husband and wife had sufficient incomes before marriage, they usually experienced a successful marriage. An important finding in McKain's research centered on how husbands and wives managed their financial resources and spent their income. Those couples who pooled their financial resources and jointly spent their income were more likely to be happily married than those couples who had reservations about their financial resources and did not jointly spend their combined income. The pooling of resources and joint spending of income probably reflects a sense of solidarity and closeness.

The arrangement for sharing property and income or giving it to children was important in predicting marriage success because it indicated the priority one spouse held in the eyes of the other. The December marriage was more likely to be successful if each marriage partner had first claim on the financial resources of the other.

In conclusion, December marriages tend to be very successful. For many older persons who are alone, marriage offers a great potential for satisfying many emotional and social needs.

Grandparenthood

An increasing number of people are becoming grandparents. Approximately 70 per cent of older persons today have living grandchildren.[38] More and more people will be experiencing the role of grandparent in the future as medical technology improves, the standard of living continues to rise, and the length of life increases. Most young persons now can expect to enjoy many years as grandparents in the future because life expectancy is now approximately seventy-six years for women and sixty-eight years for men.

IMPORTANCE OF GRANDPARENTHOOD

Grandparenthood is quite often beneficial to grandchildren and older persons alike. Grandparents provide a positive influence in the development of grandchildren. Among these positive influences are the following:

1. Contact with grandparents can provide grandchildren with a greater sense of family solidarity and family history. The child who has an affectionate relationship with grandparents has the added joy of being loved by adults other than parents, which can be a source of emotional security.
2. A moderate amount of contact with grandparents can contribute to grandchildren developing an expanded understanding and acceptance of older persons. There is evidence that youth who have moderate contact with older persons tend to have a more positive attitude toward them than those who have little or no contact.[39]
3. Grandparents can provide additional models of identification for grandchildren. Many grandchildren admire their grandparents very much and learn from them effective ways of reacting to various situations. They can learn from their grandparents how to cope with frustration and failure, how to go about achieving a goal, and how to develop positive ways of relating to people. They may learn from their grandparents how to enjoy leisure-time activity.
4. Grandparents can provide a sense of emotional stability for grandchildren. This potential contribution of grandparents may become even more important as the pace of life becomes increasingly hectic in our highly industrialized and technological society.

   Children today grow up in a very busy world. Demands on children and their parents create a harried life-style that cannot help but have its impact upon children. Some adjust to this life-style well, but for others it is disturbing.

   Grandparents can provide a calming life-style that is psychologically beneficial to children. Free from the demands of employment, they often have the time to spend with children in a relaxed and enjoyable manner.
5. Grandparents can assist in the role of child rearing. One way that some grandparents help in the rearing of their grandchildren is taking care of them while the mother and father are both employed outside the home. Grandparents also frequently serve as baby-sitters with their grandchildren while the parents go out in the evenings or vacation alone.

   The importance of grandparents in the lives of young children has been demonstrated most dramatically outside the family situation in the foster-grandparent programs with institutionalized children. The employment of older persons as substitute grandparents has alleviated depression, depressed intellectual functioning, and social immaturity among institutionalized children.[40]

BENEFITS OF GRANDPARENTHOOD TO OLDER PERSONS

Most older persons find pleasure and satisfaction in being a grandparent. What do they feel is most satisfying about this role? Research by Bernice Neugarten and Karol Weinstein [41] indicates what grandparents have reported to be the major sources of satisfaction.

Biological Renewal. Many older persons feel young again through their grandchildren, experiencing a renewed enthusiasm and excitement for life. Many grandparents also see their lives going on into the future as grandchildren become a symbol of continuation of the family line.

Emotional Fulfillment. Grandparenthood provides a sense of emotional fulfillment for many older persons. Much joy and satisfaction results from a relationship with a grandchild that is primarily one of affection and recreation and involves very few responsibilities of child rearing. For many, grandparenthood offers the opportunity to succeed in a new emotional role; this role becomes a major source through which their "I'm OK" position is reinforced. Many feel themselves to be better grandparents than they were parents. Some see grandparenthood as an opportunity to rectify mistakes they made as parents. One grandfather stated:

> I can be, and I can do for my grandchildren things I could never do for my own kids. I was too busy with my business to enjoy my kids, but my grandchildren are different. Now I have the time to be with them.[42]

Being a Teacher or Resource Person. For a small proportion of individuals, being a grandparent gives the opportunity to be a teacher or resource person. Grandparents in this role derive great satisfaction from contributing to the grandchild's knowledge and development as a person. Associated with the role of teacher or resource person are feelings of being important to and needed by the grandchild.

Experiencing Achievements Vicariously Through the Grandchild. Many grandparents enjoy experiencing achievements vicariously through their grandchildren. They can observe their grandchildren attaining goals that neither the grandparents nor their children achieved.

PROBLEMS OF GRANDPARENTHOOD

Whereas most persons delight in being grandparents some individuals do not enjoy it. Neugarten and Weinstein [43] found that approximately one third of the people in their study were having difficulty in their role as grandparents and were uncomfortable because their self-image conflicted with the role of grandparent. Some individuals harbor negative attitudes and stereotypes about the grandparent role, and when they become grandparents these attitudes and stereotypes are then generalized to themselves. A few grandparents in the study by Neugarten and Weinstein felt indifferent about the care and responsibility concerning the grandchild, yet they also felt guilty about their indifference. Some grandparents had been involved in disputes with the parents regarding child-rearing practices, and this conflict was a source of strain and disappointment.

One of the major sources of dissatisfaction with the grandparent role is a sense of remoteness from the grandchildren. In the study by Neugarten and Weinstein, 27 per cent of the grandmothers and 29 per cent of the grandfathers reported feeling distant from their grandchildren and that grandparenthood had very little significance in their lives. Other research also indicates that older persons may not feel close to their grandchildren.[44]

One of the major causes for this feeling of remoteness is that grandparents are often separated by great distances from their grandchild. The child may know grandparents only as "shadowy" figures who appear once a year for a visit of a few days.

Another reason for the remoteness stems from the philosophy in our society that children should be autonomous and independent of their parents. Parents tend to find themselves separated from their children and, as a result, grandparents are separated even more from their grandchildren.[45]

Strong peer relationships among children in American society often result in children having little time or inclination to be with older persons. Peer relationships are strongest during adolescence. This is one reason why grandparents enjoy their grandchildren more when the children are young. As children get older, they often spend less time with their grandparents.[46]

STYLES OF GRANDPARENTHOOD

What are the different ways that people perform the role of grandparent? Research by Neugarten and Weinstein [47] identified five distinct styles of grandparenting.

The Formal Style. This describes grandparents who follow what they regard as the proper and traditional role. They maintain a constant interest in their grandchildren but take care not to offer advice on child rearing. They preserve clearly defined lines between being a parent and a grandparent. All parental responsibilities belong strictly to the parents.

The Fun Seeker. This grandparent's relationship to the child is characterized by playfulness and informality. The grandchild is a source of leisure activity, fun, and enjoyment. Authority lines with the child and parents are not considered too important because this is a relationship in which both the grandparents and the grandchild have fun.

The Substitute Parent. This style of grandparenting is engaged in primarily by grandmothers usually through parental request. The grandmother actually assumes child-rearing responsibilities temporarily while the mother and father are working during the day, while they are out in the evenings, or when the parents vacation alone.

The Reservoir of Family Wisdom. This style represents an authoritarian type of relationship in which the grandparent is a source of wisdom and knowledge. The grandparent becomes the dispenser of special knowledge, wisdom, and skills and is regarded as an authority by the young parents who assume a subordinate position. This style of grandparenting was found infrequently in the research by Neugarten and Weinstein.

The Distant Figure. This grandparent has only scarce contact with the grandchildren and may see them only on special occasions, such as Christmas. Although the grandparent may be interested in the grandchild, for various reasons, he remains remote in the children's lives. At most, the grandparent becomes an occasional Santa Claus.

CHANGING NATURE OF GRANDPARENTHOOD

The relationship of grandparents to grandchildren is increasingly becoming one of recreation and affection with little involvement in child-rearing responsibilities. Authority aspects of the relationship are becoming less important. The interaction of grandparents with grandchildren seems to be moving toward greater indulgence and permissiveness. The grandparents are more permissive toward the grandchildren than the parents are.[48] Evidence indicates that children see their grandmothers as being more permissive and more responsive to their needs than their mothers.[49]

References

1. Stinnett, Nick; Linda M. Carter; and James E. Montgomery. "Older Persons' Perceptions of Their Marriages." *Journal of Marriage and the Family*, vol. 34, 1972, pp. 665–670
2. Havighurst, Robert J., and Ruth Albrecht. *Older People.* New York: Longmans, Green, 1953.
   Rose, A. M. and W. A. Peterson. *Older People and Their Social World.* Philadelphia: F. A Davis, 1965.
   Montgomery, James E. "Social Characteristics of the Aged in a Small Pennsylvania Community." *Home Economics Research Publication 233.* University Park, Pa.: Pennsylvania State University.
   Stinnett, Nick; Janet Collins; and James E. Montgomery. "Marital Need Satisfaction of Older Husbands and Wives." *Journal of Marriage and the Family*, vol. 32, 1970, pp. 428–434.
3. Atchley, Robert C. *The Social Forces in Later Life.* Belmont, Calif.: Wadsworth, 1972.
4. Fried, Edrita G., and Karl Stern. "The Situation of the Aged Within the Family." *American Journal of Orthopsychiatry*, vol. 18, 1948, pp. 31–54.
   Lipman, Aaron. "Role Conceptions and Morale of Couples in Retirement." *Journal of Gerontology*, vol. 16, 1961, pp. 267–271.
   Stinnett, Collins, and Montgomery, op. cit.
5. Riley, Matilda W., and Ann Foner. "Aging in Society." *An Inventory of Research Findings*, vol. I. New York: Russell Sage Foundation, 1968.
6. Fried and Stern, op. cit.
7. Stinnett, Carter, and Montgomery, op. cit.
8. Ibid.
9. Ibid.
10. Lipman, op. cit.
11. Stinnett, Carter, and Montgomery, op. cit.
12. Atchley, op. cit.
13. Lipman, op. cit.
14. Kalish, Richard A. *Late Adulthood: Perspectives on Human Development.* Monterey, Calif.: Brooks/Cole 1975.
15. Riley and Foner, op. cit.
16. Lipman, op. cit.
17. Ibid.
    Stinnett, Collins, and Montgomery, op. cit.
    Stinnett, Carter, and Montgomery, op. cit.
18. Clark, Margaret, and Barbara Anderson. *Culture and Aging.* Springfield, Ill.: Thomas, 1967.
19. Lipman, op. cit.
20. Atchley, op. cit.
21. McKain, Walter C. *Retirement Marriage.* Storrs, Conn.: University of Connecticut Press, 1969.
22. Atchley, op. cit.
23. Ibid.

24. McKain, op. cit., p. 127.
25. Atchley, op. cit.
26. Dean, Stanley R. As reported in *Geriatric Forces,* vol. 5, 1966, p. 2.
27. McKain, op. cit., p. 8.
28. Ibid.
29. Ibid.
30. Goolsby, Greta. "Attitudes of Older Husbands and Wives and Attitudes of College Students Concerning Marriage During the Later Years: A Comparison." Masters thesis, Oklahoma State University, 1971.
31. McKain, op. cit., p. 35.
32. Ibid., p. 36.
33. Ibid., p. 37.
34. Ibid., p. 41.
35. Ibid., p. 46.
36. Ibid., p. 125.
37. Atchley, op. cit.
38. Ibid.
39. Stinnett, Nick, and James E. Montgomery. "Youth's Perceptions of Marriages of Older Persons." *Journal of Marriage and the Family,* vol. 30, 1968, pp. 392–396.
40. Troll, Lillian E. "The Family of Later Life: A Decade of Review." *Journal of Marriage and the Family,* vol. 33, 1971, pp. 263–290.
Saltz, Rosalyn. "Evaluation of a Foster Grandparent Program." In *Child Welfare Services: A Source Book,* edited by A. Kalushin. New York: Macmillan, 1970.
41. Neugarten, Bernice L., and Karol K. Weinstein. "The Changing American Grandparent." *Journal of Marriage and the Family,* vol. 26, 1964, pp. 199–204.
42. Ibid., pp. 201–202.
43. Ibid.
44. Troll, op. cit.
Cumming, Elaine, and William Henry. *Growing Old.* New York: Basic Books, 1961.
45. Young, Leontine. *The Fractured Family.* New York: McGraw-Hill, 1973.
46. Clark, Margaret. "Cultural Values and Dependency in Later Life." In *The Dependencies of Old People,* edited by Richard Kalish. Ann Arbor: Institute for Gerontology, 1969.
47. Neugarten and Weinstein, op. cit.
48. Updegraff, Sue G. "Changing Role of the Grandmother." *Journal of Home Economics,* vol. 60, 1968, pp. 177–180.
49. Crase, Dixie R., and Norejane Hendrickson. "Maternal Grandmothers and Mothers." *Journal of Home Economics,* vol. 60, 1968, pp. 181–185.

17 Divorce and Remarriage

Photo by Walker Montgomery

Nothing except a battle lost can be half so melancholy as a battle won.

Arthur Wellesley

The Increase in Divorce

Divorce is a way of terminating a marriage situation in which one or both partners cannot relate to each other in a satisfying manner or cannot interact together without psychological injury to one or both. In transactional analysis terms, the couple have established a pattern of reinforcing each other's "I'm not OK" position and are receiving more negative psychological strokes than positive strokes from each other. Because they cannot or will not change this pattern, divorce is selected as a way out of the unhappy interaction.

The decision to choose divorce as a response to an unsatisfying marriage relationship is most often made during the first three years of marriage. There has been a marked increase in the frequency of divorce. For example, in 1915 the divorce rate was one per 1,000 population. As of 1975 the divorce rate had reached approximately 4.7 per 1,000 population.[1] The increased incidence of divorce is also reflected in the ratio of divorced persons (who have not remarried) to persons with intact marriages. This ratio has increased from 35 divorced persons for every 1,000 persons who were married and living with their spouse in 1960 to a level of 63 per 1,000 in 1974. What percentage of marriages eventually end in divorce? On the basis of figures compiled by the National Vital Statistics Division, an estimated 25 per cent of marriages now end in divorce. Although the divorce rates have increased markedly, the number of people who enter marriage remains very high. There were approximately 2,223,000 marriages in 1974 as compared to 970,000 divorces.[2]

Growth in the divorce rate does not mean that there is a larger proportion of unhappy marriages than in the past, but rather that divorce now is simply easier to obtain. The following factors have contributed to the increased divorce rate:

1. The divorce courts have become more lenient toward divorce and the grounds for divorce have multiplied.
2. There is a more liberal attitude among the public concerning divorce. No longer is the stigma and shame attached to the divorced person that was true in the past.

Figure 17-1 Marriage and Divorce Rates Since 1890

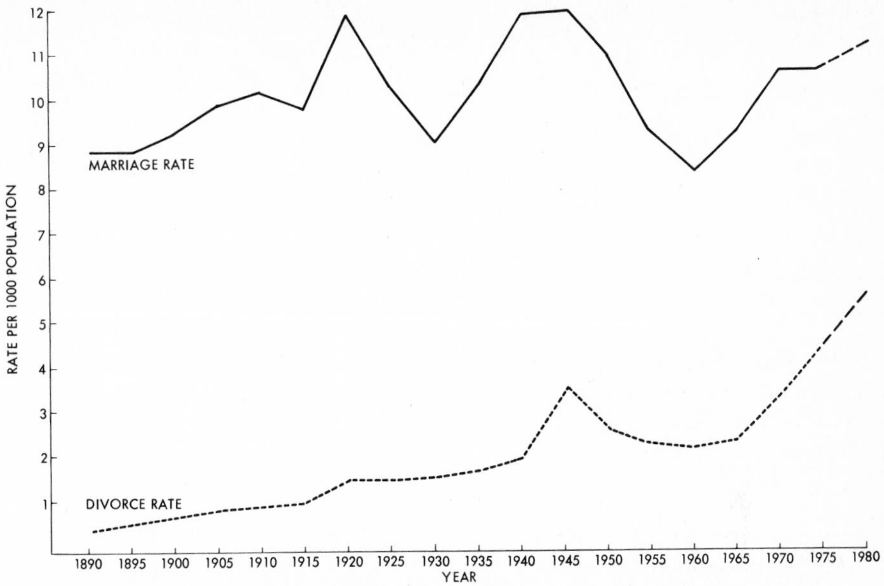

MARRIAGE AND DIVORCE RATES PROJECTED TO 1980 BASED ON 1969-1974 DATA.

From *Statistical Abstract of the United States, 1975,* 96th ed. (Washington, D.C.: U.S. Bureau of Census, 1975); Births, Marriages, Divorces, and Deaths for March 1975 in monthly *Vital Statistics Report,* Vol. 24, No. 3 (Rockville, Md.: Division of Vital Statistics, National Center for Health Statistics, Public Health Service, May 27, 1975).

3. Control by the community over the behavior of individuals has declined as a result of industrialization and urbanization, which serve to give the individual greater anonymity. The control by the community is also lessened by a decline in religious authority and by the weakening of extended family ties. Evidence indicates that attitudes toward divorce are less negative, and divorce rates are high in urban areas where there is a high migration rate.[3]
4. Women are better able to support themselves financially and thus have greater independence and freedom of choice concerning whether they will remain in a marriage relationship or not.
5. A higher standard of living has enabled more people to afford the financial expense of divorce.
6. There is a tendency to underestimate the problems and difficulties associated with divorce and instead to emphasize the beneficial aspects of escaping from an undesirable marriage.
7. The comfort-loving orientation of individuals in the United States and a refusal to tolerate discomfort and inconvenience has been suggested as one factor contributing to the high divorce rate.[4]

8. The standards for measuring marriage success now place more emphasis upon happiness and personal satisfaction within the marriage relationship than was true in the past. These goals are more difficult to achieve than were the less psychologically oriented expectations for marriage success in the past, such as permanence, production of children, and cooperation for economic production and survival.

The Divorce Process

One of the reasons why the engagement is such a happy experience is the excitement and anticipation of entering a union with another person. The adventure of building and sharing life with the person who has been selected over all others is truly a rewarding sensation. Conversely, one reason why divorce is so unpleasant and depressing is the realization that one is now taking steps to separate from the person with whom one once eagerly anticipated establishing a union. Now many ties that have been established since marriage must be rejected.

Separating oneself from a spouse is complex and difficult. The process is complicated and hard because, as Paul Bohannan [5] has noted, at least six different types of separation experiences occur simultaneously:

1. The emotional divorce, which centers around the emotional problems of the deteriorating marriage relationship.
2. The legal divorce, which is concerned with the grounds for divorce.
3. The economic divorce, which focuses upon finances and property settlement.
4. The coparental divorce, which is concerned with child custody, single-parent home, and visitation.
5. The community divorce, which centers around the changes of community and friendship patterns associated with most divorces.
6. The psychic divorce, which involves the problem of regaining individual autonomy.

A better understanding of each of these types of separation experiences gives us greater insight and empathy concerning divorce.

THE EMOTIONAL DIVORCE

A marriage relationship necessarily involves the emotional interaction and interdependence of the partners to some degree. At least at the time the couple married, the emotional feelings about one another were positive and supportive. However, at the time of divorce, the tone of emotional interaction typically becomes negative or indifferent. The couple's emotional feelings tend to concentrate upon the weak points of each other's personalities and upon the weak points of the relationship.[6] In short, the couple have decided that their emotional relationship with each other is no longer satisfactory. One or both partners then gradually find it desirable to separate emotionally from each other as much as possible.

Divorce is the second most severe crisis, in terms of emotional stress involved, which anyone experiences in life. It is surpassed only by the death of a spouse. The emotional divorce often results in a feeling of losing a loved one almost as much, though by a different type of experience, as does the death of a mate.[7] Grief or disorientation is the natural reaction to the loss of a loved one. In some instances, grief is the reaction even if the loved one has become a hated one. It is natural to mourn the loss of any intimate relationship in which there was a high degree of involvement and a backlog of some happy memories. The amount of mourning that one experiences depends upon the degree of emotional involvement in the relationship. Mourning over the emotional divorce may last for months or years. Not all couples, of course, experience grief, but few can divorce without feeling disoriented.

Bohannan [8] has suggested that the emotional divorce is particularly difficult because it entails deliberate rejection of one person by another. For some people the emotional divorce is more disturbing than is the loss of a mate through death, perhaps because they have thought about divorce and wished for it. This emotional frustration must typically be borne alone as our society recognizes no way of mourning a divorce. The distress over the emotional divorce is somewhat eased after divorced persons make new arrangements for living and establish a new daily living rouine.

THE LEGAL DIVORCE

Couples who become emotionally separated from each other and decide to dissolve their relationship must obtain a legal divorce. Before society will recognize the couple as being divorced, certain legal procedures must be carried out. The legal orientation of many courts is to determine the grounds for divorce and identify the "guilty party." Historically, the legal divorce has been seen primarily as a way of punishing the guilty party and protecting the innocent party.

Whatever the emotional problems and conflict the couple have experienced in living together, whatever the reason they feel they can no longer live with each other, these real situations as revealed to their lawyers must be taken by the lawyers and translated into language that the law will accept. When the divorce action goes to court, it must be written in a way that the court can legally accept; specifically this means that there must be grounds for the divorce and that the grounds listed in the divorce action must be among those that are legally recognized by the particular state in which the divorce is being sought.[9]

Grounds for Divorce. A very common legal grounds for divorce today is cruelty, which constitutes a high percentage of all divorces that are granted. Another frequently used grounds for divorce is desertion.

Cruelty is a very broad reason for divorce and in some states is synonymous with incompatibility. Behavior that falls under the category of cruelty may range from physical violence to mental cruelty. Divorces have also been granted on the grounds of cruelty for such seemingly absurd reasons as a husband requiring his wife to retire at nine o'clock and a woman's pet goldfish being used as bait by her husband.[10]

The grounds listed often are not the true reasons for the divorce. For example, a couple may be so incompatible and their marriage relationship may be so unsatisfactory that one or both of them may commit adultery. Committing adultery would be classified as grounds for the divorce but would not be the basic reason in this particular case; rather, it would be a symptom of a deeper problem in the marriage relationship.

There is considerable variation from state to state concerning grounds for divorce, as is illustrated in Table 17–1. Many states have several grounds, whereas others have only a few. There is also variation regarding minimum residence requirements before a divorce can be granted.

The necessity of obtaining grounds for divorce frequently increases feelings of anger because it encourages the couple to dwell upon each other's "faults" and to select one of these as the reason for the divorce. In fact, the mere process of going through the legalities of divorce (going to court and each partner having a lawyer) creates an atmosphere conducive to hostility and enmity.

It is interesting that whereas couples marry by mutual consent, they cannot, according to the laws in many states, divorce by mutual consent. When one partner wants a divorce and brings suit against the other on some grounds defined by law as acceptable, the divorce is normally granted. However, if both partners desire a divorce and there are no clear grounds, in order to satisfy the legal requirements, they may be forced to agree that one partner will allege certain grounds and the other partner will make no defense. In other words, they must perjure themselves in court to demonstrate that one partner was guilty and one was innocent in order to satisfy the court and obtain the divorce. Such agreement is common but is defined by the court as collusion, and if discovered the court may dismiss the suit.[11]

Table 17–1 Grounds for Divorce

State	No Fault	Adultery	Cruelty	Desertion	Non-Support	Habitual Drunkenness	Felony	Impotency	Pregnancy at Marriage	Drug Addiction	Fraudulent Contract	Other Grounds	Residence Time
Alabama	X	X	X	X	X	X	X	X	X	X		Crime against nature, imprisonment for 2 years, incompatibility, insanity for 5 years, separation for 2 years, breakdown of marriage with no reasonable likelihood of preservation.	6 months
Alaska		X	X	X		X	X	X		X		Incompatibility, insanity for 18 months, indignities.	Must be resident of state
Arizona	X											None	90 days
Arkansas		X	X	X	X	X	X	X				Indignities, separation with no cohabitation for 3 years, insanity for 3 years, bigamy.	60 days
California	X											Incurable insanity.	6 months
Colorado	X											None	90 days
Connecticut	X	X	X	X	X	X	X				X	Incompatibility, insanity for 5 years, separation with no cohabitation for 18 months due to incompatibility.	1 year
Delaware	X	X		X		X	X			X		Mental illness, incompatibility, bigamy, homosexuality, venereal disease.	90 days
Dist. of Col.		X		X			X					Separation with no cohabitation for 1 year, separation for 1 year after separation decree.	1 year
Florida	X											Insanity for 3 years.	6 months

Table 17–1 Grounds for Divorce (*Continued*)

State	No Fault	Adultery	Cruelty	Desertion	Non-Support	Habitual Drunkenness	Felony	Impotency	Pregnancy at Marriage	Drug Addiction	Fraudulent Contract	Other Grounds	Residence Time
Georgia	X	X	X	X		X	X	X	X	X	X	Insanity for 2 years with prognosis as incurable, consanguinity, mental incapacity at time of marriage.	6 months
Hawaii	X											Separation for 2 years.	1 year
Idaho	X	X	X	X	X	X	X					Separation with no cohabitation for 5 years, insanity for 3 years with prognosis as incurable.	6 weeks
Illinois		X	X	X		X	X	X		X		Bigamy, communication of venereal disease, attempted murder.	1 year
Indiana	X						X	X				Insanity for 2 years with prognosis as incurable.	6 months
Iowa	X											None	1 year
Kansas		X	X	X		X	X					Insanity for 3 years, incompatibility, gross neglect of duty.	60 days
Kentucky	X											None	6 months
Louisiana		X					X					Separation with no cohabitation for 1 year, separation for 1 year after decree for separation.	1 year
Maine	X	X	X	X	X	X		X		X		None	6 months
Maryland		X		X			X	X				Separation with no cohabitation for 12 months, insanity for 3 years, any cause rendering marriage null and void.	1 year
Massachusetts		X	X	X	X	X		X		X		Sentence to confinement for 5 years or more.	Must be resident of state

Michigan	X										None	6 months
Minnesota	X					X	X			X	Commitment for mental illness, separation for 1 year after decree for separation, course of conduct detrimental to the marriage relationship of party seeking divorce, serious marital discord affecting attitude of one or both parties toward marriage.	1 year
Mississippi		X	X	X		X	X	X	X	X	Insanity for 3 years with prognosis as incurable, consanguinity, bigamy, insanity at time of marriage (unknown to complaining party).	1 year
Missouri	X										None	3 months
Montana	X										Separation with no cohabitation for 6 months, serious marital discord adversely affects attitude of one of parties.	3 months
Nebraska	X										None	1 year
Nevada											Insanity for 2 years, separation with no cohabitation for 1 year, incompatibility.	6 weeks
New Hampshire	X	X	X	X	X	X	X	X			Joining religious order which professes to believe relationship of husband and wife is unlawful, treatment which injures health or endangers reason, willing absence of either party for two years without consent of other.	1 year

Table 17–1 Grounds for Divorce (*Continued*)

State	No Fault	Adul-tery	Cruelty	Deser-tion	Non-Sup-port	Habitual Drunken-ness	Felony	Impo-tency	Pregnancy at Marriage	Drug Addic-tion	Fraudu-lent Contract	Other Grounds	Residence Time
New Jersey		X	X	X		X				X		Imprisonment for 18 or more consecutive months, deviant sexual conduct performed without consent of plaintiff, insanity for 2 years, separation for 18 months.	1 year
New Mexico		X	X	X								Incompatibility.	6 months
New York		X	X	X								Separation with no cohabitation for 1 year pursuant to written separation agreement, separation for 1 year pursuant to decree for separation, imprisonment for 3 years.	1 year
North Carolina		X						X	X			Crime against nature, bestiality, insanity for 3 years, separation with no cohabitation for 1 year.	6 months
North Dakota	X	X	X	X	X	X	X					Insanity for 5 years with prognosis as incurable.	1 year
Ohio		X	X	X		X	X	X			X	Procurement of out-of-state divorce, gross neglect of duty, bigamy. Separation without cohabitation for 2 years (or 4 years when one party is confined to mental institution).	6 months
Oklahoma		X	X	X		X	X	X	X		X	Incompatibility, insanity for 5 years, procurement of out-of-state divorce, gross neglect of duty.	6 months

Oregon	X											Circumstances justifying annulment.	6 months
Pennsylvania		X	X	X			X				X	Indignities, consanguinity, bigamy, insanity for 3 years, incapability of procreation.	1 year
Rhode Island	X	X	X	X	X	X	X	X		X		Any gross misbehavior or wickedness, separation with no cohabitation for 5 years, marriage was originally void.	1 year
South Carolina		X	X	X		X				X		Separation with no cohabitation for 3 years.	1 year
South Dakota		X	X	X	X	X	X					Insanity for 5 years.	Must be resident of state
Tennessee		X	X	X	X	X	X	X	X	X		Indignities, bigamy, attempted homicide, wife separating herself from husband for 2 years without reasonable cause, separation for 2 years following decree for separation.	No length of residence required if plaintiff is resident of state at time of filing suit, otherwise there is residence requirement of 6 months.
Texas	X	X	X	X			X					Confinement in mental institution for 3 years, separation with no cohabitation for 3 years, incompatibility.	6 months
Utah		X	X	X	X	X	X	X				Separation for 3 years after decree for separation, permanent insanity.	3 months

Table 17–1 Grounds for Divorce (*Continued*)

State	No Fault	Adultery	Cruelty	Desertion	Non-Support	Habitual Drunkenness	Felony	Impotency	Pregnancy at Marriage	Drug Addiction	Fraudulent Contract	Other Grounds	Residence Time
Vermont		X	X	X	X		X					Separation with no cohabitation for 6 months, insanity for 5 years.	6 months
Virginia		X	X	X			X					Separation without cohabitation, sodomy.	6 months
Washington	X											None	Must be resident of state
West Virginia		X	X	X		X	X			X		Separation with no cohabitation for 2 years, permanent insanity.	1 year
Wisconsin		X	X	X	X	X						Separation with no cohabitation for 1 year, separation for 1 year after decree for separation, committed to imprisonment for 3 years or more, committed to mental institution for 1 year.	6 months
Wyoming		X	X	X	X	X	X	X	X			Indignities, separation with no cohabitation for 2 years, insanity for 2 years, vagrancy of husband.	60 days

SOURCE: Martindale-Hubbell Law Dictionary, Vol. VI, Law Digests, Uniform Acts, A.B.A. Section. One Hundred and Eighth Year, 1976 (Chicago: R.R. Donnelley and Sons Company, 1975).

It frequently happens that neither partner wishes to be identified as the guilty party. In these instances, when one partner sues for divorce, the other partner (the defendant) countercharges the plaintiff with being guilty also of an offense that constitutes grounds for divorce. This countercharge is called recrimination, and sometimes when this happens, the divorce is granted to neither party because there is not a guilty and innocent party. A few states, such as Nevada, make exceptions for this. When both partners have committed offenses that constitute grounds for divorce, the court can grant a divorce to the party who is judged as being less at fault.[12]

No-Fault Divorce. The present system of requiring specific grounds for divorce and requiring that one partner be a guilty party contributes to frustration and hostility between the couple who may have no intention of maintaining a marriage. In an effort to improve this system, the concept of no-fault dissolution of marriage is increasingly becoming accepted as a means of legally terminating marriage.[13]

Under the no-fault system, it is not necessary to have a guilty party and an innocent party. A person may file for dissolution of the marriage without making accusations against the spouse. The grounds in this instance are irreconcilable differences or an irretrievably broken marriage. A growing number of states now list these as grounds.[14]

The Dissolution of Marriage law enacted in California served as a model for other states. This law removed fault, and the question of whether wife or husband is to blame has been eliminated. The grounds in California have been reduced to incurable insanity or irreconcilable differences. If the court finds either of these two grounds present, the marriage is dissolved and the decree is final within six months. California also simplified the property allocation with the enactment of the no-fault system. Property is generally divided equally.[15]

THE ECONOMIC DIVORCE

The economic aspect of divorce is often the most underestimated part as far as the implications for the couple. The economic aspects of divorce include legal fees, court costs, division of property, alimony, and child support.

Legal Fees and Court Costs. Many persons are surprised to learn the price of legal fees and think they are being overcharged by lawyers. However, many lawyers regard the fees set by the court as too low. Such lawyers may make additional charges for the other services they perform for their clients. Most divorce lawyers work on an hourly rate and adjust the rate to the particular income level of clients. In most divorce cases, legal fees for both husband and wife are paid by the husband.[16]

Court costs and legal fees depend upon the community, region of the country, income of the persons getting the divorce, whether the divorce is contested, property involved, and the difficulty of the legal questions involved. It is, therefore, very difficult to state an average cost for obtaining a divorce. If the divorce is uncontested, the court costs tend to average approximately $300. The court costs for contested divorces are higher. It is not uncommon for each lawyer's fees to be $500 or more in uncontested cases. For contested cases they are considerably more.

Division of Property. In most divorce cases the wife receives from one third to one half of the property. Often the division of property is a perplexing task and becomes a source of dispute. The property within the household is considered to be jointly owned and most items—except clothing and jewelry—are usually not the exclusive property of any one member of the family.[17] For example, to whom does the car or stereo or television set belong?

A few states, such as California, have what is referred to as a "community property" law in which the wife is considered to have made a direct financial contribution to the marriage, and property accumulated during the marriage is divided equally between husband and wife.[18] In other words, all property is considered community property and is shared equally except for possessions the spouses owned before the marriage or property that each spouse has inherited.

Alimony. Alimony is the payment of money during and after divorce, usually by the ex-husband to the ex-wife. Payment of alimony is based upon the expectation that a husband takes on the duty of supporting his wife at the time of marriage. In some states, alimony is viewed as a form of punishment of the husband for mistreating his wife. In such states, if the wife is the guilty party in the divorce, she is not entitled to alimony.[19]

Generally, the amount of alimony depends upon:

1. *The "moral" or "immoral" conduct of the wife that comes to the attention of the court.* An innocent wife is awarded more than a wife who is judged guilty of immoral conduct.
2. *Need of the wife.* The greater the economic need of the wife, the higher the alimony payments are set. In determining the need of the wife, such factors as her level of education or training, health, age, and number of children may be taken into consideration.
3. *Ability of the husband to pay.* The greater the husband's ability to pay, the higher the alimony payments awarded.

The court may be petitioned by either spouse to adjust the alimony payments as a result of a change in either the former wife's need or the former husband's ability to pay. Usually, all alimony stops at the time of the former wife's remarriage.[20]

Child Support. The responsibility for child support usually lies with the father as long as he is physically and financially able to provide or until the child reaches the age of majority. The father makes child-support payments regardless of whether his former wife remarries or not. In setting child-support payments, the court considers the father's ability to pay, his health, and the needs of the child.[21] Child-support payments usually range between one fourth and one third of the father's monthly income. However, child-support payments can constitute up to one half of the father's monthly income if several children are involved.[22]

THE COPARENTAL DIVORCE

Quite possibly the most enduringly painful aspect of divorce is the coparental divorce. Coparental divorce simply refers to the fact that the child's parents are not living with each other. Even when both parents share joint legal custody, one parent obtains physical custody of the child. Therefore, the child lives with one parent with occasional visits from the other.

Custody of the child is usually given to the mother. Generally, the father does not get custody of the child unless the court is convinced that the moral character, economic situation, or emotional instability of the mother will have a deleterious effect on the child. The court usually awards custody of all children to one parent so that children will not be separated. Custody decrees are temporary and may be challenged at any time by the parent without custody.[23]

The coparental aspect of divorce is painful, particularly when the former husband and wife differ greatly with respect to what they desire their children to become spiritually, socially, professionally, and physically. In fact, a vast difference of opinion concerning what is most important in life may have contributed substantially to the divorce and tends to continue through the children.[24]

Similarly, a man may find it very difficult to relinquish the influence he had on his children. For example, a child may develop undesirable traits similar to the mother. The man may have found these traits particularly objectionable in his former wife; in fact, they may have been major factors contributing to the divorce. As one former husband has said:

My wife is typically very dogmatic about things. I mean, she often is quite offensive about it. Her way is obviously right. Other views are wrong. Well, in the three years since our divorce, I have watched my nine-year-old son progressively become dogmatic and it just makes me sick. There isn't much I can do about it. I'm not around him enough to counteract her influence.

The divorced mother who has custody of the children is faced with the challenge of coping with a single-parent household. She must make most of the decisions concerning all aspects of the child's life, such as general life-style, education, recreation, and social and cultural activities. She generally has no one to share in making these decisions.

THE COMMUNITY DIVORCE

When a couple divorce, there is a tendency for at least one of them to move to another community. The move to a new community requires the adjustment of cultivating new friendships, a new social life, moving into a new home, and in general becoming established in another location. This is therapeutic for many persons, giving a sense of starting a new life.

Even when divorced persons remain in the same community, friendships are likely to change. Some previous friends may have taken sides during the divorce with the individual's former mate and alienated themselves from the individual. The divorced person may feel "out of place" interacting with the couples with whom he or she and a former marriage partner had socialized. The individual may associate more and more with unmarried persons. He or she may join organizations for single persons, such as "Parents Without Partners." Regardless of whether the divorced person moves to a new community, the community life as he or she knew it with a marriage partner changes.

THE PSYCHIC DIVORCE

People identify themselves with the personality and influence of their marriage partners. They come to depend upon their spouses psychologically. They think of themselves as a couple. When a divorce is obtained, separation from the influence and personality of the former spouse is finalized, and the individuals then become most aware of their psychic divorce.[25]

The psychic divorce presents the divorced person with the challenge of becoming an autonomous individual again.[26] Learning to live without a partner to depend upon means coping with daily problems and challenges alone. Psychic divorce can be a very trying process and is one area in which many divorced persons need counseling. However, the psychic divorce offers opportunities to achieve an increased self-understanding and to find a personal autonomy.

Effects of Divorce upon the Marital Partners

The effects of divorce upon the partners are not easy to determine, but they are influenced by several factors, including the quality of the previous relationship, the degree to which the partners were emotionally involved with each other, whether the divorce was not desired by one of the partners, the personality characteristics of the partners, and the couple's views concerning the sacredness and permanence of marriage. Although factors such as these make generalizations difficult, following are some effects that are commonly experienced.

PROVIDES OPPORTUNITIES TO BUILD AN "I'M OK" POSITION

Some married couples interact with each other in such a destructive manner that they damage each other's self-esteem. After years of destructive interaction, many partners feel "not OK." For these persons, divorce can be an escape from the devastating interaction and can provide an opportunity to establish new relationships that support their "I'm OK" positions. A twenty-five-year-old divorcée illustrates this:

I had become persuaded that I was a worthless person. In fact, I had stopped feeling like a person at all. My husband continually belittled and ridiculed me in subtle ways. It was not just in private either. For instance, when we would go to a social gathering, he would put me down in front of others. Also, he often turned me away sexually, which made me feel totally undesirable. About a year before we were divorced, we were separated due to a temporary job I had in another town. That separation was like a whole new world to me. I found that people liked me and treated me as though I was worth something. I found that I was a more attractive, happy person. I had vitality, was more interested in people. When I returned to the community where my husband lived, a friend remarked about the change in me. She said that she had never seen me so enthusiastic and confident before. It was during this time that I fully realized how rotten our marriage relationship was and it was during this time that I decided to obtain a divorce.

Of course, the divorce has been hard in many ways, but I have few regrets. Since the divorce, my social life has expanded. I have established new friendships with people who have a high regard for me. I date a variety of men who consider me attractive. This has done wonders for me.

Of course, the divorce wasn't all my husband's fault. I think we were just not a good team. Somehow I made him feel insecure. I guess, I didn't do anything to reassure him. This was a big reason why he felt compelled to put me down. An interesting thing is that since we have been divorced, he has seemed to become a much more considerate and secure person. It looks as though we have both prospered by getting away from each other.

A SENSE OF FAILURE IN THE MARRIAGE RELATIONSHIP

Many divorced persons are nagged by feelings that the divorce is a result of their own failure to make the relationship better,[27] that somehow had they been more considerate, more appreciative, more understanding, more loving, or more determined, they could have made the marriage satisfying and could have prevented its deterioration. Some persons may have serious doubts about their ability to maintain any intimate relationship. Others, however, view the divorce not so much as a personal failure, but more as an unwise selection of a mate. They look forward to establishing a satisfying relationship with a compatible mate in the future.

DEVELOPING A FEAR OF CLOSE INTIMATE RELATIONSHIPS

As a result of destructive relationships experienced in marriage, many divorced persons are reluctant to commit themselves to such an intimate relationship in the future. They feel far safer avoiding deep involvement with, and dependence upon, others. They adopt an if-you-stay-uninvolved-you-don't-get-hurt attitude. Such persons often develop an extremely cynical attitude toward marriage.

DEPRESSION AND ALIENATION

The depression and alienation that many persons suffer as a result of divorce are reflected in the high suicide rate among the divorced. Research evidence indicates that divorced men and women commit suicide at a rate of three to four times more often than do married persons.[28] When a marriage ends, the partners involved frequently feel that their way of life has ended and they no longer have anyone to whom they belong. The severity of their trauma depends on several factors, such as basic emotional stability and presence of other close interpersonal relationships. William Goode's research [29] concerning adjustment to divorce identified various conditions related to the degree of trauma that women experienced with divorce. These factors were as follows:

1. *Length of marriage.* The longer marriages were associated with more difficulty in adjusting to divorce because of the greater commitment to, and involvement in, the marriage relationship.
2. *Age.* Age was related to greater difficulty in adjusting to divorce, with older women experiencing more adjustment problems. The possibilities for establishing a satisfying new life may be more limited for the older woman than for the younger divorcée.

3. *Number of children.* The presence of two or more children was associated with more difficulty in adjusting to divorce. The responsibility and concerns of rearing a number of children, especially small children, is often perceived as an awesome burden and is frightening to the divorced woman.[30] There is also a tendency to worry about the effects of divorce upon the children. It seems likely that the divorced man with the task of rearing children alone would experience similar feelings.
4. *Who suggested the divorce.* The greatest amount of trauma was suffered by the woman if her husband suggested the divorce. Very likely men would also tend to experience considerable trauma if their wives suggested a divorce. Many persons are disturbed by being the rejected partner.
5. *Decisiveness about the divorce.* Unsteadiness in the decision was associated with greater difficulty in adjusting to divorce. Indecision about the divorce, or the "on again, off again" approach, creates a strain upon the psychological equilibrium of many individuals and promotes anxiety and insecurity.[31]

CHANGES IN LIFE-STYLES

Some of the changes in life-style are illustrated by the divorced man in the following example:

> You know, one of the things that was the hardest to adjust to was the change in daily habits. I had not been aware of how much a part of my life these habits had become until after the divorce. I always took my little boy to the park on Saturday morning. Now I can't because Virginia has custody of our son and has moved away. After two years I am still not accustomed to this new father-son relationship.
>
> Virginia used to fix a big breakfast for me every morning. Now I fix it myself. That is a very minor thing, but I can tell you, it took me a while to get accustomed to it. I found it hard to reorganize my friendships and my social life. I gradually stopped seeing most of the couples we used to go out with. I did not fit anymore.
>
> I suddenly found myself living a completely different type of life. I developed some new hobbies, and participated more in group activities, such as dancing lessons, mostly to combat the loneliness. It was very difficult to accept the fact that I no longer had a regular sex life. I had taken sex for granted. It was not pleasant when it dawned on me that regular sex was no longer there.
>
> The most difficult times since the divorce have been at Christmas. Always before I had spent Christmas with Virginia and my son. We bought presents together, read Christmas stories aloud, and decorated the tree. Then I found myself spending Christmas alone, and I was not going through all these rituals anymore. I literally hurt with depression at Christmastime.

Divorce inevitably forces the people involved to make great changes in their daily routines, social-life patterns, and general life-styles. The longer the couple have been married, the greater the shock associated with a forced change in life-style.

The Continuous Nature of the Relationship After Divorce

A seemingly contradictory and important aftermath of divorce is that the relationship between the couple tends to continue. From his research, reported in *World of the Formerly Married,*[32] Morton Hunt has concluded that a divorce generally is never quite final. Many persons divorce with the expectation that they will completely cut off the relationship with their former spouse, only to find, in reality, that although the relationship is greatly altered and their contact with each other is markedly reduced, the relationship does tend to persist in various ways.

Many divorced persons see each other regularly. The form of this ongoing relationship varies. Some couples may have dinner or lunch together on a regular basis. One divorced woman states:

> For about a year after we were divorced, my former husband came over two or three evenings a month for dinner. Our friends couldn't understand this, but in a strange way I think it helped both of us. Neither of us wanted a complete break immediately.

When there are children, of course, the parent-child bond promotes the continuation of the relationship between the former spouses. The mate who does not have custody of the child nearly always has visitation rights. As this person visits the children, or the children visit him or her, the couple can hardly avoid interacting with each other. The child is a bond between the couple, and the divorced parents most probably will talk with each other about the child's future plans, school progress, success, health, and problems.

Not infrequently one of the divorced partners has established a close relationship with the parents of the former partner. This relationship may be so loving that the person maintains contact with the in-laws after the divorce. Contact with the parents of the former partner results in a continuation of the relationship with that partner in subtle ways, as much of the conversation with the in-laws would inevitably revolve around the former spouse. Mention would naturally be made concerning the former spouse's health, plans, accomplishments, and problems, as well as of memories of happy and special events the couple had shared in the past.

In some cases divorced couples continue to be good friends after the divorce. They may attend various social functions together. They may exchange Christmas and birthday presents, and they may help each other in solving various problems.

A very small percentage of divorced couples find this supportive friendship so meaningful that they eventually remarry each other.

Occasionally, some divorced couples continue to have a sexual relationship with each other after the divorce. As one woman said:

> My former husband who lives in another town visits our children on a regular basis, and when he comes, he usually stays overnight and we have sexual intercourse. Our sexual relationship always was good. Since the divorce, neither of us has had a regular sex life, so that when we are together, it seems natural to continue the sexual relationship.

Effects of Divorce upon Children

A male college student gives his reactions to his parents' divorce:

> I was in the tenth grade when my parents divorced. It didn't come as a surprise because I was well aware that things were not good between them. But I loved them both and when Dad moved out and the divorce was final, I had some big adjustment problems during the remaining two years of high school. At one point I almost dropped out. I lived with my mother, but I still felt very close to Dad. I've accepted it now, of course, but sometimes it still bothers me.

A more positive reaction is given by a female college student concerning the divorce of her parents:

> There is no doubt that a divorce was the best thing my parents could have done. I know I was a lot happier after they divorced. It was one vicious battle after another. They hated each other and I knew it. I felt relieved when they separated. Sure, I had some problems adjusting. One of the biggest adjustments I had was accepting a stepfather when my mother remarried. But I made it all right and I know that I was better off with the divorce than I would have been had they stayed together.

Approximately one million children are affected by divorce each year. Many adjustments are required, and there is no doubt that children experience major problems as a result of their parents' divorce. Even preschool children often experience reactions of shock and depression. For example, researchers at the University of Michigan Children's Psychiatric Hospital conducted a study that included observations of the behavior of preschool children whose parents were separating or divorcing. The children were not psychiatric patients but were in a normal nursery school setting.

Some major changes were observed in the behavior of most of the children. Common reactions were shock, anger, and despair. Many showed symptoms of severe grief. The children became more quarrelsome, restless, and bored at nursery school. Some of the children began to avoid once favorite stories that involved family relationships. Others began to see the teacher as a substitute parent and made excessive demands for approval and affection.[33]

A divorce affects children differently, depending on such factors as the age of the child at the time of divorce and how the child viewed the home situation before learning of an impending divorce. Divorce is more traumatic for older children and for those children who had perceived the home as being happy.[34]

However, not all research has indicated that divorce has a negative influence upon children's lives. For example, Lee Burchinal found no significant differences in the personal and social adjustments of adolescents from unbroken families, broken families, and families where remarriage had taken place.[35] In another study, Judson Landis concluded that the experience of living in an unhappy home is just as devastating for children as the experience of living in a divorced home.[36]

There is evidence that children are often better off in a one-parent family than living in a very unhappy, two-parent home characterized by conflict, bitterness, and mental and physical cruelty. Some research studies have found that, as a group, children in broken homes tended to have better adjustment, less delinquent behavior, and less psychosomatic behavior than did children living in unhappy, unbroken homes.[37]

Seven potentially traumatic situations that may exist for the child of divorcing parents include

1. Having to adjust to the knowledge that divorce will probably take place.
2. Having to adjust to the fact of divorce.
3. Being "used" by one or both parents as a weapon against the other.
4. Having to redefine relationships with the parents.
5. Having divorced parents may require readjustments with the peer group.
6. Recognizing the implications of their parents' failure in marriage.
7. Adjusting to stepparents if the parents remarry.[38]

William Goode, in his study of divorced women, found that most mothers worried about the influence of divorce upon their children. However, most of those who had remarried felt that their children's lives had improved after the divorce.[39]

The attitudes and reactions of the single parent with whom the child is living may have a great influence upon how the child is affected by divorce. For example, one study found that many widowed parents worried about what would happen to their children, while the divorced parents, in addition to worrying about the effects on their children, also had feelings of guilt, anger, and shame concerning their marital status.[40]

Whether or not children of divorce sustain less negative effects than children of unhappy, conflict-ridden, unbroken homes, it is certain that children of divorce do experience problems, particularly where the child loves both parents and experiences a feeling of divided loyalty. Many children also feel that they were somehow responsible for the divorce.

Few generalizations can be made about the effects of divorce upon the child. It depends upon many factors:

1. Age of the child.
2. Quality of the child's relationship with both parents.
3. Whether the parent the child is living with remarries and the quality of the child's relationship with the stepparent.
4. Personality and emotional stability of the child and the parent.
5. Availability of parent substitutes for the child.
6. Financial situation of the one-parent family.

Recommendations

Divorce is a symptom of a relationship that has deteriorated. The concern of legislators and educators should not be with divorce so much as with the goal of promoting healthy, satisfying relationships in marriage and family life. This goal will not be accomplished by concentrating on divorce.

Recommendations for promoting marriage success that would also help to decrease the number of unhappy marriages and high divorce rates include the following:

1. Family-life education and human-relationships education should be established in our public school system from kindergarten through college. Factors contributing to satisfying, happy human relationships and marriage success should be identified and education for more effective mate selection should be emphasized.
2. Research indicates that divorce rates are from two to four times greater among persons who marry before the age of twenty than among persons who marry during their twenties.[41] In view of this evidence, there seems to be merit in more states adopting plans similar to California. California has taken legislative action so that everyone under the age of eighteen must obtain a court order and also any premarital counseling the court deems necessary before a marriage license is granted.[42] Perhaps mandatory premarital counseling for everyone, regardless of age, would be desirable.

3. Marriage and family counseling services should be made more available to couples throughout their marriage. There might be merit in requiring couples to go through a period of counseling before a divorce is granted. This would enable some couples to work out their problems and develop a more positive, satisfying relationship. Others who have no intention of preserving the marriage might be helped to develop a greater understanding of themselves, of what contributed to their marriage deterioration, and of the type of person with whom they might be most compatible in the future.

Remarriage

The majority of both men and women who experience divorce do eventually remarry.[43] In fact, the marriage rates for persons who have been divorced are higher than for single persons of the same age and sex groups. Approximately 90 per cent of those who divorce before the age of forty remarry. There is a tendency to remarry rather soon after the divorce. The average time between the divorce and the remarriage is less than three years.[44]

CHARACTERISTICS OF THE REMARRIAGE

Remarriage of a divorced person has characteristics very different from the first marriage. First, those who remarry are prone to choose a person with a similar marital status. A divorced person tends to remarry another divorced person.[45] Interestingly, divorced persons also follow a pattern of remarrying someone of a different religion.[46] Perhaps finding someone who has also been divorced becomes more important than finding someone who has the same religious beliefs.

Remarriages are different from first marriages in that they are much less likely to involve presents, showers given by friends, a reception, or a honeymoon. Remarriages in which one or both partners have been divorced receive less enthusiastic support and celebration from family and friends than do first marriages. There is less optimism among family and friends concerning the remarriage. This pattern holds true regardless of how accepting the attitudes of friends and families are toward divorce.[47]

Remarriage of divorced persons is much more likely to be characterized by opposition from family members. For example, if one partner has not been married before, his or her family may express concern and doubt about the success of the marriage. "Why did the other person's first marriage fail?" "Does that person possess characteristics which also make failure of the present marriage likely?" "Since that person's first marriage failed, is there any reason to expect that the present one will be any more successful?" Such doubts and suspicions are not uncommon among family members. Both partners in the remarriage frequently must learn to cope with these doubts.

The divorced person's family is likely to compare a new marriage partner with the previous one. The new marriage partner naturally senses these comparisons and may have some difficulty in accepting them.

Many remarriages involve children from the previous marriage, which contributes to the remarriage being different from a first marriage. This situation presents the challenge of adjusting to being a stepparent. An individual may not experience immediate acceptance by the children. Rapport, trust, and love must be developed in relationships with the children, and this takes time. Some individuals also find it difficult to adjust to the fact that the spouse's former marriage partner has visitation rights with the children. The couple may also experience financial pressure if the husband has to pay alimony and child support in addition to supporting his present family.

SUCCESS OF DIVORCED PERSONS' REMARRIAGE

How successful are remarriages of the divorced? Most who remarry *do* remain married to the second marriage partner. The remarriages of many divorced persons are successful, particularly if they marry nondivorced persons.

Jessie Bernard's study [48] found that over half of the divorced persons regarded their remarriage as happy. Marriages frequently fail primarily due to a lack of maturity. Often a remarriage is very successful because the divorced person is so much more mature than in a first marriage. A divorced person may also have achieved better understanding of self and of the type of person who makes a compatible mate through the experience of a first marriage. Divorced persons have often learned a great deal more about how to develop a successful marriage relationship.

Unfortunately, some persons experience extreme dissatisfaction and find their second marriages ending in divorce just as their first marriages did. Research studies, in fact, indicate that the remarriages of divorced persons are more likely to result in divorce than first marriages.[49] Remarriages between two persons who have *both* been divorced once are about twice as likely as first marriages to end in divorce. The probability of divorce increases with each subsequent remarriage of a divorced person. For example, approximately eight out of ten remarriages between partners who have been divorced two or more times result in divorce.[50] These findings suggest that for many persons, the problems that contributed to the termination of their first marriage are perpetuated in their second and third marriages. Perhaps the trouble does not lie so much in their choice of a marriage partner as it does in their manner of interacting and responding in interpersonal relationships. This emphasizes the need for making human-relationships education and remarriage education available to divorced persons.

REMARRIAGE AND CHILDREN

One of the major adjustments in a remarriage involves the relationship between the child and the stepparent. Many children have little trouble in adjusting and achieve very positive relationships with their stepparents. There are others, however, who experience considerable difficulties.

Age of the child is an important factor in the child's adjustment. Younger children have a closer and more affectionate relationship with stepparents than do older children, and very young children and adult children accept a stepparent much more easily than do adolescents. Children adapt more readily to stepparents when the previous marriage has been broken by divorce rather than death.[51]

Other interesting findings concerning the relationship between children and stepparents are as follows:

1. Stepchildren more often express a preference for one parent or the other (either the stepparent or their biological parent) than do children who live with both biological parents.
2. Children perceive that their stepparents discriminate against them more often than their biological parents and that stepparents of the opposite sex discriminate against them than most. Children feel that the stepmother discriminates against them more often than the stepfather.
3. Female children involved in remarriages express feelings of being rejected by parents more often than do male children.
4. Both male and female children involved in remarriages more often desire to emulate their biological parent rather than their stepparent.[52]

The majority of reconstituted families are reasonably successful. However, a study by Jessie Bernard, [53] which examined attitudes of men and women toward children acquired through remarriage, found that one third of the divorced men and 44 per cent of the divorced women were not affectionate toward children they had acquired through remarriage.

The relationship between stepparents and stepchildren is susceptible to certain unique problems that are prone to create additional tensions and family conflict.[54] A major factor contributing to adjustment problems between stepparents and stepchildren is the existence of social norms that make it difficult and inappropriate for the stepparent to assume the parent role completely.[55] A clinical study by Irene Fast and Albert Cain [56] suggested that regardless of how strong the stepparent's determination to be a parent to the stepchild and regardless of how skillful the efforts, he or she cannot completely succeed.

Stepparents must usually share the parental role with the previous parent. The child may idealize the biological parent, particularly the father, from whom he or she is separated.[57] At the same time, the stepparent may be expected to completely replace the biological parent from whom the child is separated. The stepparent can easily become disillusioned and resentful when this expectation is not realized, thus adding tension to the relationship with the stepchild.

Another problem that often complicates the strained relations between stepparents and stepchildren occurs when each parent brings children into a remarriage. Competition and rivalry may arise among the children. Also, there may be a tendency for each parent to favor his or her own children.[58]

Following are other factors that can create problems between children and stepparents:

1. An expectation that there will automatically be instant love and an instant family feeling between stepparents and children.
2. Hypersensitivity by the stepparent to various events and responses from the child as proof that he or she is not regarded by the child as a "parent."
3. A tendency for the stepparent, particularly the stepmother, to interpret any behavior or emotional difficulties of the stepchild as being due to her personal shortcomings as a parent.
4. An attitude that there should only be positive feelings between stepparents and stepchildren.
5. An expectation that if the stepparent or stepchild were the biological parent or child, the relationship would be more loving and positive.
6. An expectation that the stepparent, particularly the stepmother, will be unloving toward the children.
7. A tendency for both stepchild and stepparent to misinterpret certain actions of each other as representing rejection and lack of love.

Many problems between stepparents and children, as can be seen from the previous list, are caused by unrealistic and negative expectations as well as by a tendency to misinterpret various responses as representing rejection. Problems can be minimized and more positive relationships between stepparents and stepchildren may be developed by:

1. Family members identifying and at least partially resolving some of the unrealistic and negative expectations before the remarriage takes place. Family therapy may be beneficial both during the time that the new marriage is being planned and shortly after the marriage has occurred.[60]

2. Each member of the new family understanding and appreciating the different situations and adjustments that every family member is experiencing.[61]
3. Both stepparents and stepchildren realizing that they are entering new relationships and, as with most new relationships, time is needed to develop mutual trust, affection, and a feeling of closeness.

References

1. U.S. Bureau of Census. *Statistical Abstract of the United States*, 1975. 96th ed. Washington, D.C., 1975.
2. U.S. Department of Commerce. "Population Characteristics: Population Profile of the United States: 1974." *Current Population Reports*. Series P-20, no. 279, March 1975. Washington, D.C.: U.S. Government Printing Office.
3. FENELON, BILL. "State Variation in the United States Divorce Rates." *Journal of Marriage and the Family*, vol. 33, 1971, pp. 321–327.
4. BOWMAN, HENRY A. *Marriage for Moderns*. New York: McGraw-Hill, 1974.
5. BOHANNAN, PAUL. "The Six Stations of Divorce." In *Divorce and After*, edited by Paul Bohannan. New York: Doubleday, 1970.
6. Ibid.
7. Ibid.
8. Ibid.
9. Ibid.
10. BOWMAN, op. cit.
11. Ibid.
12. Ibid.
13. KOLLER, MARVIN R. *Families: A Multigenerational Approach*. New York: McGraw-Hill, 1974.
    WALKER, TIMOTHY B. "Beyond Fault: An Examination of Patterns of Behavior in Response to Present Divorce Laws." *Journal of Family Law*, vol. 10, 1971, pp. 267–299.
14. PETERS, JACK W. "Iowa Reform of Marriage Termination." *Drake Law Review*, vol. 20, 1971, pp. 211–226.
15. COX, FRANK D. "Separation, Divorce, and Remarriage." In *American Marriage: A Changing Scene?*, edited by Frank D. Cox. Dubuque, Iowa: Brown, 1972.
16. BOHANNAN, op. cit.
17. Ibid.
18. WILLIAMSON, ROBERT C. *Marriage and Family Relations*. New York: Wiley, 1972.
19. BOHANNAN, op. cit.
20. Ibid.
21. Ibid.
22. Women in Transition. *Women's Survival Manual: A Feminist Handbook on Separation and Divorce*. Philadelphia: Women in Transition, 1972.
23. Ibid.

24. BOHANNAN, op. cit.
25. Ibid.
26. Ibid.
27. EPSTEIN, JOSEPH. *Divorced in America.* New York: Penguin Books, 1974.
28. CASHION, BARBARA G. "Durkheim's Concept of Anomie and Its Relationship to Divorce." *Sociology and Social Research,* vol. 55, 1970, pp. 72–81.
29. GOODE, WILLIAM J. *After Divorce.* New York: Free Press, 1956.
30. BELL, ROBERT R. *Marriage and Family Interaction.* Homewood, Ill.: Dorsey Press, 1971.
31. Ibid.
32. HUNT, MORTON. *World of the Formerly Married.* New York: McGraw-Hill, 1966.
33. NEUHAUS, ROBERT, and RUBY NEUHAUS. *Family Crisis.* Columbus, Ohio: Merrill, 1974.
34. LANDIS, JUDSON T. "The Trauma of Children When Parents Divorce." *Marriage and Family Living,* vol. 22, 1960, pp. 7–13.
WALTERS, JAMES, and NICK STINNETT. "Parent-Child Relationships: A Decade of Research." *Journal of Marriage and the Family,* vol. 33, 1971, pp. 70–118.
35. BURCHINAL, LEE G. "Characteristics of Adolescents from Broken, Unbroken, and Reconstituted Families." *Marriage and Family Living,* vol. 26, 1964, pp. 44–50.
36. LANDIS, JUDSON T. "A Comparison of Children from Divorced and Nondivorced Unhappy Marriages." *The Family Life Coordinator,* vol. 11, 1962, pp. 61–65.
37. BURGESS, JANE K. "The Single Parent Family: A Social and Sociological Problem." *The Family Coordinator,* vol. 19, 1970, pp. 137–144.
38. LANDIS, 1960, op. cit.
39. GOODE, op. cit.
40. BURCHINAL, op. cit.
41. COX, op. cit.
42. Ibid.
43. BERNARD, JESSIE. *The Future of Marriage.* New York: World, 1972.
44. KEPHART, WILLIAM M. *The Family, Society and the Individual.* Boston: Houghton Mifflin, 1972.
LANDIS, JUDSON T., and MARY G. LANDIS. *Building a Successful Marriage.* Englewood Cliffs, N.J.: Prentice-Hall, 1973.
45. KEPHART, op. cit.
46. ROSENTHAL, ERICH. "Divorce and Religious Intermarriage: The Effect of Previous Marital Status upon Subsequent Marital Behavior." *Journal of Marriage and the Family,* vol. 32, 1970, pp. 435–440.
47. KEPHART, op. cit.
LANDIS and LANDIS, op. cit.
48. BERNARD, JESSIE. *Remarriage: A Study in Marriage.* New York: Holt, Rinehart and Winston, 1956.
49. KEPHART, op. cit.
50. LANDIS and LANDIS, op. cit.
51. WALTERS and STINNETT, op. cit.
52. BOWERMAN, CHARLES E., and DONALD P. IRISH. "Some Relationships of Stepchildren to Their Parents." *Marriage and Family Living,* vol. 24, 1962, pp. 113–121.
WALTERS and STINNETT, op. cit.
53. BERNARD, 1956, op. cit.

54. SCHULMAN, GERDA L. "Myths That Intrude on the Adaptation of the Stepfamily." *Social Casework,* vol. 53, 1972, pp. 131–139.
55. WALTERS and STINNETT, op. cit.
56. FAST, IRENE, and ALBERT C. CAIN. "The Stepparent Role: Potential for Disturbance in Family Functioning." *American Journal of Orthopsychiatry,* vol. 36, 1966, pp. 485–491.
57. SCHULMAN, op. cit.
58. Ibid.
59. Ibid.
FAST and CAIN, op. cit.
60. SCHULMAN, op. cit.
61. Ibid.

18 Nontraditional Life-Styles

Photo by Skip Butler

The beating of my own heart was all the sound I heard.

Richard Monckton Milnes

Increased Interest in Nontraditional Life-styles

During recent years, interest in an examination of a variety of life-styles suggests that more people today accept the idea that a traditional marriage may not suit everyone. Increasingly, attention has been focused on the following nontraditional life-styles:

1. *Cohabitation.* Living together without legal marriage is becoming increasingly prevalent among the young and is accepted on numerous college campuses.
2. *Communes.* An estimated 3,000 communes exist throughout the nation.
3. *Group Marriage.* The phenomenon of group marriage, popularized by novels such as *The Harrad Experiment* by Robert Rimmer and *Stranger in a Strange Land* by Robert Heinlein, is being tried as an alternative way of life by some couples.
4. *Extramarital Affairs.* Extramarital affairs are more prevalent today for both men and women than they were a generation ago.
5. *Swinging.* Some husbands and wives choose to recruit other couples who are interested in exchanging partners in order to increase their opportunities for a variety of sexual encounters.
6. *Homosexual Marriage.* There has been a surprising growth of churches established for homosexual persons where homosexual wedding ceremonies are performed.
7. *One-Parent Families.* A less controversial life-style that is not always voluntarily chosen is the one-parent family.

Obviously, the life-style a couple chooses affects a couple's relationship, but, in addition, the chosen life-style affects children as well. A growing number of children are being reared in nontraditional homes. The number of youth and adults who have adopted nontraditional life-styles has increased dramatically during the last decade; however, the total number represents only a small minority of the total population. Perhaps more important is the greater acceptance by the general public of nontraditional life-styles. Several conditions in our society contribute to the selection, however tentative, of different life-styles.

GREATER DIVERSITY

As a nation we are evolving toward a greater fragmentation and diversity in material goods, art, education, and culture.[1] An endless range of choices in consumer products, education, and recreation has also been accompanied by a wider range of choice concerning life-styles. The fragmented and diversified society in which we live is conducive to the emergence of nontraditional choices.

AN INCREASINGLY PERMISSIVE SOCIETY

As our society has become industrialized and urbanized, a more permissive atmosphere concerning behavior that differs from the norm has emerged. For example, much less stigma is now attached to divorce than in the past, and there is currently a more permissive attitude concerning sexual encounter among persons who are not legally married. An attitude of "do your own thing" has become popular and many young people feel pressure from their peer group to adopt behavior and attitudes that are different from the "establishment." Many people feel freer to experiment with a variety of life-styles. For some, such experimentation is of temporary duration but, for others, it represents a sincere, determined decision to adopt a new life-style.

GREATER INDIVIDUALISM AND ALIENATION

Erich Fromm has stated that the greatest need any person has is the need to overcome separateness and achieve a sense of union and relatedness with others.[2] It is difficult to achieve this in a highly industrialized, urbanized, and mobile society. Families move often to different geographic locations to take advantage of better job opportunities, leaving behind relatives and old friends. There is little emphasis upon a group identity even within many nuclear families. Increasingly, a husband and wife follow separate careers and their children participate in their own activities to the point that activity as a family unit is limited.

Two thirds of our population now live in metropolitan areas, and with metropolitan living comes anonymity. Anonymity provides privacy, but at the same time it stimulates feelings of being separate and alienated from others. One middle-class executive expressed his sense of alienation:

> You know, I am with people during practically all of my waking hours, on the subway, at work, and at home, yet I feel alone. Everyone is so busy pursuing his own goals that no one takes time to get to know anyone else. This is true at work. No one there would feel any grief or loss if I were run over by a truck. I'd be replaced in a day or two and no one would even notice the difference.[3]

FAMILY INSTABILITY

The recent upsurge of interest in nontraditional life-styles is, in part, due to disillusionment with human relationships in general. For example, some research indicates that persons most in favor of alternate life-styles have a low level of need to be with people and a low level of need to both give and receive help—suggesting a sense of alienation.[4] People need close, satisfying relationships that reinforce their OK position. Most people count a satisfying marriage and family life as one of their most important dreams. Yet hundreds of thousands of people fail to achieve this goal. Many more families today are broken by separation, desertion, and divorce than fifty years ago. In 1915, the divorce rate was one per thousand population. Today, the divorce rate has climbed to approximately 4.7 per thousand population, and many couples remain together who are very dissatisfied with their marriages.

Increased instability and the lack of understanding within families has contributed to more persons becoming disillusioned with traditional marriage. Not surprisingly, research evidence indicates that the youth most in favor of life-styles other than traditional marriage are those who have experienced negative parent-child relationships.[5] More persons are selecting other alternatives in an attempt to find the satisfying, close relationships they desire but have not found in their own families.

THE MARKETING OF LIFE-STYLES

Because of their differentness, nontraditional life-styles are newsworthy. They are written about in magazines and newspapers, and presented on television and in the movies. Yet rarely do these media objectively communicate the actual experiences, advantages, and problems experienced by those involved. The marketing of nontraditional life-styles is done in such a way that many people believe they have society's permission to choose and consume life-styles just as people choose and consume commercial products.[6] An unfortunate aspect of the marketing of life-styles is that people too frequently adopt a life pattern on the basis of the marketing that implies a particular life-style is "fashionable."

A life-style involves principles, values, and habits that provide guidelines by which we make daily decisions and organize our lives. Its selection is important because it shapes our lives in the present and in the future.

What are the effects of such life-styles as cohabitation, communal living, group marriage, extramarital affairs, swinging, gay marriage and one-parent families? Do such life-styles bring people closer together or alienate them further from each other? Do alternate life-styles offer any suggestions to improve the quality of traditional marriage and family living?

Cohabitation

WHAT IS COHABITATION?

The answers to the question, "What exactly is cohabitation?" are varied. One of the best definitions is offered by Eleanor Macklin who examined cohabitation practices at Cornell University. She defines cohabitation as, "To share a bedroom for at least four nights per week for at least three consecutive months with someone of the opposite sex." Cohabitation is more often associated with a "going steady" stage of a relationship than with engagement. Macklin's study found that

> . . . living together was seldom the result of a considered decision, at least initially. Most relationships involved a gradual (and sometimes not so gradual) drifting into staying together. The general pattern was to stay over one night; in several weeks, if all was well, to stay for the weekend; in another few weeks to add a week night; in another few weeks, a second week night and so forth.[7]

The couples in Macklin's study insisted that living together is a natural progression in the man-woman relationship; that as time passes and they share more of their lives, sharing an apartment or other living arrangement is the next logical step.

INCIDENCE

The actual number of people who live together without the sanction of legal marriage is unknown. However, many authorities of family life believe that a growing number of people are choosing cohabitation either as a temporary or permanent replacement for marriage.

REASONS FOR COHABITATION

The largest growth in cohabitation appears to be with younger age groups, and particularly college students. For this reason, Donald Bloch[8] placed an advertisement in eight college newspapers, seeking unmarried college students living together who were willing to participate in group discussions of "alternate ways of family life" with psychiatrists from the Family Institute in New York City.

From the discussion groups that resulted, Bloch was unable to stereotype the persons who participated in cohabitation. Some students felt that establishing a household before marriage served as a trial or preparation for marriage. Some sought cohabitation as a means of rebelling against institutionalism. And a few viewed living together as a temporary convenience.

Other personal reasons given for cohabitation are the search for a meaningful relationship without the superficial "dating game"; the psychological fulfillment that stems from living with someone with whom one is emotionally involved; the search for individual growth compatible with the growth of the relationship; and the desire "to try out" a relationship before considering permanency.[9]

Some environmental trends that have been suggested as reasons for youth establishing unmarried households are as follows:

1. Changes in dormitory regulations concerning curfews, coed dormitories, and off-campus living regulations that permit greater flexibility in students' living patterns.
2. Rejection of the dating game and a widespread questioning of the institution of marriage.
3. The increased popularity of the view that living together is a very effective way to "test the relationship."
4. The increased popularity of the view that it is financially and emotionally desirable to live with someone that you care for.[10]

On the basis of her study of Cornell students, Macklin reported that the benefits of cohabitation as seen by cohabiting couples include gaining a greater knowledge of what is involved in living with someone else; increased ability to relate to others; gaining a greater understanding of what they desire in a marriage; and an increase in emotional maturity.

Those in Bloch's study who were not planning to marry gave various reasons: fear of marriage, desire to continue the extension of the dating relationship, importance of other goals (usually a career with which they felt marriage might interfere), or fear that marriage would destroy the spontaneity of the present relationship. Others felt too immature and too unsettled emotionally for a permanent commitment. Living together, they reported, was giving them time to come to grips with their own ambivalent feelings.

TRIAL MARRIAGE

While some living-together situations have no intention of permanence, some couples are sincerely interested in building interpersonal relationships of an enduring nature. Many of these people have experienced the negative effects of divorce within their own families, and because they desire to avoid divorce, some believe that a trial period of marriage is desirable.

Professional ideologies differ widely on trial marriages, as was demonstrated by the 1969 National Council on Family Relations Workshop in which opposing views were presented. Some participants believed trial marriage should be morally sanctioned by society as an alternative, whereas others believed trial marriage was not a valid preparation for marriage.[11] It has been pointed out that commitment is de-emphasized by the very nature of trial marriage.

DOES COHABITATION INVOLVE FEWER PROBLEMS THAN MARRIAGE?

> By living together we avoid the problems and suffocating bondage of marriage. The piece of legal paper doesn't mean you're married. It just means you have to go through a lot of red tape to get a divorce if it doesn't work out. Living together avoids that mess. You can split anytime you want.[12]

This statement of a thirty-year-old medical technician expresses one commonly cited benefit of cohabitation—avoidance of the problems of marriage and freedom to terminate the relationship without legal hassles.

However, awareness is growing among unmarried couples that they cannot escape the pressures and problems of marriage by eliminating the legal bonds.

"Young people are kidding themselves if they think living together is much different from marriage," reports Don Harvey, Director of Counseling for the Harvard Community Health Plan in Boston. Harvey and many marriage counselors across the nation indicate an increasing number of unmarried couples are seeking counseling assistance.[13]

Boston Family Services caseworker Sallyann Roth has stated, "When the unmarried man and woman are committed to each other—and they usually are if they go to the trouble of seeking counseling—the problems are strikingly similar to those of marrieds." Other counselors and psychologists, such as Houston clinical psychologist Marlene Welte Hodge, relate that they counsel unmarried couples with such problems as sexual maladjustment, inability to share or compromise, and fights with parents and in-laws.[14] Even though cohabiting couples are not legally married, the dynamics of the relationship are much the same. It is particularly interesting that counselors have observed that couples who come for counseling concerning relationship problems usually marry each other.[15]

SOME UNIQUE PROBLEMS OF COHABITATION

In addition to having some of the same problems that traditional marriage often involves, there are problems unique to cohabiting couples.

Guilt. Guilt feelings, which may be experienced because of religious reasons or because the couple is involved in a life-style that is not accepted or approved by parents, some friends, or society in general, are perhaps more prevalent than is commonly assumed. The couple may never express guilt feelings verbally, even to each other, but yet may experience lingering guilt feelings. It is difficult to adopt a life-style that is not approved by the surrounding society even though an individual maintains that he or she does not care what society thinks. Robert Whitehurst interviewed cohabiting couples across the nation and reported that some couples feel guilty that they could not or did not make their relationship work on what they themselves believed to be a higher level of morality.[16]

Instability of Relationships. Instability of relationships is one real problem involved in cohabitation. One study indicated that one third of the cohabitation relationships last an average of only four and one half months.[17] Relationships may become more temporary and less meaningful as people move from partner to partner. According to Jessie Bernard, one hazard of cohabitation is that some individuals make themselves miserable shifting from one partner to another, ever hoping that the next relationship will be better.[18]

One factor that may contribute to the instability of cohabitation relationships is that the nature of cohabitation, such as the freedom from legal bonds, creates a situation in which commitment may be de-emphasized. That a lower degree of commitment may be associated with the cohabiting life-style is suggested by the findings of a study reported by Nancy Catlin, James Keller, and James Croake who found an unusually low degree of religious participation among cohabiting couples. One possible explanation these researchers offered for this finding was a relationship between an unwillingness to commit oneself to a partner in contractual marriage and lack of commitment to a religious sect.[19]

Double-Life Conflict. After interviewing cohabiting couples across the nation, Robert Whitehurst concluded that the "double-life conflict" was a prominent problem.[20] Pretending to be legally married can create an inner conflict, a fear of being found out, and a sense of hypocrisy. Some couples find themselves referring to their relationship as a marriage and even label each other as husband and wife.

Inability to Share Lives with Others. A particularly frustrating problem for cohabiting couples who are deeply devoted to each other is that frequently they cannot share an important part of their lives with others. The couple may hide the fact that they are living together because their parents and some friends would not approve. Another possibility is that parents may be aware of the relationship and strongly disapprove. In either case, the couple is prevented from communicating or sharing an important part of their lives with their families. The inability to share their relationship with those who play significant roles in their lives, such as family and friends, can contribute to a sense of alienation and isolation and denies the couple the benefit of support that family and friends provide for their relationship.

Loss of Other Relationships. One of the problems of cohabitation is that it can be limiting and prevent an individual from experiencing a broad range of friendships. Many friendships may never develop because of a fear that the cohabiting relationship would not be approved. Cohabitation may also greatly restrict the number of persons an individual dates. This dating limitation may restrict learning experiences concerning the types of persons with whom that person is most and least compatible. One study reported approximately half of the individuals involved in cohabitation believed that they experienced a problem of overinvolvement in the cohabitation relationship. This overinvolvement included feelings of losing individual identity and a lack of opportunity to engage in other activities or be with other friends.[21]

The Living Arrangement. Another area of frustration for cohabiting couples involves the living arrangement. Apartment complexes maintained primarily for unmarried couples usually are located in large metropolitan areas and not in small towns and cities.

Some couples are successful in finding apartments or single dwellings where the landlord does not know of their arrangement or is not really concerned as long as the rent is paid promptly. But for many couples, simply finding a place where they can live together poses a problem. Such considerations as whose name appears on the mailbox, or whether both names should appear, also creates areas of conflict, especially if the neighbors think of the couple as married.

The cohabitation living arrangement itself is illegal in twenty-five states. Penalties for cohabitation range from "up to five years" in jail and/or "up to $1,000" fine. Although it is true that in many of these states a conviction must be based on an "open and notorious" clause, this is often left to the discretion of the courts; such a conviction could cause problems for the couple and their families.[22]

Different Expectations. Often a couple enters a cohabitative relationship with quite different expectations of the outcome. These different expectations can result in disappointment and conflict. One study of cohabiting couples found that for the males future marriage was not relevant to the relationship, but that the female partners expressed a desire for marriage. In contrast, it was found that among a group of noncohabiting, steadily dating couples, both partners were much more equally committed to marriage.[23]

One of the implications of these findings is that if the absence of desire for marriage by the male is a permanent characteristic, and if the woman's desire for marriage results in pressure on the male, he might respond by finding a new partner. The woman may well feel that she has been exploited.

Children. Children born to unwed couples have the stigma of illegitimacy and experience many problems as a consequence. The situation may be worsened if the couple breaks up and the child is left with the mother and, perhaps, with inadequate financial support.

Legal Problems. Those involved in cohabitation often state that one of the advantages is that the legal bonds of marriage and the legal hassle of divorce are avoided. However, cohabiting couples may also encounter legal problems, such as community property laws, which consider the property of a marriage to be commonly owned by both husband and wife. The cohabiting couple have no joint ownership rights concerning their communal property. Instead, the property belongs to the person whose income was used to purchase it.

Another legal problem of cohabitation arises when one partner dies. The surviving partner is considered by law as a stranger and cannot inherit anything from the deceased partner unless it has been specified in a valid will. It is doubtful if many cohabiting couples write wills. If in a cohabitative relationship the man dies and no will has been written, his former wife, his parents, or children by a previous marriage can take all of his property.

Cohabitation is also at a legal disadvantage in cases of automobile accidents caused by the negligence of a third person. A surviving marriage partner can, of course, sue for monetary damages resulting from the death of a spouse (due to the negligence of the third party); such an option is not available to a partner in a cohabitative relationship.

A legal problem that could be tragic for couples who live together for many years involves Social Security benefits. Take as an example a couple who has lived together for thirty years. Upon the man's death the woman is not entitled to Social Security benefits unless they live in one of the thirteen states that still recognizes common-law marriages.[24]

COMMENT

An increasing number of individuals are experimenting with the cohabitation life-style because they feel it frees them from the legal bondage of marriage and enables them to avoid many of the common problems of marriage. However, many individuals have difficulty terminating cohabitation relationships and experience the same problems as married couples. In addition, they also encounter several unique problems. Cohabiting couples and their children may face frustrating legal problems, such as illegitimacy and inheritance. It is possible that the nature of cohabitation, with its emphasis upon being free from any legal commitment, at the same time also tends to result in a decreased emphasis upon interpersonal commitment in general.

Communes

INCREASE IN COMMUNAL LIVING

The decade of the 1960s witnessed an increase in the communal movement. Ten thousand persons were estimated to have settled in more than 500 communes across the nation by 1969. Today the number has soared to approximately 3,000 communes with no estimate of the total number of residents.[25] "Commune" has become a household word. The communal movement now has its own newspapers and journals, such as *Modern Utopia*.

Regardless of how unsuccessful they are and regardless of whether a person agrees with communal living as a life-style, much can be learned from them because they give some indication of the needs that have not been adequately met in the lives of those who choose to live in communes.

CHARACTERISTICS OF COMMUNE MEMBERS

Who are the people who make up the estimated 3,000 or more communes in the United States? Most of those who adhere to communal living today are under the age of thirty. They tend to be concentrated in the age range of twenty to twenty-eight. Typically, young people living in communes have been reared in middle- or upper-class families. Persons from poverty backgrounds or minority groups rarely live in communes. This may be due to the fact that individuals from less affluent backgrounds have had all the experience they desire in sharing living quarters with several others and consequently do not view this as a Utopian experience.[26]

Communes have been composed of such diverse groups as political radicals, return-to-the-land homesteaders, intellectuals, pacifists, hippies and dropouts, ex-drug addicts, behavioral psychologists following B. F. Skinner's *Walden Two*, humanistic psychologists interested in environments for self-actualization, Quakers in South America, ex-monks in New Hampshire, and Hasidic Jews in

Boston.[27] There are indications that in many respects the communal movement has been taken over by a stable, serious-minded people. They are composed of individuals who feel there is something basically wrong about how people live and think; therefore, they have chosen to remove themselves from the mainstream of the system.

GOALS OF COMMUNES

Intimate Relationships. A desire for close, meaningful human interaction seems to be what commune members most strongly seek from their group-living experience. A common personal characteristic among commune members is a childhood emotional isolation associated with a desire to experience love and security in a new kinship environment. Many are attempting to attain the loving, accepting family relationships that were either lost in their own families or never existed at all.[28]

That today's communes are seeking to be like extended families in their warmth and intimacy is indicated by the names many adopt. For example, a commune in California referred to itself as "The Lynch Family"; a New Mexico commune called itself "The Chosen Family"; and a New York City commune chose the name of "The Family."

Personal Growth. Many commune members are seeking personal growth through the small-group processes they may experience in some communes. They attempt to criticize and support each other openly and honestly in encounter and sensitivity groups which, in some groups, are major parts of the commune's activities. The group process often is utilized to settle disagreement, regenerate commitment, and to develop a sense of intimate involvement.

A Spiritual Rebirth. Several communes have indicated that through the communal living experience they are trying to find themselves spiritually, that they are trying to experience a spiritual rebirth. This desire is reflected by the emphasis upon spiritual meditation. In some communes the study of yoga and various Eastern religions is common.

A Desire to Get Back to Nature. One of the major goals of many communes is to reunite with nature, to work the soil and grow their own organic food. Many insist upon natural childbirth. For some, the practice of birth-control methods is considered unnatural. There is characteristically a deep respect and reverence for nature and the ecological system.

A Desire to Rebel Against the Establishment. For many, a basic motivation for living in a commune is to rebel against the establishment or to demonstrate their rejection of their parents' way of life. It is a way of saying "No" to the work ethic, "No" to competition, "No" to industrialism and technology.

PROBLEMS

Many who adopt the communal life-style achieve their goals and find communal living satisfying, feeling that through the communal way of life they grow as persons, and experience closer, more meaningful relationships as well as greater spiritual awareness. However, there is evidence that others do not achieve what they seek. One indication of this is the high degree of instability that characterizes most of the groups.

One investigator, Elia Katz,[29] who was sympathetic to the commune dwellers, indicated that there are major problems in communal living. Katz toured communes across the nation and reported finding unhappy individuals who were even more dissatisfied by living in such groups. He reported that he repeatedly encountered hypocrisy among commune members, and that in the groups investigated, there was little room for individualism since persons are encouraged to get rid of all characteristics that make them unique.

Interpersonal Relationships. Although establishing close, meaningful relationships is one of the major goals of commune members, there is evidence that the close, intimate relationships people seek are not always found. Relationships are often found to be more superficial than what had been experienced before joining the commune. One reason seems to be that with several people living together in close quarters, it becomes difficult to establish an intimate, intense relationship with any one person. An individual's interaction, affection, and time are diffused.

It is quite difficult to find four or more persons from different families and backgrounds who can live together harmoniously in a family-type situation. When a large group of individuals lives in close quarters, especially if there is no authority structure, the possibilities for interpersonal conflict are greatly multiplied. Arguments, conflict, and jealousy have been found to be disruptive forces.

After having lived in a middle-class, well-educated commune in the northwest called The Community, David French suggests that communal life is as alienating as more traditional life-styles. He reports that building interpersonal relationships over time in a commune depends upon people "stretching" themselves in uncomfortable directions, and most people are unwilling to make a genuine effort to do so.[30]

Authority and Structure. Lack of authority and little or no structure contribute greatly to the instability of communes. In order to survive, certain daily tasks have to be performed. Someone must cook the food; someone has to buy, grow, or hunt the food; and someone must be responsible for providing fuel to keep warm.

However, many groups place so much emphasis upon "doing your own thing" and have so much sentiment against authority and structure that no one is responsible to anyone else and no one is really responsible for any particular task. As a result, many essential tasks never get done. The research evidence indicates that the most successful and permanent communes are structured and have definite authority patterns, which are frequently of a religious nature.[31]

Lack of Privacy. Few problems have been more apparent in communal living than the lack of privacy. Many of the communes are overcrowded to the point that it is impossible for a person to have a room of his or her own. A common practice in open-land communes is for an individual to walk off into the woods or fields in order to have privacy and solitude.

Commune members find it very difficult to give up privacy, and many are discovering what Skinner indicated in his book *Walden Two:* in a world of communal living the greatest treasure a person may have is a room of his or her own. Of course, there are groups in which each member has a private room. But even in these communes, group living infringes on an individual's privacy and freedom.[32]

Community Relations. A critical problem of communes is community relations, as such groups frequently find themselves in conflict with authorities or unfriendly neighbors. Many commune members are aware that there have been good reasons for hostility on the part of surrounding communities toward communes, and many leaders of such groups are attempting to correct this situation. An editorial in one underground paper in Hawaii advised hippie commune members to stop creating problems for themselves by antagonizing members of the "straight" community through such acts as leaving a trail of garbage over the land.

Lack of Stability. Perhaps the most glaring problem experienced by communes is their instability. People enter and leave groups with little feeling of commitment. For example, the turnover at Twin Oaks in Virginia during one year was approximately 70 per cent.[33]

With this high rate of turnover, it is difficult to attain a sense of group identity and family closeness that many commune members desire. Also, those who leave are frequently the most competent who still expect to receive special recognition for their talents.[34] Feelings of not being appreciated apparently motivate some to leave. Those groups that welcome with open arms anyone who wants to join have often experienced the unstabilizing effect of individuals who drop in for a short period of time, get what they can, and leave.

Financial Instability. Although members ideologically de-emphasize materialism and money, financial problems persistently plague communes. Conflict arises over how limited funds should be spent and frequently basic necessities are not obtained because of lack of money. Malnutrition and ill health are often found among members and are directly related to inadequate funds.

The *Whole Earth Catalog* is a popular source book for people living in communes because it offers information on how to make a better go of it financially. The catalog lists tools and books that will assist an individual in making furniture; repairing cars; building houses from styrofoam, car tops, or mud; raising bees for honey; and other helpful information.

Sanitation. Although sanitation is a problem in some urban communes housed in run-down, rat-infested buildings, the greatest sanitation problems have perhaps been more evident in the open-land communes, which have limited, if any, sanitation systems.

At one open-land commune called Wheeler's, it was reported that six chemical toilets had been installed on the ranch in order to comply with county sanitation requirements. The overall sanitation system at Wheeler's ranch was haphazard and the water was contaminated. Until people adjusted to the water, they experienced dysentery. There were also periodic outbreaks of hepatitis, streptococcic throat infections, crabs, gonorrhea, and scabies.[35]

Legal Problems. Because communes lack a legal identity, they face certain legal problems. For example, fourteen youths had formed a commune in which the members considered themselves a family.

> They had to go to court in order to answer to the application of local zoning laws which prohibit more than four persons from living in the same dwelling unless they were members of one family. The decision of the court was that simply living together and considering themselves to be a family did not constitute a legal family. The judge concluded that communes have voluntary and changing memberships with no legal obligations of support and cohabitation, and that they are legally indistinguishable from such traditional groups as residence clubs and religious communities. The judge further concluded that the right to form communes was protected by the constitution, but the right of commune members to live under the same roof in any part of the city which they desire is not upheld by the constitution.[36]

Communes also face legal problems of property ownership and legitimacy of children.

SEXUAL RELATIONSHIPS

Sexual behavior varies from commune to commune. Many practice sexual exclusivity and others have no restrictions. The most stable communes are those that practice monogamous sexual relationships and reflect a high degree of commitment in these relationships.[37] Exclusive monogamous sexual relationships is a norm that is common. Although some groups do not wish to practice sexual exclusivity, the permissive ideology of, "If my partner wants to have sexual relations with someone else, it is better that this desire be satisfied than unsatisfied," may cause intense conflict among group members.[38]

Herbert Otto, in his investigation of communes, found that although there was considerable permissiveness in some communes, there was also a high degree of pairing and a tendency toward commitment in a continuing relationship. Nudism was observed to be casual and accepted, but group sex was found to occur quite rarely.[39]

COMMUNES AND CHILDREN

Advantages of Communal Child Rearing. Some potential strengths and advantages of communal living for children have been listed by several investigators.[40]

1. Children can experience a strong sense of belonging to an extended type of family.
2. Children are exposed to many adult-role models. They have close contact with several men and women.
3. There is a decreased dependency on the two parents. Children may, instead, feel that they have several parents or at least several family members on whom to depend. If one of the natural parents is absent, the child and the remaining parent still have a number of close, caring relationships with other adults in the commune.
4. Communal children may experience an easier transition to adult life, as they are frequently given the opportunity to make needed contributions to the communes. They develop a sense of responsibility by having their own chores to perform, and they develop a sense of being a vital part of the group.
5. If the commune has its own enterprise, the child can see work and family life being integrated. Children can see their own parents work and may work with them, which can create a strong sense of solidarity and togetherness.
6. Children have the opportunity to become cooperative as cooperation is a necessary and important part of daily living.
7. If the commune runs its own school, then parents and adults can more easily participate in the lives of children, and children can more easily participate in the lives of parents and adults.

8. It is believed that communal children will not grow up feeling alienated from adults, as many children now do in traditional nuclear families, because communal children are consistently involved with adults.

Disadvantages of Communal Child Rearing. There is much unanswered about rearing children in communes. More time is necessary to determine what the actual effects are. Most of the children who have been observed are still young; however, several problems and potential disadvantages of communal child rearing are indicated:

1. Conflict and resentment emerges among the adults concerning the discipline of children. This is particularly a problem when child rearing is considered a responsibility of all the adult members of the group.
2. There is often a problem concerning the education of the children. If the children do not attend a public school, there are few alternatives, because educational practices within the commune are rarely sufficient.
3. Child-rearing practices in communes are often so overtly permissive that children may not be able to develop enough self-discipline to cope with frustration and achieve goals.[41]
4. The high turnover rate of communes can diminish children's sense of security and stability. As other mothers and fathers and brothers and sisters enter and leave the group, children may become fearful of getting closely attached to anyone because they could leave at any time.
5. Quite possibly, some children living in communes do not receive the care and attention they need. Research studies indicate that adult members often think of themselves as children, viewing their futures as uncertain and their lives as unsettled. Partially as a result of this view, adult members are generally not willing to sacrifice their personal search for identity and meaning in order to devote full time to the rearing of children. In a sense, rearing children involves certain obligations to which many commune members have not committed themselves.[42]

   Also, some adult commune members view all children as worthy of love and respect but not necessarily of attention. As children outgrow physical dependence upon adults they are treated like other adult members of the communal family.[43] While this view could have some positive effects, it could also easily result in the needs of many children being ignored and unmet.

ECONOMIC SUPPORT AND PROPERTY

Commune members ideally seek economic self-sufficiency, yet the major source of support in most groups seems to be welfare payments, unemployment compensation, and food stamps. Commune members seem aware of this dilemma but have no solution for it.[44]

In many instances the members work at outside jobs, at least on a part-time basis, and give the money they earn to the group, which operates with a common treasury. Some have their own businesses, such as farming, crafts, toy manufacturing, and gas stations. However, subsistence farming and small-craft industries generally do not provide enough income to meet the necessary expenses of food, utilities, mortgage, rent, or machinery.

As a consequence, many groups are forced to depend on public welfare, benefactors, inheritances, or generous parents. This also puts pressure upon commune members to seek employment with employers or institutions within what they consider the establishment culture. This, of course, contradicts some of the commune members' major objectives, such as getting away from alienating work and congested, polluted cities.[45]

Members are often discouraged from becoming too involved in any special skills they possess, because involvement in one's special talents is often regarded as that person's "ego trip," which may distract from the solidarity of the total group.[46]

WHAT MAKES COMMUNES STABLE?

Research studies have indicated that the most stable and successful communes share the following characteristics:

1. Monogamous sexual relationships.
2. Large age range.
3. Religious orientation.
4. Presence of authority and structured delegation of tasks.
5. Respect for individual privacy.
6. Noncompetitive achievement orientation.
7. Stable source of income.
8. No use of hard drugs such as amphetamines and heroin.
9. Good relationships with the surrounding community and local law-enforcement authorities.[47]

COMMENT

Individuals, to a great extent, join communes in a search for more intimate relationships and an extended family-type experience. The increase in communal living arrangements within the last decade has been substantial. However, only a minority of persons will be attracted to communes and most who do experiment with communal living will return to their former traditional life-styles after a few weeks or months.[48]

Most commune members are trying to escape the loneliness, restrictiveness, hypocrisy, and materialism they believe characterize the establishment. Yet, many of the same problems occur in communes as in more traditional life-styles.

A contributor to the *Whole Earth Catalog* summarized his experiences with communal living. He stated that if the commune is to survive, "It must be authoritarian, and if it is authoritarian, it offers no more freedom than conventional society. Those communes based on freedom inevitably fail, usually within a year." [49]

The values and goals to which commune members aspire include,

1. A respect for and desire to get closer to nature.
2. A desire to establish a brotherhood and sisterhood of close familylike relationships with each other, and taking the time to do things with each other.
3. Becoming more *people* oriented and less *thing* oriented.
4. A desire to move away from manipulation and dishonesty in relationships.
5. A desire to establish work as an activity in which the individual can experience fulfillment and peace.

There is much that remains unanswered about communal living. We need to know more about the long-range effects upon adults as well as upon children. Also, little is known about the personality characteristics that seem to be most compatible with communal living.

Group Marriage

A MARRIAGE OF THREE OR MORE

Group marriage has been defined as consisting of three or more persons who consider themselves married to each other and who live together on a communal basis, sharing money, home, work, children, love, and, theoretically at least, sexual intimacy.

Group marriage is not really new but has received renewed interest in recent years. It has existed throughout history and usually has been present during the transitional stages in societies undergoing drastic reorganization.[50]

A GROWING INTEREST

An increasing number of persons have expressed interest in group marriage during recent years. A national survey conducted among readers of *Psychology*

Today found that approximately 25 per cent were interested in or favored group marriage.[51] However, Maxine Edwards and Nick Stinnett, in a national study of college students' perceptions concerning various life-styles, found that only 6 per cent indicated that group marriage would be personally acceptable for them.[52] Possibly, much of the growing interest in group marriage has been generated by popular novels by such authors as Robert Rimmer (*The Harrad Experiment, Proposition 31,* and *You and I Searching for Tomorrow*) and Robert Heinlein, the famed science-fiction writer. In addition to these novels, newspaper and magazine articles dealing with group marriage have become more abundant. Also, group-living publications such as *The Modern Utopian* and *The Harrad Newsletter* have generated interest in an examination of group marriages.

How many group marriages are in existence in the United States today? No one knows, though there is agreement that the number is quite small. Larry and Joan Constantine, leading researchers in the area of group marriage, have reported on thirty-five group marriages in the United States. The difficulty in locating group marriages suggests that this is a very exceptional life-style. The Constantines state: "Pressed for an estimate, we would guess there may be fewer than a hundred, almost certainly less than a thousand group marriages in the United States."[53]

Most of the interest in group marriages has surfaced in fictional works, which have idealized and oversimplified their nature. Very little professional research has been done on this topic. As the Constantines note, the reality of living within a group marriage is quite different from the theory and fictional accounts. They further suggest that a person who enters this life-style on the basis of Robert Rimmer's characters and their experiences as described in his books is in for quite a surprise and, perhaps, serious difficulty.[54]

REASONS FOR GROUP MARRIAGES

What is it that attracts some people to group marriage? Following are some reasons that have emerged from research with group-marriage participants.

1. To many participants, traditional marriage and family leads to monotony, restrictiveness, possessiveness, sexual deprivation, and the destruction of romantic love. Some have had negative, unsatisfying experiences with monogamous marriage and see group marriage as an improved alternative.
2. The participants of group marriage see the greater sexual variety that is possible as an advantage. The group marriage, in a sense, sanctions and legitimizes variety in sexual relationships. Some adherents believe that this keeps them sexually alive and gives them a greater ability to tolerate marriage.

3. Many advocates of group marriage see this living arrangement as a way of increasing their circle of loving, intimate relationships. Not wishing to limit themselves to an intimate relationship with only one person, they feel that within a marriage with multiple partners, they will attain greater satisfaction.
4. Many seek to restore a sense of community and to expand their feelings of family identity. Group marriage is partly an attempt to overcome the isolation caused by the lack of strong friendship and kinship ties experienced in urban and suburban communities.
5. The cooperative living arrangements of most group marriages are seen by participants as having definite economic and social advantages. The participants share housing and food expenses as well as household tasks and baby-sitting. The benefits of children being exposed to more than two parents are often cited.
6. For some, group marriage represents a rebellion against the establishment, reflecting an interest in alternatives to contemporary social institutions and problems.

CHARACTERISTICS OF GROUP-MARRIAGE PARTICIPANTS

Individuals who enter group marriage have often had previous experience with swinging, mate swapping, or other forms of extramarital sexual encounter. Persons with this type of background sometimes desire to make their arrangements permanent and achieve more commitment. The Constantines report that 50 per cent of the group-marriage participants in their study had previous swinging or mate-swapping experiences. Most reported disappointment with the swingers' emphasis on gymnastics and felt that swinging was not a productive way to work toward intimate relationships.[55]

Group marriages are composed primarily of couples who are already married to each other. The general pattern is for one married couple to act as a nucleus around which other couples or single persons are drawn. As might be expected, persons who join group marriages tend to hold very liberal attitudes toward sexual behavior. Sexual fidelity is not valued highly or viewed in the same manner as in monogamous marriage.[56]

According to one study, the members of group marriages were not exclusively young, but ranged in age from twenty-two to sixty. More than half were over thirty with two distinct age clusters occurring in the midtwenties and midthirties. The median age was thirty-one.[57] Most group marriages have children who range in age from infancy to young teens, and the children are fully aware of their parents' involvement and relationships with each other.[58]

The participants in group marriages represent a wide range with respect to both occupation and income. Some are full-time students and housewives, others include physicians, commercial artists, high school teachers, custodians, rehabilitation aides, postal carriers, and ballet teachers.

THE MARRIAGE

Most group marriages involve four persons, and some include three partners. Although it seems especially easy to establish triads, this arrangement seems to be questionable psychologically as there is a tendency among the group members to equalize the sex ratio.

Relationships within a group marriage are typically intense and intimate, similar to an encounter group. Each individual is pressured to be open, provide spontaneous self-disclosure and grow toward self-actualization. However, the Constantines caution that group marriage differs from an encounter group in that it is both leaderless and exitless.

The participants of group marriage are generally equalitarian in principle concerning their orientation toward roles. There is some reduction in traditional sex roles; however, group-marriage participants tend to believe that their potential for greater role freedom has been largely unfulfilled. The most noticeable expression of role freedom has been more than average participation by men in child rearing and household activities.[59] Most of the group-marriage participants in the Constantines' study expressed the desire and intention that their group-marriage relationships be permanent or long lived. Many view group marriage as a major step in settling down after a period of previous experimentation.

SEX

According to the Constantines, the majority of men and women in group marriage indicate that they particularly enjoy sexual variety in the secure context of a marriage. They feel that their marriage arrangement provides a depth of emotional commitment and involvement not associated with most extramarital relationships. Group marriage also satisfies their desire for sexual variety without the high emotional cost of extramarital affairs or impersonal mate swapping.[60]

Sexual sharing among members of the group marriage is, of course, the dominant pattern. However, some participants do not restrict their sexual involvements to members of their marriage, but become involved with close friends and sometimes with casual acquaintances outside the group. Participants generally accept or advocate group sex and bisexual activities verbally, although group sex and bisexual activities rarely occur. Multiple-couple sex is very rare in group marriage, probably because it contributes to jealousy and competition. It seems to facilitate destructive competition among males and in some cases has apparently caused temporary impotence.[61]

Jealousy has been a problem in group marriages and has frequently been facilitated by the sexual relationships. Eighty per cent of the group-marriage participants in the Constantines' study considered jealousy to be a problem. However, it was less often a major problem among the older group marriages, suggesting that participants learn with time to cope more effectively with jealousy.[62]

CHILDREN

Most group-marriage participants ideally intend that the children involved regard all adults in the group as their parents. Generally, all adults assume some parental responsibilities in the rearing of the children. Although discipline of the children may generally be administered by all of the adults in the group, most group marriages indicate that the nature of discipline for any particular child is primarily determined by the biological parents. Discipline of children can be a source of conflict if two couples have different child-rearing patterns.

What are the effects of group marriage on children? How do they adjust to it? Before any conclusion can be reached, detailed research and observation will be required over a period of several years. The Constantines believe that most of the very young children in their study seem to adjust well. However, their research data indicate that some children experience difficulty with their parents' group-marriage relationships. Older children are more likely to experience problems as a result of being replaced as the center of attention, and some children seem concerned that they and their parents are different from other families and are aware of social disapproval when teachers and friends discover how their parents are living.[63]

PROBLEMS OF GROUP MARRIAGE

Individuals who enter group marriage usually encounter difficulties from the beginning. The Constantines reported that the majority of group marriages they have located have dissolved after a median life of sixteen months because the normal problems in traditional monogamous marriage are multiplied in group marriage. Because of the multiple relationships, there is more potential for problems.[64]

Compatibility. Many intelligent people experience great difficulty finding even one person of the opposite sex with whom they can live harmoniously and whom they can fully trust. This is illustrated by the high divorce rate in our society. It is easy to understand the tremendous selection problem involved when people try to find several persons that they can successfully relate to in a group marriage.[65] When children are involved, this selection problem of compatibility can be complicated even more because it is important that the children be compatible with their new parents and with their new brothers and sisters.

Jealousy. As mentioned earlier, 80 per cent of the group-marriage participants in the Constantines' study considered jealousy to be a problem. Jealousy seems to be related to the multiple sexual relationships. This is probably due in large part because people involved in group marriage, just as other people, deeply desire to be "number one" and have the exclusive love of one other person.

Sexual Arrangements. Related to the problem of jealousy is the mechanical process of deciding who sleeps with whom and when. Much energy is expended in making the sleeping arrangements. In many instances a highly organized rotating system is used in order to avoid favoritism, jealousy, and feelings of rejection. However, the rotating system leaves much to be desired as it tends to destroy spontaneity.[66]

Daily Responsibilities. One of the greatest problems that plagues group marriage is the organization and delegation of everyday responsibilities both within and outside the home. A consistent disappointment is the unfinished work that no one wishes to do and which usually falls on the individual who is least assertive of his or her rights or the individual who has the greatest need for order.[67] Conflicts and frustrations about such things as whose turn it is to wash dishes, clean house, or buy groceries form what have been called the tremendous trifles of family living.

Financial Management. Another major problem of group marriage and the source of much conflict is financial management. The more people involved, the more difficult it is to reach decisions satisfactory to everyone concerning the budgeting of money for such items as clothing, food, and recreation. Some group marriages attempt to solve this problem by having each member remain financially autonomous and independent rather than sharing a collective income. However, this acts to destroy group cohesiveness.

Sensory Overload. One problem that has been observed in group marriage is called "sensory overload." This simply refers to the great intensity of interaction that is generated by multiple emotional involvement and by the emphasis upon an encounter type of interaction.[68] Group marriage has been referred to as a marathon encounter group. Intense interaction may make it necessary for an individual to withdraw periodically into solitude and privacy to survive emotionally. However, even this can present problems, such as when and where one can go for privacy.

In this encounter type of atmosphere, members are pressured to grow toward self-actualization and to become more open and intimate in interactions. Some group marriages create an unreasonable and disruptive force on their members to achieve this growth. In such marriages unreasonable pressure tends to fall primarily on one person who is frequently the youngest and/or the least secure.[69]

Denial of Individualism. Some advocates maintain that group marriage provides greater opportunity for individual development. However, one source of individual frustration is that the security and stability of the marriage requires a denial of one's individualism and sometimes a denial of an individual's opportunities for personal advancement. Cross-cultural data indicate that in societies where polygamy is practiced or the extended family system is strong, individualism is obtained only at great costs to both family and the individual.

Social Unacceptability. One built-in problem of group marriage not present in traditional monogamous marriage is that of social unacceptability. Being socially unacceptable probably adds more of a strain on the relationships than the participants are willing to admit. Conflict and estrangement may be caused by the fact that participants of the marriage are usually living in open rebellion against society and against their parents in particular. If they do not choose to live in open rebellion but rather keep their unorthodox marriage arrangements a secret, then problems can evolve as a result of deception.

COMMENT

It has been predicted that the growth of group marriage in the future will be limited and will remain a life-style for a minority largely because of:

1. The difficulty of finding three or more adults who can live together harmoniously in a marriage situation.
2. The presence of jealousy and love conflicts.
3. The difficulty of coordinating the daily schedules of several people.
4. The high instability of present group marriages.[70]

It is estimated that far less than 1 per cent of the nation's population is involved in group marriage. Very likely that proportion will not increase greatly in the future.[71] Looking back to history and the experiences of various cultures over the world, it is significant that even in those cultures where group marriage has been accepted, it tends to be practiced by only a small minority of people. A review of much of the available research and information concerning group marriage suggests that the problems encountered are too great for most persons to overcome, and if stability is any criterion of success, then the prognosis for group marriage is not favorable.

Extramarital Sexual Relationships

CONFUSION

An estimated 60 per cent of husbands and 35 to 40 per cent of wives in the United States become involved in an extramarital sexual relationship at some time during their marriage.[72]

Although the incidence of extramarital sexual relationships has apparently increased, most people, even those involved in affairs, continue to disapprove of extramarital sexual relationships. A national poll conducted for *McCall's* magazine found that a large majority condemned adultery under almost all circumstances. Half of the respondents indicated they had never condoned, or felt sympathy with, extramarital affairs, even of friends.[73]

Morton Hunt, author of *The Affair,* indicated that a large majority of the individuals in his study disapproved of adultery. Those who had experienced affairs themselves were more tolerant; however, even the majority of this group generally disapproved of extramarital sexual relationships.[74]

A national survey of college students found that 80 per cent of the students reported extramarital sexual relationships *with* the consent of their spouse would not be an acceptable life-style for them personally, and 85 per cent indicated that extramarital sexual relationships *without* the consent of their spouse would not be an acceptable life-style for them personally.[75] These findings, in addition to much clinical evidence, suggest that the psychological climate in our society is not conducive to an acceptance of, and participation in, extramarital sexual relationships.

CHARACTERISTICS OF THOSE INVOLVED

What are the characteristics of those who become involved in extramarital sexual relationships? The peak incidence of involvement in extramarital relationships among women occurs in the age group thirty-six to forty and in the very young years among men. These coincide with the different stages of greatest sexual drive and interest for the male and female.

Concerning level of education, the Kinsey studies found that for males in the early years of marriage the incidence of extramarital relationships was highest among the less educated. However, after several years of marriage, the rate was greater among those at the higher educational levels.

Those who are less devout religiously or who have no religious conviction have the highest incidence of extramarital affairs. Individuals involved in affairs are more likely to be children of parents with very permissive moral values.[76] Some research indicates that "low strength of conscience" is associated with becoming involved in extramarital sexual relationships.[77]

The research by Morton Hunt has illustrated that many persons who become involved in a series of casual extramarital affairs have a history of casual premarital sexual affairs in which they dissociated sex from love. After marriage the same dissociation makes casual extramarital relationships guilt-free and easy.[78] Those who indulge in extramarital sexual relationships are more likely to live in urban areas, which offer anonymity, or in suburbs where such relationships are not severely condemned.

Feelings of alienation seem to be common among those engaged in extramarital sexual relationships.[79] For example, a study by Robert Whitehurst [80] indicated that 80 per cent of all men participating in extensive extramarital involvement were characterized by a high degree of alienation. Alienation was measured by a series of questions which reflect feelings of powerlessness, meaninglessness, normlessness, and social isolation. This study further indicated that men with a high degree of alienation had more casual affairs than the men characterized by a low degree of alienation.

Another finding by Whitehurst was that those low in alienation expressed more satisfaction and happiness in their marriages. Of those characterized by a low degree of alienation, 83 per cent said they remained faithful to their wives for moral or religious reasons or because of a sense of family responsibility.

Often, individuals who participate in extramarital sexual relationships have a lower degree of sexual and marital satisfaction within their marriages.[81] Many either do not desire or cannot manage a high level of involvement with their marriage partners. These individuals feel that discreet extramarital sexual relationships should not adversely influence their marriage relationships.[82]

However, the relationship between dissatisfaction in marriage and participation in extramarital relationships is not as conclusive as might be expected. For example, a study by Gerhard Neubeck and Vera M. Schletzer [83] found little difference between those highly satisfied with their marriages and the low-satisfaction group with respect to involvement in extramarital sexual relationships.

REASONS FOR ENTERING EXTRAMARITAL SEXUAL RELATIONSHIPS

Social and Cultural Encouragement. Many people engage in extramarital relationships because of pressure to do so in various social situations in which they are regularly involved. For example, at some business parties, sexual involvements are expected, and some otherwise monogamous husbands and wives do participate in extramarital sexual activities at these times.[84] Robert Whitehurst reports, for instance, that 41 per cent of his sample indicated that the crucial factors in determining fidelity to their wives were the places and people that presented opportunities for liaisons.[85]

Curiosity and Desire for Sexual Variety. Some individuals enter an extramarital sexual relationship primarily out of curiosity to find out what it would be like to have a sexual encounter with someone other than the spouse. Many state a desire for sexual variety as the major reason for extramarital affairs.

Escape from Boredom. One basic reason given by middle- and upper-class persons for engaging in extramarital relationships is to escape boredom. Many individuals who lead highly routinized, dull, unadventurous lives, both at home and at work, see an affair as one of the few ways they can experience excitement and adventure.[86]

Reinforcement of an "I'm OK" Position. An affair is often more an attempt to reinforce an "I'm OK" position and to feel desirable and attractive than to obtain sexual satisfaction. Many men and women have disturbing feelings of "I'm not OK" and of inadequacy. They have nagging doubts concerning themselves and tend to feel that they are not really masculine or feminine unless they continually win the attentions of members of the opposite sex.

Avoidance of Problems. A husband or wife who is having problems with a mate or with a job can forget them for a little while in the companionship of another person. People may also use the extramarital relationship as a way to create other problems that can, in a sense, be substituted for those they wish to avoid.[87]

Breakdowns in the Marriage Relationship. Many individuals become involved in extramarital relationships because of breakdowns in their marriage relationships. This may happen when a couple find their incompatibility growing and conflict becoming a continuous experience.

Retaliation and Rebellion. In some situations the major motivation for becoming involved in an adulterous relationship is not sexual interest in another person, but to "get even" and to hurt a spouse for some "wrong" he or she has committed. Closely associated with retaliation as a motivational factor is rebellion. The rebellion may be against social codes or norms the individual feels are unreasonable and unduly restrictive. It may also be directed against a marriage partner whom the individual feels has restricted or thwarted him or her in some way.

Search for Emotional Intimacy. Some who engage in extramarital relationships are seeking to have certain emotional needs satisfied. These needs may be unfulfilled within the marriage relationship, or there may simply be a desire to expand emotional intimacy to persons outside of the marriage.

Encouragement by the Spouse. Some individuals may enter extramarital relationships primarily because their spouse encourages them to do so. The Kinsey study found that some husbands encouraged their wives to engage in extramarital activities in order to justify their own extramarital affairs. Mate swapping or swinging initially often involves this type of encouragement.

Desire to Destroy Relationships. Some individuals, because they are in an "I'm not OK" position have an unconscious or conscious desire to destroy relationships. These persons apparently base their lives on the assumption that good relationships do not exist and their behavior is oriented toward "proving" this assumption.[88] One illustration of this is when an individual establishes an extramarital relationship that "just happens" to break up the extramarital partner's marriage. After the marriage has been destroyed, the extramarital relationship itself "just happens" to break up. The individual with this destructive orientation toward relationships has structured the situation in a way that "proves" that the other person's marriage relationship was not good and neither was the extramarital relationship. This type of person is expressing an "I'm not OK—You're not OK" approach to relationships.

EFFECTS OF AFFAIRS

Effects on the Marriage. The view that extramarital sexual relationships may indeed improve the quality of a marriage has increasingly been voiced by some writers. However, the research evidence indicates the probability is high that the marriage will be negatively affected.

The National Statistical Institute reports that 87 per cent of divorces are, in fact, caused by adultery regardless of the cause cited.[89] Most estimates are considerably lower than this. However, there is wide agreement that adultery does play an important role in contributing to divorce.

Over a third of the respondents in Hunt's study [90] were eventually divorced as a direct result of their extramarital sexual relationships. Only a small percentage reported that their marriage relationship improved as a result of the extramarital affairs. Only one out of ten reported that an affair had brought them emotionally closer to their spouses or had increased sexual satisfaction within marriage.

The results of a five-year longitudinal study by Stephen Beltz [91] of couples involved in extramarital sexual relationships contradicted the view that these relationships could improve the quality of a marriage relationship. A very important conclusion of this study was that persons involved in extramarital sexual relationships begin to use new patterns of behavior that are similar to the dating and seductive patterns found in courtship. Because these behavior patterns tend to conflict with stable marriage patterns, the clash between the two will probably become so great that either the extramarital sexual relationship will have to be stopped to maintain the marriage, or else dissolution of the marriage by divorce will ultimately occur.

Evidence indicates that one important consequence of an extramarital sexual relationship is that it tends to minimize the enrichment and enjoyment of the positive qualities of the spouse. William Masters, Virginia Johnson, and Robert Levin in *The Pleasure Bond* [92] observe that extramarital affairs communicate two messages in the marriage: first, one spouse is not capable of meeting the other's emotional and physical needs; second, one spouse does not consider the other a unique and irreplaceable source of satisfaction. The effect of such messages would be to reinforce an "I'm not OK" position in a spouse. An individual who restricts his or her affectional and sexual expression to the marriage partner learns to look more deeply into the positive qualities possessed by that spouse.[93]

The Internal Conflict. Extramarital affairs often cause intense feelings of conflict within the individual between a desire to maintain the marriage and a desire to continue the extramarital relationship. People soon learn that the more open they are to the extramarital relationship, the more they are pressured to shut out the marriage relationship. The more they seek to preserve the marriage, the more they must repudiate the extramarital relationship. These individuals often discover that they can end the dilemma only by choosing one relationship and abandoning the other.[94]

This internal conflict manifests both physical and emotional symptoms. Some individuals have digestive disturbances, cannot sleep, or find themselves disturbed by nightmares. Many are unable to concentrate on their work and become forgetful. Some become extremely irritable and emotional. A number experience depression; they become withdrawn and unable to interest themselves in anything. Such persons sometimes require medication, psychotherapy, or even hospitalization.[95]

In commenting on the eventual outcome of this internal struggle, one researcher [96] reports that if the marriage of a person involved in an extramarital sexual relationship is not satisfying, and if the extramarital affair is very rewarding and secure, the extramarital relationship is apt to win the struggle. However, if the extramarital partner is an unwise choice and the marriage relationship is basically rewarding and satisfying, disillusionment with the extramarital affair and a new appreciation of the marriage relationship are likely.

When the Spouse Finds Out. One important aspect of the effects of extramarital sexual relationships involves the reaction of the spouse. It was found in Hunt's study [97] that only 25 per cent of those involved in extramarital sexual relationships reported their spouse's reactions as understanding, happy, or tolerant; 75 per cent indicated that their spouses reacted in a negative manner, including fear, rage, jealousy, humiliation, and great depression.

A person who discovers a mate's involvement in an extramarital affair and will not express anger or hurt toward the spouse may, instead, focus these negative feelings on himself or herself. Turning anger and hurt inward can take the form of suicide attempts, neglect of health, accidents, or other self-destructive behavior.[98]

Some persons react to the discovery of a spouse's involvement in an extramarital sexual relationship by threatening divorce. In fact, Hunt [99] found that approximately one third of those who learned of their spouse's affairs threatened divorce if the affair was not terminated.

After the Divorce. The outcome of an extramarital affair rarely results in marriage to the extramarital partner. Of those persons Hunt interviewed, only one in ten had married or intended to marry the person with whom they were having the affair. Whereas over a third of those in Hunt's study had been divorced as a result of their extramarital affairs, only part of the divorces were sought in order to marry the extramarital partner, and even when they were, the intended marriages took place only about 50 per cent of the time.[100]

Marriage to the extramarital partner usually does not take place largely because the selection of an extramarital partner is often poor in terms of compatibility. Often the relationship is much less compatible than is the relationship with the spouse.

Personality and Effects. The effects on those involved in an extramarital affair depend upon the personalities of the individuals. For example, for conscience-controlled people, especially puritan-romantics who had or desired to have a totally involved and committed marriage, it is rare for the extramarital sexual relationship to remain emotionally casual.

For this personality type, the affair tends to be a disruptive and dynamic experience that either grows at the expense of the marriage or is diminished in significance by the marriage. Consequently, the affair is neither an amusement nor a casual comfort, but rather a crisis that must be resolved in one direction or the other. For other types of persons, extramarital sexual relationships tend to have less significant emotional effects.[101]

DURATION OF EXTRAMARITAL AFFAIRS

Extramarital affairs are likely to be short-lived and, compared to marriage relationships, they are much less stable. One research study found that between 10 and 25 per cent of first affairs last for only one day. Approximately 10 per cent endure longer than a day but less than a month. Approximately 50 per cent last for more than one month but less than a year. And about 25 per cent of first affairs last for two or more years, but of these only a few endure for four years or more. Subsequent extramarital affairs generally have a similar pattern of duration.[102]

COMMENT

Many social scientists predict that extramarital sexual relationships will become more prevalent in the future. Undoubtedly, quite a few persons feel that they receive emotional and sexual satisfaction in such liaisons that they do not obtain with their marriage partner. Others feel that the affair adds variety to the emotional and sexual fulfillment they already experience with a marriage partner.

However, considering the long-range effects, the probability is high that the affair will result in someone, if not everyone involved, getting hurt emotionally. For example, a husband may experience the stress of being torn between his wife and his extramarital partner; the extramarital partner may feel that she has second-class status; and the wife may feel rejected.

Most of us deeply desire to have a close one-to-one relationship with another who has a strong commitment to us. William Masters and Virginia Johnson have noted that when one marital partner has an affair, the spouse is likely to feel that the commitment has diminished and may feel less secure in the relationship.[103] If extramarital sexual relationships become more common in the future, there may also be an increase in anxiety, insecurity, and emotional stress because of the way we have learned to view these relationships.

Swinging

WHAT IS SWINGING?

Swinging is a unique type of extramarital sexual relationship involving two or more couples who mutually decide to exchange sexual partners or to engage in group sexual activities. Sexual behavior in swinging is primarily viewed as recreational and as an end in itself. Emotional involvement is deliberately avoided or minimized.

Swinging is engaged in jointly by husband and wife. This differs from the affair, which usually involves dishonesty and emotional involvement. Swinging adheres to a single standard of sexual behavior, which emphasizes that behavior acceptable for the husband is also acceptable for the wife.[104] Generally, the husband initiates the swinging. Some evidence indicates that women are usually pressured psychologically, and sometimes physically, into swinging by their husbands.[105] Single individuals may also be included in swinging either with another individual, with a couple, or as a part of a large group sexual experience.

CHARACTERISTICS OF SWINGERS

Most of the studies that have been conducted on swingers have emphasized their normality. They tend to be average individuals except for their involvement in swinging. Surprisingly, swingers are fairly conventional and conservative in their life orientation. One major study indicated that though alcohol is consumed among swingers, they tend to oppose the use of other drugs, including marijuana.[106]

There is some evidence that swingers value their marriages and make a great effort to establish rules to structure swinging activities in a manner that does not threaten their marriage relationships. This is why swingers emphasize emotional uninvolvement and keeping the interaction strictly on a physical level.

Swingers have higher levels of education than the general population. One study indicated that 50 per cent of the swingers were college graduates, and 80 per cent had attended college.[107] The age of swingers ranges from the late teens to, in a very few cases, seventy. The estimated median age is about twenty-nine for women and thirty-two for men.

Exactly how do swingers differ from nonswingers? There is not enough research to know definitely. However, evidence indicates that swingers have a background of more numerous premarital sexual relationships than nonswingers. As might be expected, swingers more frequently believe that love and sex are too different needs than do nonswingers.[108]

Perhaps another important characteristic of swingers is that they tend to avoid organized religious services, though they usually consider themselves to be religious.

SWINGING VS. THE AFFAIR

Many swingers have engaged in extramarital affairs previous to their participation in swinging. Most of these couples believe that once the swinging begins, the extramarital affairs and the need for them end.[109]

Why do couples become involved in swinging rather than having extramarital affairs? Some of the reasons they give are:

1. Swinging is less time consuming and less expensive.
2. There is more variety.
3. The emotional involvement is not as high and much less effort is required.
4. Husband and wife are honest with each other and participate in swinging jointly, thus removing the deception that is a major aspect of affairs.
5. The danger of breaking up the marriage because of infidelity is decreased.

LACK OF EMOTIONAL INVOLVEMENT

Perhaps the most important rule in swinging is that the participating individuals must not become emotionally attached to each other. Emotional involvement is feared as it may endanger the marriage by producing jealous reactions. In swinging activities, very strict ground rules are established which are designed to protect the marriage.

For example, many swingers interact with another couple only once. If two couples swing together more than five times, they generally stop seeing each other or else they develop a true friendship and continue to see each other but without sexual activity.[110]

Swingers tend to prefer large parties as the scene for their activities. One reason is that the large crowd minimizes the risk of emotional involvement. With all the drinking, dancing, and other distractions, there is neither time nor a conducive environment for an individual to learn much about the personal nature of the swinging partners.

SWINGING AND CHILDREN

Most swingers have children. In fact, one study reported that 87 per cent of the swinging couples had two or three children.[111] Most parents make certain their children are out of the home on swinging nights. In one study only six of the couples reported that they would rear their children in the same liberal spirit by which they lived. Many swingers take care to prevent their children from listening to telephone conversations, reading mail, or finding photographs of other couples. These parents feel that knowledge of their swinging activities would result in emotional problems for the children.[112]

MAKING CONTACTS

There is evidence that swingers' magazines are important in promoting swinging. The major purpose of these magazines is to run personal advertisements. Fees are charged to place advertisements and to forward letters. For the majority of swingers, the magazines provide the primary method of meeting others. In Gilbert Bartell's research it was found that for the majority of the couples, swingers' magazines played a vital role in their decision to enter the swinging scene. Approximately 95 per cent of the couples had placed advertisements at some point in their swinging career.[113]

Couples also may make contact with other swingers by visiting bars catering exclusively to swingers. These bars usually operate as private clubs and require membership. Organizers are frequently present and circulate among the guests, arranging parties and informing couples of parties that have been scheduled. Swinging parties also provide an opportunity for couples to meet, exchange phone numbers, and extend private party invitations to each other.

PROBLEMS OF SWINGING

Although swinging has increased in recent years and has become more widely publicized, it does remain the life-style of a very small minority. Several serious problems are associated with swinging.

Monopolization of Time and Interests. One common problem of swinging is that swingers become so preoccupied with it that it monopolizes their time and interests. It dominates their thoughts and activities to the extent that they have very few other hobbies or interests.

Suburbanite swingers generally have far less outside interests and activities than nonswinging suburbanites of the same socioeconomic class. The study by Bartell indicated that most suburban swingers take part in few activities other than swinging and watching television. Some swingers spend their annual vacations swinging. These couples arrange for their children to attend summer camp or to stay with relatives and then spend their vacation traveling to other parts of the country and swinging.

Swinging can become so time consuming, some couples report this as the major reason for dropping out. Making telephone calls, writing and reading advertisements, meeting people, and trying to find couples who are compatible with both the husband and wife becomes too much of a hassle to continue.[114]

Anxiety. Anxiety is a major problem in swinging and appears to be a common experience. Sexual performance is emphasized, and both men and women are very concerned about whether the persons with whom they swing consider them sexually desirable and competent. They feel they must arouse and satisfy all their partners because the outcome of the sexual encounter is communicated to many people through the swingers' gossip circle. Perhaps the greatest fear of swingers is that someone will put them down sexually and pronounce a negative evaluation of their sexual adequacy.

The Put Downs. One of the most psychologically damaging aspects of swinging is the inclination of many swingers to belittle others in the one area of greatest vulnerability—their sexual adequacy and desirability.

Bartell [115] found that when swingers get together, they continually discuss everything associated with swinging, including, of course, other swingers. There is a tendency to compare and evaluate the sexual performance of individuals, which promotes anxiety and uncomfortableness. As a result, many persons place more emphasis on their performance, rather than upon sexual enjoyment. They are very concerned with "measuring up" so that they will be accepted, avoid the "put downs" and be invited to future parties.

Lack of Involvement and Commitment. The lack of emotional involvement swingers consider desirable is also one of the greatest problems. There are indications that this lack of involvement may be the greatest source of dissatisfaction among swingers and a major reason for terminating swinging activities.

Most persons desire positive and satisfying interpersonal relationships and like to feel that others are committed to them. These qualities are absent in swinging because of the built-in rejection of emotional involvement. Many swingers find this disillusioning and unsatisfying. Bartell in his study reported that lack of involvement and commitment was the major reason for the more intellectually inclined, more sensitive persons dropping out of swinging. These individuals felt that

> . . . the practice of more or less indiscriminate swinging is much too mechanistic; that there is a loss of identity, and absence of commitment; and that this total noninvolvement—at least to them—represents the antithesis of sexual pleasure and satisfaction.[116]

Concern About Public Exposure. Many swingers are very apprehensive about their activities becoming known to children, friends, relatives, or their employers.

Such exposure could cost them severe social disapproval or even the loss of their job. Some worry about blackmail.

Fear of being exposed is why many couples emphasize the requirement of discretion in the advertisements they place in swinger publications. This fear is also the reason that swinger publications use code numbers to protect those placing advertisements. A response to the advertisement must then go through the publisher.[117]

Jealousy. Jealousy and quarrels frequently occur when a spouse feels that the mate enjoyed sexual activities with others more than with the spouse, or when one spouse seems to have a much better time than the other.[118] Women may become jealous of each other as a result of competing for the attentions of men. Some even maintain a record of how many men approach them during a party. A woman who attracts few men may feel resentful and jealous of a woman who attracts many. Jealousy may easily be aroused between male swingers because of their tendency to compete.[119] A man who feels this strong sense of competition may become envious of younger men or of male swingers who tire less easily.

Research evidence also indicates that couples may become jealous of other couples with whom they have been swinging. This is understandable as the emphasis upon popularity is conducive to couples competing with each other to be the most sought-after.[120]

The Spread of Venereal Disease. Because of the multiple sexual contacts in swinging, a swinger may eventually encounter venereal disease and therefore has a high probability of contracting it. Venereal disease can spread rapidly within swinging circles, as some swingers have contacts with as many as two new couples each week. Those couples, in turn, contact other new couples and, as a result, many individuals could be infected within a few weeks.[121]

Superficiality. A major problem of swinging is that it is based on superficiality. The entire system of interaction is such that a person's worth is judged almost exclusively in terms of physical attractiveness and, to a lesser extent, youth.[122]

The younger, more physically attractive couples are considered more desirable and popular. An older and less physically attractive couple may frequently be rejected or ignored.

COMMENT

On the basis of available research, and according to the predictions of social scientists, swinging will probably remain the life-style of only a few persons. There are three basic reasons for this.

First, swinging does not offer the emotional closeness and involvement, the commitment, the security, or the wholeness in interpersonal relationships that marriage does. The relationships are deliberately restricted to the mechanical aspects of sexual interaction and psychological intimacy is avoided. For many persons this decreases sexual pleasure.

Second, for many who enter swinging it is a short-lived experience. This is largely because judgments of an individual's worth are superficial and based on physical attractiveness and youth. Eventually, a swinging couple will age and, according to the standards of the younger swingers, will become less attractive and desirable.

Third, a fear of rejection and of not performing adequately appears to be so prevalent among couples who swing that it is doubtful the psychological effects of swinging are desirable for many people.

The swingers actually find themselves in a self-deluding, contradictory situation. They frequently attempt to convince themselves that they are not having sexual relationships with complete strangers by calling swinging companions "friends." But at the same time they deliberately avoid any emotional involvement and keep the relationships on a strictly physical basis.[123]

Homosexual Marriages

CHANGING ATTITUDES

Greater tolerance and understanding—if not acceptance—of homosexuality has been evidenced in recent years. We have gone from a time when individuals were jailed for openly loving, in a sexual sense, others of the same sex. Today, many homosexuals picket as an aggrieved minority, homosexual relationships have been the recurring theme of several major films and novels, and a number of churches ministering to homosexuals have been founded. England's laws have been rewritten so that homosexual acts between consenting adults are no longer a crime. In the United States, several states recognize the rights of homosexuals to pursue their own life-styles.[124]

Estimates of the number of homosexuals in the United States vary widely. Kinsey's 1953 figures, which are recognized as being accurate estimates of overt behavior by the Institute for Sex Research, indicate approximately 4 per cent of males and 2.5 per cent of females are *exclusively* homosexual throughout their lives.[125] When individuals who are homosexual for only part of their lives and those whose homosexuality is undetected are included, the estimates for incidence go as high as 10 to 17 per cent of the population.

GAY MARRIAGE

A study by Evelyn Hooker revealed that many homosexuals wish to develop long-lasting relationships. These permanent relationships are often termed *gay marriages.*[126] Use of the term *marriage* may not seem correct since it usually refers to a male-female legalized union. However, social scientists have begun to apply it to any close, intimate relationship. Larry and Joan Constantine, leading researchers in group marriage, state that what "makes two people married to each other is that they perceive themselves to be married, bonded, committed."[127]

Some social scientists foresee an increase in the number of gay marriages in the future. Some also feel that homosexual couples will adopt children in time. Indeed, a number of homosexual couples are already rearing children from previous heterosexual marriages.[128]

BENEFITS

The gay marriage seems to offer advantages and benefits to persons who are homosexual. Research indicates several important benefits including the following:

1. Male homosexuals tend to feel more adequate if they are homosexually married.[129]
2. There are indications that the healthiest, happiest homosexuals are the ones who reject entirely the group-oriented gay life and, instead, establish a homosexual marriage.[130]
3. Homosexual marriages help to solve some of the problems associated with the group-oriented gay life, such as short-term and unstable relationships, superficiality in relationships, jealousy, and promiscuity.
4. Homosexual marriage provides a way to fulfill the need of homosexual persons to have someone to care for in a long-term relationship of mutual commitment.

PROBLEMS

Research studies have indicated that homosexual persons tend to have a negative view of themselves and homosexuality. Gordon Westwood reported that more than half of his subjects had made at least one attempt to terminate all homosexual activity. They failed and experienced depression and self-loathing.[131] These negative attitudes toward themselves and their own sexuality provide a built-in potential for a greater than average amount of conflict in homosexual relationships.

Because many homosexuals have incorporated in their own consciences the prohibitions against homosexual relationships, they experience guilt and negative self-concepts as a result of a sustained homosexual relationship. The gay marriage itself may be a constant reminder that the individual is defying societal rules and prohibitions.[132]

Social prohibition is also experienced in the lack of institutionalization of the homosexual marriage by church and state. The authority of church and state acts in heterosexual marriages to see that couples keep voluntary but binding promises. In gay marriage the only bond may be the couple's devotion to one another since there are no legal sanctions to hold the couple together, probably no children, and usually few common goals. Another problem encountered in gay marriage involves the reaction of family and friends. In many cases the whole network of family relations may be so disrupted that renewal of good relationships is impossible. It is not uncommon for the family to urge their homosexual son or daughter to seek psychiatric aid or a heterosexual relationship to effect a cure, or to disown the homosexual child. Not surprisingly, many homosexuals reveal a strong desire to keep family and friends from learning about their homosexual relationships.[133]

Another problem area for the homosexual couple involves the pressures of living in two worlds. Many wear heterosexual masks in their professional and social lives. Because of this presumed heterosexual role, their mates cannot be included in their professional or social lives. This often creates dissatisfaction and feelings of alienation between partners. Some couples even maintain separate households to avoid suspicion. This is expensive as well as leaving much to be desired in terms of emotional support and psychological need fulfillment for the couple.

For some couples, making a place in the homosexual and in the heterosexual worlds simultaneously poses problems too slight to even be noticed. For other couples the problems are so great that the marriage relationship breaks.

Within the homosexual relationship itself, there may be problems of jealousy, competitiveness, insecurity, and malice. This is partially due to the power struggles that often characterize homosexual relationships and also due to infidelity and promiscuity. Undoubtedly, some of the conflict also arises from the homosexuals' negative feelings about themselves. Despite claims of "I'm gay and proud," many still feel deviant and undesirable.[134]

COMMENT

In 1973, the American Psychiatric Association removed homosexuality as a mental disorder from its diagnostic manual, and increasingly there are indications in the business and legal community that more people believe sexual behavior should be left to personal preferences so long as it involves relationships between consenting adults.[135] However, sexual behavior cannot be viewed separately from the society in which it occurs, and it would appear that homosexuality is still viewed by the mainstream of America as undesirable. It is likely that changes in attitude will occur, but it may be some time before homosexuality is viewed as one of several acceptable life-styles.

One-Parent Families

A PARENT ALONE

Millions of adults today find themselves in the situation of rearing children without the presence or assistance of a marriage partner. One-parent families currently represent over 8 per cent of all United States families. The great majority of the more than four million one-parent families in the United States with children under the age of eighteen are mother-only, or female-headed.[136]

The one-parent family is presently in the process of changing. While the term *one-parent family* was once reserved for those who had experienced widowhood, divorce, separation, or desertion, it is now being extended to the "never married." Unwed mothers wanting to keep their children with increasing frequency, more single persons seeking to adopt children, as well as gradual changes in our concepts of family life and child-rearing practices, are forcing a re-examination of the one-parent family life-style.

BY DEATH

The most numerous and the most respected one-parent families are those resulting from the death of one parent. Widows constitute the largest percentage of all female family heads. The most frequently noted advantage of the widowed person left to rear a family, in comparison to being a single parent by divorce or desertion, is the attitude of others. Since the status of widowhood is unplanned and unintentional, the community provides the bereaved spouse with respect, acceptance, and assistance. Such respect, acceptance, and assistance are less often extended to the nonwidowed counterpart.

BY DIVORCE, SEPARATION, OR DESERTION

Divorce, separation, and desertion involving children also create one-parent families. However, there are considerable differences between loss of a parent through death and loss of a parent through divorce or separation. The major difference is that legal dissolvement of a marriage represents the breakdown of a relationship between the parents, which often results in feelings of guilt, shame, failure, and anger.

Divorce affects over one million American children under the age of eighteen. The number of children affected by desertion is unknown, but is thought to be quite high—over 250,000 a year.

Some of the problems divorced persons face begin long before legalities are settled and continue for indefinite periods of time. Some divorced persons and those who are separated regret that they have not achieved whatever it is that binds the remaining majority of marriages together. However, many adjust to their divorced status well and function more effectively than when they were married.

PROBLEMS OF ONE-PARENT FAMILIES

Many problems are encountered in one-parent families. These problems are based on readjusting from one life orientation to another, from life as a couple to life as a one-parent family. The problems that face all parents in daily life take on greater magnitude when there is no spouse with whom to share them. Specific problems often experienced include financial problems, role conflicts and shifts in roles, isolation and loneliness, and child-rearing problems.

Finances. Although female-headed households compose less than 8 per cent of all households in the United States, they represent about 25 per cent of American families in poverty—a disproportionate share. Finances constitute a problem for most one-parent families at some point in the family life-cycle. For one-parent families, in comparison with most two-parent families, the period of time when finances are a problem is considerably longer. In cases of divorce or separation with the subsequent child support and alimony payments, few men can afford to support two households on an adequate level—if by adequate we include those "necessities" that each parent enjoyed before divorce or separation. The deserted mother normally has more serious financial problems than widows or divorcées because she receives no support payments, no financial settlement from her husband, nor does she receive any income from his financial investments.

Financial problems cause most single mothers to enter the labor force. For those who worked before marriage or were working at the time they became single mothers, the shift to employment as the sole "breadwinner" poses fewer problems than for those who have never worked or those with few marketable skills. Some women find that after being out of the labor market for several years, their former jobs no longer exist and they must retrain to find work, or their employer's location has changed and they must move to return to their former position.

By some companies' standards, single parents with young children are not the most desirable employees. Schoolchildren's hours do not fit in with the working parent's nine-to-five schedule. School hours often begin after the parent has gone to work and are over before the parent returns. School holidays are too numerous and too lengthy for working parents.

Thus, the working parent must locate some type of day care for young children. Day care centers have been a great assistance to the working single parent. However, for many with low incomes, day care centers are often costly and other, less expensive arrangements must be made for their children.

Role Conflict and Shift. The parent with whom the child lives often feels as though he or she must play a dual role, being both mother and father. Since one parent cannot adequately serve as both a mother and a father, the result is frequently confusing for the child and exhausting for the parent.

Many family-life educators believe if the one parent can serve as a clear image of his or her own sex role and provide adequate images for the other sex role through friends or relatives, the children will be less confused in their identity development. This not only allows the parent to portray the image of what a real mother or father is, but also gives the parent the opportunity of assisting the child in his or her relationships with those of the opposite sex.[137]

Many of the one-parent family heads eventually remarry. At this point, the parent again experiences a shift in roles—from being everything to the child to returning to a position of sharing parental responsibilities.

Being Alone. Being alone is the most universal problem that single parents must face. Not all one-parent families contend with financial crises, the problems of employment, or unsatisfactory social relationships. Some do not even experience serious problems in child rearing, but without exception, single parents must face life as one rather than two.

Death creates a vacuum of emptiness for which time may be the only remedy. The divorced face their own special problems. Even though legal dissolvement of marriage may have been desirable for both parties, special feelings, regardless of how minute, exist between the couple, creating a feeling of loss in their lives.

Fortunately, for many people who have lost a spouse, feelings of isolation and loneliness are only temporary. Readjustment eventually is achieved, enabling them to function reasonably well. For some the readjustment process may seem more painful than the loneliness. How much being alone influences the single parent depends on many factors, among which are the magnitude and duration of the negative feelings associated with being alone.

Some individuals believe they should not return to an active social life because by doing so, they run the risk of being hurt again. In an effort to avoid this, they may turn inward and withdraw from social contacts.[138] Readjustment to social life is frequently a major source of anxiety for single parents because both men and women often find it difficult to feel comfortable in social activities as singles.

Child Rearing. Common to all one-parent families is child rearing, which frequently involves anxiety and frustration. Widowed mothers may worry about the effects that death and the consequent fatherlessness have upon their children. Divorced or deserted parents are concerned over the negative emotions their children experience as a result of the marital conflict that preceded the divorce or desertion and the resulting loss of one parent. These parents frequently experience a sense of guilt and anger over their new single status.

Many single parents who work feel they do not spend enough time with their children. Some indicate that when they are with their children, they are often too tired to enjoy them because they must now assume all of the child-rearing and household responsibilities in addition to working. Finding adequate day care for children is a problem for single parents who work.

A common concern of single parents is that their children have contact with two-parent families so that they will grow up with an image of what family life is like when both parents are present. A frequent worry is whether the children will find an adequate substitute for the missing parent.

THE UNWED MOTHER

The unwed mother is becoming of greater concern to society as the illegitimacy rate increases and as more unwed mothers elect to keep their children and rear them in one-parent homes. Homes for unwed mothers now are operating at lower than capacity, whereas the number of unwed pregnancies continues to increase. In 1940 the number of illegitimate births was reported to be 89,500. In 1970 the number had increased to 398,700 illegitimate births. By 1980, this figure is expected to rise to approximately 500,000.

The unwed mother faces all the same difficulties of other one-parent family heads. Finances, employment, role conflicts, loneliness, social life, day care and child rearing may pose problems for her. However, many of these problems are intensified for the unwed mother because of her status in society. Because the unwed mother is often young and may have left school or college, she may have difficulty securing enough education to support herself and her child adequately.

ONE-PARENT ADOPTIONS

Nearly all adoption agencies recognize and support the two-parent family as the best environment for child rearing. However, faced with the difficulty of finding ideal placement for all adoptive children, many agencies are beginning to turn to single persons as an alternate solution.

The California State Department of Social Welfare was the first to revise its adoption regulations, allowing single persons to qualify as adoptive parents in 1965. Other states followed California's progressive lead. Single-parent adoptions have occurred in several states throughout the country.

Presently, single-parent adoptions are not extensive, nor are they likely to become so, though they will become more common. Single-parent adoptions open wider avenues to affectionate and supportive permanent homes for children who might otherwise spend their formative years in less than desirable institutions or in a series of foster homes.

Agencies, in an effort to determine if the one-parent applicant is a good choice for a child in need of a home, carefully screen the applicant's emotional stability, interpersonal relationships, health status, income, child-care plan, and motivation.[139]

Much of the concern over single-parent adoptions as well as one-parent families in general centers upon the question of whether the child's emotional and social adjustment, and specifically the child's sex-role identification, will be adversely affected by having only one parent. It should not be assumed, however, that children being reared by single adoptive parents will necessarily develop in significantly different ways as a result of being reared by one parent.

Many children currently being reared in homes where one parent is absent display no adjustment problems. For those who do experience behavioral problems, the cause cannot always be linked to the fact that they are in a one-parent home. A review of research on one-parent homes and children's adjustment and development in a single-parent family does not lend strong support to the idea that this is a hazardous context for child rearing.[140]

SERVICES TO THE ONE-PARENT FAMILY

The general public needs to gain a greater awareness of the needs of one-parent families. Social service agencies might well be supported to provide family counseling to single parents of all socioeconomic groups. Such agencies could provide professional assistance to single parents in overcoming their fears and doubts concerning their capacity to fulfill new social roles, and financial counseling could also be offered.

Day care for children is another service that is greatly needed by single parents, and social activities need to be provided to assist the single parent in overcoming a sense of alienation in returning to the mainstream of life.

At the present, such services are not commonly available. However, one international organization dedicated to the needs of single-parent families is Parents Without Partners, Inc., whose overall purpose is to help alleviate the isolation and alienation that make it difficult to achieve a normal family life. Educating single parents in child rearing is also a major goal of this organization.

COMMENT

Because of different circumstances and types of one-parent families, they cannot be categorized into one group. However, there are several characteristics they share. All experience the difficulty and challenge of rearing a child alone. Most experience loneliness to some degree. Most face financial problems. Many encounter problems in adjusting to their social life as a single parent.

Although there are many problems experienced by one-parent families, many of them are very happy. Research does not support the idea that a child of a one-parent family will inevitably develop in a significantly different manner than other children, nor does it support the notion that the one-parent child will necessarily be less well adjusted than the two-parent child.

References

1. TOFFLER, ALVIN. *Future Shock.* New York: Random House, 1970.
2. FROMM, ERICH. *The Art of Loving.* New York: Harper & Row, 1956.
3. STINNETT, NICK and CRAIG WAYNE BIRDSONG. *The Family and Alternate Life Styles.* Chicago: Nelson-Hall, 1977.
4. STINNETT, NICK and CRAIG WAYNE BIRDSONG. "Relationship of Personality Needs to Perceptions Concerning Alternate Life Styles." *The Journal of Genetic Psychology,* vol. 128, 1976, pp. 301–302.
5. STINNETT, NICK and SHERRY G. TAYLOR. "Parent-Child Relationships and Perceptions of Experimental Life Styles." *Journal of Genetic Psychology,* vol. 129, 1976, pp. 105–112.
6. TOFFLER, op. cit.
7. MACKLIN, ELEANOR. D. "Heterosexual Cohabitation Among Unmarried College Students." *The Family Coordinator,* vol. 21, 1972, pp. 463–472.
8. BLOCH, DONALD. "Unwed Couples." *Redbook,* vol. 132, April 1969, pp. 90, 140–141.
9. MACKLIN, op. cit.
10. BLOCH, op. cit., p. 142.
11. BERGER, MIRIAM E. "Trial Marriage: Harnessing the Trend Constructively." *The Family Coordinator,* vol. 20, 1971, pp. 38–43.
12. STINNETT and BIRDSONG, 1977, op. cit.
13. "The Tie That Binds." *Newsweek,* vol. 80, December 11, 1972, p. 114.
14. Ibid., p. 116.
15. "Single Couples Seek Help from Counselor." *The Ponca City News,* September 20, 1972, p. 22.

16. KOPECKY, GINI. "Unmarried—But Living Together." *Ladies Home Journal*, vol. 89, July 1972, pp. 64–68.
17. MACKLIN, op. cit.
18. BERNARD, JESSIE. *The Future of Marriage.* New York: World, 1972.
19. CATLIN, NANCY; JAMES F. KELLER; and JAMES W. CROAKE. "Religion in the Lives of Unmarried Cohabiting College Couples." *Journal of Humanics*, vol. 2, 1975, pp. 1–5.
20. KOPECKY, op. cit.
21. MACKLIN, op. cit.
22. RHODES, RICHARD. "Sex and Sin in Sheboygan." *Playboy*, August 1972, pp. 129–130, 186–190.
23. LYNESS, JUDITH L.; MILTON E. LIPITZ; and KEITH E. DAVIS. "Living Together: An Alternative to Marriage." *Journal of Marriage and the Family*, vol. 34, 1972, p. 305.
24. REISINGER, JOSEPH C. "Legal Pitfalls of Living Together." *Single*, vol. 1, August 1973, pp. 58, 104–105.
25. OTTO, HERBERT. "Communes: The Alternate Life-Style." *Saturday Review*, vol. 54, April 24, 1971, pp. 16–21.
26. DOWNING, JOSEPH. "The Tribal Family and the Society of Awakening." In *The Family in Search of a Future*, edited by Herbert A. Otto. New York: Appleton-Century-Crofts, 1970, pp. 119–135.
27. KANTER, ROSABETH. "Communes." *Psychology Today*, vol. 4, July 1970*a*, pp. 53–57.
28. DOWNING, op. cit.
29. KATZ, ELIA. *Armed Love.* New York: Holt, Rinehart and Winston, 1971.
30. FRENCH, DAVID. "After the Fall." *New York Times Magazine*, vol. 21, October 3, 1971, p. 35.
31. KRIPPNER, STANLEY, and DON FERSH. "Spontaneous Paranormal Experience Among Members of Intentional Communities." In *Marriage and Family in a Decade of Change*, edited by Gwen B. Carr. Reading, Mass.: Addison-Wesley, 1972, pp. 220–223.
32. FONZI, GAETON. "The New Arrangement." *Philadelphia Magazine*, January 1970, pp. 126–135.
33. OTTO, op. cit.
34. Ibid.
35. DAVIDSON, SARA. "Open Land." *Harper's Bazaar*, vol. 240, June 1970, pp. 91–100.
36. COX, FRANK D. "Communes: A Potpourri of Ideas." In *American Marriage: A Changing Scene?*, edited by Frank D. Cox. Dubuque, Iowa: Brown, 1972, pp. 237–245.
37. KRIPPNER and FERSH, op. cit.
38. BERGER, BENNETT; BRUCE HACKETT; SHERRI CAVAN; GILBERT ZICKLER; MERVYN MILLAR; MARILYN NOBLE; SUSAN THEIMAN; RICHARD FARRELL; and BENJAMIN ROSENBLUTH. "Child-Rearing Practices of the Communal Family." In *Family in Transition*, edited by Arlene S. Skolnick and Jerome H. Skolnick. Boston: Little, Brown, 1971, pp. 509–523.
39. OTTO, op. cit.
40. KANTER, ROSABETH M. "Information on Communes." Paper given at White House Conference on Children. Forum 14, December 15, 1970*b*.
41. BLOIS, MARSEN S. "Child-Rearing Attitudes of Hippie Adults." Ph.D. dissertation, University of Washington, 1970.
42. BERGER, BENNETT; BRUCE HACKETT; and MERVYN MILLAR. "The Communal Family." *The Family Coordinator*, vol. 21, October 1972, pp. 419–427.

43. Ibid.
44. Ibid.
45. KANTER, 1970*a*, op. cit.
46. BERGER, HACKETT, and MILLAR, op. cit.
47. OTTO, op. cit.
    KRIPPNER and FERSH, op. cit.
48. DOWNING, op. cit.
49. "The American Family: Future Uncertain." *Time*, vol. 96, December 28, 1970, pp. 34–39.
50. NIMKOFF, M. F., ed. *Comparative Family Systems*. Boston: Houghton Mifflin, 1965.
    ELLIS, ALBERT. "Group Marriage: A Possible Alternative?" In *The Family in Search of a Future*, edited by Herbert A. Otto. New York: Appleton-Century-Crofts, 1970, p. 85.
51. ATHENASION, ROBERT; PHILLIP SHOVER; and CAROL TAVIS. "Sex." *Psychology Today*, vol. 41, July 1970, pp. 39–52.
52. EDWARDS, MAXINE, and NICK STINNETT. "College Students' Perceptions of Alternate Life Styles." *Journal of Psychology*, vol. 87, May 1974.
53. CONSTANTINE, LARRY L., and JOAN M. CONSTANTINE. "The Group Marriage." In *The Nuclear Family in Crisis: The Search for an Alternative*, edited by Michael Gordon. New York: Harper & Row, 1972*a*, p. 206.
54. Ibid.
55. CONSTANTINE, LARRY L., and JOAN M. CONSTANTINE. "Sexual Aspects of Multilateral Relations." *Journal of Sex Research*, vol. 7, August 1971*a*, pp. 204–225.
56. KILGO, REESE. "Can Group Marriage Work?" *Sexual Behavior*, vol. 2, March 1972, p. 14.
57. CONSTANTINE and CONSTANTINE, 1971*a*, op. cit.
58. CONSTANTINE and CONSTANTINE, 1972*a*, op. cit.
59. Ibid.
60. Ibid.
61. Ibid.
62. CONSTANTINE, LARRY L. and JOAN M. CONSTANTINE. *Group Marriage*. New York: Macmillan, 1973.
63. CONSTANTINE, LARRY L., and JOAN M. CONSTANTINE. Comment in "Can Group Marriage Work?" *Sexual Behavior*, vol. 2, March 1972*b*, p. 13.
    KILGO, op. cit.
64. CONSTANTINE and CONSTANTINE, 1972*a*, op. cit.
65. ELLIS, 1970, op. cit.
66. CONSTANTINE and CONSTANTINE, 1972*a*, op. cit.
67. KILGO, op. cit.
    CONSTANTINE and CONSTANTINE, 1971*a*, op. cit.
68. CONSTANTINE and CONSTANTINE, 1972*a*, op. cit.
69. Ibid.
    KILGO, op. cit.
70. HUNT, MORTON. "The Future of Marriage." *Playboy*, August 1971, pp. 168–175.
71. Ibid.
72. HUNT, MORTON. *The Affair: A Portrait of Extra-Marital Love in Contemporary America*. New York: World, 1969.
73. BLUM, SAM. "When Can Infidelity Be Justified or Forgiven?" *McCall's*, vol. 93, May 1966, pp. 73, 135–140.

74. HUNT, 1969, op. cit.
75. EDWARDS and STINNETT, op. cit.
76. BELL, ROBERT R. *Marriage and Family Interaction.* Homewood, Ill.: Dorsey Press, 1971.
77. NEUBECK, GERHARD, and VERA M. SCHLETZER. "A Study of Extramarital Relationships." In *Extramarital Relationships,* edited by Gerhard Neubeck. Englewood Cliffs, N.J.: Prentice-Hall, 1969.
78. HUNT, 1969, op. cit.
79. EDWARDS, JOHN N. "Extramarital Involvement: Fact and Theory." *Journal of Sex Research,* vol. 9, 1973, pp. 210–224.
80. WHITEHURST, ROBERT N. "Extramarital Sex: Alienation or Extension of Normal Behavior." In *Extramarital Relationships,* edited by Gerhard Neubeck. Englewood Cliffs, N.J.: Prentice-Hall, 1969.
81. JOHNSON, RALPH E. "Some Correlates of Extramarital Coitus." *Journal of Marriage and the Family,* vol. 32, 1970, pp. 449–455.
EDWARDS, op. cit.
82. HUNT, 1969, op. cit.
83. NEUBECK and SCHLETZER, op. cit.
84. ELLIS, ALBERT. "Healthy and Disturbed Reasons for Having Extramarital Relationships." In *Extramarital Relationships,* edited by Gerhard Neubeck. Englewood Cliffs, N.J.: Prentice-Hall, 1969.
85. WHITEHURST, op. cit.
86. ELLIS, 1969, op. cit.
87. Ibid.
88. LANTZ, HERMAN R., and ELOISE C. SNYDER. *Marriage.* New York: Wiley, 1969.
89. COLTON, HELEN. "Are We a Nation of Adulterers?" *Harper's Bazaar,* vol. 104, October 1971, pp. 125–126.
90. HUNT, 1969, op. cit.
91. BELTZ, STEPHEN E. "Five Year Effects of Altered Marital Contracts (A Behavioral Analysis of Couples)." In *Extramarital Relationships,* edited by Gerhard Neubeck. Englewood Cliffs, N.J.: Prentice-Hall, 1969.
92. MASTERS, WILLIAM H., and VIRGINIA E. JOHNSON, in association with ROBERT J. LEVIN. *The Pleasure Bond: A New Look at Sexuality and Commitment.* Boston: Little, Brown, 1974.
93. BELTZ, op. cit.
94. HUNT, 1969, op. cit.
95. Ibid.
96. Ibid.
97. Ibid.
98. Ibid.
99. Ibid.
100. Ibid.
101. Ibid.
102. Ibid.
103. MASTERS, JOHNSON, and LEVIN, op. cit.
104. BELL, ROBERT R. " 'Swinging'—The Sexual Exchange of Marriage Partners." *Sexual Behavior,* vol. 1, 1971, pp. 70–79.
105. BARTELL, GILBERT D. *Group Sex.* New York: Wyden, 1971.
106. Ibid.

107. DENFELD, DUANE, and MICHAEL GORDON. "The Sociology of Mate Swapping." *Journal of Sex Research*, vol. 7, 1970, pp. 85–99.
108. SCHUPP, CHERIE E. "An Analysis of Some Social-Psychological Factors which Operate in the Functioning Relationship of Married Couples Who Exchange Mates for the Purpose of Sexual Experience." Ph.D. dissertation, United States International University, 1970.
109. BARTELL, op. cit.
110. BELL, 1971, op. cit.
111. BARTELL, op. cit.
112. Ibid.
113. Ibid.
114. Ibid.
115. Ibid.
116. Ibid., p. 216.
117. BELL, 1971, op. cit.
118. BARTELL, op. cit.
119. BELL, 1971, op. cit.
120. BRECHER, EDWARD M. *The Sex Researchers*. Boston: Little, Brown, 1969.
121. MACE, DAVID. Comment in " 'Swinging'—The Sexual Exchange of Marriage Partners." *Sexual Behavior*, vol. 1, 1971, p. 76.
122. Ibid.
123. BARTELL, op. cit.
124. "The Militant Homosexual." *Newsweek*, vol. 78, August 2, 1971, pp. 45–48.
125. KINSEY, ALFRED C.; WARDELL POMEROY; CLYDE MARTIN; and PAUL H. GEBHARD. *Sexual Behavior in the Human Female*. Philadelphia: Saunders, 1953.
126. HOOKER, EVELYN. "Male Homosexuals and Their Worlds." *Sexual Inversion*, edited by Judd Marmor. New York: Basic Books, 1965.
127. CONSTANTINE, LARRY B., and JOAN M. CONSTANTINE. "Group and Multilateral Marriage: Definitional Notes, Glossary, and Annotated Bibliography." *Family Process*, vol. 10, June 1971*b*, pp. 157–176.
128. TOBIN, KAY, and RANDY WICKER. *The Gay Crusaders*. New York: Paperback Library, 1972.
129. DICKEY, BRENDA A. "Attitudes Toward Sex Roles and Feelings of Adequacy in Homosexual Males." *Journal of Consulting Psychology*, vol. 25, 1961, pp. 116–122.
130. KARLEN, ARNO. *Sexuality and Homosexuality*. New York: Norton, 1974.
131. WESTWOOD, GORDON. *A Minority*. London: Longmans, Green, 1960.
132. GREEN, MAURICE R., ed. "Interpersonal Psychoanalysis." *The Selected Papers of Clara M. Thompson*. New York: Basic Books, 1964.
133. LEZNOFF, MAURICE, and WILLIAM A. WESTLEY. "The Homosexual Community." *Sexual Deviance*, edited by John Gaynon and William Simon. New York: Harper & Row, 1967.
134. KARLEN, op. cit.
135. "Gays on the March." *Time*, vol. 106, September 8, 1975, pp. 32–43.
136. U.S. Department of Commerce. "Household and Family Characteristics: March 1974," *Current Population Reports*. Series P-20, no. 276. Washington, D.C.: U.S. Government Printing Office, 1975.
    SCHLESINGER, BENJAMIN. *The One Parent Family*. Toronto, Ont.: University of Toronto Press, 1969.

137. BURGESS, JANE K. "The Single-Parent Family: A Social and Sociological Problem." *The Family Coordinator*, vol. 19, 1970, p. 141.
138. SCHLESINGER, op. cit.
139. KADUSKIN, ALFRED. "Single Parent Adoptions: An Overview and Some Relevant Research." *The Social Service Review*, vol. 44, September 1970, pp. 263–272.
140. BURGESS, op. cit.
SCHLESINGER, op. cit.

19 Families of Tomorrow

Photo by Nancy Stinnett

Every man takes the limits of his own field of vision for the limits of the world.

Arthur Schopenhauer

Predicting the Future

What will families of the future be like? No one knows exactly because predictions are particularly difficult to make in a society that undergoes rapid and unexpected change. Predictions are tentative at best and are based almost entirely upon current trends, which provide a fairly dependable basis. It should be recognized, however, that throughout history trends have sometimes reversed so that society does ~~not inevitably~~ continue to develop in the same direction.

The basis for predictions about the family of the future is provided by current major developments and trends, and among the important ones are the changes in sex roles and biological innovations.

Changing Sex Roles

Masculine and feminine roles have been rather rigidly and differentially defined in the past. Masculinity has traditionally been associated with such qualities as achievement, independence, physical strength, aggressiveness, competitiveness, and sexual prowess; whereas qualities associated with femininity have included nurturance, supportiveness, understanding, passivity, lack of aggressiveness and competitiveness, and dependency. Such sex-related stereotyping begins in the earliest years of life.[1]

Rigidly defined sex roles have had the disadvantage of limiting males and females in fulfilling their human potential, and have often acted as major barriers between men and women understanding one another because they interact in terms of masculine-feminine stereotypes rather than as persons.

The differences in sex roles have been due far more to cultural values and socialization processes than to biological factors.[2] Several cultural changes now taking place are contributing to greater flexibility and overlapping of sex roles.

THE WOMEN'S LIBERATION MOVEMENT

One development with far-reaching implications for family as well as men-women relationships in the future is the women's liberation movement, a growing movement that has achieved significant political power and attracted national attention. The modern version of women's liberation is commonly considered to have gained impetus with the publication in 1963 of *The Feminine Mystique,*[3] by Betty Friedan. This book elaborated upon the frustration and emptiness many women experienced because they were not using their talent and potential. Friedan maintained that the basic reason women were not using their skills and potential was because of the cultural expectation that a woman's place (and her only place) was in the home as a wife and mother. Friedan urged women to raise their self-esteem and increase their self-fulfillment by furthering their education and becoming involved in careers.

Since the publication of *The Feminine Mystique* the movement has grown rapidly. Various women's liberation groups have emerged, ranging from basically conservative and establishment-oriented to very radical.

An example of the more conservative groups is NOW (the National Organization of Women), which was organized in 1966 by Betty Friedan and others and is primarily concerned with achieving economic, occupational, legal, and political equality for women. Briefly stated, the goal of NOW is "an equal partnership with men."

Examples of the most radical groups are the Feminists, New York Radical Women, WITCH (Women's International Terrorist Conspiracy from Hell), and SCUM (Society for Cutting Up Men). Many of the women who helped form these groups came out of the civil-rights and peace movements where they complained of sex discrimination.[4]

Radical elements of the women's liberation movement tend to view the traditional family system as oppressive to women. They propose changing the marriage and family system drastically or eliminating it completely. They see themselves in a real war, with men as the oppressors.

The Feminists, for example, maintain that the oppression of women starts in the family and that from an early age little girls are taught to support the male ego and assume dependent roles in relation to men. This unequal relationship in the family is seen as the root of women's problems. The Feminists believe there can be no real equality until the relationship between the sexes is restructured.

What do members of the women's rights movement hope to accomplish?

1. To achieve educational, employment, legal, and political equality.
2. To restructure the socialization process so that children can develop behavior that is in accord with their individual predisposition rather than in terms of rigid, cultural stereotypes.[5]

3. To assist women in becoming psychologically and socially prepared to take advantage of increasing opportunities.[6]
4. To stimulate a basic reorientation in the general public's expectations concerning masculine and feminine behavior so that there is more flexibility and overlapping of sex roles.[7]
5. To increase the number of adequate day care centers and nurseries, which will better enable women to pursue careers.
6. To obtain a single standard in sexual relationships; some wish to dissociate sexual behavior from the traditional family framework.[8]
7. To encourage human relationships in which women are viewed as persons rather than as sexual objects.

Much has been accomplished by the women's movement. Interest in the equal rights of individuals has been supported largely through the promotion of the Equal Rights Amendment, which specifies that equal rights shall not be denied because of a person's sex and that women are to have identical legal privileges as men. This amendment was designed to help all people to achieve equal employment, economic, legal, and political opportunities.[9]

What are the effects of the women's rights movement? Women are beginning to enter traditionally male occupations, play a more prominent role in managerial positions, and participate in political matters. Sex stereotyping in textbooks has been markedly reduced. The legalization of abortion is also considered a major accomplishment for women's liberation.

The movement has encouraged a growing number of women to seek employment outside the home. The percentage of married women employed in the labor force in 1890 was only 4.6 per cent. This percentage has now increased to over 44 per cent.[10]

The women's rights movement, as most movements, has both advantages and disadvantages, according to numerous writers. The greatest advantages are:

1. Seeking equal opportunities and more alternatives for women.
2. Contributing to more flexibility of sex roles and to the elimination of rigid masculine and feminine stereotypes.
3. Helping women to be viewed as individual persons rather than as sex objects or in terms of feminine stereotypes.
4. Contributing to a men's liberation movement giving men more freedom of choice.

Writers have also identified two major disadvantages of the movement.

1. Many liberationists insist that women who choose to be full-time homemakers and mothers are squandering their potential and are domestic slaves.[11] Some insist that a woman is wasting her talents unless she follows a career rather

than just holding a job; some even maintain that a woman should not teach unless it is at the college level. Unfortunately, this view soon leads to the equating of personal worth with amount of salary and prestige of jobs.

This aspect of the women's liberation movement is a disadvantage because, as Judith Viorst [12] has noted, it is simply encouraging women to exchange one set of rigid role expectations (women can only find fulfillment by being full-time homemakers and mothers) for another, equally as rigid (women can only find fulfillment by working outside the home and following a career). This view overlooks the fact that many women as well as men who work in a profession are not fulfilled. In fact, quite a few women and men are frustrated by their work.

2. The devaluing of marriage, family, and motherhood by many in the women's movement has the effect of causing some women who have chosen to be full-time homemakers to feel discontented and apologetic for their chosen roles. Such devaluing of marriage and family could seriously weaken family life.

CHANGING WOMEN'S ROLES

The roles of women are rapidly undergoing major changes:

1. Women are achieving financial independence and now have a broader range of alternatives on which to base their lives.
2. There is a changing psychological orientation among women that includes a greater degree of emotional independence, aggressiveness, competitiveness, and desire to achieve. Some evidence indicates a trend toward women assuming more masculine personality traits. A study by Aletha Stein [13] reported that the increased incidence of maternal employment may be resulting in female children growing up with more masculine personality characteristics. Stein's study found that the amount of time the mother had been employed was positively related to the daughter's possessing masculine personality characteristics and negatively related to the daughter's possessing certain feminine personality characteristics.
3. Bearing and rearing children are becoming less important to a woman's sense of self-esteem. The women's movement and concern with the population problems of the world have largely contributed to this change.
4. The negative connotation associated with women remaining unmarried is decreasing.[14] As a result, some women now feel more free to remain single.

CHANGING MEN'S ROLES

As role alternatives for women change, making it possible for them to enter traditionally male-dominated occupations, men have to redefine their roles in order to adjust to a society in which masculine and feminine roles are less dichotomized. Many men face the dilemma of interacting with women as equal partners, but yet are still influenced by tradition that has provided encouragement for them to take the initiative and assume a dominant role in a variety of situations.[15]

During this transition period when the concept of masculinity is being broadened, men are understandably confused about what masculinity is. The criteria of dominance, aggressiveness, and accomplishment in work are becoming less important in the definition of masculinity. Although this change is difficult for men now, it promises increased alternatives and freedom in the future. As a consequence of the broadened definition of masculinity, men will feel less compulsion, as well as less anxiety, to prove their masculinity.

Another important modification in the masculine role is that men are assuming expressive characteristics traditionally considered feminine, such as sensitivity, being understanding and considerate, showing warmth and nurturance. It is becoming more acceptable for men to communicate their feelings, problems, and concerns to others. Men are becoming more emotionally responsive. Since expressive qualities are important in the success of interpersonal relationships, the increased internalization of such qualities will tend to improve men's skills in interpersonal relationships within as well as outside of marriage.

A change that will significantly affect family life in the future is that men are beginning to assume greater responsibility in child rearing. As a result, children may experience closer relationships with their fathers than they have in the past; it will also provide boys with a better male model with whom to identify more readily.

Other Changes in the Family

Other changes—besides sex-role changes—will exert a profound influence on what the family will become in the future.

TRANSFER OF MAJOR FUNCTIONS FROM THE FAMILY

Major functions the family performed in the past, such as economic production, protection, recreation, and education, have been largely transferred to other institutions. The family of the past was held together by these functions, which represented tangible, utilitarian, and materialistic bonds. Now the family is held together by less tangible, psychological qualities of love, happiness, and the fulfillment of basic emotional needs.[16] The major function of the family today involves meeting basic emotional needs of individual members.

MORE FRAGMENTED FAMILY LIFE

Our technological and industrialized society has made life fast-paced and complex, resulting in an individual's family life becoming fragmented. People are pressured to be involved in occupational matters and in various civic activities. These demands often leave little time for family life, interaction with spouse and children, or performance of family roles. These pressures become a major problem for families. As Anne Lindbergh notes in *Gift from the Sea*,[17] an individual whose life is extremely fragmented tends to be less in communion with self and family members.

LESS EXTENDED FAMILY CONTACT

As our society has become more industrialized and urbanized, we have experienced greater geographical and social mobility. Approximately forty million people in America change their home addresses at least once each year. The average American moves fourteen times in a lifetime.[18] Greater geographic and social mobility has resulted in fewer close interpersonal relationships with extended family members, and as a consequence the influence of aunts, uncles, cousins, and grandparents is less than in the past.

DECREASED FAMILY SIZE

The size of families in the United States has steadily decreased. The average number of persons per family was 5.8 in 1790, yet only 3.4 in 1974. This change is due in part to the move away from the extended family system and also to the fact that the number of children per family has decreased from an average of 3.43 in 1800 to approximately 1.15 in 1974.[19]

MARRIAGE AT EARLIER AGE

Age at marriage in the United States has decreased during the twentieth century. In 1890 the median age for marriage was 26.1 for males and 22.0 for females; today it has dropped to 23.1 for males and 21.1 for females.[20] An increase in younger marriages is largely the result of greater affluence and a higher level of living, increased willingness and ability of parents to support married children attending college, and the increased employment of women after marriage. Another factor is dating and steady dating at an earlier age. Several studies show a positive relationship between early dating and early marriage.[21]

CHANGING CHILD-REARING PATTERNS

Parents in America, particularly in the middle and upper classes, are relinquishing authoritarian child-rearing methods and are, increasingly, emphasizing democratic parent-child relationships. Parents are becoming less rigidly demanding and are guiding children to make their own decisions. Democratic methods used include appealing to the child's reason, explaining rules, and providing a reasonable degree of freedom in which the child can express desires and feelings.

Children today are encouraged to develop a high degree of autonomy and independence from parents. In a sense, separatism from adults, including parents, is emphasized. As a result, peer groups have assumed an increasingly prominent role in child rearing, particularly during adolescence.

INCREASED DIVORCE

Although the divorce rate has grown considerably during this century, it does not necessarily mean that there is more marriage unhappiness today, but rather that divorce is easier to obtain legally and is more socially acceptable now than in the past. Also, the general affluence of the United States has been increasing over the last hundred years, and a positive relationship exists between divorce rates and economic prosperity. In times of prosperity, couples can more easily afford to divorce.

One picture of contemporary family life in America that may be drawn from these major changes is that the family is more focused upon the fulfillment of emotional needs, more individualized, more fragmented, more temporary, and less stable than in the past.

The Biological Revolution

Many astonishing biological discoveries of recent years may revolutionize our life-styles and bring about major changes in marriage and family relationships. Ideas that only a few years ago were topics for science fiction have become real possibilities because of recent advances in biological research. These advances make it increasingly possible to redesign individual bodies as well as our whole way of life. The following possibilities in the biological revolution are all feasible based on what we now know. Transsexual surgery is already a reality, and embryo transplants have been done on a very limited basis. Many scientists believe that all could become realities within this century.

GENETIC DESIGNING

Recent breakthroughs in biological knowledge make it increasingly possible to manipulate human genes and thus control human heredity and characteristics of future generations. For example, the ability to control the sex of the unborn child is well within the range of possibility. We can now determine the sex of the unborn child, and many scientists believe that controlling the sex of the child is only a step away.[22] This has, in fact, already been done with some animals, such as rabbits. One of the advantages would be that it would enable us to eliminate sex-linked disease. A danger in controlling the sex of the child is, of course, that too many parents might prefer one sex over the other. This could result in a large imbalance of men to women or of women to men, thus creating tremendous problems for society.[23]

Genetic designing offers the real possibility of being able to control IQ, skills, and physical characteristics of children. Alvin Toffler in *Future Shock*[24] observes that through genetic manipulation we would be able to breed children with superior musical or artistic skills, superior vision, hearing, or muscular skills. Although this new knowledge would enable us to produce improved qualities in future generations, it would also enable us to manufacture inferior qualities. Various writers and scientists question whether we would create all persons equal or choose to create a superior group and an inferior group. We could produce a ruling class and a slave class similar to that described in Aldous Huxley's *Brave New World.*[25]

When we have the ability to determine mental, physical, and emotional characteristics, we immediately face the question of how many people with extremely high IQ's does society need? How many doctors and lawyers, how many laborers and white-collar workers do we need? Who decides what characteristics a person will have and the type of life each will have in the future?

EMBRYO TRANSPLANTS

Embryo transplant refers to a process in which a fertilized egg cell (embryo) is implanted in the uterus of a woman; but the ovum and the sperm that produced the embryo are from another man and woman. The embryo-transplant procedure has been successfully done with animals for some time.

One advantage of embryo transplants is that it could provide childless couples with the opportunity of having children. It would also be an alternative for single women who wish to bear and rear a child.

Several writers speculate that as embryo transplants become common, embryo storage banks will be established. The purchaser of the embryo would, in effect, shop around for an embryo with desired characteristics, and would then know in advance such things as the eye and hair color, sex, and probably IQ of the embryo.[26] A woman could go to the embryo storage bank where she would buy a frozen embryo and then take it to her physician who would transplant it in her uterus. She would carry the transplant for the nine months and then give birth to a child as though it had been conceived in her body.[27]

CLONING

Cloning is one of the most fantastic possibilities suggested by the biological revolution. Cloning is a process in which offspring are produced without the use of sperm or egg cells. Cloning would involve taking a cell from a particular person, making the genetic data in that cell accessible, and from the nucleus of this cell growing a new organism. The new organism would, in a sense, be a human copy and would have the same genetic characteristics of the person who contributed the cell.[28]

Cloning has been successfully done with frogs, rabbits, and other animals. The success of these experiments are proof that the genetic information necessary to produce an organism is coded in the nucleus of each cell in the organism.[29]

IN VITRO BABIES

Many scientists believe that it may soon be possible to conceive and grow babies *in vitro* (in laboratory glassware). By this process an egg would be fertilized with sperm in a laboratory container where it would be nurtured and raised to maturity. It would, therefore, be possible to conceive and nurture babies to maturity outside the human body.[30] In fact, an Associated Press article reported that three apparently normal babies have already been conceived in test tubes. Dr. Douglas Bevis, professor of obstetrics and gynecology at Leeds University, reported that the three babies were conceived by placing eggs and sperm in a nutrient solution in test tubes. Approximately one week later the fertilized eggs were removed from the test tubes and implanted in women's wombs.[31] Currently, most of these attempts are not successful. Even in the rare cases that are, the fertilized egg cannot be nurtured for long in the test tube. However, it is staggering to realize that *in vitro* babies, an idea Huxley effectively presented in *Brave New World*, are now very much a possibility.

A person might think that even if *in vitro* babies become a successful reality, most people will not choose to have children that way. Actually, there are indications that when *in vitro* babies can effectively be accomplished on a consistent basis, it could become an accepted practice. In the past, we have not failed to adopt work-saving and time-saving devices. Women using this method would not have to miss work or go through the physical discomforts of pregnancy and birth. This convenience would have popular appeal. Also, the *in vitro* method might make it easier to prevent birth defects.

The acceptance of the *in vitro* method would probably be similar to that of artificial insemination. The first suggestion undoubtedly seemed ridiculous and repulsive to many. Yet, today it is commonly accepted and thousands of husbands and wives collaborate with physicians and sperm donors in conceiving through artificial insemination.

ORGAN TECHNOLOGY

Organ technology (organ transplants and production of artificial organs) is an area in which tremendous progress has been made in recent years and promises to have far-reaching implications for life in the future. Successful heart, kidney, liver, pancreas, and ovary transplants have been reported.

The limited availability of organs for transplants has motivated production of artificial ones. This means that in the future we could have plastic or electronic substitutes for such organs as the liver and heart. Many scientists believe that artificial replacements for tissues and organs will be common by 1984. In fact, much has already been done in this area. Several thousand cardiac patients carry within their chest cavities "pacemaker" devices that send electrical pulses to activate and regulate the heart. Many others have artificial heart valves and implantable hearing aids.[32] The length of life may be extended significantly as a result of continued discoveries in this area.

TRANSSEXUAL SURGERY

It is, of course, now possible to perform transsexual surgery. Many people have already surgically altered their sex. This has opened up unprecedented alternatives for individuals who are dissatisfied with their particular sex.

EFFECTS OF THE BIOLOGICAL REVOLUTION

The possibilities we have discussed—genetic designing, embryo transplants, cloning, *in vitro* babies, organ technology, and transsexual surgery—can have profound influences upon human relationships, values, and the family. Following are only a few possible influences:

1. Our concept of parenthood and family may change. As childbearing is separated from its traditional biological base (a life conceived by a man and woman united in a sexual relationship who then become the parents of the child), many alternative types of parenthood and families will emerge. For example, there may be an increase in one-parent families.[33]
2. Our values concerning human life may change. As *in vitro* babies and embryo storage banks become common and people are able to buy embryos, will the value of human life diminish? Would we begin to view human life as a commodity to be purchased? We may be forced to make decisions about who will receive an organ transplant and who will not. This will force us to decide who is worthy to live and who is not. Leroy Augenstein in *Come Let Us Play God*[34] observes that the biological revolution can quickly place us in the position of making Godlike decisions and can drastically change our value of human life. He suggests that we can prevent being forced into situations and decisions for which we are not prepared by being aware of biological breakthroughs and by carefully controlling the use of the knowledge gained from biological research.
3. Future generations may consist of persons with superior intellectual, physical, and personality traits. Far fewer people may be born with birth defects. However, people may also be produced with inferior characteristics to perform menial tasks in society.
4. The life-span may be lengthened and the quality of life enhanced. The physical aspects of aging could be slowed.
5. Our traditional ideas about sex might be greatly altered. Sexual relationships may become further removed from procreation. As this occurs and as our concept of family changes, sexual relationships would probably become less restricted to the traditional marriage setting.[35]

The Future

What will marriage and family be like in the future? Following are the major predictions most frequently voiced concerning family life in the future.

MARRIAGE

Nearly all social scientists agree that monogamous marriage will remain the prevalent form of man-woman relationship.[36] Most people will continue to reflect the desire for an intimate relationship characterized by a high level of commitment with one person of the opposite sex.

There is some basis for making the optimistic prediction that marriage relationships will become closer and more intimate in the future. The growing desire in our society to improve the quality of human relationships is illustrated by the phenomenal growth in recent years of human potential groups, sensitivity groups, and similar types of group encounter. This type of experience is not only reaching families, but industry and education as well.[37]

These encounter groups emphasize the development of genuine intimate relationships and may improve marriage relationships in the future by encouraging less artificialness, less psychological game playing, less stereotyping, more sensitivity to needs, and greater ability to communicate inner feelings among husbands, wives, and children.

The roles of husbands and wives will become increasingly similar. There will be greater equality, particularly concerning homemaking, parenting, careers, and decisions influencing family life.

Husbands will participate more actively in child-rearing and housekeeping tasks. More men will choose to remain at home and care for the children while the wife is employed outside the home. This pattern has existed in Sweden for some time.

Marriage will be less frequently viewed as a relationship in which the wife is dependent financially or otherwise upon her husband. Women will place less emphasis upon the motherhood role.[38]

Serial marriage will become more common, as many predict a continued rise in the divorce rate. Morton Hunt [39] has suggested that even if divorce greatly increases, it would not destroy marriage. Divorce would simply become a more frequently experienced aspect of marriage, with the majority of divorced persons remarrying as they do today.

Most social scientists believe that sexual behavior will follow present trends and become more permissive. It is predicted that there will be greater acceptance of premarital and extramarital sexual relationships in the future. Many social scientists expect the more permissive sexual relationships because of a growing tendency to dissociate sex and parenthood, improved methods of birth control, and a weakening of the religious and moral sanctions restricting sexual behavior.

Albert Rosenfeld has suggested that sexual permissiveness and an altered moral environment pose some interesting questions as to the ultimate effects upon people and upon relationships. For example, if sexual infidelity becomes extremely common, how would it influence the husband or wife who is subject to jealous apprehensions? Such a person might become insecure and frustrated with the awareness that a spouse was having sexual relations with others. Would there be, in fact, an increase in the emotions of insecurity and jealousy in our society as a whole? Also, if sexual relations become much more casual and more restrictions are removed, is it possible that the quality and intenseness of the sexual experience might decline? [40]

Alternate life-styles will remain. Many social scientists predict that more persons will choose cohabitation, communes, group marriage, extramarital relationships, swinging, homosexual marriage, and one-parent families. Less stigma will be associated with an individual adopting any of these life-styles in the future. However, most of these life-styles will still be the choice of only a small minority of people. Major interpersonal relationship problems, instability, and frequent failure to satisfy emotional needs will prevent these alternate life-styles from becoming dominant.[41]

PARENT-CHILD RELATIONSHIPS

Parents will establish more of a person-to-person relationship with their children.[42] Parental authoritarianism or extreme permissiveness will give way to more democratic relationships; underlying the democratic relationships will be the important factor of parents and children interacting with each other as persons. Parent-child interaction will go beyond the stereotyped package of roles we call "parent" and "child," leading to greater respect, better communication, and a decrease in the generation gap.

One indication of this trend is the development of family encounter groups in which parents learn about themselves and their children from their children; and children learn about themselves and their parents from their parents. A major goal of family encounter groups is to build authentic person-to-person relationships between parents and children. Another indication of the trend toward improved relationships between parents and children is the emergence of a type of parent education in which respect for the parent as a person with rights and feelings is emphasized as well as respect for the child.[43]

Our society will become increasingly concerned that each child has the best possible parents. Restrictions may be established to determine who can become a parent. There is already sentiment among many that persons with serious hereditary disease or major mental disorders should not have children. Concern with world population problems contributes to the increased likelihood of strict selection of persons to be parents. Social scientists predict that it will soon be possible to inoculate girls against ovulation at an early age.[44] Such inoculations would allow fairly easy control of who becomes a parent.

Parents will have fewer children primarily as a result of concern with the population problem and perfected birth control. The trend toward having fewer children will increase the probability that those children who are born will be wanted and will receive the love, affection, and security they need. This would reduce many behavioral and emotional problems that have their origins in children being unwanted and rejected by parents.

More children will be reared at least part of their lives in one-parent families. This change will be largely due to the growing number of divorces, one-parent adoptions, and unmarried women who choose to have babies.

Many social scientists predict that parents will share a larger part of the socialization and education of children with child-development specialists.[45] Children will spend more time in nursery schools and day care centers; this trend will be largely the result of the women's movement and the growing number of women employed outside the home. This trend has been under way in Russia for some time. It has been predicted that by 1980 all Soviet children over three months of age will be reared in collective schools.[46] The proportion of parents' lives devoted to childbearing and child rearing will decrease as the life-span continues to increase.[47]

THE HOME OF THE FUTURE

If predictions about the home of the future are correct, men and women will be greatly freed from homemaking chores and have expanded leisure time. The following predictions are realistic possibilities. In fact, all are presently realities restricted only by the high cost of incorporating them on a wide scale or by the need for more time to accept their innovative nature.

House cleaning will be reduced because sonic cleaning devices and air filtering systems will eliminate dirt, thereby eliminating the need for dusting and vacuuming. Cities will have air purifiers to keep dirt out of our lungs and out of houses as well. Some houses already have such air systems. Dishwashing may be eliminated completely since disposable dishes can be produced from powdered plastic by a special machine in the kitchen.[48]

Food preparation will be revolutionized. For one thing, cooking is made much faster by the use of microwave ovens. It is suggested that in the future, food preparation in the home may be so programmed and computerized that we will decide before going to bed at night what we will have for breakfast and dinner the next day by simply pushing certain buttons. The next day meals will be cooked and waiting to be placed on the table. The meals will already be planned and balanced nutritionally so that individuals may not have to worry about making choices for good nutrition.[49]

Clothes of the future will need little care as they will be easily cleaned, soil resistant, wrinkle resistant, and disposable. As more clothing becomes disposable, clothing fashions will change much faster than is the case today.[50]

There will be an increase in factory-made and prefabricated homes. Home buyers will purchase modular units or rooms from a factory, with each room coming completely wired and equipped with all the necessary plumbing and appliances. A couple might start with a modular kitchen, bedroom, bathroom, and living room, and then add other rooms as their housing needs change. The modular units will allow homeowners to rearrange the floor plan of their houses as often as they wish.[51]

The home of the future may be purchased equipped as a unit, including the furniture. Increased mobility of the family in the future may make owning and transferring one's own furniture obsolete.[52]

There will be a decrease in single-family dwellings and an increase in multi-family dwellings. It has been predicted that by the year 2000, single-family dwellings will constitute only half of all housing, whereas the other half will be comprised of multi-family dwellings, such as apartments, attached townhouses, and duplexes. This trend may accelerate quite rapidly if land becomes extremely expensive. Strict laws limiting single-family housing are already common in Europe. The trend toward multi-family dwellings would seem to be compatible with an increase in communal-type living patterns.[53]

There will be spectacular entertainment innovations in the home. For example, the video tape recorder could have great impact upon families. Prerecorded tapes might be sold by stores or rented by libraries, making available in the home a variety of offerings, such as educational courses, hit Broadway shows, and special sports events.[54] Such entertainment innovations could make the home a center of activities. As more and better entertainment and education is brought into the home by electronic devices, there may be less demand for outside activities, such as movies and concerts.[55]

What do these predictions for the home of the future mean in terms of family life? Most would agree that these predictions—if they become realities—will result in a decreased amount of time families spend together in the home. Labor-saving devices will keep housekeeping and cooking to a minimum. There will, in effect, be no need to spend as much time in the home. The one development that will counteract this is the possibility that the home will become an entertainment and educational center.

Labor-saving devices in the home along with the probability of shorter workweeks would give greater opportunity for more family interaction and greater self-fulfillment in community life, art, and education. Very likely the future will challenge us to learn to use leisure time in pleasant, growth-facilitating ways.[56]

Achieving the Potential of the Family

What are some specific ways that the potentials of marriage and family life can be better realized in the future? One of the most important ways is for each individual to value his or her marriage and family relationships; to give them attention, time, and concern. Relationships often fail, not because of dramatic events, but because they literally die for want of attention.

Another way to achieve the potential of the family in the future would be to establish comprehensive human relationships and family-life education programs extending from preschool through college. Such programs could be adapted at each age level to emphasize important factors in building satisfying interpersonal relationships.

Families could also be strengthened by establishing Marriage and Family Potential Centers across the nation. This has been recommended by Herbert Otto,[57] who suggests that couples interested in developing and improving their marriage could visit the Marriage and Family Potential Center periodically for evaluation of ways their relationships might be made better. Couples and their children could be assisted in identifying and eliminating types of behavior destructive to the relationships before a crisis ever developed. The major purpose of the Marriage and Family Potential Center would be to develop more fully the positive aspects of the husband-wife and parent-child relationships.[58]

Family life does have the potential of becoming more satisfying and significant. The current trend toward greater equality in sex roles, less stereotyping, more emphasis on genuinely close, person-centered relationships, and on meaningful communication patterns that are free of psychological game playing provide hope for the quality of marriage and family relationships in the future.

References

1. FAGOT, BEVERLY I. "Sex-Related Stereotyping of Toddlers' Behaviors." *Developmental Psychology*, vol. 9, 1973, p. 429.
2. ROSENBERG, MIRIAM. "The Biologic Basis for Sex Role Stereotypes." *Contemporary Psychoanalysis*, vol. 9, 1973, pp. 374–391.

3. FRIEDAN, BETTY. *The Feminine Mystique.* New York: Norton, 1963.
4. CLAVAN, SYLVIA. "Women's Liberation and the Family." *The Family Coordinator,* vol. 19, 1970, pp. 317–323.
5. PONZO, ZANDER, and R. WRAY STRONING. "Relations Among Sex-Role Identity and Selected Intellectual and Non-Intellectual Factors for High School Freshmen and Seniors." *Journal of Educational Research,* vol. 67, 1973, pp. 137–141.
6. BADEN, MARY ANNA. "Sex Role Change and Some Implications for Family Relations." Paper presented at 48th Annual Meeting of Southwestern Sociological Association, 1973.
7. Ibid.
8. CLAVAN, SYLVIA. "Impact of Feminism on American Family Structure." Ph.D. dissertation, Temple University, 1972.
9. DU BRIN, ANDREW J. *Women in Transition.* Springfield, Ill.: Thomas, 1972.
10. U.S. Bureau of Census. *Statistical Abstract of the United States,* 1975. 96th ed. Washington, D.C., 1975.
11. BOWMAN, HENRY A. *Marriage for Moderns.* New York: McGraw-Hill, 1974.
12. VIORST, JUDITH. "What Worries Me Most About Women's Lib." *Redbook,* vol. 143, May 1974, pp. 51–52.
13. STEIN, ALETHA. "The Effects of Maternal Employment and Educational Attainment on the Sex-Typed Attributes of College Females." *Social Behavior and Personality,* vol. 1, 1973, pp. 111–114.
14. ADAMS, MARGARET. "The Single Woman in Today's Society: A Reappraisal." *American Journal of Orthopsychiatry,* vol. 41, 1971, pp. 776–786.
15. BOWMAN, op. cit.
16. OGBURN, W. F., and M. F. NIMKOFF. *Technology and the Changing Family.* Boston: Houghton Mifflin, 1955.
17. LINDBERGH, ANNE M. *Gift from the Sea.* New York: Vintage Books, 1955.
18. PACKARD, VANCE. *Nation of Strangers.* New York: McKay, 1972.
19. U.S. Department of Commerce. "Household and Family Characteristics: March, 1974." *Current Population Reports.* Series P-20, no. 276, February 1975. Washington, D.C.: U.S. Government Printing Office.
20. U.S. Department of Commerce. "Population Characteristics: Population Profile of the United States: 1974." *Current Population Reports.* Series P-20, no. 279, March 1975. Washington, D.C.: U.S. Government Printing Office.
21. LANDIS, PAUL. *Making the Most of Marriage.* New York: Appleton-Century-Crofts, 1970.
22. ROSENFELD, ALBERT. "Science, Sex, and Tomorrow's Morality." In *American Marriage: A Changing Scene?,* edited by Frank D. Cox. Dubuque, Iowa: Brown, 1972.
23. WEATHERSBEE, CHRISTOPHER. "Toward Preselected Sex." *Science News,* vol. 94, August 3, 1968, pp. 119–20.
24. TOFFLER, ALVIN. *Future Shock.* New York: Random House, 1970.
25. HUXLEY, ALDOUS. *Brave New World.* New York: Bantam Books, 1953.
26. TOFFLER, op. cit.
27. Ibid.
28. Ibid.
29. ROSENFELD, op. cit.
    GURDON, J. B. "Adult Frogs Derived from the Nuclei of Single Somatic Cells." *Developmental Biology,* vol. 4, 1962, pp. 256–273.

30. TOFFLER, op. cit.
31. "Test Tube Babies Born." *Stillwater Newspress,* July 15, 1974.
32. TOFFLER, op. cit.
33. Ibid.
34. AUGENSTEIN, LEROY. *Come Let Us Play God.* New York: Harper & Row, 1969.
35. TOFFLER, op. cit.
36. BERNARD, JESSIE. *The Future of Marriage.* New York: World, 1972.
HUNT, MORTON. "The Future of Marriage." *Playboy,* August 1971, pp. 116, 168–175.
37. ROGERS, CARL. "Interpersonal Relationships: USA 2000." *Journal of Applied Behavioral Science,* vol. 4, 1968, pp. 265–280.
38. PACKARD, VANCE. *The Sexual Wilderness.* New York: McKay, 1968.
39. HUNT, op. cit.
40. ROSENFELD, op. cit.
41. HUNT, op. cit.
42. ROGERS, op. cit.
43. Ibid.
44. EAST, MARJORIE. "Family Life by the Year 2000." *Journal of Home Economics,* vol. 62, 1970, pp. 13–18.
45. Ibid.
46. Ibid.
47. HAUSER, PHILIP M. "Social Science Predicts and Projects." In *The Future of the Family,* edited by Richard E. Farson, Philip M. Hauser, Herbert Stroup, and Anthony J. Weiner. New York: Family Service Association of America, 1969.
48. LAWSON, HERBERT G. "The Home: Automated Living." In *Here Comes Tomorrow,* edited by Paul Lancaster. Princeton, N.J.: Dow Jones Books, 1966.
EAST, op. cit.
49. EAST, op. cit.
50. Ibid.
51. LAWSON, op. cit.
52. EAST, op. cit.
53. LAWSON, op. cit.
54. Ibid.
55. Ibid.
56. Ibid.
57. OTTO, HERBERT A. "New Light on Human Potential." *In Families of the Future,* edited by Iowa State University College of Home Economics. Ames, Iowa: Iowa State University Press, 1972.
58. Ibid.

Author Index

F

G

H

I

J

K

L

Subject Index

D

E

F

I

J

L